W9-CZZ-723

ENGLISH
FOR EVERYONE

COURSE BOOK
BUSINESS ENGLISH

FREE AUDIO
website and app
www.dkefe.com

Author

Victoria Boobyer is a freelance writer, presenter, and teacher trainer with a background in English-language teaching and teacher management. She has a keen interest in the use of graded readers and the sound pedagogical use of technology in teaching.

Course consultant

Tim Bowen has taught English and trained teachers in more than 30 countries worldwide. He is the co-author of works on pronunciation teaching and language-teaching methodology, and author of numerous books for English-language teachers. He is currently a freelance materials writer, editor, and translator. He is a member of the Chartered Institute of Linguists.

Language consultant

Professor Susan Barduhn is an experienced English-language teacher, teacher trainer, and author, who has contributed to numerous publications. In addition to directing English-language courses in at least four different continents, she has been President of the International Association of Teachers of English as a Foreign Language, and an adviser to the British Council and the US State Department. She is currently a Professor at the School of International Training in Vermont, USA.

ENGLISH
FOR EVERYONE

COURSE BOOK LEVEL ❶
BUSINESS ENGLISH

US Editors Jenny Siklos, Allison Singer
Project Editors Lili Bryant, Laura Sandford
Art Editors Chrissy Barnard, Paul Drislane, Michelle Staples
Editor Ben Ffrancon Davies
Editorial Assistants Sarah Edwards, Helen Leech
Illustrators Edwood Burn, Michael Parkin, Gus Scott
Managing Editor Daniel Mills
Managing Art Editor Anna Hall
Audio Recording Manager Christine Stroyan
Jacket Designer Ira Sharma
Jacket Editor Claire Gell
Managing Jacket Editor Saloni Singh
Jacket Design Development Manager Sophia MTT
Producer, Pre-production Andy Hilliard
Producer Mary Slater
Publisher Andrew Macintyre
Art Director Karen Self
Publishing Director Jonathan Metcalf

DK India
Senior Managing Art Editor Arunesh Talapatra
Senior Art Editor Chhaya Sajwan
Art Editors Meenal Goel, Roshni Kapur
Assistant Art Editor Rohit Dev Bhardwaj
Illustrators Manish Bhatt, Arun Pottirayil,
Sachin Tanwar, Mohd Zishan
Editorial Coordinator Priyanka Sharma
Pre-production Manager Balwant Singh
Senior DTP Designers Harish Aggarwal, Vishal Bhatia
DTP Designer Jaypal Chauhan

First American Edition, 2017
Published in the United States by DK Publishing
345 Hudson Street, New York, New York 10014

Copyright © 2017 Dorling Kindersley Limited
DK, a Division of Penguin Random House LLC
17 18 19 20 21 10 9 8 7 6 5 4 3 2 1
001–290208–Jan/2017

A catalog record for this book
is available from the Library of Congress.
ISBN 978-1-4654-5267-2

DK books are available at special discounts when purchased
in bulk for sales promotions, premiums, fund-raising, or educational use.
For details, contact: DK Publishing Special Markets, 345 Hudson Street,
New York, New York 10014
SpecialSales@dk.com

Printed and bound in China

All images © Dorling Kindersley Limited
For further information see: www.dkimages.com

A WORLD OF IDEAS:
SEE ALL THERE IS TO KNOW

www.dk.com

Level ❶ Contents

How the course works — 8

01 Meeting new colleagues — 12
New language Alphabet and spelling
Vocabulary Introductions and greetings
New skill Introducing yourself to co-workers

02 Everyday work activities — 16
New language Present simple
Vocabulary Work activities
New skill Talking about workplace routines

03 Vocabulary — 20
Countries and continents

04 Business around the world — 22
New language Negative statements
Vocabulary Countries and nationalities
New skill Saying where things are from

05 Vocabulary Office equipment — 26

06 Asking questions at work — 28
New language Forming questions
Vocabulary Office equipment
New skill Asking colleagues questions

07 Exchanging details — 32
New language Short answers
Vocabulary Contact information
New skill Exchanging contact details

Level ❷ Contents see page 194

How the course works

English for Everyone is designed for people who want to teach themselves the English language. The Business English edition covers essential English phrases and constructions for a wide range of common business scenarios. Unlike other courses, English for Everyone uses graphics in all its learning and practice, to help you learn as easily as possible. The course is split into two levels, both contained in this book. The best way to learn is to work through the book in order, making full use of the audio on the website and app. Turn to the practice book at the end of each unit to reinforce your learning with exercises.

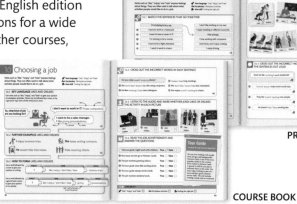

PRACTICE BOOK

COURSE BOOK

Unit number The book is divided into units. The unit number helps you keep track of your progress.

Learning points Every unit begins with a summary of the key learning points.

Modules Each unit is broken down into modules, which should be done in order. You can take a break from learning after completing any module.

Language learning Modules with colored backgrounds teach new language points. Study these carefully before moving on to the exercises.

Audio support Most modules are supported by audio recordings to help you improve your speaking and listening skills.

Exercises Modules with white backgrounds contain exercises that help you practice your new skills to reinforce learning.

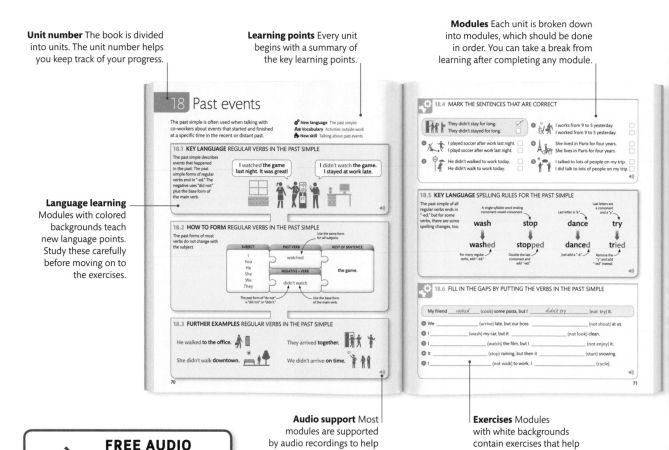

FREE AUDIO
website and app
www.dkefe.com

Language modules

New language is shown in the context of common business scenarios. Each learning module introduces appropriate English for a particular situation, as well as general points of English language to improve your overall fluency.

Module number Every module is identified with a unique number, so you can track your progress and easily locate any related audio.

Module heading The teaching topic appears here, along with a brief introduction.

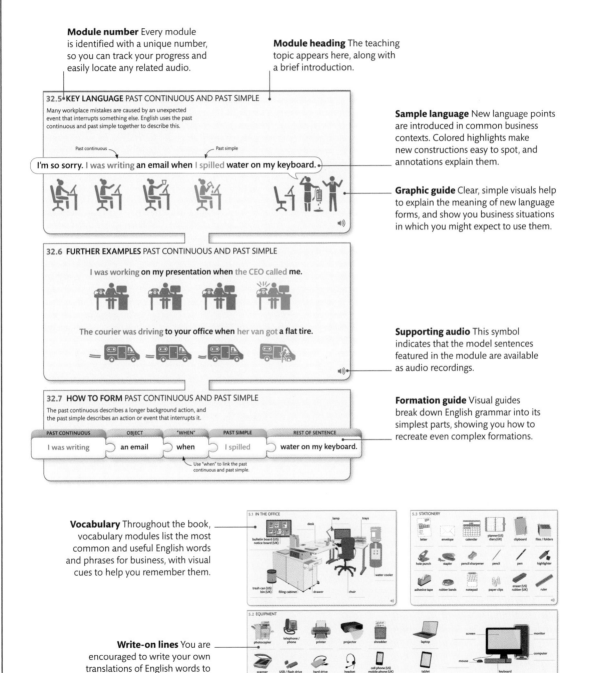

32.5 KEY LANGUAGE PAST CONTINUOUS AND PAST SIMPLE

Many workplace mistakes are caused by an unexpected event that interrupts something else. English uses the past continuous and past simple together to describe this.

Past continuous   Past simple

I'm so sorry. I was writing an email when I spilled water on my keyboard.

Sample language New language points are introduced in common business contexts. Colored highlights make new constructions easy to spot, and annotations explain them.

Graphic guide Clear, simple visuals help to explain the meaning of new language forms, and show you business situations in which you might expect to use them.

32.6 FURTHER EXAMPLES PAST CONTINUOUS AND PAST SIMPLE

I was working on my presentation when the CEO called me.

The courier was driving to your office when her van got a flat tire.

Supporting audio This symbol indicates that the model sentences featured in the module are available as audio recordings.

32.7 HOW TO FORM PAST CONTINUOUS AND PAST SIMPLE

The past continuous describes a longer background action, and the past simple describes an action or event that interrupts it.

PAST CONTINUOUS	OBJECT	"WHEN"	PAST SIMPLE	REST OF SENTENCE
I was writing	an email	when	I spilled	water on my keyboard.

Use "when" to link the past continuous and past simple.

Formation guide Visual guides break down English grammar into its simplest parts, showing you how to recreate even complex formations.

Vocabulary Throughout the book, vocabulary modules list the most common and useful English words and phrases for business, with visual cues to help you remember them.

5.1 IN THE OFFICE

lamp   trays
desk
bulletin board (US)
notice board (UK)
water cooler
trash can (US)
bin (UK)   filing cabinet   drawer   chair

5.3 STATIONERY

letter   envelope   calendar   planner (US)
diary (UK)   clipboard   files / folders

hole punch   stapler   pencil sharpener   pencil   pen   highlighter

adhesive tape   rubber bands   notepad   paper clips   eraser (US)
rubber (UK)   ruler

5.2 EQUIPMENT

photocopier   telephone /
phone   printer   projector   shredder   laptop   screen   monitor

scanner   USB / flash drive   hard drive   headset   cell phone (US)
mobile phone (UK)   tablet   mouse   keyboard   computer

Write-on lines You are encouraged to write your own translations of English words to create your own reference pages.

Practice modules

Each learning point is followed by carefully graded exercises that help to fix new language in your memory. Working through the exercises will help you remember what you have learned and become more fluent. Every exercise is introduced with a symbol to indicate which skill is being practiced.

 GRAMMAR
Apply new language rules in different contexts.

 READING
Examine target language in real-life English contexts.

 LISTENING
Test your understanding of spoken English.

VOCABULARY
Cement your understanding of key vocabulary.

WRITING
Practice producing written passages of English text.

SPEAKING
Compare your spoken English to model audio recordings.

Module number Every module is identified with a unique number, so you can easily locate answers and related audio.

Exercise instruction Every exercise is introduced with a brief instruction, telling you what you need to do.

41.6 FILL IN THE GAPS USING THE WORDS IN THE PANEL

Do you have _____enough_____ bread?

1 I've eaten _____ many chocolates.

2 How _____ glasses do we need?

3 There's too _____ sauce on this.

4 How _____ should we tip here?

much	much	many
	too	~~enough~~

Sample answer The first question of each exercise is answered for you, to help make the task easy to understand.

Space for writing You are encouraged to write your answers in the book for future reference.

Speaking exercise This symbol indicates that you should say your answers out loud, then compare them to model recordings included in your audio files.

Supporting graphics Visual cues are given to help you understand the exercises.

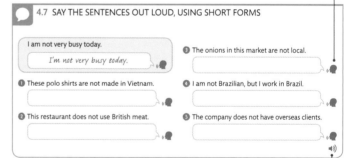

4.7 SAY THE SENTENCES OUT LOUD, USING SHORT FORMS

I am not very busy today.

I'm not very busy today.

3 The onions in this market are not local.

1 These polo shirts are not made in Vietnam.

4 I am not Brazilian, but I work in Brazil.

2 This restaurant does not use British meat.

5 The company does not have overseas clients.

Listening exercise This symbol indicates that you should listen to an audio track in order to answer the questions in the exercise.

Supporting audio This symbol shows that the answers to the exercise are available as audio tracks. Listen to them after completing the exercise.

20.6 LISTEN TO THE AUDIO, THEN NUMBER THE PICTURES IN THE ORDER THEY ARE DESCRIBED

Audio

English for Everyone features extensive supporting audio materials. You are encouraged to use them as much as you can, to improve your understanding of spoken English, and to make your own accent and pronunciation more natural. Each file can be played, paused, and repeated as often as you like, until you are confident you understand what has been said.

LISTENING EXERCISES
This symbol indicates that you should listen to an audio track in order to answer the questions in the exercise.

SUPPORTING AUDIO
This symbol indicates that extra audio material is available for you to listen to after completing the module.

FREE AUDIO
website and app
www.dkefe.com

Track your progress

The course is designed to make it easy to monitor your progress, with regular summary and review modules. Answers are provided for every exercise, so you can see how well you have understood each teaching point.

Checklists Every unit ends with a checklist, where you can check off the new skills you have learned.

07 ✓ CHECKLIST
♂ Short answers ☐   Aa Contact information ☐   👤 Exchanging contact details ☐

Review modules At the end of a group of units, you will find a more detailed review module, summarizing the language you have learned.

Check boxes Use these boxes to mark the skills you feel comfortable with. Go back and review anything you feel you need to practice further.

○ REVIEW THE ENGLISH YOU HAVE LEARNED IN UNITS 1-7

NEW LANGUAGE	SAMPLE SENTENCE	☑	UNIT
INTRODUCING YOURSELF AND OTHER PEOPLE	Good morning. My name's **Alisha Sharma.** This is **my colleague, Edward.**	☐	1.1, 1.5
PRESENT SIMPLE TO DESCRIBE ROUTINE WORK ACTIVITIES	We **have a team meeting** every Tuesday. The CEO **works** weekends if we're busy.	☐	2.1
COUNTRIES AND NATIONALITIES	These new mopeds **are** from Italy. I'm Brazilian, **but I work** in the US.	☐	4.1, 4.2, 4.3
NEGATIVE SENTENCES	I'm **not** French. I'm Canadian. The printer **doesn't work!**	☐	4.6
ASKING QUESTIONS	Do you have **an appointment?** Where is **the staff room?**	☐	6.1, 6.4, 6.8
EXCHANGING DETAILS, SHORT ANSWERS	Is this your email address? Yes, it is. Do you have a business card? No, I don't.	☐	7.1, 7.2, 7.7

29

29.2 ◀))
① It's a special one for fire safety.
② There's a nice café across the street.
③ We're meeting clients later this afternoon.
④ I have saved all the documents.

29.3 ◀))
① Is your stapler broken? You **can** use mine.
② She **doesn't have to** come to the training session. She did it last year.
③ You **have to** turn off the light if you're the last person to leave the office.
④ He **has to** test the fire alarm every Wednesday morning.
⑤ We **don't have to** wear a jacket and tie in the summer months.

29.4
① Not given ② False ③ True
④ True ⑤ False

29.8 ◀))
① Could you **tell** Jan to call me back?
② Could you **check** this report?
③ Would you mind **ordering** more pens?
④ Could you **mop** the floor, please?
⑤ Could you **come** to today's meeting?
⑥ Would you mind **calling** back later?
⑦ Would you mind **turning** the light off?
⑧ Could you **wash** these cups, please?
⑨ Could you **pass** around the reports?
⑩ Would you mind **booking** me a taxi?
⑪ Could you **show** our clients around?

29.9
① False ② False ③ True ④ True

29.10 ◀))
1. Could you book a meeting room?
2. Could you send Sam Davies an email?
3. Could you call our supplier?
4. Would you mind booking a meeting room?
5. Would you mind sending Sam Davies an email?
6. Would you mind calling our supplier?

Answers Find the answers to every exercise printed at the back of the book.

Exercise numbers Match these numbers to the unique identifier at the top-left corner of each exercise.

Audio This symbol indicates that the answers can also be listened to.

01 Meeting new colleagues

You can use formal or informal English to introduce yourself and greet colleagues or co-workers, depending on the situation and the people you are meeting.

⚙ **New language** Alphabet and spelling
Aa Vocabulary Introductions and greetings
🧩 **New skill** Introducing yourself to co-workers

1.1 KEY LANGUAGE INTRODUCING YOURSELF

English uses a variety of polite phrases for introducing yourself and greeting your co-workers.

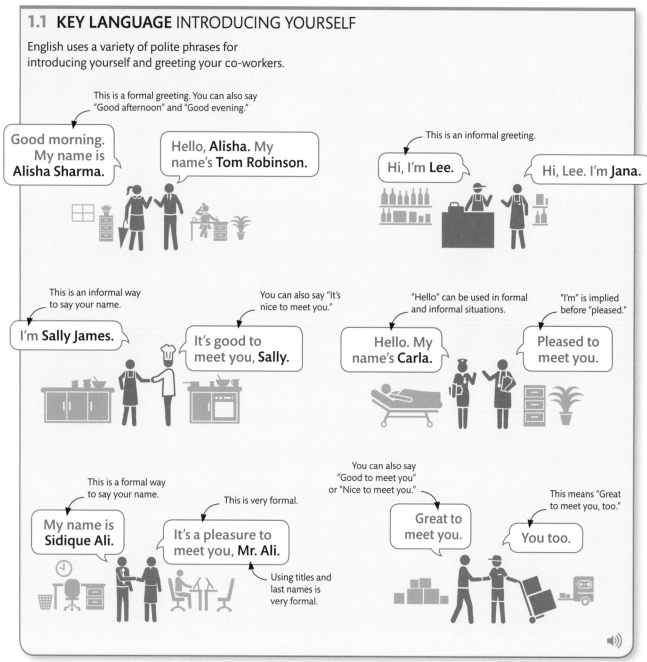

This is a formal greeting. You can also say "Good afternoon" and "Good evening."

Good morning. My name is **Alisha Sharma.**

Hello, **Alisha. My** name's **Tom Robinson.**

This is an informal greeting.

Hi, I'm **Lee.**

Hi, Lee. I'm **Jana.**

This is an informal way to say your name.

I'm **Sally James.**

You can also say "It's nice to meet you."

It's good to meet you, **Sally.**

"Hello" can be used in formal and informal situations.

Hello. My name's **Carla.**

"I'm" is implied before "pleased."

Pleased to meet you.

This is a formal way to say your name.

My name is **Sidique Ali.**

This is very formal.

It's a pleasure to meet you, **Mr. Ali.**

Using titles and last names is very formal.

You can also say "Good to meet you" or "Nice to meet you."

Great to meet you.

This means "Great to meet you, too."

You too.

1.2 FILL IN THE GAPS USING THE WORDS IN THE PANEL

It's good to _____*meet*_____ you.

1 Hello. My _____ Sebastian.

2 Good _____ . My name is Joe Carr.

3 Hi, Marie. _____ Clive.

4 It's great to meet you, _____ , Sven.

5 It's a _____ to meet you.

afternoon	pleasure	~~meet~~
I'm	name's	too

1.3 PRONUNCIATION THE ALPHABET

Listen to how the letters of the alphabet are pronounced in English when they are said individually.

Aa Bb Cc Dd Ee
Ff Gg Hh Ii Jj Kk
Ll Mm Nn Oo Pp
Qq Rr Ss Tt Uu
Vv Ww Xx Yy Zz

1.4 LISTEN TO THE AUDIO AND MARK THE NAMES YOU HEAR

GEORGE A / JORGE B

1 KATIE A / KATY B

2 FRANCIS A / FRANCES B

3 LAURA A / LORNA B

4 SANDRA A / ZANDRA B

5 BORIS A / DORIS B

1.5 KEY LANGUAGE INTRODUCING OTHER PEOPLE

You can also use polite formal and informal phrases to introduce your co-workers to each other.

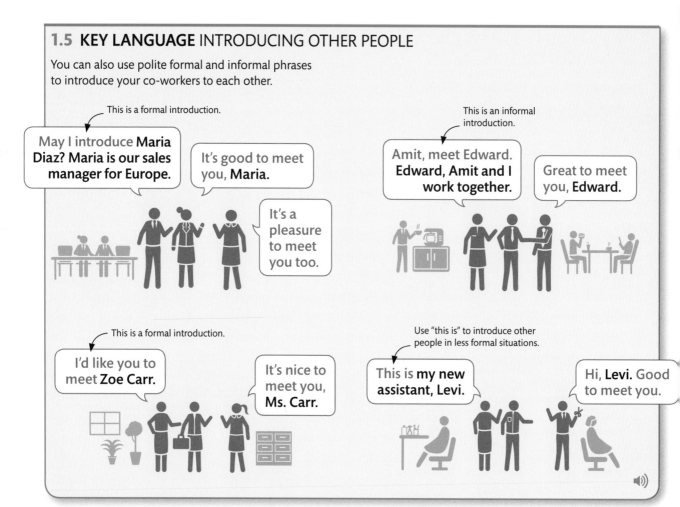

This is a formal introduction.

May I introduce **Maria Diaz**? Maria is our sales manager for Europe.

It's good to meet you, **Maria**.

It's a pleasure to meet you too.

This is an informal introduction.

Amit, meet Edward. **Edward, Amit and I work together.**

Great to meet you, **Edward**.

This is a formal introduction.

I'd like you to meet **Zoe Carr**.

It's nice to meet you, **Ms. Carr**.

Use "this is" to introduce other people in less formal situations.

This is **my new assistant, Levi.**

Hi, **Levi**. Good to meet you.

1.6 REWRITE THE SENTENCES, CORRECTING THE ERRORS

Hello, Sam. Nice meet you.
Hello, Sam. Nice to meet you.

❶ To meet you, it's a pleasure, too.
_____

❷ Hi, I'm name's Adedeyo.
_____

❸ Greet to meet you.
_____

❹ This my new colleague, Martin.
_____

❺ Marisa, meeting Roula, my partner.
_____

❻ It's good to meet to you, Katherine.
_____

❼ I may introduce Claudia Gomez, our new CEO?
_____

1.7 LISTEN TO THE AUDIO AND ANSWER THE QUESTIONS

Jill has started a new job. She goes to a meeting with her new colleagues, Mr. Singh and Daniel.

What is Jill's role at the company?
Design assistant ☐
Finance manager ☑
Intern ☐

❶ What is Jill's last name?
Greene ☐
Cheam ☐
Green ☐

❷ How long has Mr. Singh been working with Spandone and Co.?
14 years ☐
15 years ☐
16 years ☐

❸ What is Mr. Singh's role at Spandone and Co.?
Lawyer ☐
CEO ☐
Accountant ☐

❹ Which two people are meeting for the first time?
Jill and Daniel ☐
Jill and Mr. Singh ☐
Daniel and Mr. Singh ☐

1.8 SAY THE SENTENCES OUT LOUD, FILLING IN THE GAPS USING THE WORDS IN THE PANEL

May I __introduce__ Marta Lopez? Marta and I __work__ together.

❶ Hello, Mr. Lucas. It's a _____ to meet _____ .

❷ Ashley, _____ André. André and I work on the _____ project.

❸ _____ , Sophie. My _____ Rachel Davies. Great to meet you.

❹ _____ is my colleague, Hayley. We went to college _____ .

❺ It's _____ to meet you, Cori. _____ name's Angel.

❻ Hello, James. _____ really nice ____ meet you. My name's Alex.

good	together	It's	My	to
~~introduce~~	name's	pleasure	Hello	
meet	same	you	This	~~work~~

🔊

02 Everyday work activities

Use the present simple to talk about things that you do regularly, such as your daily tasks or everyday work routines.

🌀 **New language** Present simple
Aa **Vocabulary** Work activities
🧩 **New skill** Talking about workplace routines

2.1 KEY LANGUAGE THE PRESENT SIMPLE

Use the present simple to talk about things that happen regularly as part of a routine.

Every morning, we prepare the food and Justin sets the tables.

🔊

2.2 HOW TO FORM THE PRESENT SIMPLE

With regular verbs, use the base form of the verb to make the present simple with "I," "you," "we," and "they." With "he," "she," and "it," add "s" to the base form.

SUBJECT	VERB	REST OF SENTENCE
I / You / We / They	prepare	the food every morning.
He / She	prepares	

2.3 FURTHER EXAMPLES THE PRESENT SIMPLE

"Be" with "I" is "I am."
The short form is "I'm."

 I'm a lifeguard at the local pool.

Present simple form of "be" with "he," "she," and "it."

 Mia is an excellent tour guide.

 They have a meeting every morning.

 We usually stop for tea and coffee at 11.

Present simple form of "be" with "we," "you," and "they."

 Stephanie works from home on Mondays.

We are always busy in the evening.

🔊

2.4 MATCH THE PICTURES TO THE CORRECT SENTENCES

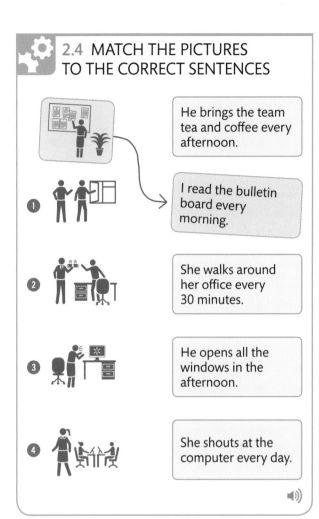

He brings the team tea and coffee every afternoon.

I read the bulletin board every morning.

She walks around her office every 30 minutes.

He opens all the windows in the afternoon.

She shouts at the computer every day.

2.5 FILL IN THE GAPS USING THE WORDS IN THE PANEL

We __have__ a meeting every day.

1 She _____ a hairdresser.

2 He _____ by train every morning.

3 She _____ work at 6pm every day.

4 She _____ coffee twice a day.

5 He _____ lunch at a local café.

| eats | is | drinks |
| leaves | ~~have~~ | travels |

2.6 LISTEN TO THE AUDIO AND ANSWER THE QUESTIONS

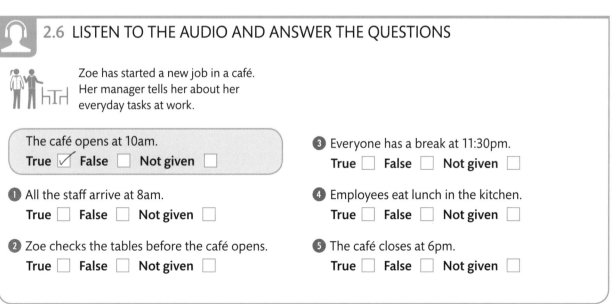

Zoe has started a new job in a café. Her manager tells her about her everyday tasks at work.

The café opens at 10am.
True ☑ **False** ☐ **Not given** ☐

1 All the staff arrive at 8am.
True ☐ **False** ☐ **Not given** ☐

2 Zoe checks the tables before the café opens.
True ☐ **False** ☐ **Not given** ☐

3 Everyone has a break at 11:30pm.
True ☐ **False** ☐ **Not given** ☐

4 Employees eat lunch in the kitchen.
True ☐ **False** ☐ **Not given** ☐

5 The café closes at 6pm.
True ☐ **False** ☐ **Not given** ☐

2.7 ⚠ COMMON MISTAKES THE PRESENT SIMPLE WITH "HE," "SHE," AND "IT"

It's easy to forget to add "s" to the base form of the verb in the present simple with third-person singular pronouns, "he," "she," and "it."

Add an "s" to the base form of the verb.

The CEO works on Sundays. ✔

The CEO work on Sundays. ✖

This is wrong.

2.8 CROSS OUT THE INCORRECT WORD IN EACH SENTENCE

She ~~make~~ / makes tea and coffee before the team meeting every Friday.

1 The head of marketing speak / speaks for about an hour at every team meeting.

2 Arianna and Gabriel read / reads their emails first thing every morning.

3 The photocopier stop / stops working if we don't load the paper carefully.

4 The owners of the hotel visit / visits it at the end of every month.

5 The cleaner start / starts work at 6am every day. The office is always clean in the mornings.

2.9 USE THE CHART TO CREATE EIGHT CORRECT SENTENCES AND SAY THEM OUT LOUD

I work from Monday to Friday.

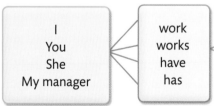

I	work	from Monday to Friday.
You	works	a meeting every morning.
She	have	
My manager	has	

OUR TEAM

Meet the manager

Our Head of Customer Services describes a typical working day

Sumiko Akimoto, our Head of Customer Services, describes a typical day at work. "Every morning, even in the winter, I ride my bicycle to work. I arrive at work early and then walk through the departments to talk to the staff. It is important for me to know what is happening in the company so that I can share any useful information with clients. Next, I read my emails and use them to help me write a list of things to do during the day. I rarely do everything on the list, but it's useful to help me plan my day.

During my morning coffee break, I talk to my team members about my list and sometimes delegate tasks to them. At lunchtime, many of my colleagues go to a local Italian restaurant to eat, but I stay in the office and eat a packed lunch. I like to deal with all my emails by 5 o'clock. Sometimes I can leave work at 5:30, but I usually leave at 6 o'clock. To help me relax after work, I turn off my phone as soon as I get home."

Sumiko cycles to work every day.	True ☑ False ☐

❶ She reads her emails first thing every morning.　　True ☐　False ☐

❷ She writes a list of things to do that day.　　True ☐　False ☐

❸ She meets her colleagues to talk about the day's work.　　True ☐　False ☐

❹ Sumiko goes to a local restaurant for lunch every day.　　True ☐　False ☐

❺ She tries to deal with all her emails by 5 o'clock.　　True ☐　False ☐

❻ Sumiko always leaves work at 6 o'clock.　　True ☐　False ☐

❼ She turns her phone off when she gets home.　　True ☐　False ☐

02 ✔ CHECKLIST

⚙ Present simple ☐　　**Aa** Work activities ☐　　🧩 Talking about workplace routines ☐

3.1 COUNTRIES

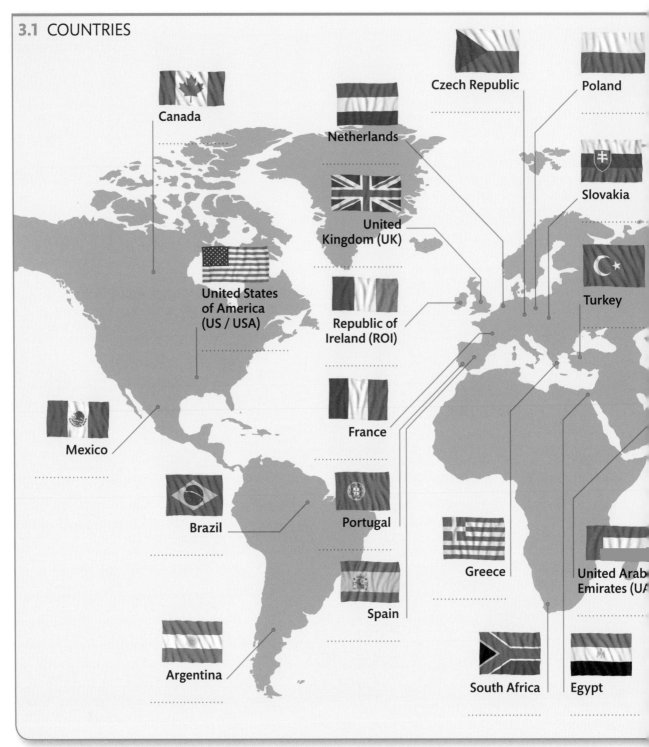

Canada

Netherlands

Czech Republic

Poland

Slovakia

United Kingdom (UK)

United States of America (US / USA)

Republic of Ireland (ROI)

Turkey

France

Mexico

Brazil

Portugal

Greece

United Arab Emirates (UA...

Spain

Argentina

South Africa

Egypt

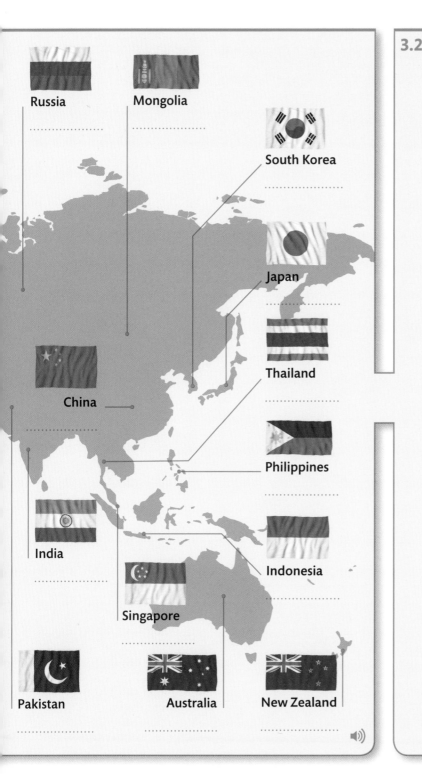

Russia

Mongolia

South Korea

Japan

China

Thailand

Philippines

India

Indonesia

Singapore

Pakistan

Australia

New Zealand

3.2 CONTINENTS

North America

South America

Europe

Africa

Asia

Australasia

21

Business around the world

English uses "from" or nationality adjectives to talk about where products or people come from. "From" can also refer to your company or department.

⚙ **New language** Negative statements
Aa Vocabulary Countries and nationalities
New skill Saying where things are from

4.1 VOCABULARY NATIONALITY ADJECTIVES

Nationality adjectives are based on country names. Most end in "-ese," "-an," "-ish," "-ean," or "-ian," but some are irregular.

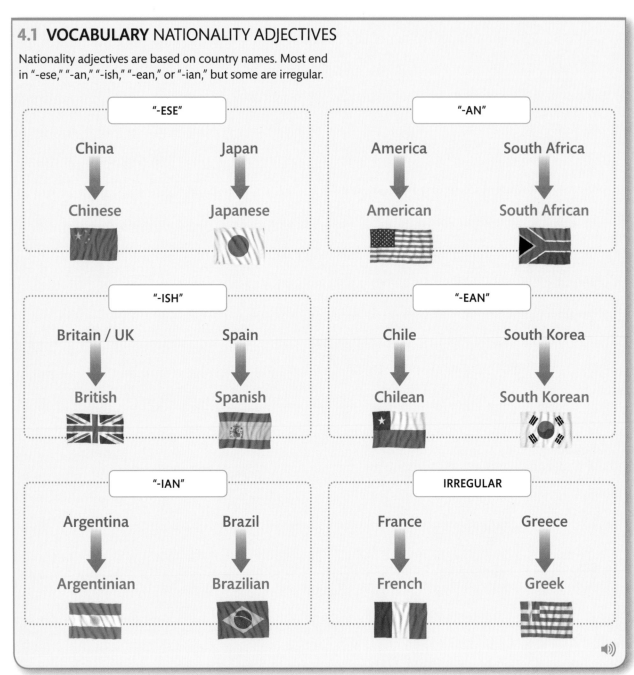

"-ESE"

China → Chinese

Japan → Japanese

"-AN"

America → American

South Africa → South African

"-ISH"

Britain / UK → British

Spain → Spanish

"-EAN"

Chile → Chilean

South Korea → South Korean

"-IAN"

Argentina → Argentinian

Brazil → Brazilian

IRREGULAR

France → French

Greece → Greek

4.2 KEY LANGUAGE COUNTRIES AND NATIONALITIES

To talk about where products were made or what country people come from, use "from" with a country name, or a nationality adjective.

"FROM" + COUNTRY

These new mopeds are from Italy.

NATIONALITY ADJECTIVE

These new mopeds are Italian. ◀))

4.3 FURTHER EXAMPLES COUNTRIES AND NATIONALITIES

These smartphones are from Japan.

The new CEO is from Switzerland.

These Indian dresses are excellent value.

I'm Russian, but I regularly visit the US. ◀))

4.4 CROSS OUT THE INCORRECT WORD IN EACH SENTENCE

These monitors are from China / ~~Chinese~~.

❶ I'm on the Europe / European sales team.

❷ Our Chile / Chilean office is in Santiago.

❸ We sell leather shoes from Spain / Spanish.

❹ My job is to watch the Asia / Asian markets.

❺ Book a trip to Mexico / Mexican with us.

◀))

4.5 LISTEN TO THE AUDIO AND MATCH THE PRODUCTS TO THE PLACE NAMES

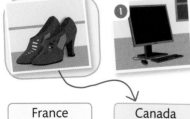  

| France | Canada | Asia | Italy | Africa | India |

4.6 KEY LANGUAGE CONTRACTED NEGATIVES

Adding "not" makes a positive statement negative.
"Not" is often used in its contracted form.

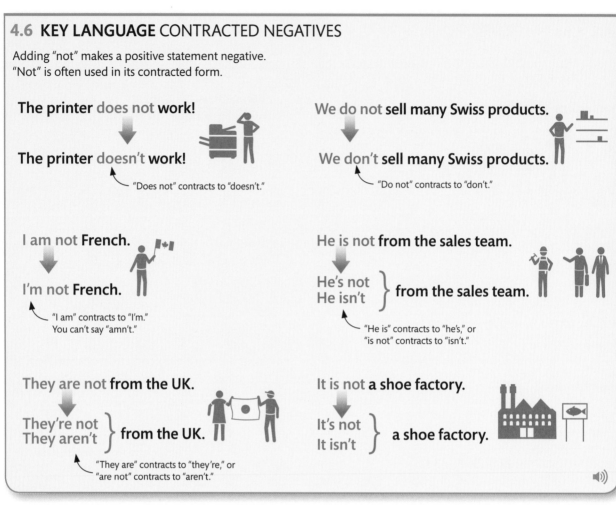

The printer does not work!

The printer doesn't work!

"Does not" contracts to "doesn't."

We do not sell many Swiss products.

We don't sell many Swiss products.

"Do not" contracts to "don't."

I am not French.

I'm not French.

"I am" contracts to "I'm."
You can't say "amn't."

He is not from the sales team.

He's not
He isn't } from the sales team.

"He is" contracts to "he's," or
"is not" contracts to "isn't."

They are not from the UK.

They're not
They aren't } from the UK.

"They are" contracts to "they're," or
"are not" contracts to "aren't."

It is not a shoe factory.

It's not
It isn't } a shoe factory.

4.7 SAY THE SENTENCES OUT LOUD, USING SHORT FORMS

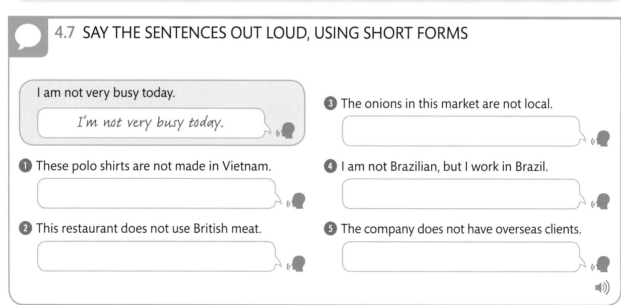

I am not very busy today.

I'm not very busy today.

❶ These polo shirts are not made in Vietnam.

❷ This restaurant does not use British meat.

❸ The onions in this market are not local.

❹ I am not Brazilian, but I work in Brazil.

❺ The company does not have overseas clients.

4.8 KEY LANGUAGE SAYING WHERE YOU WORK

"From" can also refer to a company or department.

I'm George. I'm from the marketing department in New York.

And this is Barbara. She's from QuickStyle Printers.

I'm Nisha. I'm from finance.

People often leave out "the" and "department" when they say what department they are from.

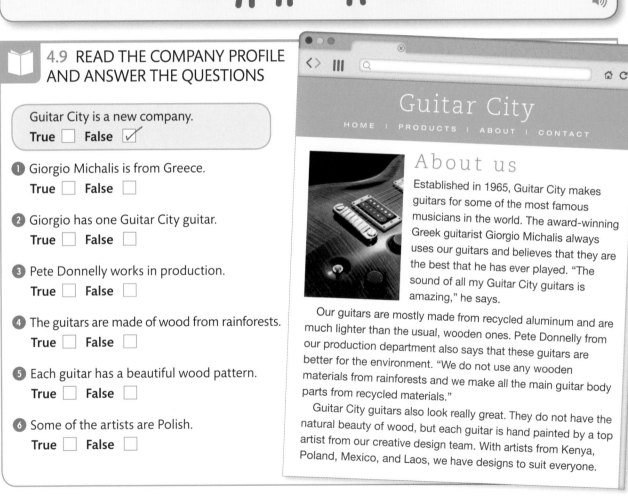

4.9 READ THE COMPANY PROFILE AND ANSWER THE QUESTIONS

Guitar City is a new company.
True ☐ **False** ☑

① Giorgio Michalis is from Greece.
True ☐ **False** ☐

② Giorgio has one Guitar City guitar.
True ☐ **False** ☐

③ Pete Donnelly works in production.
True ☐ **False** ☐

④ The guitars are made of wood from rainforests.
True ☐ **False** ☐

⑤ Each guitar has a beautiful wood pattern.
True ☐ **False** ☐

⑥ Some of the artists are Polish.
True ☐ **False** ☐

Guitar City

HOME | PRODUCTS | ABOUT | CONTACT

About us

Established in 1965, Guitar City makes guitars for some of the most famous musicians in the world. The award-winning Greek guitarist Giorgio Michalis always uses our guitars and believes that they are the best that he has ever played. "The sound of all my Guitar City guitars is amazing," he says.

Our guitars are mostly made from recycled aluminum and are much lighter than the usual, wooden ones. Pete Donnelly from our production department also says that these guitars are better for the environment. "We do not use any wooden materials from rainforests and we make all the main guitar body parts from recycled materials."

Guitar City guitars also look really great. They do not have the natural beauty of wood, but each guitar is hand painted by a top artist from our creative design team. With artists from Kenya, Poland, Mexico, and Laos, we have designs to suit everyone.

Vocabulary

5.1 IN THE OFFICE

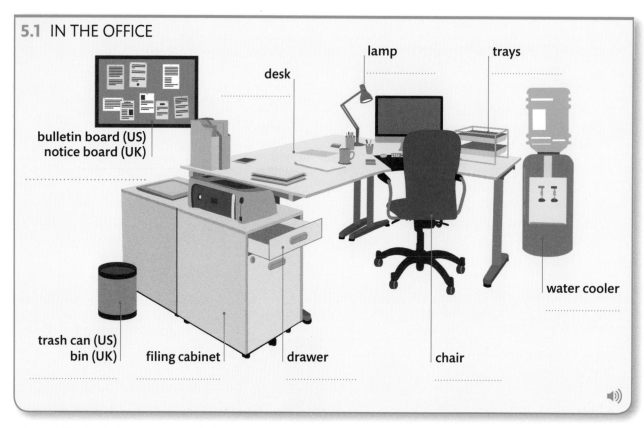

lamp

trays

desk

bulletin board (US)
notice board (UK)

water cooler

trash can (US)
bin (UK)

filing cabinet

drawer

chair

5.2 EQUIPMENT

photocopier

telephone /
phone

printer

projector

shredder

scanner

USB / flash drive

hard drive

headset

cell phone (US)
mobile phone (UK)

5.3 STATIONERY

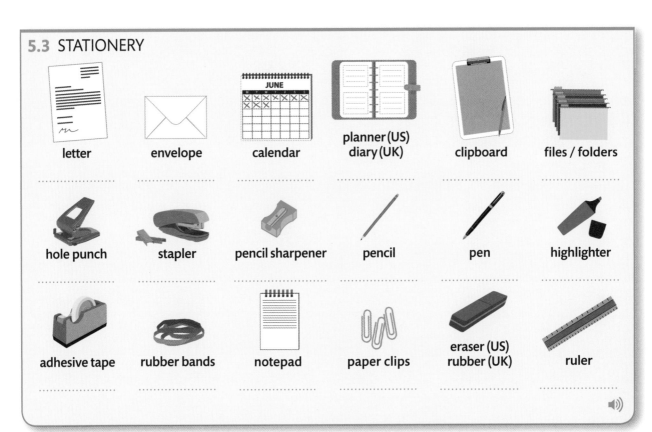

letter	envelope	calendar	planner (US) diary (UK)	clipboard	files / folders
hole punch	stapler	pencil sharpener	pencil	pen	highlighter
adhesive tape	rubber bands	notepad	paper clips	eraser (US) rubber (UK)	ruler

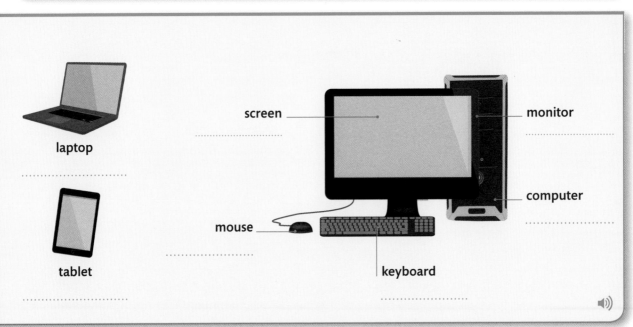

screen

monitor

laptop

computer

mouse

tablet

keyboard

06 Asking questions at work

It is important to use the correct word order and question words in English questions, depending on whether the questions are open-ended.

⚙ **New language** Forming questions
Aa **Vocabulary** Office equipment
🧩 **New skill** Asking colleagues questions

6.1 KEY LANGUAGE SIMPLE QUESTIONS WITH "TO BE"

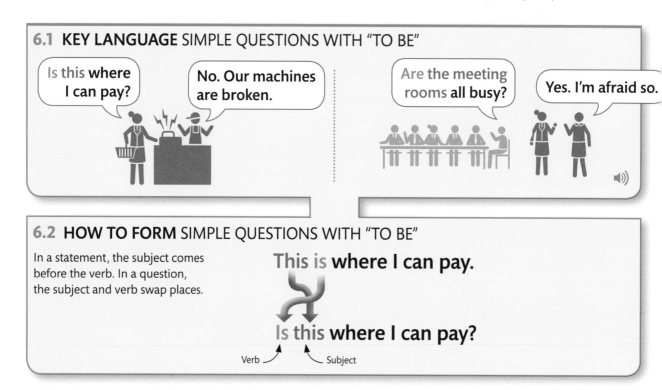

Is this **where I can pay?**

No. Our machines are broken.

Are the meeting rooms **all busy?**

Yes. I'm afraid so.

6.2 HOW TO FORM SIMPLE QUESTIONS WITH "TO BE"

In a statement, the subject comes before the verb. In a question, the subject and verb swap places.

This is **where I can pay.**

Is this **where I can pay?**

Verb — Subject

6.3 REWRITE THE QUESTIONS, PUTTING THE WORDS IN THE CORRECT ORDER

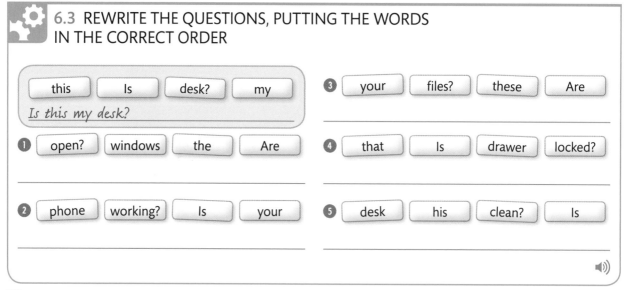

| this | Is | desk? | my |

Is this my desk?

① open? windows the Are

② phone working? Is your

③ your files? these Are

④ that Is drawer locked?

⑤ desk his clean? Is

28

6.4 KEY LANGUAGE SIMPLE QUESTIONS WITH "DO"

To form questions in sentences without the verb
"to be," start the question with "do" or "does."

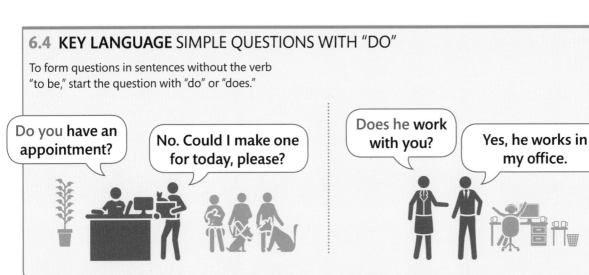

Do you **have an appointment?**

No. Could I make one for today, please?

Does he **work with you?**

Yes, he works in my office.

6.5 HOW TO FORM SIMPLE QUESTIONS WITH "DO"

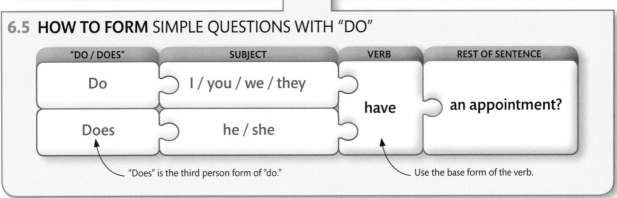

"DO / DOES"	SUBJECT	VERB	REST OF SENTENCE
Do	I / you / we / they	have	an appointment?
Does	he / she		

"Does" is the third person form of "do."

Use the base form of the verb.

6.6 FILL IN THE GAPS USING "DO" OR "DOES"

___Do___ they come in early?

1 _____ he have a key for this drawer?

2 _____ your laptop have a DVD drive?

3 _____ Jim and Tom have new screens?

4 _____ you keep pens in your desk drawer?

5 _____ Sarah write the minutes?

6 _____ all employees have wall calendars?

6.7 LISTEN TO THE AUDIO AND NUMBER THE QUESTIONS IN THE ORDER YOU HEAR THEM

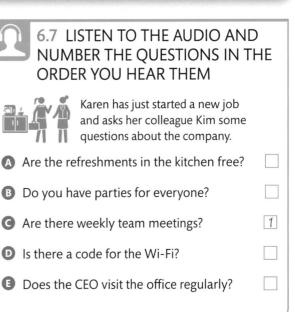

Karen has just started a new job and asks her colleague Kim some questions about the company.

A Are the refreshments in the kitchen free? ☐

B Do you have parties for everyone? ☐

C Are there weekly team meetings? ☐ *1*

D Is there a code for the Wi-Fi? ☐

E Does the CEO visit the office regularly? ☐

6.8 KEY LANGUAGE ASKING OPEN QUESTIONS

Use question words such as "when," "where," "how," or "why" to ask questions that can't be answered with "yes" or "no."

Where is the staff room?

Go down to the second floor.

When does Mia start work?

She usually starts at nine.

6.9 FURTHER EXAMPLES OPEN QUESTIONS

The auxilary "do / does" comes before the subject.

How does the scanner work?

What would you like to drink?

Invert the subject and the verb to form open questions with "to be."

Where is the cafeteria?

Why is he late?

The main verb comes at the end in questions without "to be."

Who is giving the presentation?

When does the meeting start?

6.10 CROSS OUT THE INCORRECT WORD IN EACH QUESTION

When / ~~What~~ are you going on vacation?

1 Where / How are the cups?

2 Who / What is the photocopier code?

3 Why / How do I turn off the screen?

4 Why / Who is this drawer always locked?

5 Where / When does the cafeteria open?

6 Why / Who do I ask for printer ink?

7 What / When do you discuss at meetings?

6.11 MATCH THE QUESTIONS TO THE CORRECT ANSWERS

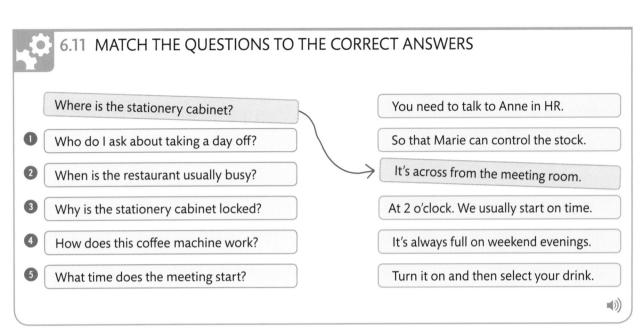

Where is the stationery cabinet?

1 Who do I ask about taking a day off?

2 When is the restaurant usually busy?

3 Why is the stationery cabinet locked?

4 How does this coffee machine work?

5 What time does the meeting start?

You need to talk to Anne in HR.

So that Marie can control the stock.

It's across from the meeting room.

At 2 o'clock. We usually start on time.

It's always full on weekend evenings.

Turn it on and then select your drink.

6.12 MARK THE QUESTIONS THAT ARE CORRECT

Who is in your team? ☑
What is in your team? ☐

1 What I can do to help you? ☐
What can I do to help you? ☐

2 Do you know where the key is? ☐
Does you know where the key is? ☐

3 When does the store open? ☐
When do the store open? ☐

4 Who do I connect the keyboard? ☐
How do I connect the keyboard? ☐

5 Why is her desk always a mess? ☐
Why does her desk always a mess? ☐

6.13 SAY THE QUESTIONS OUT LOUD, FILLING IN THE GAPS USING THE WORDS IN THE PANEL

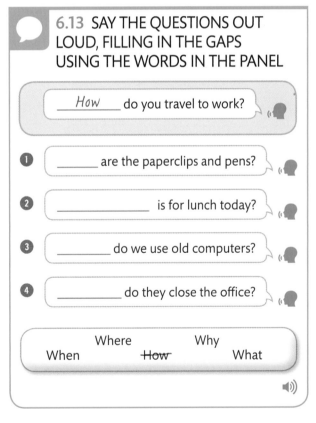

How do you travel to work?

1 _____ are the paperclips and pens?

2 _____ is for lunch today?

3 _____ do we use old computers?

4 _____ do they close the office?

When   Where   Why   ~~How~~   What

06 ✓ CHECKLIST

⚙ Forming questions ☐   **Aa** Office equipment ☐   🧩 Asking colleagues questions ☐

31

Exchanging details

When making new business contacts, there are several phrases you can use to ask for their details and offer yours in return.

⚙ **New language** Short answers
Aa Vocabulary Contact information
🧩 **New skill** Exchanging contact details

7.1 KEY LANGUAGE EXCHANGING CONTACT DETAILS

It is useful to know how to ask for contact information from a client or co-worker. Certain stock phrases can be adapted to many different situations.

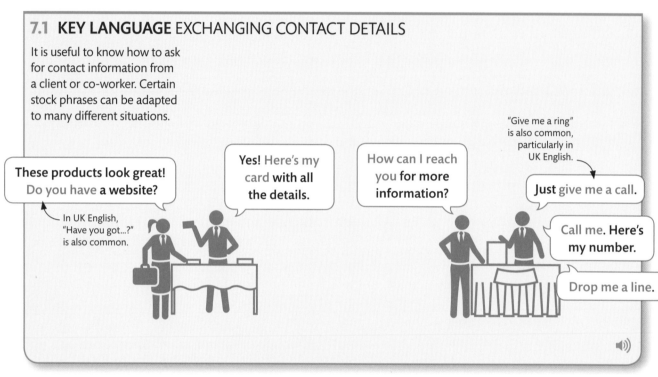

These products look great! **Do you have a website?**

In UK English, "Have you got...?" is also common.

Yes! Here's my card **with all the details.**

How can I reach you **for more information?**

"Give me a ring" is also common, particularly in UK English.

Just give me a call.

Call me. **Here's my number.**

Drop me a line.

7.2 VOCABULARY BUSINESS CARDS

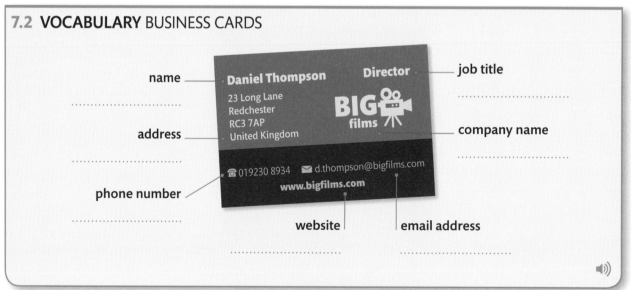

name

Daniel Thompson Director

job title

23 Long Lane
Redchester
RC3 7AP
United Kingdom

address

BIG films

company name

☎ 019230 8934   ✉ d.thompson@bigfilms.com
www.bigfilms.com

phone number

website

email address

7.3 PRONUNCIATION EMAIL ADDRESSES

There are set conventions for how to pronounce email address symbols such as "@" and "." in English.

at | hyphen | underscore | dot

sue@super-cleaning_team.com

This is pronounced as one word, but domains like **.co.jp** and **.co.uk** are pronounced with initials: "dot co dot yoo kay"

7.4 LISTEN TO THE AUDIO, THEN NUMBER THE EMAIL ADDRESSES IN THE ORDER YOU HEAR THEM

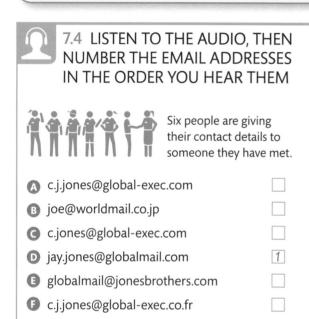

Six people are giving their contact details to someone they have met.

A c.j.jones@global-exec.com ☐

B joe@worldmail.co.jp ☐

C c.jones@global-exec.com ☐

D jay.jones@globalmail.com ☐ 1

E globalmail@jonesbrothers.com ☐

F c.j.jones@global-exec.co.fr ☐

7.5 CROSS OUT THE INCORRECT WORD IN EACH SENTENCE

Just ~~make~~ / give me a call when you're ready.

1 Do you **do** / **have** a website I can look up?

2 Your job **title** / **name** isn't listed here.

3 Just **fall** / **drop** me a line for more details.

4 How can I **reach** / **touch** you to follow up?

5 Is this your phone **number** / **address**?

6 Here's my **contact** / **business** card.

7 **Say** / **Call** me to arrange a meeting.

8 Drop me a **line** / **word** to follow up next week.

7.6 LOOK AT THE BUSINESS CARDS AND ANSWER THE QUESTIONS

McKay & Sons is a travel agent. **True** ☐ **False** ✓

1 McKay and Sons has a website. **True** ☐ **False** ☐

2 Steven McKay is a Web Designer. **True** ☐ **False** ☐

3 Nancy Li has a website. **True** ☐ **False** ☐

4 City Zoo is on Madison Avenue. **True** ☐ **False** ☐

5 Nancy works in Human Resources. **True** ☐ **False** ☐

6 Nancy has an email address. **True** ☐ **False** ☐

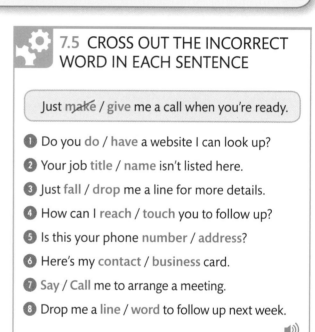

McKay & Sons
Architects
www.mckayandsons.com
Steven McKay
Managing Director
📞 1200 400 589
✉ s.mckay@mckayandsons.net

City Zoo
2045 Mason Avenue, Madison, WI 54229
Nancy Li
Assistant Zoologist
(608) 233-4487
nancyli@cityzoo.org

33

7.7 KEY LANGUAGE SHORT ANSWERS

You will often hear short answers such as
"Yes, I am" in English-speaking workplaces.
It is more polite to use a short answer than
to just answer "Yes" or "No."

TIP
You can use long
answers in more formal
conversations, or when
you want to add more
information in your
response.

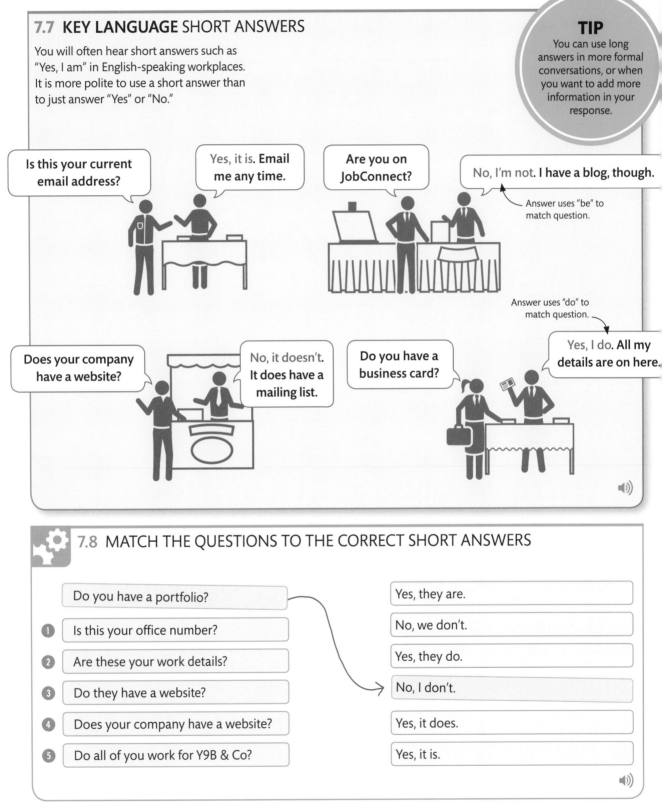

Is this your current email address?

Yes, it is. **Email me any time.**

Are you on JobConnect?

No, I'm not. **I have a blog, though.**

Answer uses "be" to match question.

Does your company have a website?

No, it doesn't. **It does have a mailing list.**

Do you have a business card?

Answer uses "do" to match question.

Yes, I do. **All my details are on here.**

7.8 MATCH THE QUESTIONS TO THE CORRECT SHORT ANSWERS

Do you have a portfolio?

1 Is this your office number?

2 Are these your work details?

3 Do they have a website?

4 Does your company have a website?

5 Do all of you work for Y9B & Co?

Yes, they are.

No, we don't.

Yes, they do.

No, I don't.

Yes, it does.

Yes, it is.

7.9 RESPOND OUT LOUD TO THE AUDIO, FILLING IN THE GAPS

Do I have your phone number?

Yes, *you do* .

④ Does your website have a contact form?

No, _____ .

① Is that your company's address?

No, _____ .

⑤ Do they have a brochure?

Yes, _____ .

② Are these details still correct?

Yes, _____ .

⑥ Do you want to arrange a meeting?

Yes, _____ .

③ Do you have a website?

Yes, _____ .

⑦ Do you have an office in the city?

No, _____ .

---

07 ✔ CHECKLIST

⚙ Short answers ☐   **Aa** Contact information ☐   🧩 Exchanging contact details ☐

↻ REVIEW THE ENGLISH YOU HAVE LEARNED IN UNITS 1–7

NEW LANGUAGE	SAMPLE SENTENCE	☑	UNIT
INTRODUCING YOURSELF AND OTHER PEOPLE	Good morning. My name's Alisha Sharma. This is my colleague, Edward.	☐	1.1, 1.5
PRESENT SIMPLE TO DESCRIBE ROUTINE WORK ACTIVITIES	We have a team meeting every Tuesday. The CEO works weekends if we're busy.	☐	2.1
COUNTRIES AND NATIONALITIES	These new mopeds are from Italy. I'm Brazilian, but I work in the US.	☐	4.1, 4.2, 4.3
NEGATIVE SENTENCES	I'm not French. I'm Canadian. The printer doesn't work!	☐	4.6
ASKING QUESTIONS	Do you have an appointment? Where is the staff room?	☐	6.1, 6.4, 6.8
EXCHANGING DETAILS, SHORT ANSWERS	Is this your email address? Yes, it is. Do you have a business card? No, I don't.	☐	7.1, 7.2, 7.7

08 Skills and experience

English uses the verb "have" to talk about people's skills, experience, and professional attributes. You might also hear "have got" in informal UK English.

New language "Have," "have got," articles
Aa Vocabulary Jobs and skills
New skill Writing a business profile

8.1 KEY LANGUAGE "HAVE"

Use "have" with nouns to talk about people's qualities or experience.

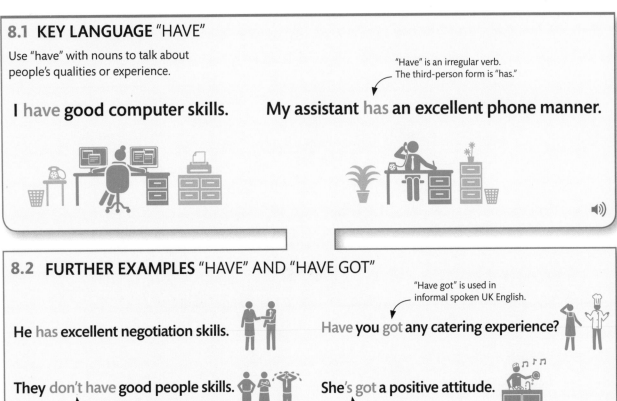

"Have" is an irregular verb. The third-person form is "has."

I have good computer skills.

My assistant has an excellent phone manner.

8.2 FURTHER EXAMPLES "HAVE" AND "HAVE GOT"

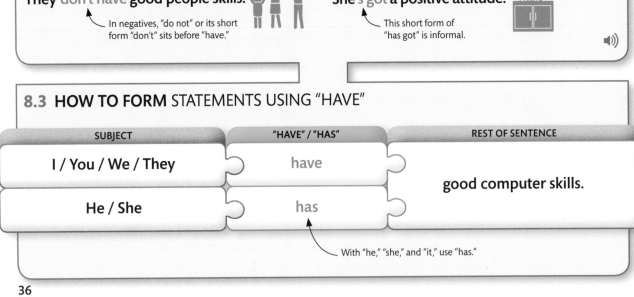

He has excellent negotiation skills.

"Have got" is used in informal spoken UK English.

Have you got any catering experience?

They don't have good people skills.

In negatives, "do not" or its short form "don't" sits before "have."

She's got a positive attitude.

This short form of "has got" is informal.

8.3 HOW TO FORM STATEMENTS USING "HAVE"

SUBJECT	"HAVE" / "HAS"	REST OF SENTENCE
I / You / We / They	have	good computer skills.
He / She	has	

With "he," "she," and "it," use "has."

8.4 CROSS OUT THE INCORRECT WORDS IN EACH SENTENCE

He ~~have~~ / has excellent typing skills.

1 They don't / doesn't have interviews today.

2 He haven't / hasn't got a diploma.

3 I don't have / don't got any experience.

4 Do you has / have good IT skills?

5 We haves / have monthly training sessions.

6 He don't / doesn't have experience with animals.

7 He's have / has a Master's degree.

8 They have / got a lot of inexperienced staff.

9 She's got / have super negotiation skills.

8.5 READ THE ONLINE PROFILE AND MARK THE STATEMENTS THAT ARE CORRECT

Sam Bradley · photographer

HOME | SKILLS | CONTACT

Experience:
I have a lot of experience in digital photography and photo editing. I love working with animals and nature, and I won my first regional competition when I was 13. In college, I chaired the Photography Club and arranged speakers, training, and field trips. I have some experience of working in an office, having spent a summer working for a nature magazine.

Skills:
- I have excellent photography and editing skills learned from my degree and many years of experience.
- I enjoy working in teams, on my own, and with animals.

Qualifications:
- **BA Dance and Drama** (2014)
- **Diploma in Pet Photography** (2016)

Sam has never edited photographs. ☐
Sam has edited photographs. ☑

1 Sam loves working with children. ☐
Sam loves working with animals. ☐

2 Sam won a regional competition. ☐
Sam won a national competition. ☐

3 Sam didn't organize field trips. ☐
Sam organized field trips at college. ☐

4 Sam worked in an office. ☐
Sam didn't work in an office. ☐

5 Sam has excellent photography skills. ☐
Sam has good negotiation skills. ☐

6 Sam's degree is is photography. ☐
Sam's degree is in dance and drama. ☐

7 Sam has a photography diploma. ☐
Sam has never studied photography. ☐

8.6 KEY LANGUAGE "A / AN / THE"

Use "a" or "an" to talk about jobs and workplaces if you are mentioning them for the first time. Use "the" to talk about something specific, or something you have mentioned before.

Use "a" because you are mentioning the restaurant for the first time.

I'm a waiter. I work in a popular restaurant.

The restaurant is always busy.

Use "the" because you have already mentioned the restaurant.

8.7 FURTHER EXAMPLES "A / AN / THE"

Use "an" before a vowel sound.

I'm an intern at an advertising agency.

Isaac is a good hairdresser.

The agency is next to a café.

The hairdresser who works weekends is terrible.

8.8 FILL IN THE GAPS USING "A," "AN," OR "THE"

He works in _____a_____ hotel.

1 Oh, yes. I know _____ hotel you mean.

2 Susan has _____ diploma.

3 Is _____ meeting on the second floor?

4 I work for _____ large recruitment agency.

5 There's _____ ad for a chef here.

6 I hired _____ PA to help me out.

7 He works at _____ hospital down the road.

8 Is there _____ office in Mexico?

8.9 LISTEN TO THE AUDIO, THEN NUMBER THE PEOPLE IN THE ORDER THEY ARE DESCRIBED

 A ☐

 B 1

 C ☐

 D ☐

 E ☐

 F ☐

8.10 KEY LANGUAGE THE ZERO ARTICLE

When English leaves out "a," "an," or "the" before a noun, this is called the zero article. Use the zero article with plurals when you are talking about things in general.

Refers to interviews in general, not specific interviews.

I get very nervous before interviews.

We're looking for people who can sell our products.

Refers to people in general, not specific individuals.

8.11 MARK THE SENTENCES THAT ARE CORRECT

> Online profiles are really useful. ☑
> The online profiles are really useful. ☐

1. He was out of the office today. ☐
   He was out of an office today. ☐

2. I have the excellent people skills. ☐
   I have excellent people skills. ☐

3. What skills do you need for this job? ☐
   What a skills do you need for this job? ☐

4. Have you read the job requirements? ☐
   Have you read a job requirements? ☐

5. She's a architect for a top company. ☐
   She's an architect for a top company. ☐

6. The new designer is very good. ☐
   A new designer is very good. ☐

8.12 READ THE COVER LETTER AND CROSS OUT THE INCORRECT WORDS

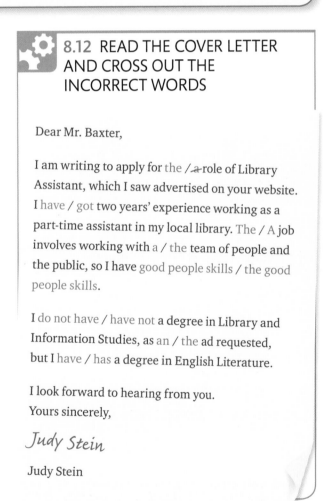

Dear Mr. Baxter,

I am writing to apply for the / a~~ role of Library Assistant, which I saw advertised on your website. I have / got two years' experience working as a part-time assistant in my local library. The / A job involves working with a / the team of people and the public, so I have good people skills / the good people skills.

I do not have / have not a degree in Library and Information Studies, as an / the ad requested, but I have / has a degree in English Literature.

I look forward to hearing from you.
Yours sincerely,

Judy Stein

Judy Stein

---

08 ✓ CHECKLIST

⚙ "Have," "have got," articles ☐   **Aa** Jobs and skills ☐   🧩 Writing a business profile ☐

09 Vocabulary

9.1 JOBS

 businessman

 businesswoman

 sales manager

 sales assistant

 receptionist

 hairdresser / stylist

 gardener

 cleaner / janitor

 train driver

 taxi driver

 electrician

 construction worker (US) / builder (UK)

 plumber

 engineer

 mechanic

 pilot

 flight attendant

 travel agent

 tour guide

 journalist

9.2 EMPLOYMENT

 full-time (F/T) [a complete working week]

 part-time (P/T) [an incomplete working week]

 permanent [a long-term, salaried position]

 temporary [a short-term position with a known end date]

 **shift** [a period of work with a set number of hours]

 waiter

 waitress

 chef

 personal assistant / PA

 scientist

 librarian

 teacher

 judge

 police officer

 firefighter

 surgeon

 doctor

 nurse

 dentist

 vet

 writer

 designer

 photographer

 artist

 musician

 manager
[the person responsible for directing employees]

 co-worker / colleague
[a person you work with in a profession]

 assistant
[someone who does routine tasks for a senior person]

 intern
[a person who works to gain experience]

 apprentice
[a person who is learning a trade]

10 Choosing a job

Verbs such as "like," "enjoy," and "hate" express feelings about things. They are often used to talk about what activities people would like to do in a job.

⚙ **New language** "Like," "enjoy," and "hate"
Aa Vocabulary Workplace activities
🧩 **New skill** Finding the right job

10.1 KEY LANGUAGE LIKES AND DISLIKES

Use verbs such as "like," "enjoy," and "hate" to give your opinion on workplace activities. These can be followed by a noun, or by a gerund ("-ing" form of the verb) and a noun.

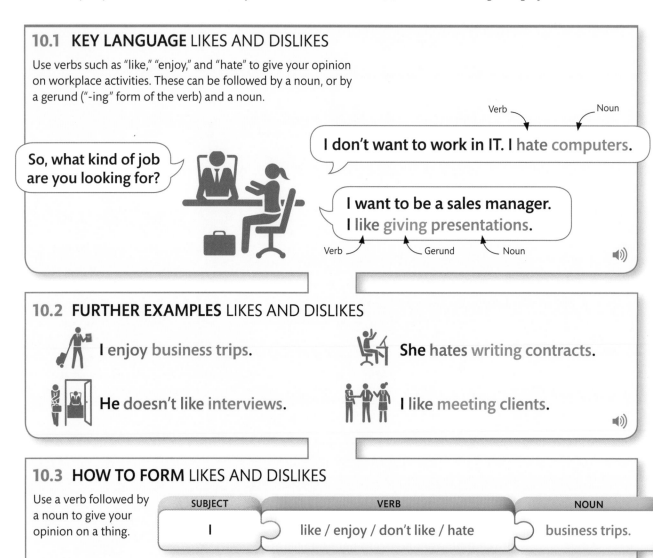

So, what kind of job are you looking for?

Verb   Noun

I don't want to work in IT. I hate computers.

I want to be a sales manager.
I like giving presentations.

Verb   Gerund   Noun

10.2 FURTHER EXAMPLES LIKES AND DISLIKES

I enjoy business trips.

She hates writing contracts.

He doesn't like interviews.

I like meeting clients.

10.3 HOW TO FORM LIKES AND DISLIKES

Use a verb followed by a noun to give your opinion on a thing.

SUBJECT	VERB	NOUN
I	like / enjoy / don't like / hate	business trips.

Use a verb followed by a gerund and a noun to give your opinion on an activity.

SUBJECT	VERB	GERUND	NOUN
I	like / enjoy / don't like / hate	giving	presentations.

Add "-ing" to the verb to form the gerund.

10.4 CROSS OUT THE INCORRECT WORDS IN EACH SENTENCE

Do you enjoy ~~meet~~ / meeting clients?

1 She don't like / doesn't like like using computers.

2 He likes training / train new colleagues.

3 I hates / hate long meetings.

4 We don't like / doesn't like lazy employees.

5 She enjoys work / working in a team.

10.5 LISTEN TO THE AUDIO AND MARK WHETHER JORDI LIKES OR DISLIKES THE ACTIVITY IN EACH PICTURE

Likes ☐
Dislikes ☑

1 Likes ☐
Dislikes ☐

2 Likes ☐
Dislikes ☐

3 Likes ☐
Dislikes ☐

4 Likes ☐
Dislikes ☐

10.6 READ THE JOB ADVERTISEMENT AND ANSWER THE QUESTIONS

The tour guide might work with children. **True** ☑ **False** ☐

1 Not many tourists go to Notwen Castle. **True** ☐ **False** ☐

2 The job involves greeting visitors. **True** ☐ **False** ☐

3 The tour guide must like working alone. **True** ☐ **False** ☐

4 The tour guide always works inside. **True** ☐ **False** ☐

5 The job involves weekend work. **True** ☐ **False** ☐

JOBS

Tour Guide

needed for top tourist attraction

Do you love working with people from all ages and backgrounds? Notwen Castle is one of the most popular castles in the country. Every visitor to Notwen Castle is special. It will be your job to welcome them to the castle. You must enjoy working as part of a team and have great customer service skills. The job includes working outside and on weekends.

10 ✔ CHECKLIST

⚙ "Like," "enjoy," and "hate" ☐   **Aa** Workplace activities ☐   🧩 Finding the right job ☐

11 Describing your workplace

One way of telling people about your company is by using "there is" and "there are." Use "Is there...?" or "Are there...?" to ask questions about a workplace.

⚙ **New language** "There is" and "there are"
Aa Vocabulary Office equipment
🧩 **New skill** Describing a workplace

11.1 KEY LANGUAGE "THERE IS" AND "THERE ARE"

Use "there is" to talk about one thing, and "there are" to talk about more than one thing.

There is always a supervisor on the factory floor.

There are six well-trained assistants on her team.

11.2 FURTHER EXAMPLES "THERE IS" AND "THERE ARE"

There's a business dress code at this company.

↳ "There is" can be shortened to "There's."

There are two printers on your floor.

↳ "There are" cannot be shortened.

There isn't a water cooler in the kitchen.

↳ Use "not" or its short form in negatives.

There aren't any elevators in the office.

↳ Use "any" for negative plurals.

Is there a set time for lunch breaks?

↳ Start questions with "Is there" or "Are there."

Are there any files in the stationery cabinet?

↳ Use "any" for plurals in questions.

11.3 REWRITE THE SENTENCES, CORRECTING THE ERRORS

> There is 10 people on the sales team.
> _There are 10 people on the sales team._

1 There are'nt any bathrooms on this floor.

_____

2 Is there any stationery cabinet in the office?

_____

3 There's staff cafeteria on the third floor.

_____

4 There isnt an elevator in this building.

_____

5 Is there any places to lock my bicycle here?

_____

6 Are there a desk ready for our new designer?

_____

7 There're lots of envelopes in the cabinet.

_____

🔊

11.4 LISTEN TO THE AUDIO AND WRITE ANSWERS TO THE QUESTIONS IN FULL SENTENCES

Alvita is showing a new colleague, Jonathan, around the office.

> What happens every Monday afternoon?
> _There is a weekly team meeting._

1 Where do people leave their wet coats?

_____

2 How many desks are in Jonathan's office?

_____

3 What is across from Jonathan's office?

_____

4 Where do staff sign in every day?

_____

11.5 USE THE CHART TO CREATE SIX CORRECT SENTENCES AND SAY THEM OUT LOUD

> _There is a staff parking lot._

| There | is / are / isn't / aren't | a / any | staff parking lot. / places to relax. / business dress code. |

🔊

12.1 MONEY

bills (US) / notes (UK)

coins

wallet

wallet (US) / purse (UK)

credit card

debit card

cash machine / ATM

withdraw money

bank

bank statement

online banking

mobile banking

receipt

currency

cash register (US) / till (UK)

safe

invoice

check (US) / cheque (UK)

deposit / pay in money

transfer money

12.2 PAY AND CONDITIONS

The company I work for pays an **hourly rate** of $15.

hourly rate
[the amount of money paid per hour]

The **salary** for this job is $35,000.

salary
[a fixed, regular payment every month, often expressed as an annual sum]

I work fewer hours now, but I had to take a huge **pay cut**.

a pay cut
[a reduction in pay]

My annual review was really positive so I'm hoping to get a **raise** next year.

a raise (US) / a pay rise (UK)
[an increase in pay]

My **bonus** this year was $2,000 so I'm going to buy a new car.

a bonus
[money added to a person's wages as a reward for good performance]

Benefits include a free gym membership.

benefits
[extras given to employees in addition to their usual pay]

I work extra hours regularly and get **overtime** pay.

overtime
[additional pay for extra hours worked]

The demand for plumbers has decreased so I **earned** half as much this year.

to earn
[to receive money in return for labor or services]

The shop has been really busy so our **wages** are increasing next week.

wage
[the amount of money paid per week or month]

I get 20 days of **annual vacation** every year.

annual vacation (US) / annual leave (UK)
[paid time off work granted by employers]

13 Personal qualities

You will encounter people with different skills and personalities at work. It is useful to be able to describe your co-workers and discuss their strengths and weaknesses.

⚙️ **New language** Possessive adjectives
Aa Vocabulary Personality traits
🧩 **New skill** Describing your co-workers

13.1 KEY LANGUAGE ADJECTIVES

Adjectives are usually placed before nouns or after some verbs such as "be," "become," "get," "seem," and "look."

Adjective comes before the noun.

Adjective comes after the verb "be."

I run a great team, but John is really lazy. It's not fair on his co-workers.

TIP
Adjectives that describe negative qualities, such as "lazy," are usually avoided in business environments.

13.2 FURTHER EXAMPLES ADJECTIVES

 Chloe is polite to clients.

 Michael is very hardworking.

 Ben seems very organized.

Use "very" or "really" before adjectives to add emphasis.

Adjectives do not change form with feminine nouns.

 Sally is always calm under pressure.

 Fatima is a creative designer.

 Ruth and Ian always look great.

Adjectives do not change form with plural nouns.

13.3 LISTEN TO THE AUDIO, THEN NUMBER THE PEOPLE IN THE ORDER THAT THEY ARE DESCRIBED

 A ☐

 B 1

 C ☐

 D ☐   E ☐

13.4 READ THE ARTICLE AND WRITE THE HIGHLIGHTED ADJECTIVES
UNDER THE CORRECT HEADING

POSITIVE

motivated

_____

_____

_____

_____

NEGATIVE

impatient

_____

_____

_____

_____

OUR TEAM

Career climbers who are moving up fast

Meet two of our new employees

A design that inspired Sam Riley

Sam Riley joins Scarlett Fashion Design after a short, steep climb to the top of his career ladder. Sam says, "I've always been an extremely motivated and ambitious person. I am sometimes a little impatient with lazy or impolite people, but I hope my new colleagues will find me to be helpful."

Alik Novozik already has a reputation as a bright and intelligent designer and we are very happy to welcome him to the Scarlett family. Alik says, "I'm looking forward to working with the design team here. Some people say I can be a little nervous. Even if I do get nervous sometimes, I'm definitely not boring."

 13.5 REWRITE THE SENTENCES, CORRECTING THE ERRORS

This is a team great. All my colleagues be really hardworkings.
This is a great team. All my colleagues are really hardworking.

1 My team leader impolite is and he is also impatient very.

_____

2 My co-workers say that I really motivated and ambitious am.

_____

3 The new young intern seems very intelligent and he really be polite.

_____

4 I'm very lucky. All my colleagues be hardworking and helpfuls.

_____

49

13.6 KEY LANGUAGE POSSESSIVE ADJECTIVES

Possessive adjectives tell you who something belongs to. Use them to talk about colleagues, work, or competitors.

Subject pronoun.

She looks busy.

Yes. Tamsin takes her work very seriously.

Possessive adjective means the work belongs to Tamsin.

13.7 FURTHER EXAMPLES POSSESSIVE ADJECTIVES

Your team is so hardworking.

Pablo is talking to his manager.

My staff is very motivated.

Their products aren't very good.

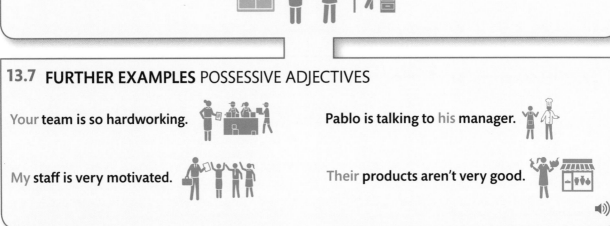

13.8 HOW TO FORM POSSESSIVE ADJECTIVES

SUBJECT PRONOUN	I	you	he	she	it	we	they
POSSESSIVE ADJECTIVE	my	your	his	her	its	our	their

13.9 FILL IN THE GAPS BY TURNING THE SUBJECT PRONOUNS INTO POSSESSIVE ADJECTIVES

Sophia is so efficient. _____*Her*_____ (She) desk is always very well organized.

1. Two of the people on _____ (I) team are new to the company, but they're settling in well.

2. _____ (They) manager is very good with people. They enjoy working with him.

3. The company is very proud of _____ (it) reputation and quality products.

4. Is this _____ (you) phone? It doesn't belong to me but I found it on my desk.

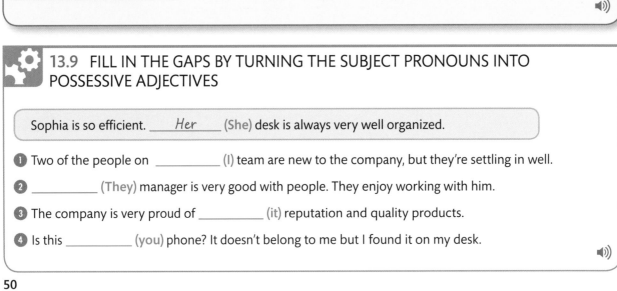

13.10 KEY LANGUAGE POSSESSIVE PRONOUNS

Use possessive pronouns to refer back to your achievements or the things you own. If you use the possessive pronoun, don't repeat the noun phrase in the question.

"Mine" sounds more natural than "my design."

Is that design yours? It looks great!

Yes, it's mine. I'm very proud of it.

13.11 HOW TO FORM POSSESSIVE PRONOUNS

POSSESSIVE ADJECTIVE	my	your	his	her	its	our	their
POSSESSIVE PRONOUN	mine	yours	his	hers	its	ours	theirs

13.12 CROSS OUT THE INCORRECT WORD IN EACH SENTENCE

This laptop is ~~their~~ / theirs.

1 We hate their product but we love our / ours.

2 They are proud of their / theirs project.

3 Our / Ours clients expect excellent service.

4 This isn't her desk. It's my / mine.

5 This is amazing. Is it her / hers project?

13.13 WRITE EACH SENTENCE IN ITS OTHER FORM

This is my computer.	This computer is mine.
1	I think these files are yours.
2 Is this his desk?	
3	These pens are hers.
4 Are those their products?	

13.14 KEY LANGUAGE POSSESSIVE APOSTROPHE

Add an apostrophe and the letter "s" to the end of a singular noun to show that what comes after the noun belongs to it.

Apostrophe with an "s" signifies ownership.

Jeremy is Pepe's line manager.

[Jeremy is the line manager of Pepe.]

Add an apostrophe with no "s" to plural nouns.

To show belonging with a plural noun, just add an apostrophe after the "s."

Jeremy is my colleagues' line manager.

[Jeremy is the line manager of multiple people.]

13.15 ⚠ COMMON MISTAKES POSSESSIVE APOSTROPHE

Never use an apostrophe and "s" after a plural noun in a statement which does not express possession.

"Colleagues" is a plural noun, but it does not refer to possession here.

My colleagues are late. ✔

My colleagues' are late. ✘

Don't use an apostrophe because "late" doesn't belong to "colleagues."

My colleague's are late. ✘

13.16 REWRITE THE SENTENCES, CORRECTING THE ERRORS

Jasons assistant often works late.
Jason's assistant often works late.

❶ The intern's work really hard.

_____

❷ All the team members' are intelligent.

_____

❸ This big room is my boss office.

_____

❹ All the bosses' have parking spaces.

_____

❺ The best thing about this product is it's strength.

_____

13.17 REWRITE THE HIGHLIGHTED PHRASES, CORRECTING THE ERRORS

**Performance Review:
Jorge Perez**

Jorge is very hardworking and he confidence has grown since his joined the company last summer. He writes excellent reports and is polite and friendly with co-workers and customers. Jorges supervisor believes that he will be promoted soon and will have an excellent future in the company. We are very pleased with his work and continued progress here.

**Performance Review:
Maria Moran**

Maria does not seem to be very happy at work at the moment. She progress is slow and she has not completed a single project yet. Her main problem is that she has difficulties working as part of a team. Co-workers complain that Maria impatient is and also unfriendly. This is a shame as she is obviously intelligent very. We hope that Maria will begin to see how important it is to be a good team player.

> *his confidence has grown*

1 _____

2 _____

3 _____

4 _____

5 _____

13.18 USE THE CHART TO CREATE 14 CORRECT SENTENCES AND SAY THEM OUT LOUD

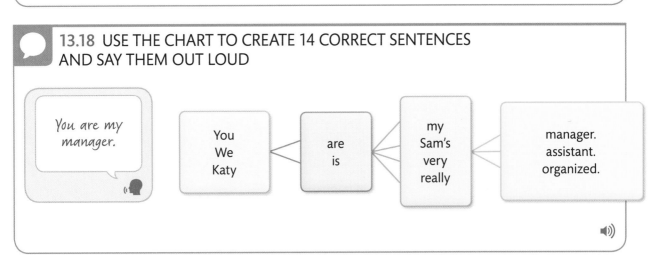

> *You are my manager.*

| You / We / Katy | are / is | my / Sam's / very / really | manager. / assistant. / organized. |

---

13 ✓ **CHECKLIST**

⚙ Possessive adjectives ☐   **Aa** Personality traits ☐   🧩 Describing your co-workers ☐

14 Describing your job

One way of telling someone about your job is to use adjectives to describe it. Adjectives can also help you to make comparisons with other roles you have had.

⚙ **New language** Adjectives and comparatives
Aa Vocabulary Money and pay
🧩 **New skill** Describing your job to someone

14.1 KEY LANGUAGE ADJECTIVES WITH "-ING" AND "-ED"

Adjectives that end in "-ing" describe the effect something has.
Adjectives ending in "-ed" describe how something is affected.

The job causes tiredness.

My job is very tiring.
I am always so tired!

The man experiences tiredness.

🔊

14.2 FURTHER EXAMPLES ADJECTIVES WITH "-ING" AND "-ED"

The building is amazing.
The tourists are amazed.

The meeting was boring.
They were bored.

The task is annoying.
She is annoyed.

The vacation is relaxing.
He is relaxed.

🔊

14.3 CROSS OUT THE INCORRECT WORD IN EACH SENTENCE

That's a very ~~interested~~ / interesting idea.

1. That meeting was really bored / boring.

2. The printer can be annoyed / annoying at times.

3. By the end of the week, I'm really tired / tiring.

4. The system is confused / confusing at first.

5. I'm very excited / exciting about my project.

6. The news was shocked / shocking.

7. I was very surprised / surprising by my raise!

🔊

54

14.4 READ THE ARTICLE AND ANSWER THE QUESTIONS

Sven is self-employed.
True ☐   False ☐   Not given ☑

1 Sven wanted to work on a space station.
True ☐   False ☐   Not given ☐

2 Sven's job is based in the US.
True ☐   False ☐   Not given ☐

3 Sven thinks everyone would like to do his job.
True ☐   False ☐   Not given ☐

4 Sven works some weekends.
True ☐   False ☐   Not given ☐

5 Sven finds his work annoying.
True ☐   False ☐   Not given ☐

Reach for the stars

This week we talk to Sven about his work

I was really excited when I first got this job. More than 3,000 people applied for it and I was thrilled to be successful. I do really interesting research on astronauts and space programs. I work in a large office in the United States and analyze data from space stations and satellites. I think the work is really fascinating, although some people might think that looking at screens of statistics from space stations is quite boring. The data arrives all the time, so the work can be quite tiring. We all work quite long hours, but we never get annoyed as we hope that the work we do will be important for scientists and other researchers.

Aa 14.5 READ THE CLUES AND WRITE THE WORDS FROM THE PANEL IN THE CORRECT PLACES ON THE GRID

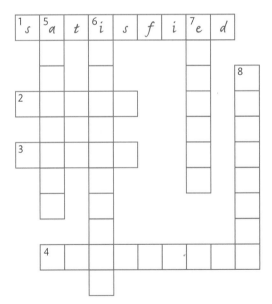

ACROSS

1 Happy or pleased with what you have.

2 Lacking interest and patience.

3 Needing sleep or rest.

4 Difficult to follow or understand.

DOWN

5 Causing irritation and frustration.

6 Something that you want to learn more about.

7 Enthusiastic and eager.

8 Unexpected, surprising, or upsetting.

bored   excited   ~~satisfied~~   tired   shocking   confusing   interesting   annoying

55

14.6 KEY LANGUAGE COMPARATIVE ADJECTIVES

Most adjectives have a comparative form that is used
to describe the difference between two things.

Do you like the new job?
I bet the salary is higher!

Add "-er" to make
the comparative.

It is, but the hours are much
longer than my old job.

Use "than" after the
comparative to compare
one thing to another.

14.7 FURTHER EXAMPLES COMPARATIVE ADJECTIVES

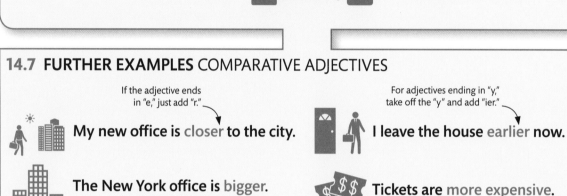

If the adjective ends
in "e," just add "r."

My new office is closer to the city.

For adjectives ending in "y,"
take off the "y" and add "ier."

I leave the house earlier now.

The New York office is bigger.

For single-syllable adjectives
ending consonant-vowel-consonant,
double the final letter and add "er."

Tickets are more expensive.

For adjectives with more than
two syllables, use "more" to
make the comparative.

Adjective
does not
change.

14.8 FILL IN THE GAPS WITH THE CORRECT COMPARATIVES

My new commute is __more expensive__ (expensive) than before, and it's _____longer_____ (long).

❶ This printer is _____ (fast) than the other, but that one is _____ (reliable).

❷ This coffee is _____ (strong) than I normally buy, but it is also _____ (tasty).

❸ This building is _____ (new) than my last workplace, and the area is _____ (quiet).

❹ This café is _____ (busy) than the other one, so the service is _____ (slow).

❺ My new uniform is _____ (comfortable) than my old one, but _____ (ugly).

14.9 KEY LANGUAGE IRREGULAR COMPARATIVE ADJECTIVES

Some common adjectives (usually short words)
have comparatives that do not follow the rules.

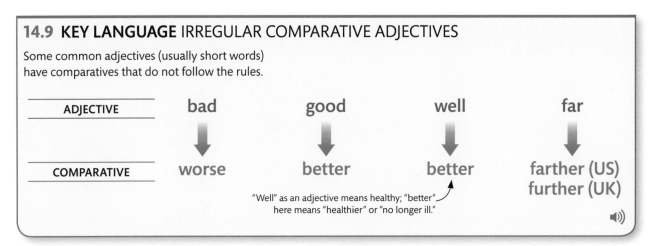

ADJECTIVE	bad	good	well	far
COMPARATIVE	worse	better	better	farther (US) / further (UK)

"Well" as an adjective means healthy; "better" here means "healthier" or "no longer ill."

14.10 MARK THE SENTENCES THAT ARE CORRECT

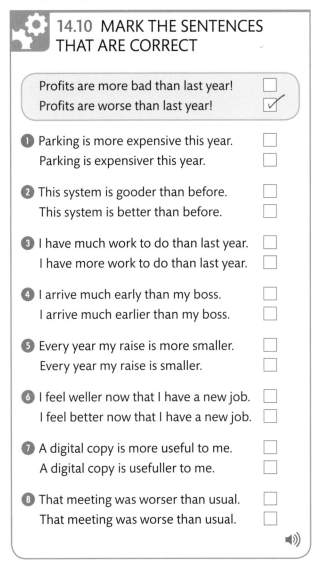

Profits are more bad than last year! ☐
Profits are worse than last year! ☑

1 Parking is more expensive this year. ☐
Parking is expensiver this year. ☐

2 This system is gooder than before. ☐
This system is better than before. ☐

3 I have much work to do than last year. ☐
I have more work to do than last year. ☐

4 I arrive much early than my boss. ☐
I arrive much earlier than my boss. ☐

5 Every year my raise is more smaller. ☐
Every year my raise is smaller. ☐

6 I feel weller now that I have a new job. ☐
I feel better now that I have a new job. ☐

7 A digital copy is more useful to me. ☐
A digital copy is usefuller to me. ☐

8 That meeting was worser than usual. ☐
That meeting was worse than usual. ☐

14.11 LISTEN TO THE AUDIO AND MATCH THE IMAGES TO THE CORRECT PHRASES

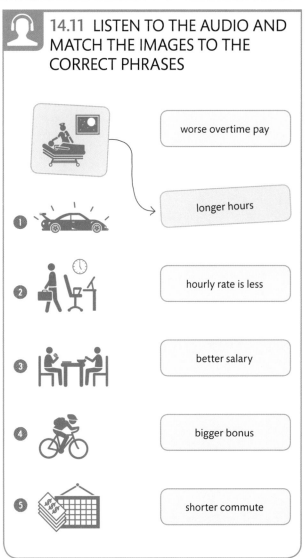

worse overtime pay

longer hours

hourly rate is less

better salary

bigger bonus

shorter commute

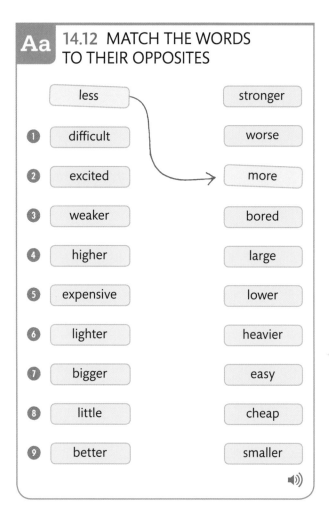

Aa 14.12 MATCH THE WORDS TO THEIR OPPOSITES

less	stronger
① difficult	worse
② excited	more
③ weaker	bored
④ higher	large
⑤ expensive	lower
⑥ lighter	heavier
⑦ bigger	easy
⑧ little	cheap
⑨ better	smaller

🔊

⚙ 14.13 REWRITE THE HIGHLIGHTED PHRASES, CORRECTING ERRORS

Join our team

Are you more efficienter than your colleagues? Are you more friendlier than others? And do you want to be more successfuller? ...then come to work with us at Sandwich Delicious. We sell morer sandwiches than any other sandwich bar in the city. We also offer more good pay than similar jobs in the area. All our co-workers at Sandwich Delicious deli get more long vacations than those working at similar companies. You will get three days off every week.

more efficient	③ _____
① _____	④ _____
② _____	⑤ _____

⚙ 14.14 MATCH THE BEGINNINGS OF THE SENTENCES TO THE CORRECT ENDINGS

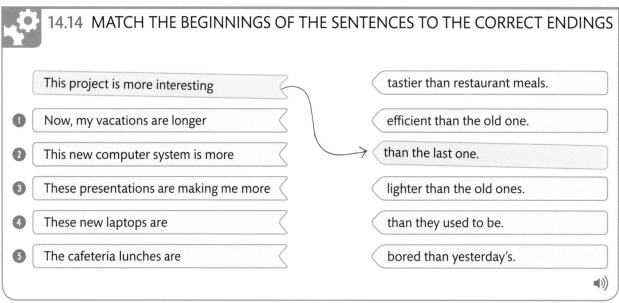

This project is more interesting	tastier than restaurant meals.
① Now, my vacations are longer	efficient than the old one.
② This new computer system is more	than the last one.
③ These presentations are making me more	lighter than the old ones.
④ These new laptops are	than they used to be.
⑤ The cafeteria lunches are	bored than yesterday's.

🔊

14.15 LISTEN TO THE AUDIO AND ANSWER THE QUESTIONS

Joe is talking about his new job and comparing it to the previous company where he worked.

Joe says the new company is more modern.
True ☑ False ☐ Not given ☐

1 Joe does not enjoy working in social media.
True ☐ False ☐ Not given ☐

2 Joe earns more money now than he did before.
True ☐ False ☐ Not given ☐

3 Joe spends more time at work now than before.
True ☐ False ☐ Not given ☐

4 Joe is bored in his new job.
True ☐ False ☐ Not given ☐

5 Joe's new boss has regular meetings with him.
True ☐ False ☐ Not given ☐

6 Joe's old workplace was not very organized.
True ☐ False ☐ Not given ☐

7 Joe's new workplace is more efficient.
True ☐ False ☐ Not given ☐

14 ⊘ CHECKLIST

⚙ Adjectives and comparatives ☐   **Aa** Money and pay ☐   🧩 Describing your job to someone ☐

♲ REVIEW THE ENGLISH YOU HAVE LEARNED IN UNITS 8–14

NEW LANGUAGE	SAMPLE SENTENCE	☑	UNIT
TALKING ABOUT YOUR SKILLS AND EXPERIENCE	I have **excellent negotiation skills.** I work in a **busy restaurant.**	☐	8.1, 8.6
LIKES AND DISLIKES	I hate **computers.** He likes giving **presentations.**	☐	10.1, 10.2
DESCRIBING A WORKPLACE	There is **a formal dress code at this company.** There are **two printers on your floor.**	☐	11.1, 11.2
DESCRIBING COLLEAGUES	Your **new team is really hard-working.** Jeremy is Pepe's **line manager.**	☐	13.1, 13.11
DESCRIBING YOUR JOB	My job is very tiring. I am always so tired!	☐	14.1
MAKING COMPARISONS	Is the salary higher in your new job?	☐	14.6

15 Workplace routines

Employees have schedules and workplaces also have their own routines and timetables. It is useful to be able to talk to colleagues about when things usually happen.

⚙ **New language** Prepositions of time
Aa Vocabulary Commuting and transportation
🧩 **New skill** Describing routines

15.1 KEY LANGUAGE PREPOSITIONS OF TIME

Use prepositions to give more information about when something happens.

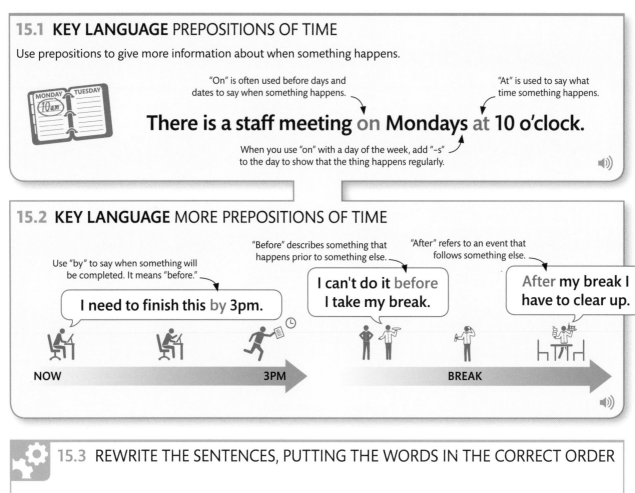

"On" is often used before days and dates to say when something happens.

"At" is used to say what time something happens.

There is a staff meeting on Mondays at 10 o'clock.

When you use "on" with a day of the week, add "-s" to the day to show that the thing happens regularly.

15.2 KEY LANGUAGE MORE PREPOSITIONS OF TIME

Use "by" to say when something will be completed. It means "before."

"Before" describes something that happens prior to something else.

"After" refers to an event that follows something else.

I need to finish this by 3pm.

I can't do it before I take my break.

After my break I have to clear up.

NOW   3PM   BREAK

15.3 REWRITE THE SENTENCES, PUTTING THE WORDS IN THE CORRECT ORDER

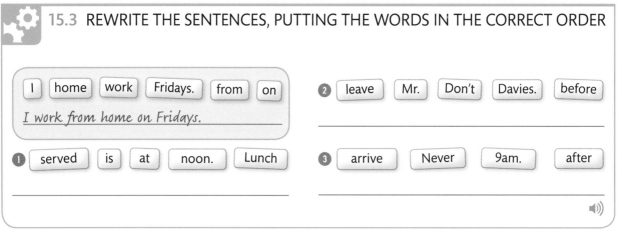

I | home | work | Fridays. | from | on
I work from home on Fridays.

2 | leave | Mr. | Don't | Davies. | before
_____

1 | served | is | at | noon. | Lunch
_____

3 | arrive | Never | 9am. | after
_____

60

15.4 KEY LANGUAGE PREPOSITIONS SHOWING DURATION

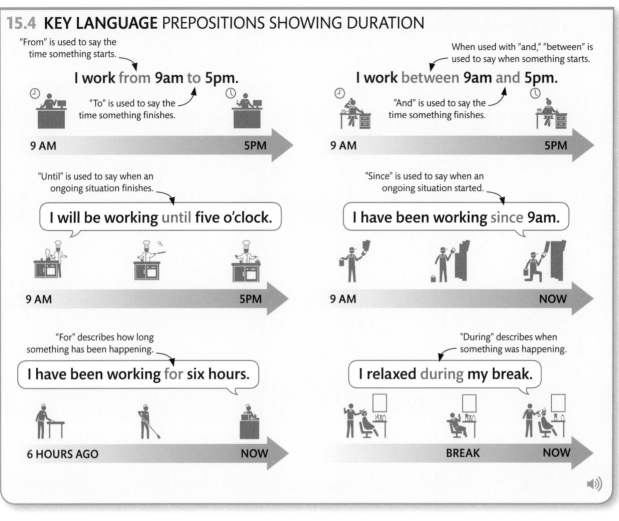

"From" is used to say the time something starts.

I work from 9am to 5pm.

"To" is used to say the time something finishes.

9 AM   5PM

When used with "and," "between" is used to say when something starts.

I work between 9am and 5pm.

"And" is used to say the time something finishes.

9 AM   5PM

"Until" is used to say when an ongoing situation finishes.

I will be working until five o'clock.

9 AM   5PM

"Since" is used to say when an ongoing situation started.

I have been working since 9am.

9 AM   NOW

"For" describes how long something has been happening.

I have been working for six hours.

6 HOURS AGO   NOW

"During" describes when something was happening.

I relaxed during my break.

BREAK   NOW

15.5 CROSS OUT THE INCORRECT WORD IN EACH SENTENCE, THEN SAY THE SENTENCES OUT LOUD

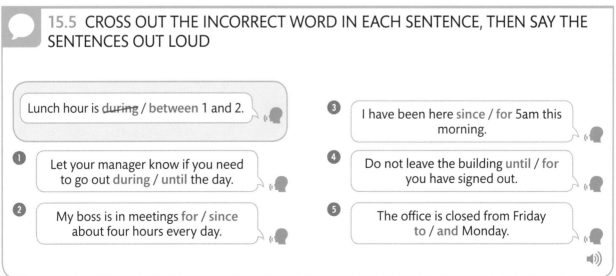

Lunch hour is ~~during~~ / between 1 and 2.

1 Let your manager know if you need to go out during / until the day.

2 My boss is in meetings for / since about four hours every day.

3 I have been here since / for 5am this morning.

4 Do not leave the building until / for you have signed out.

5 The office is closed from Friday to / and Monday.

61

15.6 KEY LANGUAGE GETTING TO WORK

There are a number of ways to describe how you get to work.

Use "take" and "catch" with forms of transportation that you do not drive or control.

I walk to work.

I cycle to work.

I drive to work.

I take the metro.

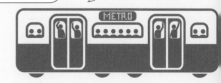

15.7 MATCH THE PAIRS OF PHRASES THAT MEAN THE SAME THING

I drive to work. → I go by car.

Sometimes I ride my bike to work.

1. I take the metro to work.

2. I cycle to work in good weather.

I normally go to work on foot.

3. I commute by train.

I go by metro.

4. I usually walk to work.

Sometimes I take a taxi to work.

5. When it rains, I go by taxi.

I take the bus.

6. I catch the bus to work.

I go by train to work.

15.8 CROSS OUT INCORRECT WORD IN EACH SENTENCE

 I usually take / ~~drive~~ the bus to work.

1. I always catch / drive to work.

2. It's usually quicker to bike / cycle.

3. When it's sunny, we go on foot / walk.

4. I don't like taking the metro / cycle.

5. I walk / foot to work to stay fit.

6. I read a book when I go on / by train.

7. I take / walk the bus when it rains.

You can't "take" or "catch" a car or a bike as these are things you control yourself.

I catch the bus.

Use "go by" + the means of transportation. The exception is "go on foot."

I go by train.

15.9 LISTEN TO THE AUDIO, THEN NUMBER THE PICTURES IN THE ORDER THEY ARE DESCRIBED

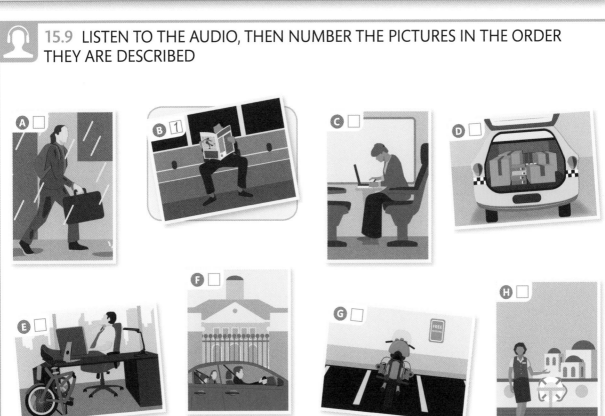

16 Vocabulary

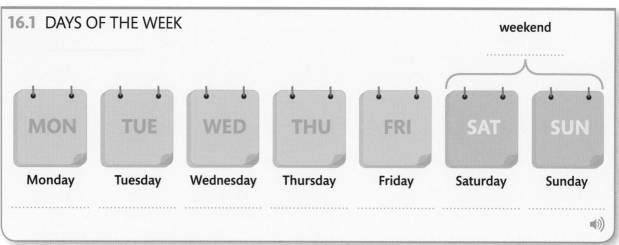

16.1 DAYS OF THE WEEK

weekend

| MON | TUE | WED | THU | FRI | SAT | SUN |
| Monday | Tuesday | Wednesday | Thursday | Friday | Saturday | Sunday |

16.2 FREQUENCY PHRASES

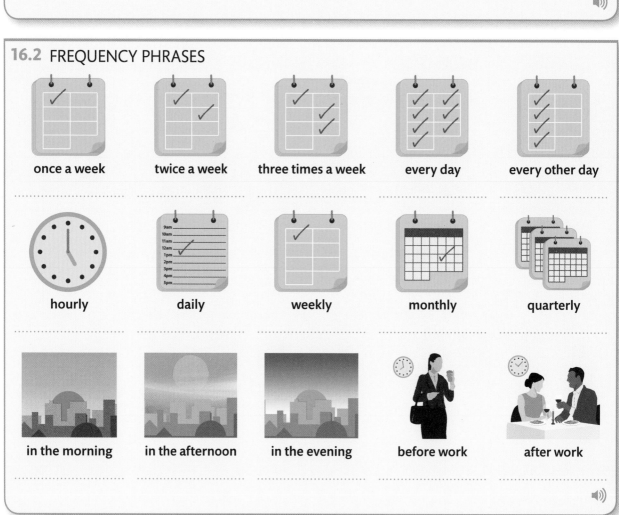

once a week   twice a week   three times a week   every day   every other day

hourly   daily   weekly   monthly   quarterly

in the morning   in the afternoon   in the evening   before work   after work

16.3 FREE TIME

read

draw

write

cook

take photos

stay (at) home

listen to music

watch television

watch a movie

see a play

visit a museum /
art gallery

meet friends

go out for a meal

go shopping

go to the gym

go cycling

walk / hike

go running

go camping

do exercise

play sports

play board
games

play video
games

play an
instrument

do yoga

17 Hobbies and habits

When talking with colleagues about your hobbies and habits, you may want to use adverbs of frequency to say how often you do the activities.

⚙ **New language** Adverbs of frequency
Aa Vocabulary Hobbies and habits
🧩 **New skill** Talking about free time

17.1 VOCABULARY ADVERBS OF FREQUENCY

Some adverbs tell you how frequently something happens.
"Always" and "never" are definite. Others, like "sometimes," are less specific.
Their position in a sentence depends on the main verbs and auxiliaries.

 100%

I **always** go to the gym after work.

Adverbs go after the verb "be."

I am **usually** happy to stay at home in the evening.

Adverbs go before other main verbs.

My company **frequently** organizes sponsored walks.

I **often** play computer games at home.

"Sometimes" and "often" can also go at the beginning or end of the sentence.

My team goes out for a meal **sometimes**.

My wife and I **occasionally** go cycling together.

I **rarely** work weekends if I have a choice.

0%

I have **never** played golf with my boss. I'm terrible at it!

Adverbs go between an auxiliary and the main verb.

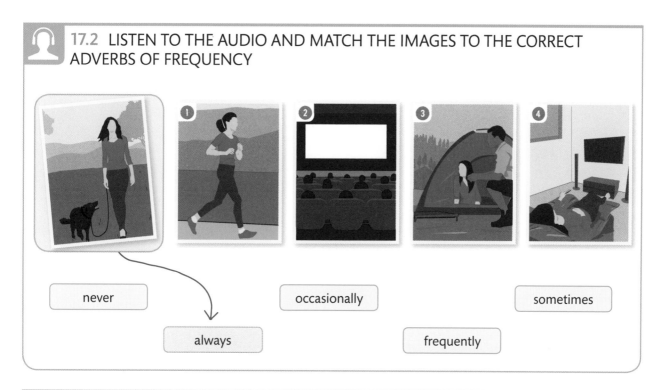

17.2 LISTEN TO THE AUDIO AND MATCH THE IMAGES TO THE CORRECT ADVERBS OF FREQUENCY

never

occasionally

sometimes

always

frequently

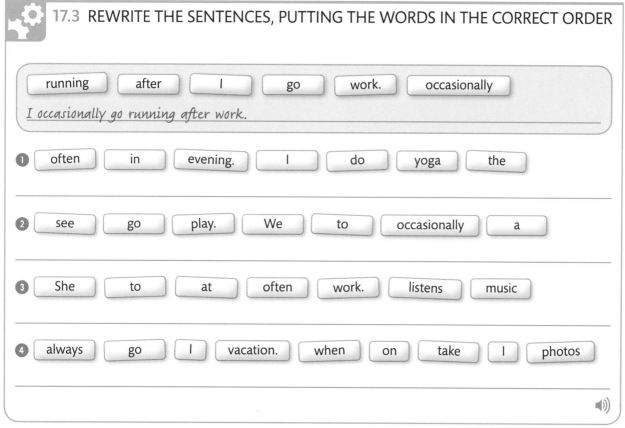

17.3 REWRITE THE SENTENCES, PUTTING THE WORDS IN THE CORRECT ORDER

running   after   I   go   work.   occasionally

I occasionally go running after work.

① often   in   evening.   I   do   yoga   the

② see   go   play.   We   to   occasionally   a

③ She   to   at   often   work.   listens   music

④ always   go   I   vacation.   when   on   take   I   photos

17.4 KEY LANGUAGE SUPERLATIVE ADJECTIVES

Superlative adjectives are used to compare two or more objects, people, or places. The superlative describes the most extreme.

"The" is used before a superlative.

Friday nights are always the loudest.

This is the most interesting gallery in town.

Long adjectives take "the most" or "the least" before the adjective to form the superlative.

◀))

17.5 HOW TO FORM SUPERLATIVE ADJECTIVES

For most short adjectives, "-est" is added to make the superlative. There are different spelling rules depending on the ending of the simple form of the adjective.

large → **largest**

If the adjective ends in "-e," "-st" is added.

easy → **easiest**

For some adjectives ending in "-y," the "-y" is removed and "-iest" added.

hot → **hottest**

For adjectives ending consonant-vowel-consonant, the last letter is doubled and "-est" is added.

◀))

17.6 FURTHER EXAMPLES SUPERLATIVE ADJECTIVES

 That's the longest run I've ever done!

 The earliest train is at 4am.

 That's the most expensive item!

 I go to the newest gym in town.

 This is the biggest launch to date.

 It's the least exciting party ever.

"The least" has the opposite meaning from "the most."

◀))

17.7 KEY LANGUAGE IRREGULAR SUPERLATIVE ADJECTIVES

Some common adjectives (usually short words) have superlatives that do not follow the rules.

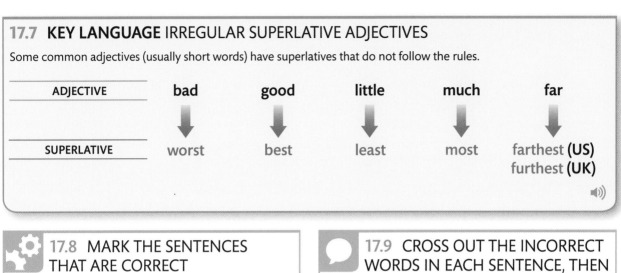

ADJECTIVE	bad	good	little	much	far
SUPERLATIVE	worst	best	least	most	farthest (US) furthest (UK)

17.8 MARK THE SENTENCES THAT ARE CORRECT

This is the best restaurant in town. ✓
This is the most good restaurant in town. ☐

1. This is the most good book I've ever read. ☐
   This is the best book I've ever read. ☐

2. The piano is most easy instrument to play. ☐
   The piano is the easiest instrument to play. ☐

3. Yannick listens to the most loud music. ☐
   Yannick listens to the loudest music. ☐

4. Shopping is the expensivest hobby I do. ☐
   Shopping is the most expensive hobby I do. ☐

5. That was the baddest play I have ever seen. ☐
   That was the worst play I have ever seen. ☐

6. Exercising is the more relaxing thing I do. ☐
   Exercising is the most relaxing thing I do. ☐

7. Let's eat at the most close restaurant. ☐
   Let's eat at the closest restaurant. ☐

17.9 CROSS OUT THE INCORRECT WORDS IN EACH SENTENCE, THEN SAY THE SENTENCES OUT LOUD

The earliest / ~~most early~~ yoga class is at 8am.

1. The interestingest / most interesting gallery I've been to is in Paris.

2. I've just finished the worst / most bad book I've ever read.

3. The most long / longest hike I've ever done is 15km.

4. The farthest / most far I've ever gone cycling is 50 miles.

5. I think that hiking is the morest exciting / most exciting hobby.

18 Past events

The past simple is often used when talking with co-workers about events that started and finished at a specific time in the recent or distant past.

🔧 **New language** The past simple
Aa Vocabulary Activities outside work
🧩 **New skill** Talking about past events

18.1 KEY LANGUAGE REGULAR VERBS IN THE PAST SIMPLE

The past simple describes events that happened in the past. The past simple forms of regular verbs end in "-ed." The negative uses "did not" plus the base form of the main verb.

I watched the game last night. It was great!

I didn't watch the game. I stayed at work late.

18.2 HOW TO FORM REGULAR VERBS IN THE PAST SIMPLE

The past forms of most verbs do not change with the subject.

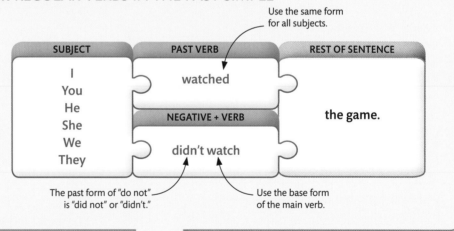

Use the same form for all subjects.

SUBJECT	PAST VERB	REST OF SENTENCE
I You He She We They	watched	the game.
	NEGATIVE + VERB	
	didn't watch	

The past form of "do not" is "did not" or "didn't."

Use the base form of the main verb.

18.3 FURTHER EXAMPLES REGULAR VERBS IN THE PAST SIMPLE

He walked **to the office.**

They arrived **together.**

She didn't walk **downtown.**

We didn't arrive **on time.**

18.4 MARK THE SENTENCES THAT ARE CORRECT

They didn't stay for long. ✓
They didn't stayed for long. ☐

① I played soccer after work last night. ☐
I playd soccer after work last night. ☐

② He didn't walked to work today. ☐
He didn't walk to work today. ☐

③ I works from 9 to 5 yesterday. ☐
I worked from 9 to 5 yesterday. ☐

④ She lived in Paris for four years. ☐
She lives in Paris for four years. ☐

⑤ I talked to lots of people on my trip. ☐
I did talk to lots of people on my trip. ☐

18.5 KEY LANGUAGE SPELLING RULES FOR THE PAST SIMPLE

The past simple of all regular verbs ends in "-ed," but for some verbs, there are some spelling changes, too.

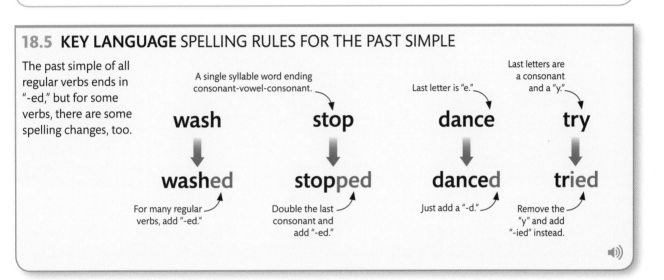

A single syllable word ending consonant-vowel-consonant.

Last letter is "e."

Last letters are a consonant and a "y."

wash → **washed**
For many regular verbs, add "-ed."

stop → **stopped**
Double the last consonant and add "-ed."

dance → **danced**
Just add a "-d."

try → **tried**
Remove the "y" and add "-ied" instead.

18.6 FILL IN THE GAPS BY PUTTING THE VERBS IN THE PAST SIMPLE

My friend ___cooked___ (cook) some pasta, but I ___didn't try___ (not try) it.

① We _____ (arrive) late, but our boss _____ (not shout) at us.

② I _____ (wash) my car, but it _____ (not look) clean.

③ I _____ (watch) the film, but I _____ (not enjoy) it.

④ It _____ (stop) raining, but then it _____ (start) snowing.

⑤ I _____ (not walk) to work, I _____ (cycle).

71

18.7 HOW TO FORM QUESTIONS IN THE PAST SIMPLE

Use "did" plus the base form of the verb
to ask a question in the past simple.

They played tennis after work.

⬇

Did they play tennis after work?

"Did" goes before
the subject.

The main verb
is in its base form.

18.8 HOW TO FORM QUESTIONS IN THE PAST SIMPLE

"DID"	SUBJECT	BASE FORM OF VERB	REST OF SENTENCE
Did	they	play	tennis after work?

18.9 REWRITE THE SENTENCES AS QUESTIONS IN THE PAST SIMPLE

He visited the art gallery with his family yesterday.
Did he visit the art gallery with his family yesterday?

① You played board games when you were young.

_____

② He cooked some pasta for lunch.

_____

③ She stayed at home and watched TV last night.

_____

④ They watched a scary movie at the movie theater.

_____

⑤ They walked home from work together.

_____

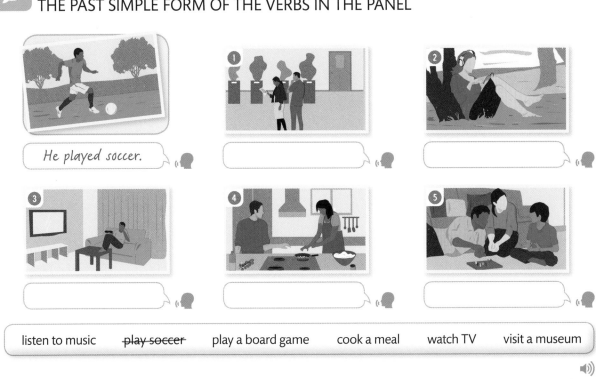

18.10 LISTEN TO THE AUDIO AND ANSWER THE QUESTIONS

Two colleagues, Jasmine and Marilyn, are talking about events from the week before.

On vacation, Jasmine watched a lot of movies.
True ☐ False ☐ Not given ☑

① Jasmine played tennis and volleyball on vacation.
True ☐ False ☐ Not given ☐

② Jasmine played four new sports.
True ☐ False ☐ Not given ☐

③ Jasmine didn't try yoga.
True ☐ False ☐ Not given ☐

④ Jasmine liked the local food.
True ☐ False ☐ Not given ☐

⑤ Jasmine and Marilyn often cook for each other.
True ☐ False ☐ Not given ☐

18.11 DESCRIBE WHAT EACH PERSON DID, SPEAKING OUT LOUD AND USING THE PAST SIMPLE FORM OF THE VERBS IN THE PANEL

He played soccer.

①

②

③

④

⑤

listen to music   ~~play soccer~~   play a board game   cook a meal   watch TV   visit a museum

---

18 ✓ **CHECKLIST**

⚙ The past simple ☐   **Aa** Activities outside work ☐   🧩 Talking about past events ☐

Dates and times

When making arrangements or talking about past or future events, it is important to talk about the time correctly. There are a number of ways to do this in English.

✿ **New language** When things happen
Aa **Vocabulary** Telling the time
🧩 **New skill** Making appointments

19.1 KEY LANGUAGE TELLING THE TIME

In spoken English, there are a few different key phrases that can be used to say what the time is.

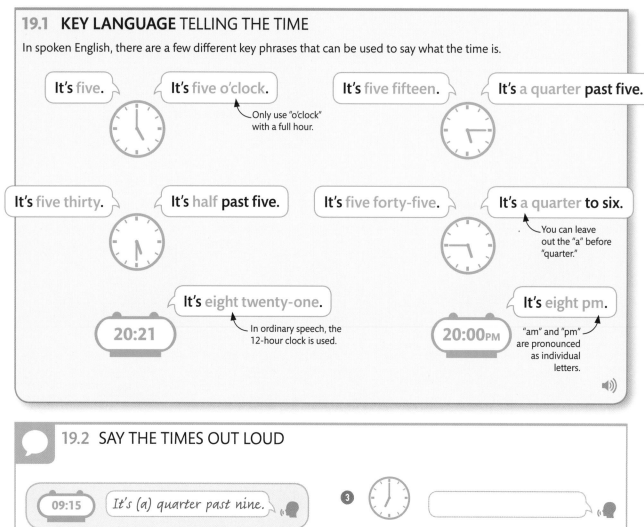

It's five.

It's five o'clock.
Only use "o'clock" with a full hour.

It's five fifteen.

It's a quarter **past five.**

It's five thirty.

It's half **past five.**

It's five forty-five.

It's a quarter **to six.**
You can leave out the "a" before "quarter."

It's eight twenty-one.
In ordinary speech, the 12-hour clock is used.

20:21

It's eight pm.
"am" and "pm" are pronounced as individual letters.

20:00PM

19.2 SAY THE TIMES OUT LOUD

09:15 *It's (a) quarter past nine.*

❶

❷ **10:45**

❸

❹

❺ **08:43PM**

19.3 VOCABULARY MONTHS OF THE YEAR

Jan January	**Feb** February	**Mar** March
Apr April	**May** May	**Jun** June
Jul July	**Aug** August	**Sept** September
Oct October	**Nov** November	**Dec** December

19.4 KEY LANGUAGE DATES AND YEARS

In the US, people often describe dates by writing cardinal numbers and saying ordinal numbers. In the UK, people use ordinal numbers to write and say dates.

In US English, the number is written after the month.

May 10 (US) — May tenth

May 10th / 10th May (UK) — May the tenth

the 10th of May (UK / US) — the tenth of May

Most years are spoken as pairs of numbers, such as "nineteen" and "seventy-five."

1975 — nineteen seventy-five

2015 — twenty fifteen

You can also say, "two thousand and..." for years between 2000 and 2019.

19.5 LISTEN TO THE AUDIO AND ANSWER THE QUESTIONS

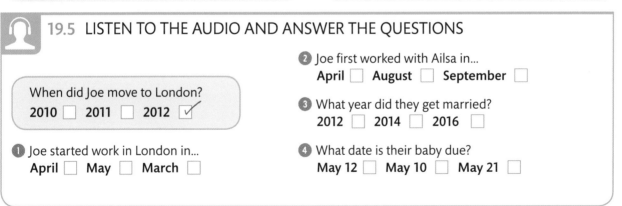

When did Joe move to London?
2010 ☐ **2011** ☐ **2012** ☑

❶ Joe started work in London in...
April ☐ **May** ☐ **March** ☐

❷ Joe first worked with Ailsa in...
April ☐ **August** ☐ **September** ☐

❸ What year did they get married?
2012 ☐ **2014** ☐ **2016** ☐

❹ What date is their baby due?
May 12 ☐ **May 10** ☐ **May 21** ☐

19 ✓ CHECKLIST

⚙ When things happen ☐   **Aa** Telling the time ☐   👥 Making appointments ☐

20 Career history

When you meet new co-workers or attend an interview, people may ask about your previous jobs. It is important to use correct verb forms when talking about the past.

⚙ **New language** Past simple irregular verbs
Aa Vocabulary Jobs and workplaces
🧩 **New skill** Talking about previous jobs

20.1 KEY LANGUAGE PAST SIMPLE IRREGULAR VERBS

Many common English verbs have irregular forms in the past simple. The verb "be" changes form in the past depending on the subject.

What did you do before?

Past simple form of the verb "be" with "I," "he," "she," and "it."

I **was** a waitress in a café. My co-workers **were** really nice.

Past simple form of the verb "be" with "you," "we," and "they."

20.2 FURTHER EXAMPLES PAST SIMPLE IRREGULAR VERBS

Other past simple irregular verbs do not change form with the subject.

We **had** a very demanding boss.

He **got** very tired working night shifts.

I **spent** all day stacking shelves.

I **left** my job because it was badly paid.

Jo **met** our new clients yesterday.

They **went** on a business trip to Paris.

Past simple verbs do not change form in the third person.

20.3 KEY LANGUAGE PAST SIMPLE IRREGULAR VERBS

BASE FORM	be	have	spend	meet	get	leave	go
	↓	↓	↓	↓	↓	↓	↓
PAST SIMPLE	was/were	had	spent	met	got	left	went

20.4 FILL IN THE GAPS BY PUTTING THE VERBS IN THE PAST SIMPLE

My first job _____was_____ (be) in a busy restaurant kitchen.

1 When I was a gardener, I _____ (spend) the majority of my time outside.

2 I _____ (meet) lots of famous people when I worked as a reporter.

3 Benjamin _____ (go) to nearly 100 countries as a pilot.

4 In his last job, he _____ (have) a dog as a partner.

20.5 MATCH THE QUESTIONS TO THE CORRECT ANSWERS

Why did you leave your first job?   → I left it because it was boring.

1 What did you wear in your first job?   I met lots of famous musicians.

2 What was the best thing about being a DJ?   I spent a lot of time in museums.

3 How did you get a job as a chef?   As a police officer, I had a uniform.

4 Where did you work as a tour guide?   I went to catering school.

20.6 LISTEN TO THE AUDIO, THEN NUMBER THE PICTURES IN THE ORDER THEY ARE DESCRIBED

A ☐   B ☐ 1   C ☐   D ☐   E ☐

BUSINESS BULLETIN

Sadim Nalik: Mailroom to boardroom

He started in the mailroom at his father's company, but Sadim Nalik is now a respected business executive. He tells us what he learned from his first job.

I always wanted to work in my father's company, but my father told me that I had to go to college first. He always said that education was the most important thing in life. He taught himself to read and write and wanted the very best for me. I chose to study engineering in college. When I left college with a top degree, I thought that my father would give me a good job in his company. I remember he sent me an email congratulating me on my university success and offering me a job in the mailroom at the company. I felt really angry at the time because I wanted a better job. I wrote to my father that I would look for a job at another company. He then called me and said I could one day be CEO, but only if I knew the company from top to bottom. After the mailroom, I worked in the kitchen, in the HR department, as a personal assistant, and as his deputy CEO. I finally understood what hard work was like in different areas of the company. The experience taught me to respect all employees and understand that every part of the company must be working well for the whole company to succeed. My father made me CEO five years ago and my daughter, Myra, began working in the mailroom two months ago.

What did Sadim's father tell him to do?

He told Sadim to go to college.

❶ What did Sadim choose to study in college?

_____

❷ What did Sadim think his father would do?

_____

❸ Why did Sadim feel angry?

_____

❹ What did Sadim write to his father?

_____

❺ What did his father say he could be one day?

_____

❻ What did Sadim finally understand?

_____

❼ What did Sadim's work experience teach him?

_____

❽ When did Sadim's father make him CEO?

_____

❾ When did Myra begin working in the mailroom?

_____

20.8 REWRITE THE SENTENCES, CORRECTING THE ERRORS

I choosed to study medical science in college.
I chose to study medical science in college.

❶ I feeled really happy when I left college with a top degree.

_____

❷ My manager sayed that one day I could be CEO of the whole company.

_____

❸ My tutor teached me that it was important to check my own work.

_____

❹ I maked my girlfriend a big cake to celebrate her new job.

_____

20.9 RESPOND TO THE AUDIO, SPEAKING OUT LOUD

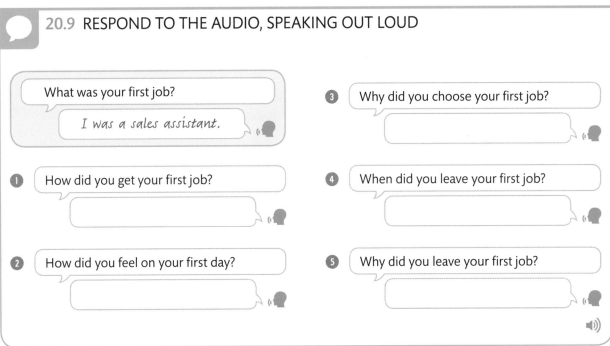

What was your first job?

I was a sales assistant.

❶ How did you get your first job?

❷ How did you feel on your first day?

❸ Why did you choose your first job?

❹ When did you leave your first job?

❺ Why did you leave your first job?

20 ✓ CHECKLIST

⚙ Past simple irregular verbs ☐   **Aa** Jobs and workplaces ☐   🧩 Talking about previous jobs ☐

21 Company history

The past simple can be used to describe repeated or single actions in a company's history. These actions can last for a short or long time.

⚙ **New language** Past simple with time markers
Aa Vocabulary Describing trends
🧩 **New skill** Describing a company's history

21.1 KEY LANGUAGE THE PAST SIMPLE WITH TIME MARKERS

To talk about specific events in the past, such as landmarks in a company's history, use the past simple with a time marker.

I founded Transtech in 1996.

Past simple of the verb "to found," which means "to set up a company."

Time markers specify when an event happened.

21.2 FURTHER EXAMPLES THE PAST SIMPLE WITH TIME MARKERS

Time markers can go at the start of a sentence.

At first, we only had five employees.

We launched a new range of laptops last year.

Time markers that are adverbs go immediately before the verb.

"Ago" means "before now."

Ten years ago, we opened a new flagship store.

We recently merged with Alphaelectrics.

21.3 FILL IN THE GAPS USING THE WORDS IN THE PANEL

At _____*first*_____ , we only sold products in store, but now we sell online.

1 We opened our tenth store two months _____ .

2 The company _____ merged with one of its competitors.

3 Jane Hunt opened the first Hunt Bags store _____ 1995.

4 A new CEO started working here _____ year.

| last |
| recently |
| ago |
| ~~first~~ |
| in |

21.4 LISTEN TO THE AUDIO, THEN NUMBER THE SENTENCES IN THE ORDER YOU HEAR THEM

A CEO is giving a presentation on the company history.

A At first, business was quite slow and the salon was often empty. ☐

B They opened a second hair salon in London in 1988. ☐

C By 1995, they were stylists for many top celebrities. ☐

D Brisar Styling was founded by Brian and Sarah Paterson in 1984. ☑ 1

E Five years later, they launched their hair product range. ☐

F Last year, Brisar Styling merged with our beauty product company, Wilson's. ☐

21.5 READ THE ARTICLE AND ANSWER THE QUESTIONS

> What did Cake & Crumb report last year?
> *It reported a record rise in profits.*

① When did Ahmed found Cake & Crumb?

_____

② Where did Ahmed work at first?

_____

③ What were sales like in the company's first year?

_____

④ When did the company open its first store?

_____

⑤ When did Cake & Crumb employ 2,000 bakers?

_____

⑥ What happened two years ago?

_____

BUSINESS WORLD

A slice of the market

This week, we look at the history of Cake & Crumb

CAKE & CRUMB IS NOW one of the biggest and most popular bakeries in the US. Last year, the company reported a record rise in profits. But Cake & Crumb had much smaller beginnings.

Ahmed Hassan founded the company in 2003. At first, Ahmed worked from his kitchen in his small apartment and sold cakes to customers online. In the company's first year, sales remained steady, but in 2005, sales increased and Ahmed opened the first Cake & Crumb store.

Now, the company has stores all over the US. By 2010, Cake & Crumb employed 2,000 bakers. Two years ago, the company launched a catering service for children's parties. With the launch of this service and rebranding, Cake & Crumb became one of the most successful companies in the catering industry.

21.6 KEY LANGUAGE DESCRIBING TRENDS

English also uses the past simple with time markers to describe business trends.
Note that some verbs for describing trends have irregular past simple forms.

Ice cream sales { increased / went up / rose } over the summer.

"Rise" has an irregular past simple form.

House prices { stayed the same / remained steady / stabilized } during the last quarter.

Demand for new cars { decreased / went down / fell } last year.

"Fall" is also an irregular verb.

21.7 FILL IN THE GAPS BY PUTTING THE VERBS IN THE PAST SIMPLE

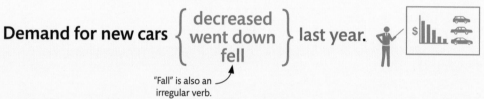

Visitor numbers at the luxury hotel _____*fell*_____ (fall) by 20 percent last year.

❶ The number of people going to festivals _____ (go up) last year.

❷ Fortunately, the cost of fuel for transportation _____ (stabilize) recently.

❸ In the really wet summer of 2010, sales of umbrellas _____ (rise) a lot.

❹ The number of people downloading music _____ (stay the same) last month.

❺ The numbers of students earning MBAs _____ (remain steady) last year.

21.8 CROSS OUT THE INCORRECT WORDS IN EACH SENTENCE, THEN SAY THE SENTENCES OUT LOUD

Our sales figures ~~increased up~~ / went up in 2011, but ~~falled~~ / fell in 2012.

1. At / In first, the value of the company stayed / stay the same.

2. Marketing costs increasing / increased and sales also rose / rosing.

3. Last / Recent summer, umbrella sales increased / increasing because it was rainy.

4. The number of customers decrease / decreased, but profits go / went up.

5. Two years ago / past, we launched an online delivery service and our sales rised / rose.

21 ✓ CHECKLIST

⚙ Past simple with time markers ☐   **Aa** Describing trends ☐   🧩 Describing a company's history ☐

↻ REVIEW THE ENGLISH YOU HAVE LEARNED IN UNITS 15-21

NEW LANGUAGE	SAMPLE SENTENCE	☑	UNIT
PREPOSITIONS OF TIME AND DURATION	There is a staff meeting on Mondays. I work from 9am to 5pm.	☐	15.1, 15.4
ADVERBS OF FREQUENCY	I always go to the gym after work.	☐	17.1
SUPERLATIVE ADJECTIVES	Friday nights are always the loudest.	☐	17.4
PAST SIMPLE	I watched the game last night. Did they play tennis after work?	☐	18.1, 18.7
PAST SIMPLE IRREGULAR VERBS	I was a waitress. We had a very demanding boss.	☐	20.1, 20.2
PAST SIMPLE WITH TIME MARKERS	I founded Transtech in 1996.	☐	21.1, 21.2

22.1 MAKING ARRANGEMENTS

morning

afternoon

evening

running late

planner (US) /
diary (UK)

calendar

appointment

agenda

invitation

to invite someone

to accept an invitation

to decline an invitation

boardroom

conference room

meeting room

reception

to book a
meeting room

to chair a meeting

to attend a meeting

to miss a meeting

office

café

restaurant

refreshments

22.2 ACCEPTING AND DECLINING

I'm afraid I'm busy today.

to be busy
[to have lots to do]

10am is good for me. See you then!

good for me
[I am free at that time]

Yes, I am free on Wednesday and Thursday this week.

to be free
[to be available]

Yes, the café suits me.

to suit someone
[to be convenient]

I can't make the meeting on Monday. I will reschedule it for Tuesday.

to reschedule
[to decide on a new time and date for a meeting]

2pm is fine. I look forward to meeting you then.

to look forward to
[to be pleased about something that is going to happen]

I'm really busy this morning. Can we postpone the meeting?

to postpone
[to delay a meeting or an event]

I won't be at the meeting. Something unexpected has come up.

to come up
[to occur unexpectedly]

I'm afraid I have to cancel the team meeting on Friday.

to cancel
[to decide that a planned event will not happen]

Apologies, but I'm unable to attend due to other commitments.

to be unable to attend
[cannot go to]

23 Talking about your plans

One way of making plans with a co-worker or client is by using the present continuous to talk about what you are doing at the moment, or plans in the future.

⚙ **New language** The present continuous
Aa Vocabulary Making arrangements
🧩 **New skill** Talking about your plans

23.1 KEY LANGUAGE THE PRESENT CONTINUOUS

The present continuous is mostly used to describe ongoing events that are happening right now.

Are you busy at the moment?

Yes, I'm writing this report for Susan.

23.2 HOW TO FORM THE PRESENT CONTINUOUS

SUBJECT + "BE"	VERB + "-ING"	REST OF SENTENCE
I'm	writing	this report.

Short form of "I am."

This is the present participle. It is the same as the gerund ("-ing") form.

23.3 FURTHER EXAMPLES THE PRESENT CONTINUOUS

She's having **lunch downtown.**

He is printing **the report.**

We are not enjoying **this meal.**
Add "not" after "be" to make the negative.

They're having **a discussion.**

She is meeting **a new client.**

I'm not working **on my own.**

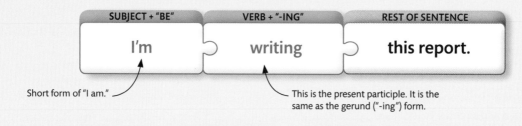

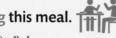

23.4 LISTEN TO THE AUDIO, THEN NUMBER THE PICTURES IN THE ORDER THEY ARE DESCRIBED

A □

B 1

C □

D □

E □

F □

G □

H □

23.5 FILL IN THE GAPS BY PUTTING THE VERBS IN THE PRESENT CONTINUOUS

The team _isn't having_ (not have) much success this year, so we ___are trying___ (try) new things.

1 Sales _____ (increase) at the moment, so we _____ (get) a bigger bonus.

2 Fashions _____ (change), so we _____ (adapt) to new trends.

3 Travel costs _____ (rise) this year, so we _____ (call) each other more instead.

4 Profits _____ (drop), so we _____ (cut) costs in all areas of the business.

5 We _____ (sell) a lot to Asia, so we _____ (plan) to open an office there next year.

6 I can't believe you _____ (work) late. You _____ (miss) the staff party!

7 I _____ (wait) for my interview to start, and I _____ (feel) nervous.

8 The company _____ (lose) money, so we _____ (consider) a restructure.

🔊

87

23.6 KEY LANGUAGE QUESTIONS IN THE PRESENT CONTINUOUS

Questions in the present continuous can be formed by inverting the subject and "be," adding a question word for open questions.

To turn a statement into a question, swap the subject and "be."

Subject and "be" are inverted.

Who are we waiting **for?**

I'm not sure. Is James coming to this meeting?

Question words can be used before the verb to form open questions.

23.7 HOW TO FORM QUESTIONS IN THE PRESENT CONTINUOUS

QUESTION WORD	FORM OF "BE"	SUBJECT	VERB + "-ING"	REST OF SENTENCE
Who	**are**	**we**	**waiting**	**for?**

Using a question word like "where," "what," or "who" makes the question more open.

23.8 REWRITE THE SENTENCES, PUTTING THE WORDS IN THE CORRECT ORDER

| you | What | writing? | are |

What are you writing?

3 | we | selling | Are | that? |

_____

1 | they | this? | Are | buying |

_____

4 | him? | meeting | Are | you |

_____

2 | working | now? | it | Is |

_____

5 | promoting? | Who | they | are |

_____

88

23.9 MATCH THE QUESTIONS TO THE CORRECT ANSWERS

Where are you going?	Yes, I'm running two workshops.
1 Why aren't they selling coffee?	He's giving a presentation.
2 Who is giving this presentation?	I'm going to meet my new client.
3 Are you doing any staff training?	No, I'm on the bus at the moment.
4 What is Marco doing now?	That's Giorgio. He's a great speaker.
5 Is he buying the company?	No, it's out of toner. I'm refilling it now.
6 Are you taking the train home?	Yes, I think he is.
7 Is the photocopier working?	There is no hot water left.

 23.10 REWRITE THE STATEMENTS AS QUESTIONS IN THE PRESENT CONTINUOUS WITHOUT USING QUESTION WORDS

Mariam is working on the new project today.
Is Mariam working on the new project today?

1 The company is buying everyone new laptops.

2 Maria is giving her first presentation at the moment.

3 Rakesh is designing the packaging for the new gadget.

4 We are all going to the team meeting now.

5 They are trying to improve sales in North America.

23.11 KEY LANGUAGE THE PRESENT CONTINUOUS FOR FUTURE ARRANGEMENTS

You can also use the present continuous to talk about fixed future plans. A clear date, day, or time is normally given.

I'm free next week. What are you doing on Monday?

This refers to fixed plans that have already been made.

I'm working from home all day.

Specific time reference is given.

23.12 MARK THE SENTENCES THAT ARE CORRECT

What are you doing on Monday? ☑
What are you doing on Mondays? ☐

1. I'm not coming to work tomorrow. ☐
   I not coming to work tomorrow. ☐

2. Are you meeting the team today? ☐
   Is you meeting the team today? ☐

3. I can't go. I'm not leaving until 8pm. ☐
   I can't go. I'm not leave until 8pm. ☐

4. Are we coming back here next year? ☐
   Will we coming back here next year? ☐

5. You are coming to the party later? ☐
   Are you coming to the party later? ☐

6. I'm not taking notes today. Are you? ☐
   I'm not take notes today. Are you? ☐

7. I'm having lunch at noon tomorrow. ☐
   I having lunch at noon tomorrow. ☐

8. Are you going to Asia this winter? ☐
   Will you going to Asia this winter? ☐

23.13 LISTEN TO THE AUDIO AND ANSWER THE QUESTIONS

Julia is calling a client, Jerome, to arrange a meeting.

Who is Julia trying to arrange a meeting for?
Julia and Jerome ☐
Jerome and Sylvie ☐
Jerome and Marie ☑

1. How long is Jerome staying in the city?
   Until Monday ☐
   For 10 days ☐
   He does not say ☐

2. When is Jerome taking Sylvie to the airport?
   Right now ☐
   Next Monday morning ☐
   Every Monday morning ☐

3. Where is the meeting taking place?
   In the bookstore ☐
   At the airport ☐
   In Marie's office ☐

23.14 READ THE SCHEDULE, THEN RESPOND TO THE AUDIO, SPEAKING OUT LOUD

What are you doing on Monday morning?

I'm meeting the new client.

MONDAY

10am:
Meet the new client (reception).

TUESDAY

2pm:
Meet HR team.

WEDNESDAY

Train to Paris departs 9am.
Return at 4pm. Home at 7:15pm.

THURSDAY

Finish at 3pm for dentist appointment.

FRIDAY

Lunch break:
Monica's leaving party (cafeteria).

❶ Who are you meeting on Tuesday afternoon?

❷ Where are you going on Wednesday?

❸ How are you traveling on Wednesday?

❺ What time are you finishing on Thursday?

❹ When are you getting home on Wednesday?

❻ Who is leaving work on Friday?

---

24 Giving opinions

English speakers often use set phrases to signal that they want to interrupt without being rude. There are a number of ways to communicate your opinion politely.

⚙ **New language** Interruptions and opinions
Aa Vocabulary Environmental issues
🧩 **New skill** Giving opinions politely

24.1 KEY LANGUAGE INTERRUPTING POLITELY

First, try to catch the speaker's eye or raise your hand. If you still do not get the chance to speak, starting your sentence with one of these phrases will help your interruption be polite.

This is why we plan to—

Sorry to interrupt, but...

If I could just come in here...

Could I just say...?

Excuse me, but...

I'm sorry, but...

24.2 MARK WHETHER EACH INTERRUPTION IS POLITE OR IMPOLITE

"Could I just say, this isn't the only option."
Polite ✓   **Impolite** ☐

❶ "What? I don't agree at all."
Polite ☐   **Impolite** ☐

❷ "I'm sorry, but I agree with Nick on this point."
Polite ☐   **Impolite** ☐

❸ "Excuse me, but I have some different figures."
Polite ☐   **Impolite** ☐

❹ "That's wrong and everyone knows it."
Polite ☐   **Impolite** ☐

❺ "Say that again. I don't believe it."
Polite ☐   **Impolite** ☐

❻ "If I could just come in here and mention losses."
Polite ☐   **Impolite** ☐

❼ "You don't know what you're talking about."
Polite ☐   **Impolite** ☐

24.3 KEY LANGUAGE EXCHANGING OPINIONS

It is also important to introduce your opinion respectfully, and it is polite to ask others for their thoughts.

You can soften your interruption by introducing your point politely.

In my opinion we need to focus on recycling.

What do you think?

Follow up your comments by asking others for their opinions.

24.4 FURTHER EXAMPLES EXCHANGING OPINIONS

I can see your point, but...

This structure can be followed by a noun or a gerund.

What do you think about doing this?

What do you think about this idea?

I'm not sure I agree. I think...

How about you?

24.5 RESPOND OUT LOUD TO THE AUDIO, FILLING IN THE GAPS USING THE WORDS IN THE PANEL

This is clearly the best approach.

I'm sorry, but I'm not sure I _____*agree*_____ .

1 We will lose thousands of customers.

Sorry to _____ , but my figures are different.

2 It's the same problem as last year.

I'm not sure. What do you _____ about new outlets?

3 These will never sell in Asia.

I'm sorry, but in my _____ they will sell well.

opinion

~~agree~~

interrupt

think

93

24.6 LISTEN TO THE AUDIO AND ANSWER THE QUESTIONS

The head of green policy at RonMax is holding a meeting to discuss the company's environmental strategy.

The meeting is about past environmental policy.	True ☐	False ☑	Not given ☐

❶ RonMax currently recycles all its waste. True ☐ False ☐ Not given ☐

❷ RonMax currently pays a company to take away waste paper. True ☐ False ☐ Not given ☐

❸ Some rooms will not have lights on all the time. True ☐ False ☐ Not given ☐

❹ Everyone agrees with the environmental strategy. True ☐ False ☐ Not given ☐

❺ RonMax will publicly promote their green policies. True ☐ False ☐ Not given ☐

Aa 24.7 READ THE ARTICLE, THEN COMPLETE THE COLLOCATIONS

attend	
schedule	a meeting

❶ [ ] [ ] the minutes

❷ [ ] [ ] the agenda

❸ [ ] [ ] apologies

❹ [ ] [ ] vote

❺ [ ] [ ] remarks

ATTENDING AND SCHEDULING MEETINGS

During a meeting, someone takes "the minutes" (a record of what was said). You can review these afterward. Before a new meeting, you may be sent an outline ("the agenda"). Make sure to read this beforehand, and follow it as the meeting works through it. If you cannot go to a meeting, send your apologies. These will be announced at the meeting.

Sometimes the person in charge of the meeting ("the chair") takes a vote. He or she may have the casting vote if there is a tie. The best chairs keep the opening and closing remarks short.

24.8 READ THE CLUES AND WRITE THE ANSWERS IN THE CORRECT PLACES ON THE GRID

ACROSS

1 The air, water, and land around us all

2 Make an amount or number smaller

3 Use again

4 Something that is not used or wanted

DOWN

5 Environmentally friendly

6 Process something to make it usable again

7 Things that are available to be used

8 The mark or effect that something leaves behind

1 e n v i r o n m e n t

recycle   ~~environment~~   green   footprint   reduce   waste   reuse   resources

---

24.9 CROSS OUT THE INCORRECT WORD IN EACH SENTENCE

Can we ~~attend~~ / review the minutes?

1 Tim sent / said his apologies. He can't come.

2 Let's review our environmental / recycle strategy.

3 Let's work through the agenda / remarks quickly.

4 We should look at reducing / falling our waste.

5 I'm sorry to interrupt / disturb, but I disagree.

6 What do you think about / around recycling?

7 Let's make / take a vote on the new policy.

8 The meeting chair has the casting / chasing vote.

9 I'm sorry / apologize, but I don't agree.

10 I think it's the best strategy. How about / do you?

11 I just have a few closed / closing remarks.

🔊

---

24 ✓ CHECKLIST

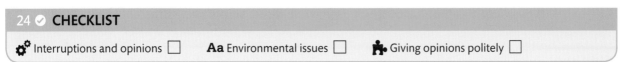

⚙ Interruptions and opinions ☐   **Aa** Environmental issues ☐   🧩 Giving opinions politely ☐

95

25 Agreeing and disagreeing

When you react to someone's opinion, it is important to be polite and respectful. This is especially important when you disagree with someone.

New language Reacting to opinions
Aa Vocabulary Agreeing and disagreeing
New skill Discussing opinions

25.1 KEY LANGUAGE AGREEING WITH AN OPINION

There are many ways to say that you agree with someone. You do not need to say very much and, sometimes, people just nod.

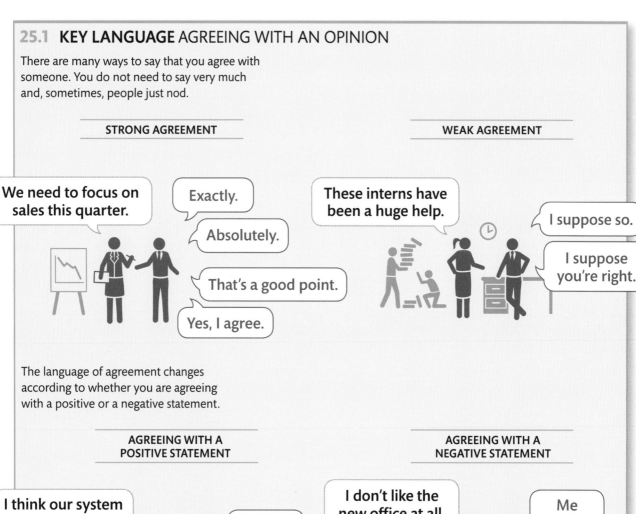

STRONG AGREEMENT

We need to focus on sales this quarter.

Exactly.

Absolutely.

That's a good point.

Yes, I agree.

WEAK AGREEMENT

These interns have been a huge help.

I suppose so.

I suppose you're right.

The language of agreement changes according to whether you are agreeing with a positive or a negative statement.

AGREEING WITH A POSITIVE STATEMENT

I think our system needs updating.

Me too.

So do I.

AGREEING WITH A NEGATIVE STATEMENT

I don't like the new office at all.

Me neither.

Nor do I.

25.2 MARK THE BEST REPLY TO EACH STATEMENT

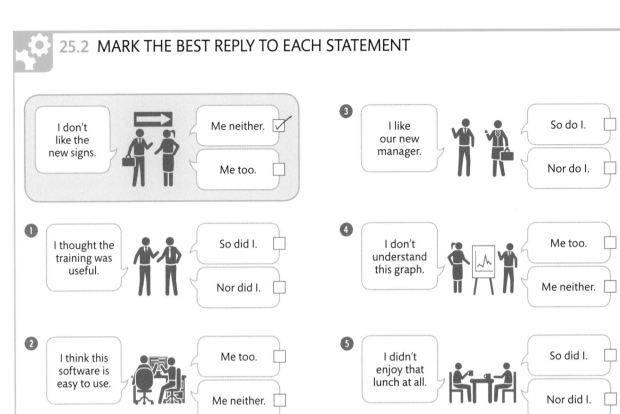

25.3 MATCH THE STATEMENTS TO THE RESPONSES

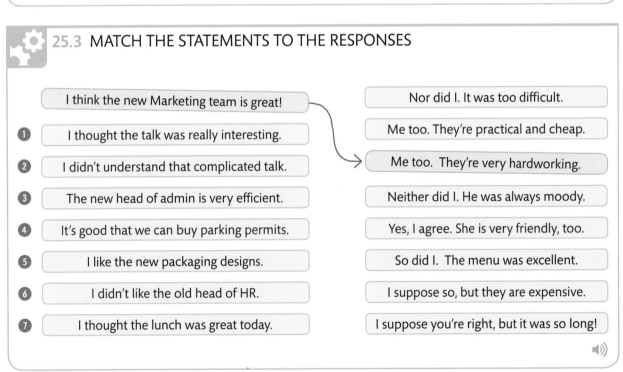

25.4 KEY LANGUAGE DISAGREEING WITH AN OPINION

English speakers often use a variety of polite phrases to express degrees of disagreement.

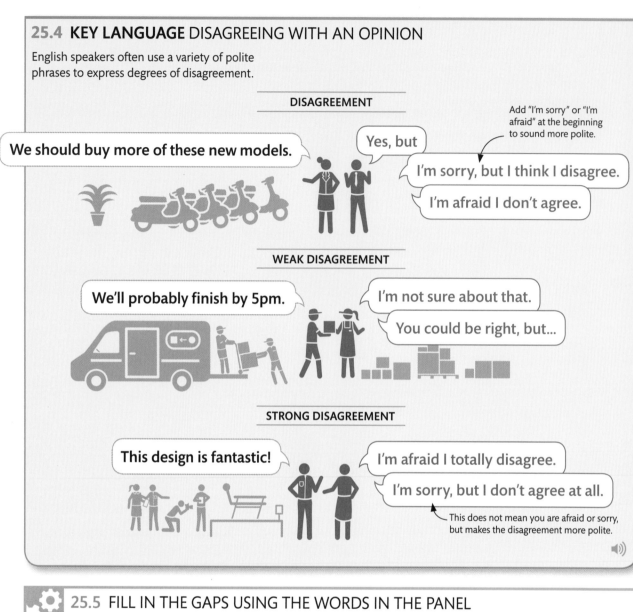

DISAGREEMENT

We should buy more of these new models.

Yes, but

Add "I'm sorry" or "I'm afraid" at the beginning to sound more polite.

I'm sorry, but I think I disagree.

I'm afraid I don't agree.

WEAK DISAGREEMENT

We'll probably finish by 5pm.

I'm not sure about that.

You could be right, but...

STRONG DISAGREEMENT

This design is fantastic!

I'm afraid I totally disagree.

I'm sorry, but I don't agree at all.

This does not mean you are afraid or sorry, but makes the disagreement more polite.

25.5 FILL IN THE GAPS USING THE WORDS IN THE PANEL

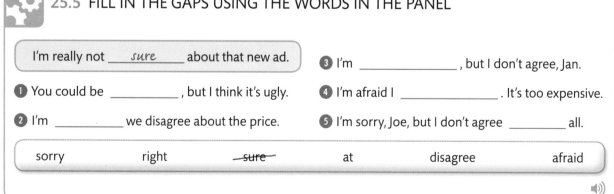

I'm really not _____sure_____ about that new ad.

❶ You could be _____ , but I think it's ugly.

❷ I'm _____ we disagree about the price.

❸ I'm _____ , but I don't agree, Jan.

❹ I'm afraid I _____ . It's too expensive.

❺ I'm sorry, Joe, but I don't agree _____ all.

| sorry | right | ~~sure~~ | at | disagree | afraid |

98

25.6 LISTEN TO THE AUDIO AND ANSWER THE QUESTIONS

Jeremy and Sian are discussing recent proposals for change in their workplace.

What does Jeremy think about the changes?
He likes all of them ☐
He likes some of them ☑
He dislikes all of them ☐

① Sian loves the idea of shower rooms.
Jeremy strongly agrees with her ☐
Jeremy agrees with her ☐
Jeremy strongly disagrees with her ☐

② Sian is looking forward to a choice of coffees.
Jeremy strongly agrees with her ☐
Jeremy agrees with her ☐
Jeremy strongly disagrees with her ☐

③ Jeremy liked having meetings on Mondays.
Sian strongly agrees with him ☐
Sian agrees with him ☐
Sian disagrees with him ☐

④ Sian is looking forward to the convention in Santiago.
Jeremy strongly agrees with her ☐
Jeremy agrees with her ☐
Jeremy strongly disagrees with her ☐

25.7 CROSS OUT THE INCORRECT WORD IN EACH SENTENCE, THEN SAY THE SENTENCES OUT LOUD

I'm ~~sure~~ / sorry, but I have to disagree with you about that.

① Yes, I suppose your / you're right about the new design.

② You could / should be right, but I need to do more research.

③ I'm sorry, but I don't agree / argue at all with that comment.

④ I'm scared / afraid I don't agree about this one issue.

⑤ I'm not sure / final about that, Sara. I don't like it.

⑥ I'm afraid I totally / finally disagree. That will never work.

---

25 ✓ CHECKLIST

⚙ Reacting to opinions ☐   **Aa** Agreeing and disagreeing ☐   Discussing opinions ☐

26 Health and safety

Many workplaces issue guidelines for how to avoid accidents and stay safe. In English, this topic often uses specialist vocabulary and reflexive pronouns.

⚙ **New language** Reflexive pronouns
Aa Vocabulary Health and safety at work
New skill Talking about safety at work

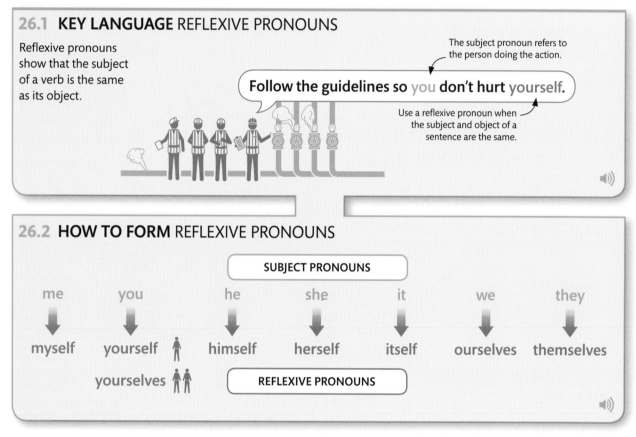

26.1 KEY LANGUAGE REFLEXIVE PRONOUNS

Reflexive pronouns show that the subject of a verb is the same as its object.

The subject pronoun refers to the person doing the action.

Follow the guidelines so you don't hurt yourself.

Use a reflexive pronoun when the subject and object of a sentence are the same.

26.2 HOW TO FORM REFLEXIVE PRONOUNS

SUBJECT PRONOUNS

me	you	he	she	it	we	they
↓	↓	↓	↓	↓	↓	↓
myself	yourself	himself	herself	itself	ourselves	themselves

yourselves

REFLEXIVE PRONOUNS

26.3 MARK WHICH SENTENCES ARE CORRECT

She cut herself on the machinery. ✓
She cut itself on the machinery. ☐

❶ They locked themselves in the fridge. ☐
They locked themselfs in the fridge. ☐

❷ He burned himself on the coffee machine. ☐
He burned herself on the coffee machine. ☐

❸ Both of you, protect yourself from the sun. ☐
Both of you, protect yourselves from the sun. ☐

❹ We booked ourself on a fire safety course. ☐
We booked ourselves on a fire safety course. ☐

❺ I fell and hurt myself on the wet floor. ☐
I fell and hurt yourself on the wet floor. ☐

26.4 READ THE ARTICLE AND ANSWER THE QUESTIONS

> The author is surprised that accidents happen at work.
> **True** ☐ **False** ☐ **Not given** ✓

❶ The author hurt himself at work last year.
True ☐ **False** ☐ **Not given** ☐

❷ The author does not think health and safety regulations are important.
True ☐ **False** ☐ **Not given** ☐

❸ You should tell your employer if you have an accident at work.
True ☐ **False** ☐ **Not given** ☐

Protect yourself at work

How to prevent accidents in the workplace

We spend a lot of our time at work, so it is not surprising that we have accidents there. But what can you do to protect yourself and help your co-workers protect themselves from injury? The first thing is to make sure that your company follows all the sensible health and safety regulations. Most accidents are caused by slips, trips, lifting, and carrying. If you do hurt yourself at work, report it to your employer and don't blame yourself. You could ask to take a first aid course so that you can protect and, if necessary, treat yourself and your co-workers.

Aa 26.5 MATCH THE PICTURES TO THE CORRECT PHRASES

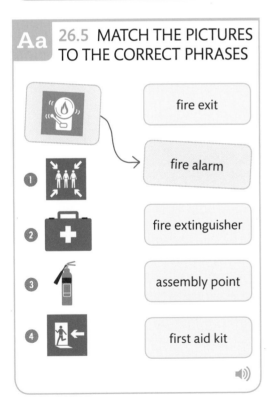

fire exit

fire alarm

fire extinguisher

assembly point

first aid kit

26.6 CROSS OUT THE INCORRECT WORDS IN EACH SENTENCE, THEN SAY THE SENTENCES OUT LOUD

> It was an accident. Don't blame ~~itself~~ / yourself.

❶ She's cut **himself** / **herself**. Get the first aid box.

❷ They paid for it **themselves** / **theirselves**.

❸ The machine started **it's self** / **itself**.

❹ Please take care of **himself** / **yourselves**.

❺ Make **yourself** / **herself** aware of the fire exits.

26 ✓ CHECKLIST

⚙ Reflexive pronouns ☐   **Aa** Health and safety at work ☐   Talking about safety at work ☐

27 Suggestions and advice

When there are everyday problems in the workplace, it is useful to know how to make suggestions and offer advice. There are several ways to do this in English.

⚙ **New language** Prefixes and suffixes
Aa Vocabulary Everyday workplace problems
🧩 **New skill** Making suggestions

27.1 KEY LANGUAGE MAKING SUGGESTIONS

You can use a number of phrases to offer advice or make suggestions. Some of these take the base form of the verb, and others need the "-ing" form.

"How about" and "what about" take the "-ing" form of the verb.

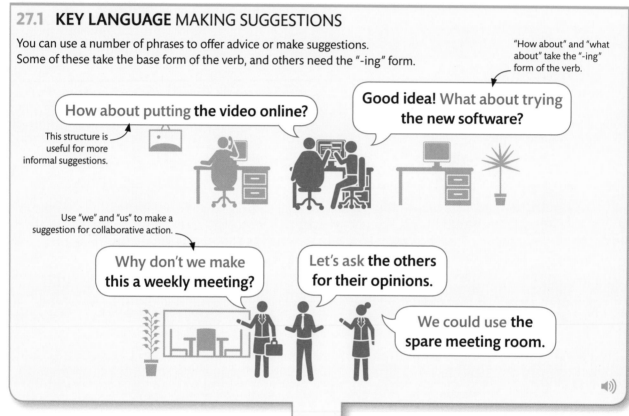

How about putting **the video online?**

This structure is useful for more informal suggestions.

Good idea! What about trying **the new software?**

Use "we" and "us" to make a suggestion for collaborative action.

Why don't we make **this a weekly meeting?**

Let's ask **the others for their opinions.**

We could use **the spare meeting room.**

27.2 HOW TO FORM SUGGESTIONS

When making a suggestion, the form of the verb depends on who you are addressing.

Informal suggestions take the "-ing" form of the verb.

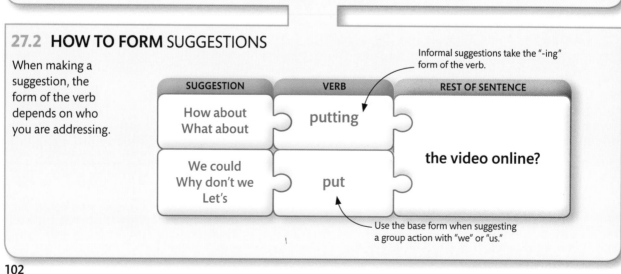

SUGGESTION	VERB	REST OF SENTENCE
How about / What about	putting	
We could / Why don't we / Let's	put	the video online?

Use the base form when suggesting a group action with "we" or "us."

27.3 REWRITE THE SENTENCES, PUTTING THE WORDS IN THE CORRECT ORDER

| building | new | about | a | How | website? |

How about building a new website?

1 | Let's | more | media. | on | do | promotion | social |

_____

2 | could | the | product. | We | redesign | packaging | this | for |

_____

3 | about | a | consultant? | software | What | hiring |

_____

27.4 KEY LANGUAGE OFFERING ADVICE WITH "SHOULD" + BASE FORM

One way to offer stronger advice is using "should" or "shouldn't," which suggests negative consequences if ignored.

You should try to keep the meeting short.

Base form of main verb

27.5 MATCH THE WORKPLACE PROBLEMS TO THE SUGGESTIONS AND ADVICE

The printer is broken.

1 The internet is down again.

2 Sara scraped the director's car.

3 There's only one package of coffee left.

4 The fridge door has been open all day.

5 Jeremy sits at the computer all day.

You should reset the router.

I should order some more.

We should call an engineer.

She should tell him before he sees it.

He should walk around the office.

We should throw away the food.

27.6 KEY LANGUAGE CHANGING MEANING WITH PREFIXES AND SUFFIXES

Prefixes and suffixes change the meaning of words that they are added to.
Sometimes this also changes the word's form (such as from a noun to an adjective).

 **careful**   **careless**

Adding "-ful" to a noun forms
an adjective with a sense of
"full of" that noun.

Adding "-less" to a noun forms an
adjective meaning "not having"
or "not affected by" that noun.

There are several
prefixes that can
be used to form
a new word with the
opposite meaning.

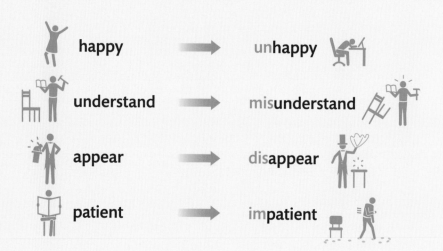

happy ➡	**un**happy
understand ➡	**mis**understand
appear ➡	**dis**appear
patient ➡	**im**patient

🔊

 ## 27.7 FILL IN THE GAPS USING THE WORDS IN THE PANEL

This time slot is ___*impractical*___ . Why don't we rearrange it?

❶ I am _____ to come in the morning. How about the afternoon?

❷ I _____ words so often. Why don't we get an editor?

❸ The machine isn't working. We should _____ it.

❹ Are you _____ ? Why don't we call a doctor for you?

❺ These tests are _____ . What about doing easier ones?

impossible
~~impractical~~
unable
disconnect
misspell
unwell

🔊

27.8 LISTEN TO THE AUDIO, THEN NUMBER THE PICTURES IN THE ORDER THEY ARE DESCRIBED

 A ☐

 B 1

 C ☐

 D ☐

 E ☐

27.9 CROSS OUT THE INCORRECT WORD IN EACH SENTENCE, THEN SAY THE SENTENCES OUT LOUD

Why don't we keep notes so we don't misunderstand / ~~understand~~ the plan?

① Let's use our old system again. This new one is so familiar / unfamiliar and slow.

② How about changing the time so that more people are able / unable to come.

③ Let's discuss the negative feedback from people who agree / disagree with our plan.

④ What about explaining the delay to stop people from becoming so impatient / patient.

⑤ I love conventions! It's so easy to connect / disconnect with new people.

⑥ I have no idea how to write this report. It seems possible / impossible!

27 ✓ **CHECKLIST**

⚙ Prefixes and suffixes ☐   **Aa** Everyday workplace problems ☐   ᐟᐞ Making suggestions ☐

28 Giving a presentation

When you are preparing a presentation, make sure it is clear and easy to follow. There are certain phrases you can use to help guide the audience through the talk.

⚙ New language Signposting language
Aa Vocabulary Presentation equipment
🧩 New skill Structuring a talk

28.1 KEY LANGUAGE BEGINNING A PRESENTATION

If you outline the structure of your presentation at the start, it makes it easier for the audience to follow what you are saying. Signposting language can help you to do this effectively.

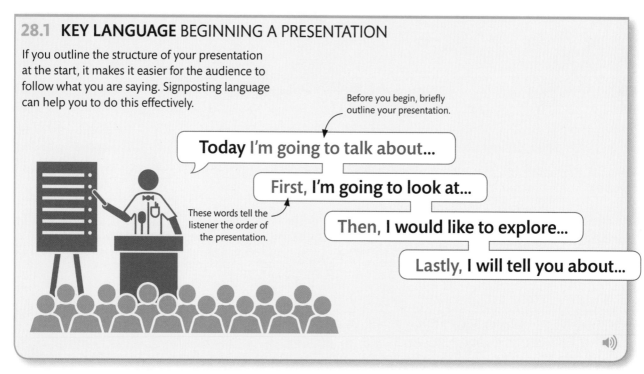

Before you begin, briefly outline your presentation.

Today I'm going to talk about...

First, I'm going to look at...

These words tell the listener the order of the presentation.

Then, I would like to explore...

Lastly, I will tell you about...

28.2 FILL IN THE GAPS USING THE PHRASES IN THE PANEL

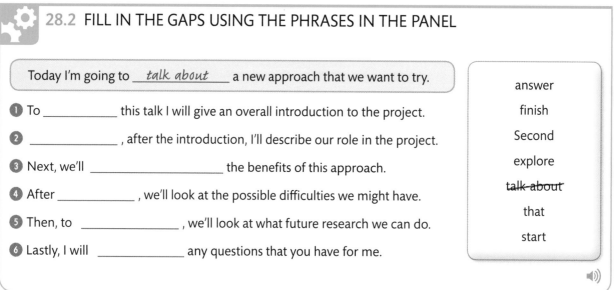

Today I'm going to __*talk about*__ a new approach that we want to try.

1 To _____ this talk I will give an overall introduction to the project.

2 _____ , after the introduction, I'll describe our role in the project.

3 Next, we'll _____ the benefits of this approach.

4 After _____ , we'll look at the possible difficulties we might have.

5 Then, to _____ , we'll look at what future research we can do.

6 Lastly, I will _____ any questions that you have for me.

answer
finish
Second
explore
~~talk about~~
that
start

28.3 KEY LANGUAGE CHANGING TOPICS

You can also use signposting language to move between topics during your presentation.

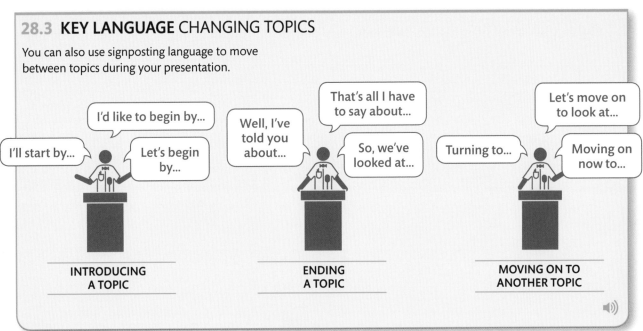

INTRODUCING A TOPIC: I'll start by... / I'd like to begin by... / Let's begin by...

ENDING A TOPIC: Well, I've told you about... / That's all I have to say about... / So, we've looked at...

MOVING ON TO ANOTHER TOPIC: Turning to... / Let's move on to look at... / Moving on now to...

28.4 LISTEN TO THE AUDIO AND ANSWER THE QUESTIONS

The head of a sales team is giving a talk about the performance.

The last three years' sales figures were good.

True ☐ False ☐ Not given ☑

❶ All the new products were successful.

True ☐ False ☐ Not given ☐

❷ The company recently started social media campaigning.

True ☐ False ☐ Not given ☐

❸ Older people liked the campaigns.

True ☐ False ☐ Not given ☐

28.5 MATCH THE DEFINITIONS TO THE PRESENTATION EQUIPMENT

a document given to an audience at a talk — flipchart

❶ an image that is shown on a large screen → handout

❷ a flat surface where people can see images and words — microphone

❸ equipment that shows slide images on other surfaces — slide

❹ equipment that makes your voice sound louder — screen

❺ large sheets of paper to write on and show others — projector

28.6 KEY LANGUAGE ENDING A PRESENTATION

At the end of your presentation, you can give a brief summary of
your points and, if you want, allow the audience to ask questions.

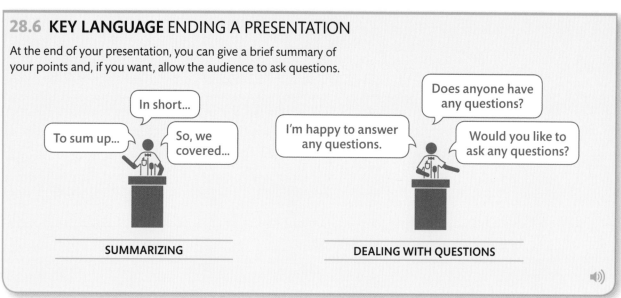

In short...

To sum up...

So, we covered...

SUMMARIZING

Does anyone have any questions?

I'm happy to answer any questions.

Would you like to ask any questions?

DEALING WITH QUESTIONS

28.7 REWRITE THE SENTENCES, PUTTING THE WORDS IN THE CORRECT ORDER

a | sum | is | To | big | year. | up, | this

To sum up, this is a big year.

① happy | questions. | I'm | answer | to | any

_____

② we've | main | So, | covered | the | issues.

_____

③ have | anyone | Does | questions? | any

_____

④ to | anything? | you | Would | like | ask

_____

⑤ next | important. | In | short, | is | year

_____

28.8 LISTEN TO THE AUDIO, THEN NUMBER THE SENTENCES IN THE ORDER YOU HEAR THEM

A company's head of marketing is talking about their new range.

Ⓐ That's all I have to say about the product. ☐

Ⓑ Does anyone have anything they want to ask? ☐

Ⓒ Let's move on to look at the promotion materials. ☐

Ⓓ I'd like to begin by showing you something new. ☐

Ⓔ So, we briefly covered the product, and the promotion. ☐

Ⓕ Today I'm going to talk about our new range of products. ☐1☐

Ⓖ I'm happy to answer any questions you may have. ☐

28.9 CROSS OUT THE INCORRECT WORD IN EACH SENTENCE, THEN SAY THE SENTENCES OUT LOUD

To / ~~For~~ start, let's look at the way the company has performed.

1 In tall / short we are very proud of our new products.

2 I'd like to beginning / begin by looking back at past sales.

3 That's all I have to say / talk about the advertising campaign.

4 Let's move up / on to talk about the packaging we've designed.

5 Does anyone have / make any questions for me?

28 ✓ CHECKLIST

⚙ Signposting language ☐   **Aa** Presentations and talks ☐   🧩 Structuring a talk ☐

↻ REVIEW THE ENGLISH YOU HAVE LEARNED IN UNITS 22–28

NEW LANGUAGE	SAMPLE SENTENCE	☑	UNIT
THE PRESENT CONTINUOUS FOR ONGOING EVENTS AND FUTURE PLANS	I'm finishing **this report.** I'm working **from home on Monday.**	☐	23.1, 23.6, 23.11
INTERRUPTING POLITELY AND EXCHANGING OPINIONS	Sorry to interrupt, but… I'm not sure I agree… How about you?	☐	24.1, 24.3
AGREEING AND DISAGREEING	I suppose you're right… I'm afraid I totally disagree.	☐	25.1, 25.4
REFLEXIVE PRONOUNS	**Follow the guidelines so** you **don't** hurt **yourself.**	☐	26.1
MAKING SUGGESTIONS AND GIVING ADVICE	How about putting **the video online?** You should try **to keep the meeting short.**	☐	27.1, 27.4
SIGNPOSTING LANGUAGE FOR PRESENTATIONS	First, **I'm going to look at…**	☐	28.1, 28.3, 28.6

29 Rules and requests

Use "can" and "have to" to talk about rules in the workplace, and verbs such as "could" to politely ask colleagues to help you solve problems.

⚙ **New language** Modal verbs
Aa Vocabulary Polite requests
🧩 **New skill** Talking about rules and regulations

29.1 KEY LANGUAGE MODAL VERBS FOR PERMISSION

Use "can" to give a colleague permission to do something.

> **You can take your lunch break at 1 o'clock.**

Use "can't" to say that a colleague is not allowed to do something.

> **There's a business dress code here. You can't wear shorts to work.**

"Have to" expresses a strong obligation to do something.

> **That's the fire alarm! We have to leave the store now.**

"Don't have to" means that something is not necessary.

> **You don't have to stay late tonight. We're not very busy.**

🔊

29.2 MATCH THE PAIRS OF SENTENCES THAT GO TOGETHER

You can listen to music at work.	It's a special one for fire safety.
1 You have to close that door.	We're meeting clients later this afternoon.
2 You don't have to eat at your desk.	Just make sure it's not too loud.
3 You can't leave early today.	I have saved all the documents.
4 You can shut the computers down.	There's a nice café across the street.

🔊

29.3 FILL IN THE GAPS USING THE WORDS IN THE PANEL

You ___can't___ park your car there. It's the CEO's space.

❶ Is your stapler broken? You _____ use mine.

❷ She _____ come to the training session. She did it last year.

❸ You _____ turn off the light if you're the last person to leave the office.

❹ He _____ test the fire alarm every Wednesday morning.

❺ We _____ wear a jacket and tie to work in the summer months.

| ~~can't~~ | have to | has to | don't have to | can | doesn't have to |

29.4 READ THE NOTICE AND ANSWER THE QUESTIONS

KITCHEN RULES:

- Kitchen staff can wear jeans and sneakers
- Waiting staff have to wear uniform at all times
- All staff can drink free tea, coffee, and soft drinks
- You have to keep cell phones in your locker
- You don't have to cut your hair, but do tie it back
- You don't have to pay for lunch or dinner
- You can keep any tips given by customers
- You can't use bad language in the restaurant
- You have to clean the kitchen before you leave
- And remember that you have to wash your hands before and after touching food

All staff are allowed to wear jeans to work.
True ☐ **False** ☐ **Not given** ☑

❶ Staff get free breakfast at the restaurant.
True ☐ **False** ☐ **Not given** ☐

❷ All staff must have short hair.
True ☐ **False** ☐ **Not given** ☐

❸ Staff are allowed to keep tips from the clients.
True ☐ **False** ☐ **Not given** ☐

❹ Staff are not allowed to leave the kitchen dirty.
True ☐ **False** ☐ **Not given** ☐

❺ Staff only wash their hands after touching food.
True ☐ **False** ☐ **Not given** ☐

29.5 KEY LANGUAGE POLITE REQUESTS WITH MODAL VERBS

Use "Could you" with a base verb, or "Would you mind" with a gerund, to politely ask for help with problems at work.

We've run out of hangers. { Could you order / Would you mind ordering } some more?

29.6 HOW TO FORM POLITE REQUESTS WITH MODAL VERBS

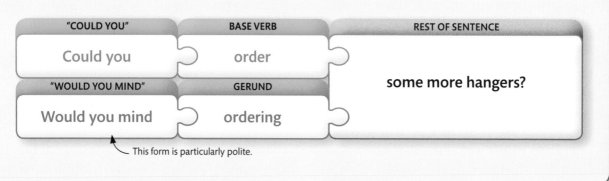

"COULD YOU"	BASE VERB	REST OF SENTENCE
Could you	order	
"WOULD YOU MIND"	GERUND	some more hangers?
Would you mind	ordering	

This form is particularly polite.

29.7 FURTHER EXAMPLES POLITE REQUESTS WITH MODAL VERBS

This box is really heavy. Could you help me lift it?

I can't find my stapler. Could you lend me yours, please?

You can add "please" to make requests more polite.

The clients are here early. Would you mind making them tea and coffee?

Our card machine isn't working. Would you mind paying with cash?

29.8 CROSS OUT THE INCORRECT WORD IN EACH SENTENCE

Would you mind close / closing the door?

1 Could you tell / telling Jan to call me back?

2 Could you checking / check this report?

3 Would you mind ordering / order more pens?

4 Could you mop / mopping the floor, please?

5 Could you coming / come to today's meeting?

6 Would you mind calling / call back later?

7 Would you mind turning / turn the light off?

8 Could you wash / washing these cups, please?

9 Could you passing / pass around the reports?

10 Would you mind book / booking me a taxi?

11 Could you showing / show our clients around?

29.9 LISTEN TO THE AUDIO AND ANSWER THE QUESTIONS

Robin is asking a co-worker, Bruno, to help him prepare for a difficult meeting with their suppliers.

Bruno has finished his presentation.
True ✓ **False** ☐

1 Robin doesn't need help with his handout.
True ☐ **False** ☐

2 The suppliers are a new company.
True ☐ **False** ☐

3 Bruno will check Robin's handouts.
True ☐ **False** ☐

4 Robin asks Bruno to call the taxi company.
True ☐ **False** ☐

29.10 USE THE CHART TO CREATE SIX CORRECT SENTENCES AND SAY THEM OUT LOUD

Could you book a meeting room?

| Could / Would | you / you mind | book / booking / send / sending / call / calling | a meeting room? / Sam Davies an email? / our supplier? |

30.1 WORK IDIOMS

The road is closed, but it's **business as usual** in the store.

business as usual
[the normal daily routine at a company]

There's so much **red tape** involved in importing food products.

red tape
[administration, paperwork, or rules and regulations]

Our sales were poor this year and we're **in the red**.

to be in the red
[to owe money]

I can't come home yet, I'm **snowed under** with work.

to be snowed under
[to have too much work to do]

I hope I can **wind down** a bit over the weekend.

to wind down
[to gradually relax]

Spending any more on that useless product would be **throwing money down the drain**.

throwing money down the drain
[wasting money]

You get a free car and the company gets good press. It's a **win-win situation**.

a win-win situation
[a situation with no negative outcome]

They have to **work around the clock** to redecorate the shop.

to work around the clock
[to work very long hours]

Sorry, he can't come to the phone. He's **tied up with** another client.

to be tied up with
[to be busy doing something else]

Take it easy! We've got another hour to finish decorating the conference hall.

to take it easy
[to relax or calm down]

Sorry, I'll have to miss lunch. I'm
swamped with invoices to file.

to be swamped
[to be really busy]

I hate being on the top floor when the
elevator is out of order.

to be out of order
[to not be working]

She's not a great team member. She
doesn't really pull her weight.

to pull your weight
[to do a fair share of work]

We've told you our final price.
The ball is in your court now.

the ball is in your court
[it is your turn to do or say something]

This report is due today. I can't
put it off any longer.

to put something off
[to delay or avoid something]

Greg is really creative and often
thinks outside the box.

to think outside the box
[to think about a something in
an original way]

They are very difficult clients because
they're always moving the goalposts.

to move the goalposts
[to change the desired end result]

If we're all here, Marcia, can
you get the ball rolling?

to get the ball rolling
[to start something]

I don't understand all these error
messages. My laptop's going haywire!

going haywire
[not acting or behaving as it should]

I want to finish by five o'clock,
so let's get down to business.

to get down to business
[to start work on something
that needs doing]

31 Discussing issues

Many common workplace problems arise from an ongoing situation in the past. You can use the past continuous tense to discuss these problems.

⚙️ **New language** Past continuous
Aa Vocabulary Work idioms
🧩 **New skill** Describing workplace problems

31.1 KEY LANGUAGE THE PAST CONTINUOUS

Use the past continuous to describe problems or situations that were ongoing in the past, but are now finished.

The action started in the past and continued for some time.

This morning was awful. My managers were complaining about my work.

PAST   NOW

31.2 FURTHER EXAMPLES THE PAST CONTINUOUS

The coffee machine wasn't working this morning. Is it fixed now?

PAST   NOW

Were you taking notes in that meeting? I can't remember what we have to do.

PAST   NOW

31.3 HOW TO FORM THE PAST CONTINUOUS

SUBJECT	"WAS / WERE"	VERB + "-ING"	REST OF SENTENCE
My managers	were	complaining	about my work.

Use "was" or "were" depending on the subject.

Add "-ing" to the main verb.

31.4 FILL IN THE GAPS BY PUTTING THE VERBS IN THE PAST CONTINUOUS

> Angel _____ was writing _____ (write) his report this morning. He still hasn't finished.

❶ Gabino _____ (not listen) during the team meeting this morning.

❷ The internet _____ (not work) all day yesterday. I had to call my clients.

❸ Hannah and Luke _____ (talk) during the CEO's presentation.

❹ I _____ (forget) to do everyday jobs, so I wrote a list.

❺ I put you on a new team because you _____ (lose) sales.

🔊

31.5 READ THE ARTICLE AND WRITE ANSWERS TO THE QUESTIONS AS FULL SENTENCES

OUR CAREER

Your problems solved

Our experts are here to help solve your workplace problems

Last week I was reading all your emails about problems with co-workers. Most of us know someone in the office who can be a little bit lazy sometimes, but Maria wrote last week to say that her co-worker was not answering important emails and leaving Maria to reply to all the sales enquiries. Well, my advice, Maria, is to talk to your co-worker first. Perhaps he was going through a difficult time. I know it is difficult if your co-worker is also your friend, but you must make sure that you don't end up doing your work and his as well!

Remember José from last month, who was feeling very tired after lunch every day? Well, he did change his diet so that he ate more salads and vegetables and said last week that he was working until 5pm every day without feeling exhausted. Great news, José!

A healthy lunch will give you more energy at work

> What was the author doing last week?
> The author was reading emails.

❶ What wasn't Maria's co-worker doing?

_____

❷ What was he leaving Maria to do?

_____

❸ What was the author's advice?

_____

❹ What was José's problem last month?

_____

❺ What did he do to solve the problem?

_____

❻ How late was José working last week?

_____

31.6 LISTEN TO THE AUDIO, THEN NUMBER THE PICTURES IN THE ORDER THEY ARE DESCRIBED

A ☐

B 1

C ☐

D ☐

E ☐

Aa 31.7 REWRITE THE SENTENCES, CORRECTING THE ERRORS

> I was **working about** the clock today
> _I was working around the clock today._

1. Sales were improving. It was **win-win** situation.
   _____

2. It's a difficult task. We must think **out** the box.
   _____

3. The team was throwing money **up** the drain.
   _____

4. Was your assistant **pushing** his weight today?
   _____

5. We were working with a lot of **blue** tape.
   _____

6. Now we're all here, let's get **in** to business.
   _____

🔊

Aa 31.8 MATCH THE PICTURES TO THE CORRECT SENTENCES

The printer was going haywire yesterday.

1. I kept putting off a difficult phone call this morning.

2. The elevator is out of order.

3. I'm tied up with these difficult reports.

4. Our sales fell last year. Now we're in the red.

🔊

118

31.9 READ THE EMAIL THEN ANSWER THE QUESTIONS, SPEAKING OUT LOUD

✉   ✕ ⌄

To: Faruk

Subject: Work stress

Hi Faruk,

It's great to hear from you. I am still working around the clock on the project we were talking about. I am trying to design the packaging for the new health tracker watch, but time's running out. Every time I show the marketing department a design, people send me so many new emails that I feel snowed under. I'm so up to my ears with silly emails that I can't do any real work for the project. This means even though I'm always on the go, I don't seem to get much work done. My husband, Mark, says that I should take it easy because I'm quite stressed and miserable at home too, but I find it hard to wind down on weekends. I know you've worked in marketing for a long time, and just wondered if you have any advice for me?

Thanks so much, Gloria

↩ ↩↩   ■ 📎 🔧

What does Gloria say about her workload?

> *She is working around the clock* 🗣

❸ Why doesn't Gloria get much work done?

🗣

❶ What project is Gloria working on?

🗣

❹ What does Mark want Gloria to do?

🗣

❷ Who sends Gloria lots of emails?

🗣

❺ Why has Gloria written to Faruk?

🗣

🔊

---

31 ✓ CHECKLIST

⚙ Past continuous ☐   **Aa** Work idioms ☐   🧩 Describing workplace problems ☐

English uses a variety of polite phrases to apologize for mistakes. Use the past continuous with the past simple to offer an explanation for a mistake.

⚙ **New language** Past continuous and past simple
Aa Vocabulary Workplace mistakes
🧩 **New skill** Apologizing and giving explanations

32.1 KEY LANGUAGE APOLOGIES AND RESPONSES

There are many formal and informal phrases that you can use to make and respond to apologies. Responses can either accept the apology to end the conversation, or reject it to ask for further action.

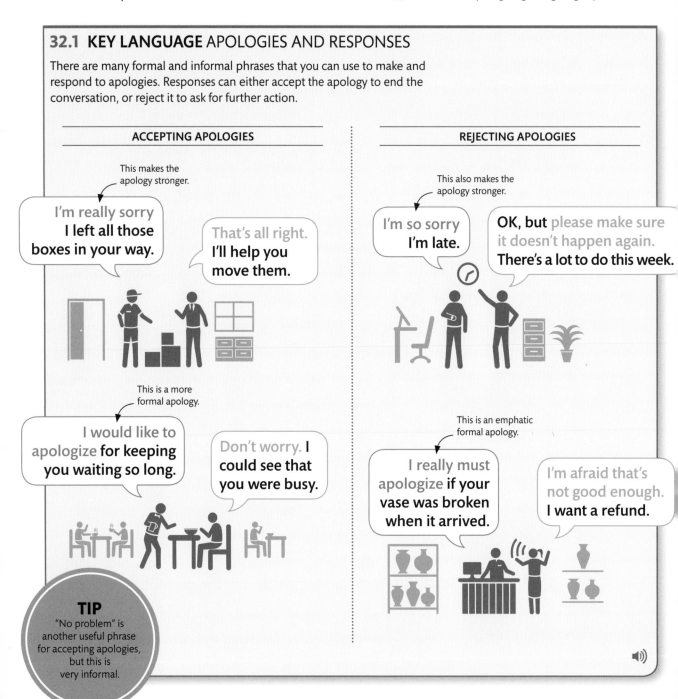

ACCEPTING APOLOGIES

This makes the apology stronger.

I'm really sorry **I left all those boxes in your way.**

That's all right. **I'll help you move them.**

This is a more formal apology.

I would like to apologize **for keeping you waiting so long.**

Don't worry. **I could see that you were busy.**

REJECTING APOLOGIES

This also makes the apology stronger.

I'm so sorry **I'm late.**

OK, but please make sure it doesn't happen again. **There's a lot to do this week.**

This is an emphatic formal apology.

I really must apologize **if your vase was broken when it arrived.**

I'm afraid that's not good enough. **I want a refund.**

TIP
"No problem" is another useful phrase for accepting apologies, but this is very informal.

Aa 32.2 MATCH THE APOLOGIES WITH THE CORRECT RESPONSES

I'm really sorry I'm late.

1 I do apologize. I've left the files at home.

2 I'm sorry. I've forgotten your last name.

3 I would like to apologize for the bad line.

4 I'm really sorry. I think I'm very early.

5 I'm so sorry. I took your cup accidentally.

Don't worry. I have copies of them here.

No need. The signal's always bad here.

That's all right. My train was delayed too.

Never mind. I've got myself another one.

No problem. It's Carson.

That's OK. We can have coffee first.

🔊

32.3 LISTEN TO THE AUDIO AND MARK WHETHER KARL ACCEPTS THE APOLOGIES

Yes ☐ No ☑

1 Yes ☐ No ☐

2 Yes ☐ No ☐

3 Yes ☐ No ☐

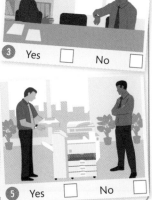

4 Yes ☐ No ☐

5 Yes ☐ No ☐

32.4 SAY THE SENTENCES OUT LOUD, FILLING IN THE GAPS

I really ____must____ apologize for not calling you back earlier. 🗣

1 I'm so _____ I was late for this morning's meeting. 🗣

2 I'm afraid that's not good _____ . I want my money back. 🗣

3 I would like to _____ for the rudeness of our receptionist. 🗣

4 That's OK, but please make _____ it doesn't happen again. 🗣

🔊

121

32.5 KEY LANGUAGE PAST CONTINUOUS AND PAST SIMPLE

Many workplace mistakes are caused by an unexpected event that interrupts something else. English uses the past continuous and past simple together to describe this.

Past continuous

Past simple

I'm so sorry. I was writing **an email when** I spilled **water on my keyboard.**

32.6 FURTHER EXAMPLES PAST CONTINUOUS AND PAST SIMPLE

I was working **on my presentation when** the CEO called **me.**

The courier was driving **to your office when** her van got **a flat tire.**

32.7 HOW TO FORM PAST CONTINUOUS AND PAST SIMPLE

The past continuous describes a longer background action, and the past simple describes an action or event that interrupts it.

PAST CONTINUOUS	OBJECT	"WHEN"	PAST SIMPLE	REST OF SENTENCE
I was writing	an email	when	I spilled	water on my keyboard.

Use "when" to link the past continuous and past simple.

32.8 CROSS OUT THE INCORRECT WORDS IN EACH SENTENCE

We ~~signed~~ / were signing the contract when our client ~~was receiving~~ / received a text message.

1 She was walking / walked into the room and saw that Clive practiced / was practicing his presentation.

2 I tried / was trying to make an important point when someone's phone started / was starting to ring.

3 The printer worked / was working fine when unfortunately the power went / was going off.

4 He opened / was opening the door and saw that we listened / were listening to his conversation.

5 We ate / were eating lunch in the cafeteria when we heard / were hearing the fire alarm.

32.9 READ THE EMAIL AND ANSWER THE QUESTIONS

Tam accepts that she deleted the document.
True ☑ **False** ☐ **Not given** ☐

1 Tam was working on a presentation.
True ☐ **False** ☐ **Not given** ☐

2 Tam's computer crashed yesterday.
True ☐ **False** ☐ **Not given** ☐

3 Tam was only editing a copy of the report.
True ☐ **False** ☐ **Not given** ☐

4 The company lost a client because of her mistake.
True ☐ **False** ☐ **Not given** ☐

5 Tam now regularly saves her documents.
True ☐ **False** ☐ **Not given** ☐

✉ ⌄ ✕

To: Kim May

Subject: Apologies

Dear Kim,
I'm writing to apologize about the season's sales report going missing. It was entirely my fault and I really am sorry for all the disruption it caused to you and our colleagues yesterday.
I was editing the report yesterday when my computer crashed. I thought I was working on a copy of the report, so when my computer restarted, I chose not to save it. Clearly, I was working on the only master copy and accidentally deleted it from all the computers.
I will rewrite the report and now back up all my work to an external hard drive every thirty minutes so that this will not happen again.
Once again, please accept my apologies.
Best wishes,
Tam

↩ ↩↩   📎 🗑

32 ✓ CHECKLIST

⚙ Past continuous and past simple ☐   **Aa** Workplace mistakes ☐   🧩 Apologizing and giving explanations ☐

33 Tasks and targets

When you are dealing with deadlines and pressure at work, you can use the present perfect to let your co-workers know how your work is progressing.

⚙ **New language** Present perfect and past simple
Aa Vocabulary Workplace tasks
🧩 **New skill** Discussing achievements at work

33.1 KEY LANGUAGE THE PRESENT PERFECT

Use the present perfect to talk about whether or not tasks are completed or goals have been met. Use "yet" for things that you expect to happen, and "just" for recent events.

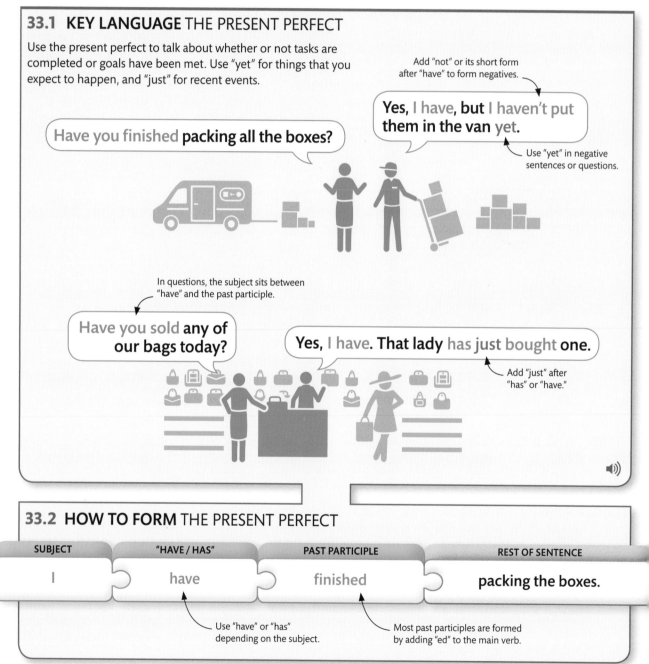

Add "not" or its short form after "have" to form negatives.

Have you finished **packing all the boxes?**

Yes, I have, but I haven't put **them in the van** yet.

Use "yet" in negative sentences or questions.

In questions, the subject sits between "have" and the past participle.

Have you sold **any of our bags today?**

Yes, I have. That lady has just bought **one.**

Add "just" after "has" or "have."

33.2 HOW TO FORM THE PRESENT PERFECT

SUBJECT	"HAVE / HAS"	PAST PARTICIPLE	REST OF SENTENCE
I	have	finished	**packing the boxes.**

Use "have" or "has" depending on the subject.

Most past participles are formed by adding "ed" to the main verb.

33.3 FILL IN THE GAPS BY PUTTING THE VERBS IN THE PRESENT PERFECT

We ___*have stopped*___ (stop) cleaning the windows because it's raining.

1 Adrian _____ (make) three flower arrangements already today.

2 I _____ (start) work on the report, but I won't finish it tonight.

3 Leah _____ (cut) four people's hair so far this afternoon.

4 It's early. We _____ (not speak) to any customers yet.

33.4 CROSS OUT THE INCORRECT WORD IN EACH SENTENCE

Have you finished the reports ~~just~~ / yet?

1 I've just / yet left work and it's very late.

2 We haven't shown this to the public just / yet.

3 Have you just / yet started selling this product?

4 She hasn't done her training course just / yet.

5 They've just / yet opened the store doors.

33.5 READ JUAN'S TO DO LIST AND ANSWER THE QUESTIONS

Juan has updated his timesheets.
True ☐ False ☑

To do list

- Update timesheets
- ~~File client documents~~
- Move files across to new server
- ~~Call the engineer~~
- ~~Book appointment with designer~~
- Buy coffee and tea
- Update the computer software
- ~~Write training manual~~
- ~~Renew parking permit~~
- Call Sam about lunch

1 Juan has called the engineer.
True ☐ False ☐

2 Juan has bought tea and coffee.
True ☐ False ☐

3 Juan hasn't written the training manual.
True ☐ False ☐

4 Juan hasn't called Sam about lunch yet.
True ☐ False ☐

33.6 KEY LANGUAGE PRESENT PERFECT AND PAST SIMPLE

Use the present perfect to talk about tasks you completed recently that still have an impact in the present.

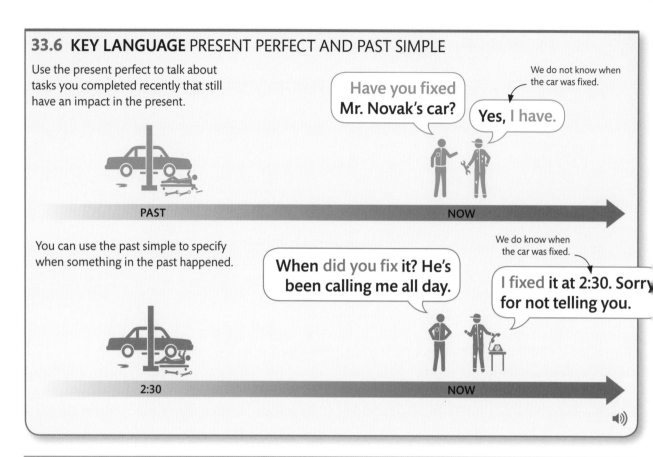

We do not know when the car was fixed.

Have you fixed Mr. Novak's car?

Yes, I have.

PAST   NOW

You can use the past simple to specify when something in the past happened.

When did you fix it? He's been calling me all day.

We do know when the car was fixed.

I fixed it at 2:30. Sorry for not telling you.

2:30   NOW

33.7 REWRITE THE SENTENCES, CORRECTING THE ERRORS

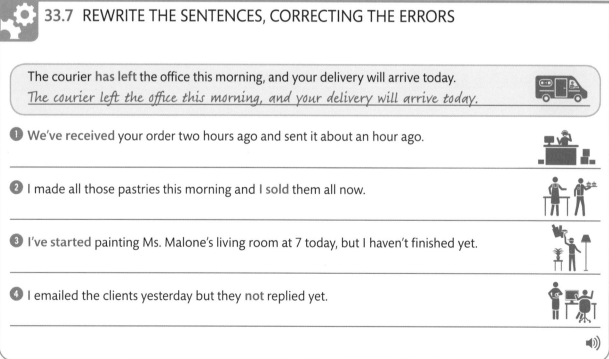

The courier **has left** the office this morning, and your delivery will arrive today.
The courier left the office this morning, and your delivery will arrive today.

❶ We've **received** your order two hours ago and sent it about an hour ago.

❷ I made all those pastries this morning and I **sold** them all now.

❸ I've **started** painting Ms. Malone's living room at 7 today, but I haven't finished yet.

❹ I emailed the clients yesterday but they **not** replied yet.

33.8 LISTEN TO THE AUDIO AND ANSWER THE QUESTIONS

Tanya and Imran are talking about their busy week at work.

What has Imran done recently?
Left his job	☐
Started a new job	☑
Won a promotion	☐

❶ Imran has met...
some of his new co-workers	☐
all his new co-workers	☐
only his manager	☐

❷ What did Imran do on Tuesday?
He had a meeting with his boss	☐
He met some of his co-workers	☐
He went to a conference	☐

❸ What did Tanya do this week?
She gave a conference talk	☐
She appeared on TV	☐
She finished her research	☐

❹ Where did Imran and Tanya both go?
A meeting for local business	☐
A marketing conference	☐
A talk on local businesses	☐

❺ What did they think of the last speaker?
Only Imran liked his talk	☐
Only Tanya liked his talk	☐
They both liked his talk	☐

33.9 RESPOND OUT LOUD TO THE AUDIO, FILLING IN THE GAPS USING THE WORDS IN THE PANEL

Have you finished the reports?

No, I haven't finished them ___yet___ .

❶ When did you start working here?

I _____ in January this year.

❷ Has Clare explained the task to you?

No, she _____ yet.

❸ Have you packed all the boxes yet?

Yes, I've _____ finished.

❹ Who has left the meeting room so messy?

Not me. I _____ been in there.

~~yet~~	just	hasn't
haven't		started

---

33 ✓ CHECKLIST

⚙ Present perfect and past simple ☐   **Aa** Workplace tasks ☐   🧩 Discussing achievements at work ☐

34 Dealing with complaints

If a customer complains about a problem, one way to offer a solution, and to make predictions or promises, is to use the future with "will."

⚙ New language The future with "will"
Aa Vocabulary Complaints and apologies
🧩 New skill Dealing with complaints

34.1 KEY LANGUAGE THE FUTURE WITH "WILL"

Use the future with "will" to make a promise to resolve a customer's problem.

I called a taxi half an hour ago, and it hasn't arrived yet.

Use "will" to make a promise and offer a solution.

I'm very sorry about that. I will contact the driver immediately.

34.2 HOW TO FORM THE FUTURE WITH "WILL"

"Will" is a modal verb, so its form doesn't change with the subject.

SUBJECT	"WILL"	BASE FORM OF VERB	REST OF SENTENCE
I The company	will	contact	the driver.

34.3 FURTHER EXAMPLES THE FUTURE WITH "WILL"

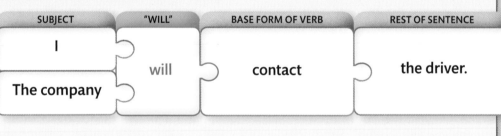

Short form of "we will." *Use the future with "will" to make an offer.*

I'm sorry the play was canceled. We'll offer you free tickets for another show.

Oh no, is your soup cold? I'll ask the chef to heat it up.

Use the future with "will" to describe a decision at the time of speaking.

34.4 READ THE LETTER AND WRITE ANSWERS TO THE QUESTIONS AS FULL SENTENCES

What type of vacation did Ms. Chang go on?

She went on a walking tour.

1 How did Ms. Chang feel about her vacation?

_____

2 What was Ms. Chang's first complaint about?

_____

3 What will the company do about phone calls?

_____

4 What was Ms. Chang's second complaint?

_____

5 What will the hotel do in the future?

_____

6 What has the company given Ms. Chang?

_____

Dear Ms. Chang,

Thank you very much for your letter of September 24 regarding your walking tour last month. We were very upset to hear that you did not enjoy your vacation, and we take full responsibility for the problems that you experienced.

We were sorry to hear that no one responded to your phone calls on the contact number that you were given when you arrived. We will ensure that every customer is now given a second contact number. Regarding the lack of a vegetarian option in the hotel restaurant, the hotel promises that they will offer both vegetarian and vegan options from now on.

By way of an apology, we have included a voucher worth $200 off your next trip with us.

Yours sincerely,
Dylan Levine

34.5 MATCH THE COMPLAINTS TO THE CORRECT RESPONSES

My train was two hours late.

1 How can I get my money back?

2 This steak is not cooked correctly.

3 These shirts are too small for me.

4 Your sales assistant was rude.

5 Where are all your wait staff?

We will refund it to your credit card.

I'll talk to him about his bad attitude.

We'll give you money off your next trip.

They'll be with you as soon as possible.

I'll take it back to the kitchen.

We'll replace them with bigger ones.

34.6 KEY LANGUAGE MAKING PREDICTIONS

You can also use "will" to make predictions about the future.

Will my taxi arrive in the next five minutes?

Yes, it will. I'm on my way now.

Use "I'm afraid" to apologize.

Short form of "will not."

No, I'm afraid it won't. The traffic is terrible.

34.7 FILL IN THE GAPS USING THE WORDS IN THE PANEL

The company will __offer__ you a discount.

1 I'm afraid your order _____ arrive today.

2 We'll _____ your appointment now.

3 I'll _____ to my manager for you.

4 We'll _____ you a replacement tomorrow.

5 I _____ contact the courier about the delay.

6 I'll _____ the chef to bring you a new meal.

7 Your delivery will _____ later today.

talk	arrive	won't
~~offer~~	ask	
will	change	send

34.8 LISTEN TO THE AUDIO AND MARK WHETHER EACH SCENARIO WILL OR WON'T HAPPEN TODAY

Will ☐   Won't ☑

1 Will ☐   Won't ☐

2 Will ☐   Won't ☐

3 Will ☐   Won't ☐

4 Will ☐   Won't ☐

5 Will ☐   Won't ☐

34.9 RESPOND OUT LOUD TO THE AUDIO, FILLING IN THE GAPS USING THE WORDS IN THE PANEL

This milk was sour when I bought it.

I'm very _sorry_ about that. Would you like a _refund_ ?

1 This part is broken and it doesn't work.

I do _____ . We'll _____ the broken part for you.

2 Can you send the replacement part today?

I'm _____ it _____ arrive until Wednesday.

3 My train was 90 minutes late!

We'll _____ you a _____ on your next trip.

Panel words:
afraid
~~refund~~
offer
apologize
won't
discount
replace
~~sorry~~

---

34 ✓ CHECKLIST

⚙ The future with "will" ☐   **Aa** Complaints and apologies ☐   Dealing with complaints ☐

↻ REVIEW THE ENGLISH YOU HAVE LEARNED IN UNITS 29–34

NEW LANGUAGE	SAMPLE SENTENCE	☑	UNIT
TALKING ABOUT RULES POLITE REQUESTS	You can't wear jeans to work. Could you send your email again, please?	☐	29.1, 29.5
DESCRIBING WORKPLACE PROBLEMS	The printer wasn't working today.	☐	31.1
APOLOGIZING AND GIVING EXPLANATIONS	I'm really sorry. I was writing an email when I spilled water on my keyboard.	☐	32.1, 32.5
DISCUSSING DEADLINES	I have finished packing the boxes.	☐	33.1
DEALING WITH COMPLAINTS	We will investigate this problem, and we'll offer you a discount.	☐	34.1

35 Vocabulary

35.1 TRANSPORTATION

car

taxi

bus

coach

plane

train

tram

metro

bicycle

motorcycle (US) /
motorbike (UK)

helicopter

airport

bus stop

train station

taxi stand (US) /
taxi rank (UK)

35.2 TRAVEL

one-way ticket

terminal

check-in

boarding pass

first class

round trip ticket (US) /
return ticket (UK)

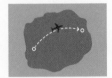
domestic flight

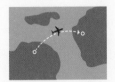
international flight

connecting flight

on time

late

delay

luggage

security

passport

passport control

departure gate

board a plane

seat reservation

aisle seat

window seat

business class

economy

transfer

hotel

36 Making travel arrangements

When you have travel plans or want to discuss the arrangements for a trip, it is useful to be able to talk about the possible results of actions and choices.

⚙ New language Zero and first conditional
Aa Vocabulary Travel
🧩 New skill Talking about actions and results

36.1 KEY LANGUAGE THE FIRST CONDITIONAL

You can use the first conditional when you want to describe a realistic action and a future result that it might lead to.

If you buy a return flight, you will save money.

36.2 HOW TO FORM THE FIRST CONDITIONAL

The first conditional is usually introduced by "if" followed by the present simple. The future with "will" expresses the result.

"IF"	PRESENT SIMPLE	COMMA	FUTURE WITH "WILL"
If	**you buy a return flight**	**,**	**you will save money.**

"If" shows that the sentence is conditional.

Present simple tense describes suggested action.

Comma separates action from result.

Future with "will" describes the result.

36.3 FURTHER EXAMPLES THE FIRST CONDITIONAL

 If you book in advance, you will get a discount.

 If they bring a lot of equipment, we will need a bigger suitcase.

 If the trip is long, I will probably fall asleep.

 We will be late for the flight **if** we don't leave soon.

You can put the "if" clause at the end of the sentence if you remove the comma.

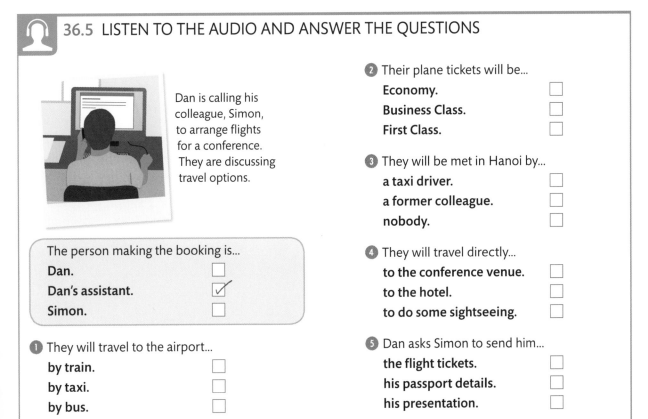

36.4 MATCH THE BEGINNINGS OF THE SENTENCES TO THE CORRECT ENDINGS

Will you buy a ticket → if I buy one, too?

1 If you go to China for business,

2 If I go to China on business,

3 If we win the contract,

4 Will you arrange a taxi

5 We won't get a discount

6 If you have a lot of luggage,

if we land late at the airport?

you will need a taxi.

if I buy one, too?

will you visit the Great Wall?

if we don't book now.

I won't have time to go sightseeing.

we will go out to celebrate.

36.5 LISTEN TO THE AUDIO AND ANSWER THE QUESTIONS

Dan is calling his colleague, Simon, to arrange flights for a conference. They are discussing travel options.

The person making the booking is...

Dan. ☐

Dan's assistant. ☑

Simon. ☐

1 They will travel to the airport...

by train. ☐

by taxi. ☐

by bus. ☐

2 Their plane tickets will be...

Economy. ☐

Business Class. ☐

First Class. ☐

3 They will be met in Hanoi by...

a taxi driver. ☐

a former colleague. ☐

nobody. ☐

4 They will travel directly...

to the conference venue. ☐

to the hotel. ☐

to do some sightseeing. ☐

5 Dan asks Simon to send him...

the flight tickets. ☐

his passport details. ☐

his presentation. ☐

36.6 KEY LANGUAGE THE ZERO CONDITIONAL

You can use the zero conditional to talk about things that are generally true, or to describe the direct result of an action.

If your bag weighs too much, we charge a fee.

36.7 HOW TO FORM THE ZERO CONDITIONAL

The zero conditional uses "if" or "when" with the present simple, followed by the present simple in the main clause.

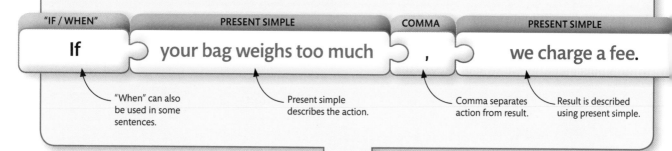

"IF / WHEN"	PRESENT SIMPLE	COMMA	PRESENT SIMPLE
If	your bag weighs too much	,	we charge a fee.

"When" can also be used in some sentences.

Present simple describes the action.

Comma separates action from result.

Result is described using present simple.

36.8 FURTHER EXAMPLES THE ZERO CONDITIONAL

"When" can sometimes be used instead of "if."

 If you book online, flights are often cheaper.

 When I pack in a hurry, I sometimes forget my passport.

 The airport has a shower **if** you need to freshen up.

 Clients get angry **if** we don't pay their expenses.

 The airline offers transfers **if** you have a connecting flight.

 If I don't carry a map, I always get lost in a new city.

36.9 REWRITE THE SENTENCES, PUTTING THE WORDS IN THE CORRECT ORDER

| fly | Business | If | there | Class, | you | a | lounge. | is |

If you fly Business Class, there is a lounge.

1. | you | transfer, | you. | book | a | When | driver | a | meets |

_____

2. | get | the | off | Passengers | if | plane | annoyed | takes | late. |

_____

3. | You | a | meal | vegetarian. | special | can | if | you're | order |

_____

🔊

36.10 CROSS OUT THE INCORRECT WORD IN EACH SENTENCE, THEN SAY THE SENTENCES OUT LOUD

Will / ~~do~~ you pick me up from the airport if I tell you my flight number?

1. If you buy food on the plane, it **was** / **is** quite expensive.

2. If you **are** / **will** in a group, it is often cheaper to go by taxi.

3. Will it be cheaper to **buy** / **bought** a return ticket if I come back the same day?

4. When you book flights early, they **are** / **is** usually cheaper.

5. Traveling is boring if you **don't** / **didn't** have anything to do on the plane.

🔊

Asking for directions

When traveling to conferences and meetings, you may need to ask for directions. Knowing how to be polite but clear is essential.

✿ **New language** Imperatives, prepositions of place
Aa Vocabulary Directions
✦ **New skill** Asking for and giving directions

37.1 KEY LANGUAGE ASKING FOR AND GIVING DIRECTIONS

When you ask for directions, be polite and listen carefully to the response. Imperatives are often used to give directions.

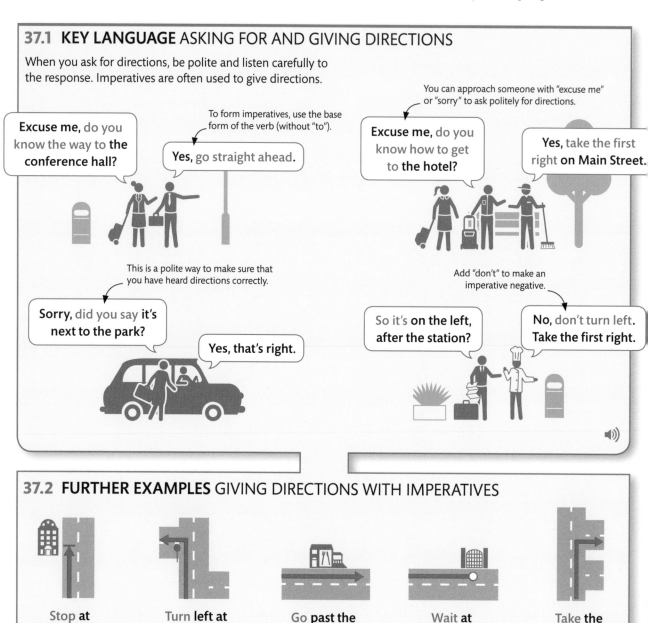

You can approach someone with "excuse me" or "sorry" to ask politely for directions.

Excuse me, do you know the way to **the conference hall?**

To form imperatives, use the base form of the verb (without "to").

Yes, go straight ahead.

Excuse me, do you know how to get to **the hotel?**

Yes, take the first right **on Main Street.**

This is a polite way to make sure that you have heard directions correctly.

Sorry, did you say **it's next to the park?**

Yes, that's right.

Add "don't" to make an imperative negative.

So it's **on the left, after the station?**

No, don't turn left. **Take the first right.**

37.2 FURTHER EXAMPLES GIVING DIRECTIONS WITH IMPERATIVES

Stop at the hotel.

Turn left at the sign.

Go past the restaurant.

Wait at the gate.

Take the second right.

37.3 VOCABULARY PREPOSITIONS OF PLACE AND OTHER DIRECTIONS

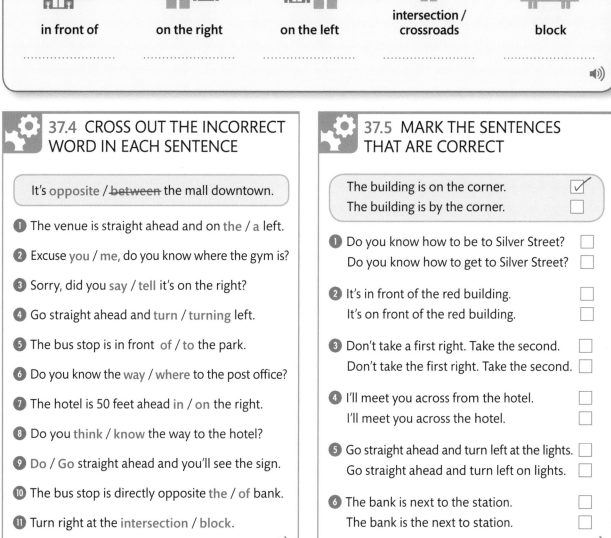

next to

opposite /
across from

between

on the corner

behind

in front of

on the right

on the left

intersection /
crossroads

block

37.4 CROSS OUT THE INCORRECT WORD IN EACH SENTENCE

It's opposite / ~~between~~ the mall downtown.

1 The venue is straight ahead and on the / a left.

2 Excuse you / me, do you know where the gym is?

3 Sorry, did you say / tell it's on the right?

4 Go straight ahead and turn / turning left.

5 The bus stop is in front of / to the park.

6 Do you know the way / where to the post office?

7 The hotel is 50 feet ahead in / on the right.

8 Do you think / know the way to the hotel?

9 Do / Go straight ahead and you'll see the sign.

10 The bus stop is directly opposite the / of bank.

11 Turn right at the intersection / block.

37.5 MARK THE SENTENCES THAT ARE CORRECT

The building is on the corner. ☑
The building is by the corner. ☐

1 Do you know how to be to Silver Street? ☐
Do you know how to get to Silver Street? ☐

2 It's in front of the red building. ☐
It's on front of the red building. ☐

3 Don't take a first right. Take the second. ☐
Don't take the first right. Take the second. ☐

4 I'll meet you across from the hotel. ☐
I'll meet you across the hotel. ☐

5 Go straight ahead and turn left at the lights. ☐
Go straight ahead and turn left on lights. ☐

6 The bank is next to the station. ☐
The bank is the next to station. ☐

37.6 REWRITE THE SENTENCES, PUTTING THE WORDS IN THE CORRECT ORDER

| way | Do | bank? | to | the | know | you | the |

Do you know the way to the bank?

1 | you | Sorry, | opposite | café? | did | say | it's | the |

___

2 | ahead | right | and | Go | turn | the | straight | at | intersection. |

___

3 | to | Do | know | to | you | get | the | how | venue? |

___

4 | past | and | post | Go | on | it's | the | left. | office | the |

___

🔊

37.7 LISTEN TO THE AUDIO AND MARK THE DIRECTIONS YOU HEAR

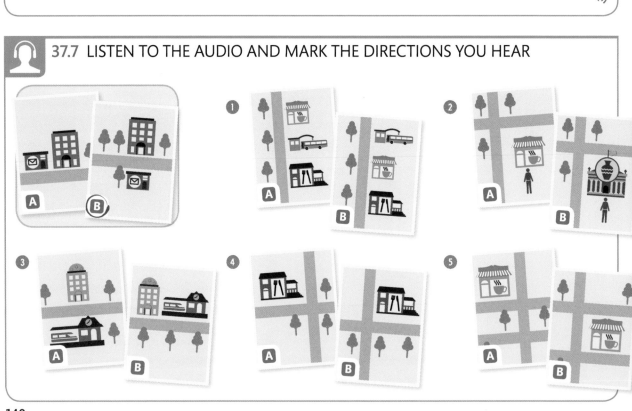

37.8 LOOK AT THE MAP, THEN RESPOND TO THE AUDIO OUT LOUD, FILLING IN THE GAPS

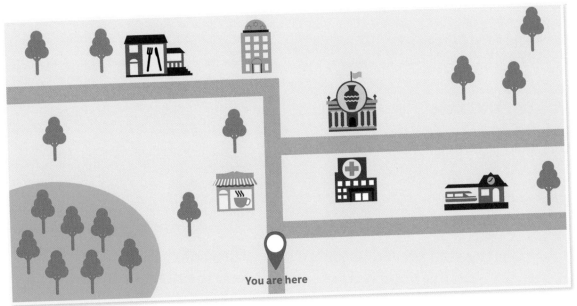

You are here

Do you know the way to the hospital?

Yes. Take the second ___*right*___ .
It's ___*opposite*___ the museum.

3 Can you tell me where the nearest hotel is?

Go straight _____ .
It's on the _____ .

1 Is there a restaurant near here?

Take the first _____ , and
go _____ the hotel.

4 Do you know the way to the train station?

Take the first _____ ,
then _____ straight ahead.

2 Could you tell me the way to the museum?

It's across from the hospital.
Take the _____ right.

5 Can you tell me the quickest way to a café?

Just go _____ ahead
and it's on the _____ .

---

37 ✓ **CHECKLIST**

⚙ Imperatives, prepositions of place ☐   **Aa** Directions ☐   🧩 Asking for and giving directions ☐

38 Describing your stay

You can describe events using either active or passive sentences. The focus in a passive sentence is on the action itself rather than the thing that caused it.

⚙ **New language** The passive voice
Aa Vocabulary Hotels and accommodation
🧩 **New skill** Using the passive voice

38.1 KEY LANGUAGE THE PASSIVE VOICE

In passive sentences, the person or thing doing the action is unknown, unimportant, or obvious.

The staff served breakfast on the hotel terrace.

In this active sentence, the focus is on the people serving breakfast.

Breakfast was served on the hotel terrace.

Here the focus is on breakfast, rather than the people who served it.

38.2 HOW TO FORM THE PASSIVE VOICE

All passives use a form of "be" with a past participle. "By" can be used to introduce the person or thing doing the action.

SUBJECT	FORM OF "BE"	PAST PARTICIPLE	REST OF SENTENCE
Breakfast	**was**	**served**	**by the staff.**

The main verb is expressed as a past participle.

38.3 FURTHER EXAMPLES THE PASSIVE VOICE

 The TV was broken when I arrived.

The hotel room was booked by my assistant.

 The Wi-Fi code is written on your keycard.

 A wake-up call was not offered.

142

38.4 MATCH THE ACTIVE SENTENCES TO THE CORRECT PASSIVE VERSIONS

The guest requested a double room.

① Maria cleaned the rooms this morning.

② Someone left the key in the door.

③ The CEO met the VIPs in the boardroom.

④ Someone put flowers in the hotel foyer.

The rooms were cleaned this morning.

The key was left in the door.

A double room was requested.

Flowers were put in the hotel foyer.

The VIPs were met in the boardroom.

38.5 REWRITE THE PASSIVE SENTENCES, PUTTING THE WORDS IN THE CORRECT ORDER

| opened | was | VIP. | a | hotel | by | The |

The hotel was opened by a VIP.

① | car | driven | chauffeur. | The | was | by | a |

② | by | the | guest. | key | The | was | found |

③ | shown | conference | around | They | the | venue. | were |

38.6 LISTEN TO THE AUDIO, THEN NUMBER THE PICTURES IN THE ORDER THEY ARE DESCRIBED

A ☐

B 1

C ☐

D ☐

38.7 READ THE REVIEWS AND ANSWER THE QUESTIONS

Hotel Gwesty is not near the airport
True ☐ **False** ☐ **Not given** ☑

① Hugh Jenkins didn't like the hotel staff.
True ☐ **False** ☐ **Not given** ☐

② Hugh Jenkins and his clients ate at the hotel.
True ☐ **False** ☐ **Not given** ☐

③ Hugh Jenkins will go back to Hotel Gwesty.
True ☐ **False** ☐ **Not given** ☐

④ Sue Vardy was impressed by Hotel Plaza.
True ☐ **False** ☐ **Not given** ☐

⑤ The Wi-Fi worked well at Hotel Plaza.
True ☐ **False** ☐ **Not given** ☐

⑥ The furniture at Hotel Plaza was bad.
True ☐ **False** ☐ **Not given** ☐

Which hotel?

HOME | REVIEWS | ABOUT | CONTACT

Hotel Gwesty: Review by Hugh Jenkins, CEO TotalData
The hotel is very conveniently located, less than two miles from the airport. From the moment we checked in, I was impressed by the staff's professional manner. They immediately took us to the meeting room to look around before our clients arrived. The meeting room was comfortable and had all the equipment we needed for presentations and discussions. Throughout the day, we had refreshments provided in the room and an excellent buffet lunch. Our clients were happy and we will be returning here for future meetings.

Hotel Plaza: Review by Sue Vardy, Director Centria32
The best part of our stay here was checking out! We booked this hotel to launch our new product, and it was a disaster. Our conference room was very dark and there was no Wi-Fi or internet connection at all. We could not turn the projector on, the furniture was falling apart, and worst of all, they forgot to pick up our client from the airport! A horrible place!

Aa 38.8 MATCH THE DEFINITIONS TO THE CORRECT PHRASAL VERBS

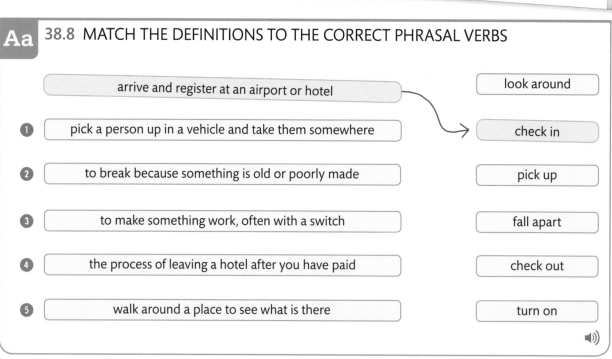

arrive and register at an airport or hotel → check in

① pick a person up in a vehicle and take them somewhere — look around

② to break because something is old or poorly made — pick up

③ to make something work, often with a switch — fall apart

④ the process of leaving a hotel after you have paid — check out

⑤ walk around a place to see what is there — turn on

38.9 LISTEN TO THE AUDIO, THEN NUMBER THE SENTENCES IN THE ORDER YOU HEAR THEM

An assistant is calling a hotel to reserve a room for her boss.

A How many rooms would you like? ☐

B Could I reserve a parking space for those days? ☐

C Would you like to book breakfast now? ☐

D I'd like to make a reservation, please. ☑1

E Can I have the name, please? ☐

38.10 RESPOND OUT LOUD TO THE AUDIO, PUTTING THE VERBS IN THE PASSIVE VOICE

What did you think of the meals during your stay?

The hotel food _____*was prepared*_____ (prepare) very badly.

1 Where did you have breakfast in the morning?

Breakfast _____ (serve) in the main restaurant.

2 Were the rooms clean and tidy?

The rooms _____ (clean) every day.

3 Who reserved your rooms?

The reservation _____ (make) by my assistant.

4 Were the rooms nice?

Yes. Very. They _____ (decorate) beautifully.

38 ✅ CHECKLIST

⚙️ The passive voice ☐   Aa Hotels and accommodation ☐   👥 Using the passive voice ☐

39.1 EATING OUT

chef	waiter	waitress	make a reservation / booking	menu
appetizer (US) / starter (UK)	entrée (US) / main course (UK)	dessert	check (US) / bill (UK)	receipt
café	restaurant	bar	tip	food allergy / intolerance
breakfast	lunch	dinner	vegan	vegetarian
broil (US) / grill (UK)	bake	roast	boil	fry

39.2 FOOD AND DRINK

food

drinks

fork

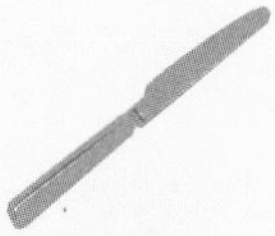

knife

spoon

napkin

cup

glass

tea

coffee

water

milk

cream

butter

cheese

meat

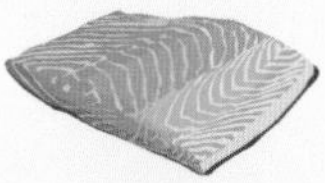

fish

seafood

fruit

vegetables

potatoes

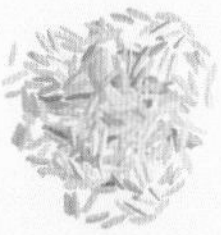

rice

pasta

bread

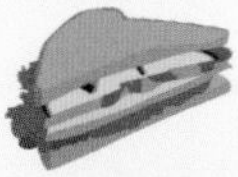

sandwich

soup

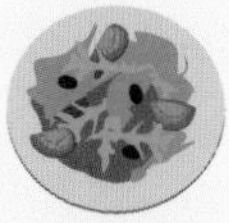

salad

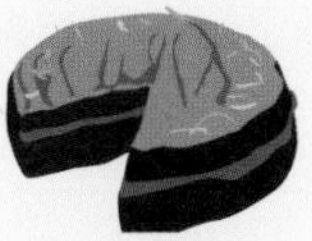

cake

chocolate

sugar

40 Conferences and visitors

Whether you are welcoming visitors, or visiting somewhere on business yourself, it is important to know how to interact politely in English.

⚙ **New language** "A," "some," "any"
Aa Vocabulary Hospitality
🧩 **New skill** Welcoming visitors

40.1 KEY LANGUAGE WELCOMING VISITORS

There are a number of phrases you can use when welcoming visitors who have come to see you on business.

40.2 MARK THE SENTENCES THAT ARE CORRECT

You are Mr. Draper. ☐
You must be Mr. Draper. ☑

Welcome **to Hanoi.**

Have you been **to Hanoi before?**

You must be Mr. Burford.

Yes, we spoke on the phone.

It's great to meet in person.

Did you have a good flight?

Can I get you anything?

1. Yes, we speak on the phone. ☐
   Yes, we spoke on the phone. ☐

2. Have you been to Mexico City before? ☐
   Have you been Mexico City before? ☐

3. I'll let Mrs. Singh know that you're here. ☐
   I'll tell Mrs. Singh know you're here. ☐

4. Would you like some tea or coffee? ☐
   Would you have some tea or coffee? ☐

5. Did you have a good flight? ☐
   Did you have a well flight? ☐

6. I've been looking forward to this visit. ☐
   I've been look forward to this visit. ☐

7. It's great to meet your person. ☐
   It's great to meet you in person. ☐

8. Did you have any trouble getting here? ☐
   Do you have any trouble getting here? ☐

9. Can I get you anything? ☐
   Can I have you anything? ☐

40.3 KEY LANGUAGE "A," "SOME," "ANY"

In English, nouns can either be countable, meaning they can be easily counted, or uncountable, meaning they aren't usually counted individually. Use "a" or "an" with single countable nouns. Use "some" with plural countable nouns and uncountable nouns. Use "any" in questions and negative statements.

Uncountable nouns can be made countable if they are placed in containers.

Would you like a cup of coffee?

Do you have any tea?

Use "any" in questions and negative statements.

I'm afraid not. Can I get you some water?

Always use "some" with uncountable nouns, not "a," "an," or a number.

40.4 REWRITE SENTENCES, CORRECTING THE ERRORS

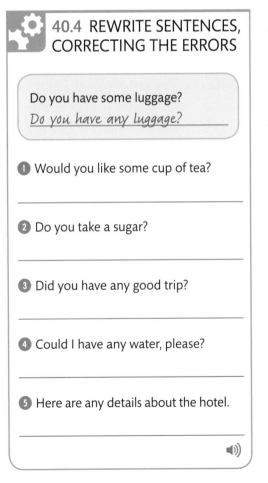

Do you have some luggage?
Do you have any luggage?

❶ Would you like some cup of tea?

_____

❷ Do you take a sugar?

_____

❸ Did you have any good trip?

_____

❹ Could I have any water, please?

_____

❺ Here are any details about the hotel.

_____

40.5 MATCH THE BEGINNINGS OF THE SENTENCES TO THE CORRECT ENDINGS

I like to drink ⟶ coffee at breakfast.

a good flight?

❶ I didn't bring — any help?

❷ Did you have — coffee at breakfast.

❸ Do you need — any luggage.

❹ Would you like to — anything to drink?

❺ There will be — meet the team?

❻ Can I get you — seat and wait here.

❼ Please take a — something to eat.

40.6 LISTEN TO THE AUDIO AND ANSWER THE QUESTIONS

Two attendees are discussing products at a marketing conference in Hanoi.

Where has Mr. Park traveled from?
London ☐
Moscow ☑
Seoul ☐

1 When was the conference's opening reception?
The morning before ☐
The evening before ☐
That morning ☐

2 What does Ben Park want to see at the conference?
A product launch ☐
Jo's presentation ☐
The closing session ☐

3 What is Jo going to give a presentation about?
Networking at conferences ☐
Social media and marketing ☐
A new product launch ☐

Aa 40.7 FILL IN THE GAPS USING THE WORDS IN THE PANEL

Collect your lanyard from ___reception___.

1 The _____ speech will start at 10am.

2 The main _____ used a lot of slides.

3 The main sponsor will _____ a new product.

4 Every attendee gets a _____ and a name tag.

5 In a workshop the _____ get involved.

6 There are lots of _____ opportunities.

~~reception~~   keynote
launch   lanyard   networking
delegates   presenter

40.8 CROSS OUT THE INCORRECT WORDS IN EACH SENTENCE

There is a / ~~any~~ / some workshop at midday.

1 They have a / some / any free food and drinks.

2 Do you have a / some / any lanyard already?

3 I have a / some / any business cards to give people.

4 I'd like to see a / some / any interesting talks.

5 Are you going to a / some / any talks today?

6 Do you have a / some / any business card?

7 Are you staying in a / some / any hotel?

8 They don't have a / some / any drinks.

9 I'm giving a / some / any presentation today.

40.9 READ THE ARTICLE AND MARK THE CORRECT SUMMARY

1 Use conferences to network. Dress professionally, act politely, and tell everyone all about yourself. ☐

2 Use conferences to network. Dress professionally, act politely, and find out about the person you are talking to. ☐

3 Use conferences to network. Dress professionally, act politely, and tell your clients about yourself. ☐

Conference tips:

Going to a conference is one of the best ways to network and make new business connections.

• It is really important to make a good first impression. Remember, you might be talking to a future client or employer.

• Dress professionally and always behave politely. Most importantly, show an interest in the person you are talking to. Find out their name; ask them what they do and ask about their family. This, in turn, will make them more likely to ask about you.

40.10 RESPOND OUT LOUD TO THE AUDIO, FILLING IN THE GAPS USING THE WORDS IN THE PANEL

Do you have any goals for the conference?

I want to start ___*networking*___ with people in my field.

1 Sorry, I didn't catch your name.

It's Leo Smart. I haven't collected my _____ yet.

2 Do you have any contact details?

Yes, here. Please take my _____ .

3 Are you going to any presentations?

Yes, and I went to an interesting _____ this morning.

workshop

business card

~~networking~~

lanyard

41 Dining and hospitality

It is important to learn local customs for dining and entertaining. At business lunches and conferences, follow these customs and use polite language.

New language "Much / many," "too / enough"
Aa Vocabulary Restaurants
New skill Offering and accepting hospitality

41.1 KEY LANGUAGE DINING IN RESTAURANTS

When dining or sharing hospitality with clients, it is important as a host or guest to be friendly and polite.

I'd like a table for two, please.

Do you have a reservation?

Yes. My name is Sarah Key.

Do you have any tables free for lunch?

How many people are in your party?

I'm afraid there is a 20-minute wait.

Are you ready to order?

"Could" is more polite than "can."

Could I have the fish?

Do you have any allergies?

Yes. I'm allergic to peanuts.

I'll have the soup, please.

Add "please" to make requests more polite.

How is everything?

There were lots of bones in my fish.

Could we have the check, please?

This is usually referred to as the "bill" in UK English.

I don't have enough cash. Can I pay by card?

There is too much cream in my soup.

41.2 REWRITE THE SENTENCES, PUTTING THE WORDS IN THE CORRECT ORDER

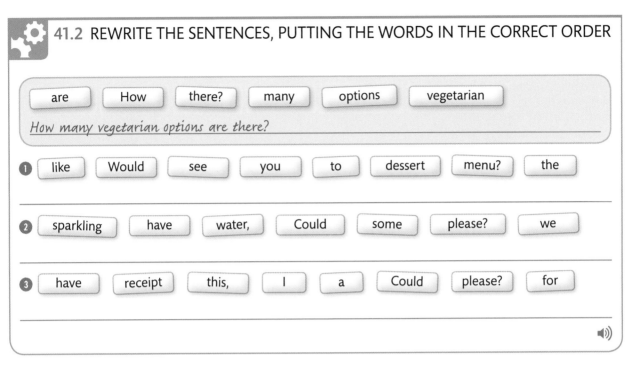

| are | How | there? | many | options | vegetarian |

How many vegetarian options are there?

1. | like | Would | see | you | to | dessert | menu? | the |

_____

2. | sparkling | have | water, | Could | some | please? | we |

_____

3. | have | receipt | this, | I | a | Could | please? | for |

_____

41.3 RESPOND OUT LOUD TO THE AUDIO, FILLING IN THE GAPS USING THE WORDS IN THE PANEL

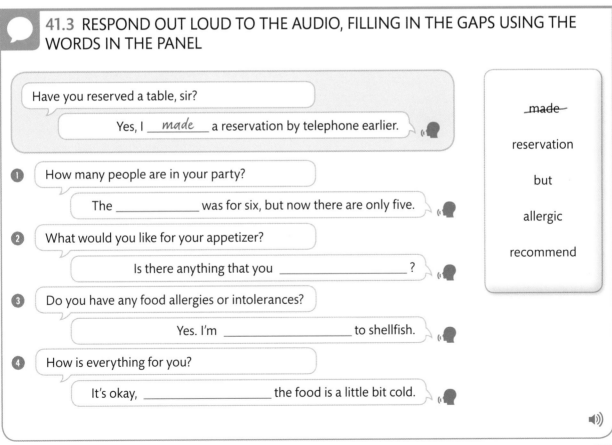

Have you reserved a table, sir?

Yes, I ___made___ a reservation by telephone earlier.

Panel:
~~made~~
reservation
but
allergic
recommend

1. How many people are in your party?

The _____ was for six, but now there are only five.

2. What would you like for your appetizer?

Is there anything that you _____ ?

3. Do you have any food allergies or intolerances?

Yes. I'm _____ to shellfish.

4. How is everything for you?

It's okay, _____ the food is a little bit cold.

153

41.4 KEY LANGUAGE TALKING ABOUT QUANTITY

Use "much," "many," and "enough" to talk about amounts and quantities.
These words can also show our feelings about the amounts and quantities.
For example, "too much" is negative, but "enough" is positive.

How much **time do we have?**

Use "much" to ask questions about
quantities of uncountable nouns.

How many **sides have you ordered?**

Use "many" to ask questions about
quantities of countable nouns.

There is too much **chili in this!**

"Too much / many" is used to talk about
quantities that are too large.

There aren't enough **waiters.**

"Enough" and "not enough" are used to talk
about countable and uncountable nouns.

41.5 MARK THE SENTENCES THAT ARE CORRECT

How many glasses will you need?	☑
How much glasses will you need?	☐

1. How much rice do you want? ☐
   How many rice do you want? ☐

2. I don't need more. There's enough here. ☐
   I don't need more. There's not enough here. ☐

3. There are too much seats here. ☐
   There are too many seats here. ☐

4. There's not enough water. ☐
   There's not many water. ☐

5. $40 for a steak! That's too many. ☐
   $40 for a steak! That's too much. ☐

41.6 FILL IN THE GAPS USING THE WORDS IN THE PANEL

Do you have ___enough___ bread?

1. I've eaten _____ many chocolates.

2. How _____ glasses do we need?

3. There's too _____ sauce on this.

4. How _____ should we tip here?

much	much	many
	too	~~enough~~

41.7 READ THE ARTICLE AND ANSWER THE QUESTIONS

You should ask all clients to business lunches.
True ☐ **False** ☑ **Not given** ☐

① The author recommends reading about local customs.
True ☐ **False** ☐ **Not given** ☐

② Guests should be given a selection of places to eat.
True ☐ **False** ☐ **Not given** ☐

③ You should go outside to answer your phone.
True ☐ **False** ☐ **Not given** ☐

④ Guests shouldn't order the most expensive meal.
True ☐ **False** ☐ **Not given** ☐

⑤ The author suggests you shouldn't eat too much.
True ☐ **False** ☐ **Not given** ☐

MEALS AND DEALS

Business lunches can be a great way to get to know your clients, but be careful about who you invite to lunch. CEOs, for example, have busy schedules, and it may be better to invite them for coffee. If you do invite someone to lunch, you should read about the local dining etiquette. You could also present your guest with several dining options before making a restaurant reservation. Once you arrive at the

restaurant, turn off your phone. Your guests should have all your attention. If you are a guest yourself, arrive on time, and make sure that you do not order the most expensive thing on the menu. Last, as host or guest, try to enjoy yourself.

---

41 ✓ CHECKLIST

⚙ "Much / many," "too / enough" ☐   **Aa** Restaurants ☐   🧩 Offering and accepting hospitality ☐

↻ REVIEW THE ENGLISH YOU HAVE LEARNED IN UNITS 35–41

NEW LANGUAGE	SAMPLE SENTENCE	☑	UNIT
THE FIRST CONDITIONAL	If you buy a return flight, you will save money.	☐	36.1
THE ZERO CONDITIONAL	If your bag weighs too much, we charge a fee.	☐	36.6
GIVING DIRECTIONS WITH IMPERATIVES	Go straight ahead.	☐	37.1
THE PASSIVE VOICE	Breakfast was served on the hotel terrace.	☐	38.1
"A," "SOME," "ANY"	Do you have any tea? Would you like a cup of coffee or some water?	☐	40.3
"MUCH / MANY," "TOO / ENOUGH"	How much time do we have? There are not enough waiters.	☐	41.4

42 Informal phone calls

In most workplaces, you can use polite but informal language to call your co-workers. English often uses two- or three-part verbs in informal telephone language.

🔧 **New language** Telephone language
Aa Vocabulary Phone numbers and etiquette
🧩 **New skill** Calling your co-workers

42.1 KEY LANGUAGE MAKING INFORMAL PHONE CALLS

Informal phone calls between co-workers often use various polite phrases for starting and ending a call and exchanging information.

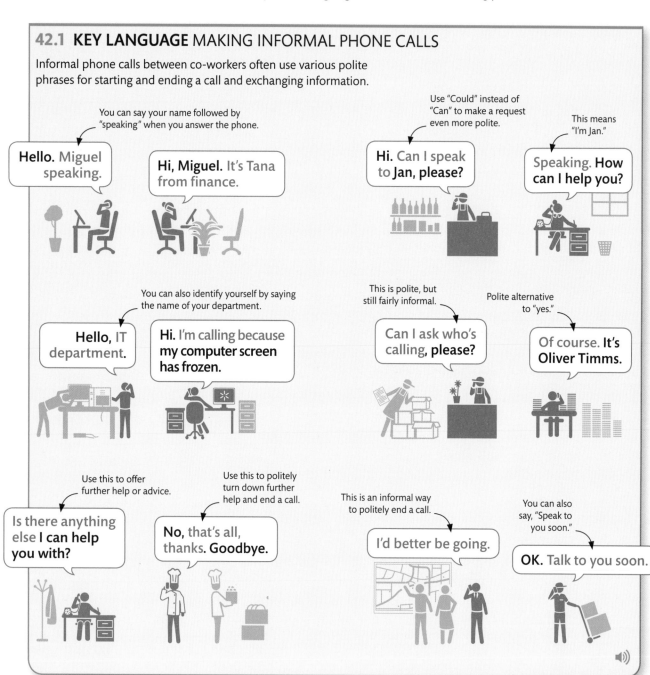

You can say your name followed by "speaking" when you answer the phone.

Hello. Miguel speaking.

Hi, Miguel. **It's Tana from finance.**

Use "Could" instead of "Can" to make a request even more polite.

Hi. Can I speak to Jan, please?

This means "I'm Jan."

Speaking. How can I help you?

You can also identify yourself by saying the name of your department.

Hello, IT department.

Hi. I'm calling because my computer screen has frozen.

This is polite, but still fairly informal.

Can I ask who's calling, **please?**

Polite alternative to "yes."

Of course. **It's Oliver Timms.**

Use this to offer further help or advice.

Is there anything else **I can help you with?**

Use this to politely turn down further help and end a call.

No, that's all, thanks. **Goodbye.**

This is an informal way to politely end a call.

I'd better be going.

You can also say, "Speak to you soon."

OK. Talk to you soon.

156

42.2 FILL IN THE GAPS USING THE WORDS IN THE PANEL

Can I ___*speak*___ to Jan, please?

1 Hi, Karl. It's Katie _____ HR.

2 Hi. I'm _____ about the Wi-Fi.

3 My client is here. I'd _____ be going.

4 Can I ask _____ calling, please?

5 Is there _____ else I can do for you?

6 Hello. Olga _____ .

7 No, thanks. That's _____ . Bye.

better	from	who's
anything		all
~~speak~~	calling	speaking

◀))

42.3 LISTEN TO THE AUDIO, THEN NUMBER THE SENTENCES IN THE ORDER YOU HEAR THEM

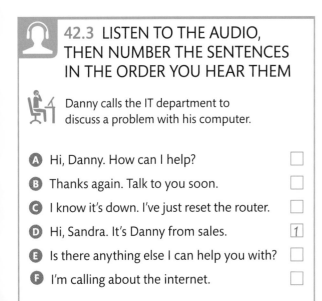

Danny calls the IT department to discuss a problem with his computer.

A Hi, Danny. How can I help? ☐

B Thanks again. Talk to you soon. ☐

C I know it's down. I've just reset the router. ☐

D Hi, Sandra. It's Danny from sales. ☐1

E Is there anything else I can help you with? ☐

F I'm calling about the internet. ☐

42.4 SAY THE SENTENCES OUT LOUD, CORRECTING THE ERRORS

I'd better be go. Goodbye.

> *I'd better be going. Goodbye.* ◀)

1 Hi. Can I speak Jacob, please?

[_____] ◀)

2 Hello, Sophie. Here Ahmed from sales.

[_____] ◀)

3 Could I say who's calling, please?

[_____] ◀)

4 Hi. Adam speaks.

[_____] ◀)

5 It's Sandy off IT.

[_____] ◀)

6 Hi. I call because the elevator is stuck.

[_____] ◀)

7 Bye then. Speaking to you soon.

[_____] ◀)

8 Can I ask who calls, please?

[_____] ◀)

◀))

42.5 KEY LANGUAGE SAYING YOUR PHONE NUMBER

There are many useful phrases for telling people your phone number.

Informal English usually shortens "phone number" to "number."

The office number is **0078 555 251.**

An extension is the last few digits of an employee's office phone number.

My extension is **3827.**

You can also say "You can call me."

You can contact me at **603-902-0691.**

42.6 PRONUNCIATION NUMBERS

In US English, the number 0 is pronounced "zero," and repeated numbers are said individually.
In UK English, many different pronunciations are possible for 0 and rows of repeated numbers.

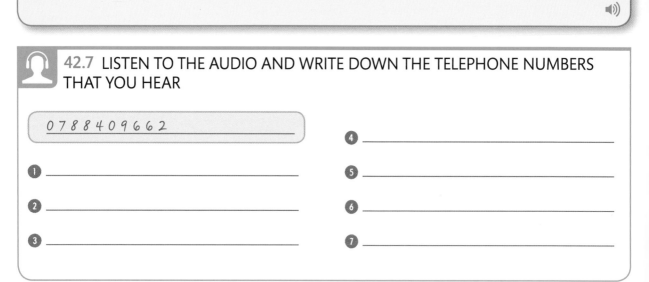

zero · "oh" · nought

0

four four · forty-four · double four

44

five five five · treble five · triple five · five double five

555

42.7 LISTEN TO THE AUDIO AND WRITE DOWN THE TELEPHONE NUMBERS THAT YOU HEAR

0 7 8 8 4 0 9 6 6 2

1 _____

2 _____

3 _____

4 _____

5 _____

6 _____

7 _____

42.8 CROSS OUT THE INCORRECT WORD IN EACH SENTENCE, THEN SAY THE SENTENCES OUT LOUD

If you want to arrange a meeting, you can / ~~will~~ contact me on 0078 555 251.

① Can / Don't you call Martin at the office? His number's 902-555-4349.

② You can / will call me on my cell phone any time. My number's 03069 991332.

③ Hi, it's Myra. Can / Do you call me back? My number's 07064 881206.

④ Would / Can you be able to call me back? I'm at the office. My extension is 8762.

⑤ If you want / should to contact Samuel later, his number's 01632 960441.

⑥ I've got a number for Hanna if you can / want to contact her. It's 321-554-8933.

🔊

42.9 LISTEN TO THE AUDIO AND ANSWER THE QUESTIONS

Tara calls her co-worker, Sven, to ask for help with some workplace problems.

What department does Sven work in?
Sales ☐
IT ☑
HR ☐

① What is Tara working on at the moment?
A project selling mobile devices ☐
A project selling shoes ☐
A project selling apps ☐

② What is her main problem?
The mobile devices do not work ☐
The Wi-Fi does not work ☐
She cannot connect to the Wi-Fi ☐

③ What is Sven's solution?
Enter a different passcode ☐
Turn them off and on again ☐
Come to a different office ☐

④ What is the passcode that Sven gives?
JG330XS ☐
GJ330XF ☐
GJ330XS ☐

⑤ What does Sven say about Tara's second problem?
He cannot fix it ☐
She cannot fix it ☐
He will fix it ☐

42.10 KEY LANGUAGE VERBS FOR PHONE CALLS

Informal spoken English, particularly in telephone language, often uses two- or three-part verbs.

> **I have to hang up now, but I'll call you back tomorrow.**

42.11 FURTHER EXAMPLES VERBS FOR PHONE CALLS

I'll just put you through to the IT department.

This line is awful! I just got cut off.

Sorry, I'm really busy. Can I get back to you in 10 minutes?

Their receptionist never picks up the phone.

42.12 CROSS OUT THE INCORRECT WORDS IN EACH SENTENCE

This line is terrible! I hope we don't get cut ~~up~~ / off / ~~on~~.

1. Anna, can I call you off / on / back later from the office?

2. Suzanna always takes ages to pick up / on / off the phone.

3. Ethan, I will get back to / with / until you later with an answer.

4. I'll put you in / back / through to Ivor now.

5. If a customer is very rude, you can hang on / off / up.

6. I'll find out the information and get off / back / on to you.

7. I'm busy now, Valeria, but I'll call you / me / us back later.

42.13 REWRITE THE SENTENCES, PUTTING THE WORDS IN THE CORRECT ORDER

| to | get | later | back | Can | you | today? | I |

Can I get back to you later today?

1 | I'll | through | sales. | you | put | to | Simone | in |

_____

2 | will | you | afternoon. | back | I | call | this | later |

_____

3 | just | were | off. | cut | about | we | Sorry | that; |

_____

🔊

Aa 42.14 READ THE ARTICLE AND WRITE THE HIGHLIGHTED PHRASES NEXT TO THEIR DEFINITIONS

| end a call | = | _hang up_ |

1 have a call interrupted = _____

2 answer the phone = _____

3 talk louder = _____

4 return your call = _____

5 becoming bad quality = _____

6 call them again = _____

BUSINESS TIPS

Problem phone call?

What to do with people who won't stop talking

We have all wanted to hang up on callers who keep talking when we are really busy at work. Sometimes, the usual, "I'd better be going" does not work. One thing you can do is to say that you have a meeting in another room and that you will get back to them later. Another tactic is to say, "Could you speak up, please? The line keeps breaking up. I hope we don't get cut off." Then put the phone down. If they call you back, don't pick up the phone!

🔊

43 Formal phone calls

When you talk to clients or receptionists, you may need to use formal language on the phone. You may also need to take or leave a phone message.

🔧 **New language** Adjective order
Aa Vocabulary Formal telephone language
🧩 **New skill** Leaving phone messages

43.1 KEY LANGUAGE FORMAL PHONE CONVERSATIONS

You can use formal language to introduce yourself, greet the speaker, and take or leave a message.

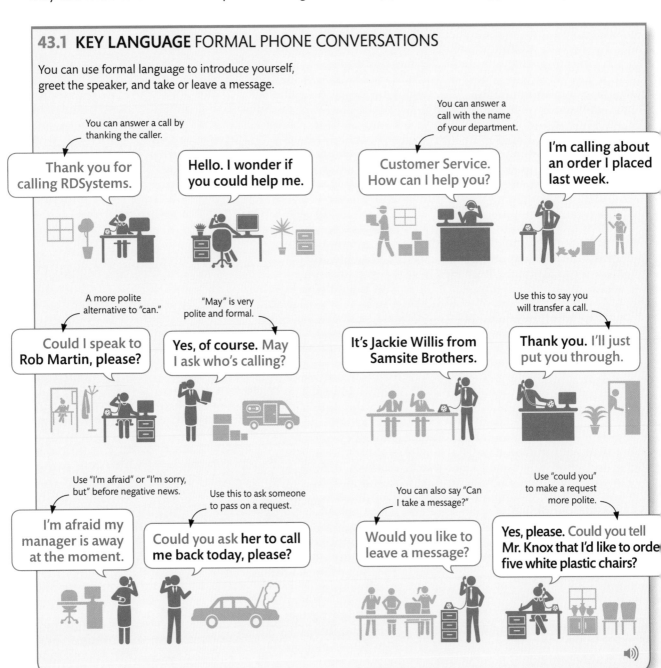

You can answer a call by thanking the caller.

Thank you for calling RDSystems.

Hello. I wonder if you could help me.

You can answer a call with the name of your department.

Customer Service. How can I help you?

I'm calling about an order I placed last week.

A more polite alternative to "can."

Could I speak to Rob Martin, please?

"May" is very polite and formal.

Yes, of course. May I ask who's calling?

It's Jackie Willis from Samsite Brothers.

Use this to say you will transfer a call.

Thank you. I'll just put you through.

Use "I'm afraid" or "I'm sorry, but" before negative news.

I'm afraid my manager is away at the moment.

Use this to ask someone to pass on a request.

Could you ask her to call me back today, please?

You can also say "Can I take a message?"

Would you like to leave a message?

Use "could you" to make a request more polite.

Yes, please. Could you tell Mr. Knox that I'd like to order five white plastic chairs?

162

43.2 MARK THE BEST REPLY TO EACH STATEMENT

Could I speak to Jia Li, please?

May I ask who's calling, please? ✓

Who are you? ☐

1 Would you like to leave a message?

I'll just put you through to HR. ☐

Can you say that I'll arrive late? ☐

2 Thank you for calling TCE Consulting.

I want the sales department. ☐

Could I speak to someone in sales? ☐

3 I'm afraid my manager is out of the office.

Can I talk to the manager? ☐

Can I leave a message for her? ☐

4 Could I talk to Myra Singh, please?

I'll get her now. ☐

Certainly. I'll just put you through. ☐

5 Customer service department. How can I help you?

Yes, please. ☐

I have a problem with an order. ☐

6 Thank you for calling EcoTech.

I'll just put you through. ☐

Hello. I wonder if you could help me. ☐

🔊

43.3 CROSS OUT THE INCORRECT WORD IN EACH SENTENCE, THEN SAY THE SENTENCES OUT LOUD

How **can** / ~~will~~ I help you?

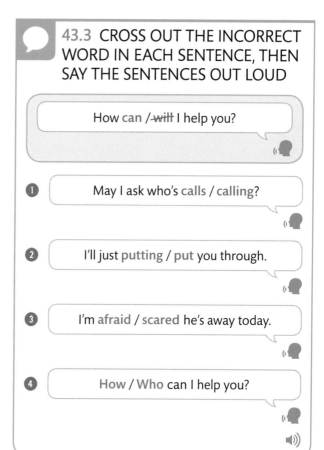

1 May I ask who's **calls** / **calling**?

2 I'll just **putting** / **put** you through.

3 I'm **afraid** / **scared** he's away today.

4 **How** / **Who** can I help you?

🔊

43.4 LISTEN TO THE AUDIO AND MARK THE CORRECT SUMMARY

Tom calls his client, Mr. Ryder, to arrange a meeting.

1 Tom and Mr. Ryder agree to meet at noon on Wednesday next week. ☐

2 Mr. Ryder is not at his desk. Tom leaves a message with the receptionist saying he will call again tomorrow. ☐

3 Mr. Ryder is not at his desk. Tom leaves a message with the receptionist saying he will meet him next week. ☐

43.5 KEY LANGUAGE ADJECTIVE ORDER

Adjectives add detail to descriptions and messages. When English uses more than one adjective before a noun, the adjectives must go in a particular order.

I've booked our team lunch at the nice little restaurant next to the office.

Adjectives describing opinions come before adjectives describing facts.

There's a large red car in the CEO's parking space. The driver needs to move it.

Fact adjectives also have their own order, depending on the type of fact.

43.6 KEY LANGUAGE ADJECTIVE ORDER IN DETAIL

English very rarely uses more than three adjectives before a noun.

	OPINION	SIZE	AGE	COLOR	MATERIAL	NOUN
I've booked the	nice	little				restaurant.
These are				white	plastic	chairs.
There's a		large		red		car.
We sell	beautiful		antique		china	cups.

43.7 WRITE THE WORDS FROM THE PANEL IN THE CORRECT GROUPS

OPINION	SIZE	AGE	COLOR	MATERIAL
useful	_____	_____	_____	_____
_____	_____	_____	_____	_____

awful   large   useful   tiny   antique

blue   wooden   new   glass   green

43.8 REWRITE THE SENTENCES, CORRECTING THE ERRORS

> I have a tiny awful old desk in my office.
> *I have an awful tiny old desk in my office.*

1 My boss has a white large friendly cat.

_____

2 My computer is a old white huge desktop from 1995.

_____

3 We're marketing a clever watch tiny new that helps you get fit.

_____

4 Have you seen the black tiny amazing briefcase she has?

_____

5 The meeting room has a modern painting very large.

_____

43.9 LISTEN TO THE AUDIO AND ANSWER THE QUESTIONS

Julio takes a phone message from Mrs. Garcia, who wants to complain about an order that she has placed.

> Julio's manager isn't at her desk.
> **True** ☑ **False** ☐ **Not given** ☐

1 Mrs. Garcia ordered an old coffee pot.
True ☐ **False** ☐ **Not given** ☐

2 Mrs. Garcia's items are broken.
True ☐ **False** ☐ **Not given** ☐

3 Mrs. Garcia does not like the color purple.
True ☐ **False** ☐ **Not given** ☐

4 Julio will send a replacement coffee pot.
True ☐ **False** ☐ **Not given** ☐

5 Mrs. Garcia must go to the post office.
True ☐ **False** ☐ **Not given** ☐

6 Julio will tell his manager about the call.
True ☐ **False** ☐ **Not given** ☐

43 ✓ CHECKLIST

⚙ Adjective order ☐   **Aa** Formal telephone language ☐   🧩 Leaving phone messages ☐

44 Writing a résumé

A résumé (or CV in UK English) is a clear summary of your skills and career history. Past simple action verbs are particularly useful for describing past achievements.

🔧 **New language** Action verbs for achievements
Aa Vocabulary Résumé vocabulary
🧩 **New skill** Writing a résumé

44.1 KEY LANGUAGE RÉSUMÉ HEADINGS

Shown below are the most common English résumé headings, and useful phrases for describing your achievements.

TIP
English résumés often leave the subject and the verb "be" out of sentences. For example, "Fluent in English, Spanish, and Italian" omits "I am."

Adriana Pires

275 Main Street, Minneapolis, MN 55401
addi123@pires456.com · 612-555-1746

An introductory statement describing a person's skills, qualities, and career goals.

PERSONAL STATEMENT
A highly motivated individual, with a proven track record in hotel reception and front-of-house work.

Describes the most significant things achieved throughout someone's career.

PROFESSIONAL ACHIEVEMENTS
Won an award for the Best Hotel Receptionist in the Midwestern Region.

A list of current and previous jobs, responsibilities, and skills.

CAREER SUMMARY
Hotel Deluxe Cite
HEAD RECEPTIONIST · May 2013–Present
• Working in a service-oriented environment
• Gained in-depth knowledge of the hospitality industry, and hands-on experience in customer service.

A list of qualifications, and the institutions where they were gained.

EDUCATION
• BA in Tourism and Hospitality
• Minor in Spanish

Other important skills, such as language skills or IT skills.

KEY SKILLS
• Fluent in Portuguese, Spanish, and English
• Proficient in IT use, including most types of booking systems

Things that someone enjoys doing in his or her spare time.

INTERESTS
Cooking, traveling, paragliding, scuba diving

References available upon request

A reference is a recommendation from a current or previous employer.

Aa 44.2 MATCH THE PHRASES TO THE CORRECT RÉSUMÉ HEADINGS

Fluent in Portuguese, Spanish, and English

1 A highly motivated individual

2 Working in a service-oriented environment

3 Won an award for the Best Hotel Receptionist

4 Diploma in Tourism and Hospitality

5 Cooking, traveling, paragliding, scuba diving

6 References available upon request

Personal statement

Interests

Key skills

References

Career summary

Education

Professional achievements

44.3 FILL IN THE GAPS USING THE WORDS IN THE PANEL

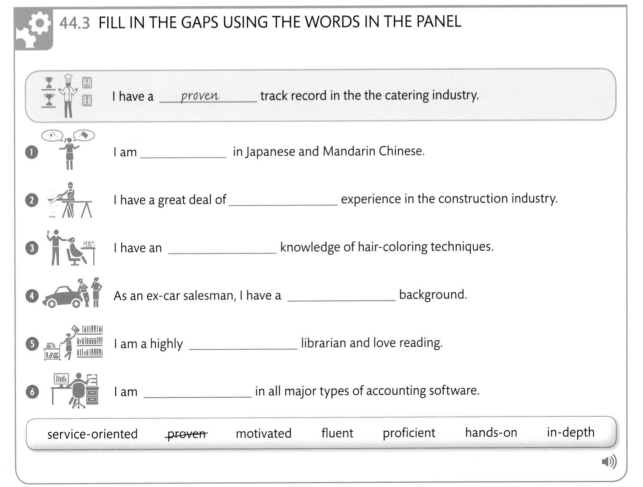

I have a ___proven___ track record in the the catering industry.

1 I am _____ in Japanese and Mandarin Chinese.

2 I have a great deal of _____ experience in the construction industry.

3 I have an _____ knowledge of hair-coloring techniques.

4 As an ex-car salesman, I have a _____ background.

5 I am a highly _____ librarian and love reading.

6 I am _____ in all major types of accounting software.

| service-oriented | ~~proven~~ | motivated | fluent | proficient | hands-on | in-depth |

167

44.4 KEY LANGUAGE PAST SIMPLE ACTION VERBS

Use past simple action verbs on your résumé to talk about the
responsibilities you have had and your past achievements.

I managed a successful
team of scientists.

I coordinated
a major product launch.

I negotiated a great price for
the company's products.

I volunteered
in a local school.

I established a
new training program.

I collaborated with designers
to produce the company logo.

44.5 CROSS OUT THE INCORRECT WORD IN EACH SENTENCE

 Last year, I managed / ~~negotiated~~ a small team of painters.

❶ Our teams established / collaborated to create the packaging design.

❷ We established / collaborated a new headquarters downtown.

❸ I coordinated / collaborated a staff training day for all departments.

❹ I managed / volunteered for a charity and built a classroom.

❺ I established / negotiated with all our suppliers and cut costs by 15 percent.

Ela Babinski

7 Gold Street
Perth
1609
elabab765@babela12.com
+61 491 570 156

I am determined and enthusiastic with practical experience in arranging and running sporting and educational activities for young adults. I have organized and supervised a number of overseas activity vacations in various countries and I have numerous health and safety certificates.

Career summary

YLHS Activity Vacations
HEAD OF ACTIVITIES • April 2013–present
YLHS Activity Vacations is a small, successful company, which combines adventure vacations with language education.

Duties:
• I create and supervise safe and exciting activity programs for 14–18 year-olds in three different countries.
• I manage teams of up to 16 activity leaders.

World Youth Language Schools
ACTIVITY LEADER • November 2011–April 2013
World Youth Language Schools run language courses around the world. Each day students have lessons followed by a sports activity.

Duties:
• I supervised up to 15 students at a time for activities.
• I also arranged transportation for students to and from each activity.

Professional achievements
Voted "Activity Leader of the Year" three years in a row by co-workers

Education
• Certificate in Activity Leadership, Level 3
• International Baccalaureate Diploma

Key skills
• Fluent in French and intermediate level Spanish
• First aid qualified
• Excellent organizer and people manager

Interests
Canoeing, climbing, and photography.

All the activities Ela organizes are in France.
True ☐ **False** ☐ **Not given** ☑

① Ela currently manages other activity leaders.
True ☐ **False** ☐ **Not given** ☐

② Ela's co-workers voted for her to receive an award.
True ☐ **False** ☐ **Not given** ☐

③ Ela was a language teacher for World Youth.
True ☐ **False** ☐ **Not given** ☐

④ Ela got her Activity Leadership Certificate last year.
True ☐ **False** ☐ **Not given** ☐

⑤ Ela can speak French and Spanish fluently.
True ☐ **False** ☐ **Not given** ☐

---

44 ✓ CHECKLIST

⚙ Action verbs for achievements ☐   **Aa** Résumé vocabulary ☐   🧩 Writing a résumé ☐

45 Making plans

English uses the future with "going to" to talk about plans and decisions that have already been made. It is useful for informing co-workers about your plans.

New language The future with "going to"
Aa Vocabulary Polite requests
New skill Making arrangements and plans

45.1 KEY LANGUAGE THE FUTURE WITH "GOING TO"

Use "going to" to tell co-workers what you have decided to do in the future.

I am going to arrange a training course.

45.2 HOW TO FORM THE FUTURE WITH "GOING TO"

To form the future with "going to" use the verb "to be" with "going to" followed by the base verb.

SUBJECT	"TO BE"	"GOING TO"	BASE FORM OF VERB	REST OF SENTENCE
I	am			
You / We / They	are	going to	arrange	a training course.
He / She	is			

"Going to" doesn't change with the subject.

45.3 FURTHER EXAMPLES THE FUTURE WITH "GOING TO"

They're really busy. They're not going to join us for the meeting.

Add "not" after "to be" to make the negative.

There's no paper for the printer. Are you going to order some more?

Switch the subject and "to be" in questions.

45.4 FILL IN THE GAPS USING THE FUTURE WITH "GOING TO"

I ___am going to order___ (order) new stationery supplies this afternoon.

1 They _____ (not invest) a lot of money next year.

2 He _____ (travel) by plane and then taxi to the meeting.

3 _____ you _____ (meet) with the suppliers next week?

4 We _____ (buy) the best quality business cards we can.

45.5 MATCH THE PAIRS OF SENTENCES

Mr. Bassir is going to arrive at 10am. → Can you please meet him at reception?

1 We're going to travel by plane.

2 She's not going to make it to the meeting.

3 We're going to give everyone leaflets.

4 You're going to join a new team soon.

5 He's going to retire at the end of the year.

It's good to work with different people.

Can you let her know what happens?

He wants to spend more time playing golf.

We should email the printers today.

Make sure you have your passports.

45.6 LISTEN TO THE AUDIO, THEN NUMBER THE PICTURES IN THE ORDER THEY ARE DESCRIBED

A ☐

B 1

C ☐

D ☐

E ☐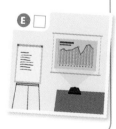

45.7 KEY LANGUAGE POLITE ALTERNATIVES TO COMMANDS

Remember that it is polite to phrase requests
as questions rather than commands.

"Can" is more direct than
"could," but it is still polite.

Add "please" to make a
request more polite.

Can you **serve the refreshments, please?**
[You have to serve the refreshments.]

Use "we" instead of "you" to make
the request particularly polite.

Could we **possibly move the time of the meeting?**
[Move the time of the meeting.]

45.8 MARK THE REQUESTS THAT ARE POLITE

Please could you call our suppliers? ☑
You must call our suppliers. ☐

1 Come to my office. ☐
Could you come to my office? ☐

2 Why don't we discuss this at the meeting? ☐
I don't have time to discuss this now. ☐

3 Can you tell me when it's finished, please? ☐
When will it be finished? ☐

4 Could we move these files? ☐
Why haven't you moved these files? ☐

5 Could you send the design to the printers? ☐
You should send the printers the design. ☐

6 Can you help me with these figures, please? ☐
I need help with these figures. ☐

45.9 REWRITE THE SENTENCES, CORRECTING THE ERRORS

Could you to serve the refreshments?
Could you serve the refreshments?

1 Can help you me move this cupboard?
_____

2 Could you being a little neater, please?
_____

3 Can you to finish the design soon, please?
_____

4 Could us meet at 5 instead of 6?
_____

5 Could you possible send me the report today?
_____

6 Can you to clean up the meeting room?
_____

45.10 READ THE EMAIL THEN ANSWER THE QUESTIONS, SPEAKING OUT LOUD

To: Gylfi Laarson

Subject: Conference preparations

Hello Gylfi,

Following our meeting yesterday, I have some more news about the plans for the sales conference. I spoke to Diego this morning about the refreshments and he's going to call ConCater Ltd today to make arrangements.

Sven is going to meet the printers about the posters and leaflets this afternoon. He's going to email us after the meeting when he has more news about prices. We need to move ahead ASAP on the printing.

I've emailed Diane and she's going to work on the Information Desk during the conference. Agnes is going to organize lanyards for all the delegates to wear. Could you arrange for the names to be printed for the lanyards, please?

I'm just going to email the venue to check that the rooms all have projectors and an internet connection. I'll email you later with a further update.

Best,
Simon

What is Diego going to do?

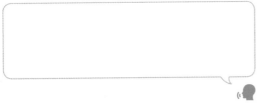

Diego is going to arrange the refreshments for the conference.

❶ Who is Sven going to meet in the afternoon?

❷ Who is going to work on the Information Desk?

❸ Who is going to wear the lanyards during the conference?

❹ What is Simon going to check when he emails the venue?

---

45 ✓ CHECKLIST

⚙ The future with "going to" ☐   **Aa** Polite requests ☐   🧩 Making arrangements and plans ☐

46.1 FORMS OF COMMUNICATION

email	letter	envelope	stamp
internal mail	mail (US) / post (UK)	courier	delivery
telephone call / phone call	voicemail	answering machine	switchboard
transfer a call	text message	formal meeting	informal meeting
presentation	conference call	web conference	online chat

social networking	website	memo	bulletin board (US) / notice board (UK)

46.2 SENDING EMAILS

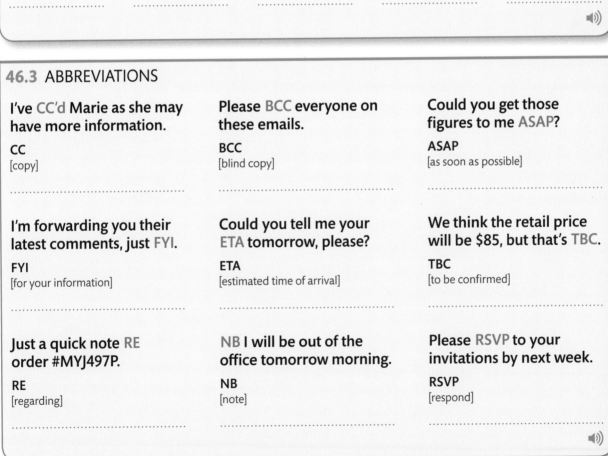

inbox	outbox	draft	junk mail / spam	trash
attachment	subject	contact	print	signature
reply	reply all	forward	flagged	sent

46.3 ABBREVIATIONS

I've CC'd Marie as she may have more information.

CC
[copy]

Please BCC everyone on these emails.

BCC
[blind copy]

Could you get those figures to me ASAP?

ASAP
[as soon as possible]

I'm forwarding you their latest comments, just FYI.

FYI
[for your information]

Could you tell me your ETA tomorrow, please?

ETA
[estimated time of arrival]

We think the retail price will be $85, but that's TBC.

TBC
[to be confirmed]

Just a quick note RE order #MYJ497P.

RE
[regarding]

NB I will be out of the office tomorrow morning.

NB
[note]

Please RSVP to your invitations by next week.

RSVP
[respond]

47 Emailing a client

Emails to clients should be polite and clearly state your future plans and intentions. Use the present continuous or "going to" to discuss plans and arrangements.

⚙ **New language** Future tenses for plans
Aa Vocabulary Polite email language
🧩 **New skill** Emailing a client

47.1 KEY LANGUAGE EMAILS TO CLIENTS

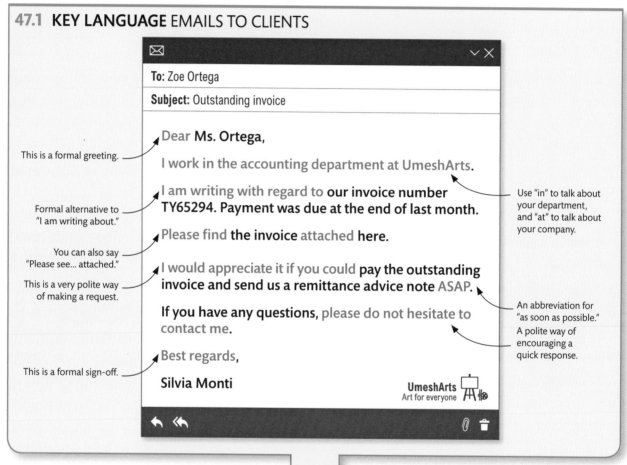

To: Zoe Ortega

Subject: Outstanding invoice

Dear **Ms. Ortega,** ← This is a formal greeting.

I work in the accounting department at UmeshArts. → Use "in" to talk about your department, and "at" to talk about your company.

I am writing with regard to **our invoice number TY65294. Payment was due at the end of last month.** ← Formal alternative to "I am writing about."

Please find **the invoice** attached **here.** ← You can also say "Please see... attached."

I would appreciate it if you could **pay the outstanding invoice and send us a remittance advice note** ASAP. ← This is a very polite way of making a request.

→ An abbreviation for "as soon as possible." A polite way of encouraging a quick response.

If you have any questions, please do not hesitate to contact me.

Best regards, ← This is a formal sign-off.

Silvia Monti

UmeshArts
Art for everyone

47.2 KEY LANGUAGE GREETINGS AND SIGN-OFFS

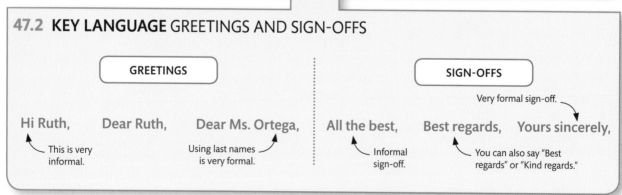

GREETINGS

Hi Ruth, — This is very informal.

Dear Ruth,

Dear Ms. Ortega, — Using last names is very formal.

SIGN-OFFS

Very formal sign-off. →

All the best, — Informal sign-off.

Best regards, — You can also say "Best regards" or "Kind regards."

Yours sincerely,

47.3 READ THE EMAIL AND ANSWER THE QUESTIONS

What is the main purpose of Zarifa's job?
Science ☐ **Recycling** ☑ **Technology** ☐

❶ What sort of companies does Zarifa work with?
Schools ☐ **Laboratories** ☐ **Technology** ☐

❷ Old microchips are currently being...
recycled ☐ **sold** ☐ **discarded to landfill** ☐

❸ What does Science Solutions want to do with waste?
Purchase it ☐ **Discard it** ☐ **Sell it** ☐

❹ What will benefit from this?
The environment ☐ **Science** ☐ **Nothing** ☐

❺ How would Zarifa like to discuss further?
Email ☐ **Telephone** ☐ **In a meeting** ☐

To: Richard McGrath

Subject: Recycling opportunity

Dear Mr. McGrath,
I work in the recycling department at Science Solutions. I deal with repurposing waste from technology companies.

It has come to our attention that the microchips you no longer deem fit for purpose are being discarded to landfill. I wonder if you are aware that we could purchase this waste from you? Such a proposition would benefit both your company and the environment.

I would welcome the opportunity to discuss this further with you in a meeting.

Best regards,
Zarifa Sahli

Science Solutions

47.4 REWRITE THE SENTENCES, CORRECTING THE ERRORS

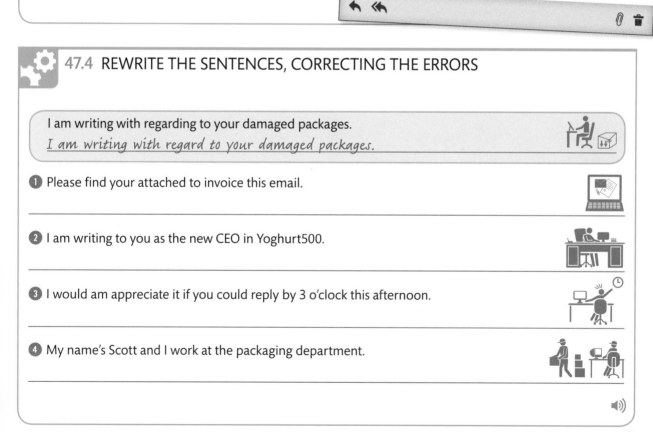

I am writing with regarding to your damaged packages.
I am writing with regard to your damaged packages.

❶ Please find your attached to invoice this email.

❷ I am writing to you as the new CEO in Yoghurt500.

❸ I would am appreciate it if you could reply by 3 o'clock this afternoon.

❹ My name's Scott and I work at the packaging department.

47.5 KEY LANGUAGE TALKING ABOUT FUTURE ARRANGEMENTS

To tell clients about future plans, you can use the present continuous, particularly if you have specified when something will happen.

I am writing to inform you that we are meeting other suppliers on Monday.

We know when this will happen.

Present continuous.

"Going to" can be used with a time marker, but it is often used instead of the present continuous to talk about plans for an unspecified time in the future.

I am writing to inform you that we are going to meet other microchip suppliers.

We don't know when this will happen.

Future with "going to."

47.6 CROSS OUT THE INCORRECT WORDS IN EACH SENTENCE

We are ~~paying~~ / going to pay your invoice very soon.

1. He is **emailing** / going to emailing all the clients this afternoon.

2. She is **to sending** / going to send vouchers to all customers.

3. They are **meet** / going to meet in Rome to discuss options.

4. I am **speaking** / going speaking with our couriers tomorrow.

47.7 FILL IN THE GAPS USING THE PHRASES IN THE PANEL

We _____ *are meeting* _____ our new clients on Friday.

1. We hope they're _____ us a discount.

2. Our CEO is _____ a merger.

3. Simone is _____ your invoice this afternoon.

4. Mark and Johan are _____ the calls later.

going to discuss

going to offer

~~are meeting~~

going to answer

sending

47.8 REWRITE THE HIGHLIGHTED PHRASES, CORRECTING THE ERRORS

with regard to the

1 _____

2 _____

3 _____

4 _____

5 _____

6 _____

47 ✓ CHECKLIST

⚙ Future tenses for plans ☐   **Aa** Polite email language ☐   🧩 Emailing a client ☐

↻ REVIEW THE ENGLISH YOU HAVE LEARNED IN UNITS 42–47

NEW LANGUAGE	SAMPLE SENTENCE	☑	UNIT
INFORMAL PHONE CALLS	Can I ask who's calling, please? **I have to** hang up **now. I'll** call you back **later.**	☐	42.1, 42.10
FORMAL PHONE CALLS	Customer Service. How can I help you? May I ask who's calling?	☐	43.1
ADJECTIVE ORDER	**I've booked a** nice little **restaurant for lunch.**	☐	43.5
WRITING YOUR RÉSUMÉ	**I have a** proven track record **in sales.**	☐	44.1
FUTURE WITH "GOING TO"	**I am** going to **arrange a training course.**	☐	45.1
EMAILS TO CLIENTS	I am writing with regard to **our invoice number TY65294.**	☐	47.1
TALKING ABOUT FUTURE PLANS	We are meeting **other suppliers** on Monday.	☐	47.5

Answers

1.2 🔊
1. Hello. My **name's** Sebastian.
2. Good **afternoon**. My name is Joe Carr.
3. Hi, Marie. **I'm** Clive.
4. It's great to meet you, **too**, Sven.
5. It's a **pleasure** to meet you.

1.4
1. B 2. A 3. B 4. A 5. B

1.6 🔊
1. **It's a pleasure to meet you**, too.
2. Hi, **I'm** Adedeyo. / Hi, **my** name's Adedeyo.
3. **Great** to meet you.
4. This **is** my new colleague, Martin.
5. Marisa, **meet** Roula, my partner.
6. It's good to **meet you**, Katherine.
7. **May I** introduce Claudia Gomez, our new CEO?

1.7
1. Greene
2. 14 years
3. Accountant
4. Jill and Mr. Singh

1.8 🔊
1. Hello, Mr. Lucas. It's a **pleasure** to meet **you**.
2. Ashley, **meet** André. André and I work on the **same** project.
3. **Hello**, Sophie. My **name's** Rachel Davies. Great to meet you.
4. **This** is my colleague, Hayley. We went to college **together**.
5. It's **good** to meet you, Cori. **My** name's Angel.
6. Hello, James. **It's** really nice **to** meet you. My name's Alex.

2.4 🔊
1. He opens all the windows in the afternoon.
2. He brings the team tea and coffee every afternoon.
3. She shouts at the computer every day.
4. She walks around her office every 30 minutes.

2.5 🔊
1. She **is** a hairdresser.
2. He **travels** by train every morning.
3. She **leaves** work at 6pm every day.
4. She **drinks** coffee twice a day.
5. He **eats** lunch at a local café.

2.6
1. False
2. True
3. False
4. Not given
5. False

2.8 🔊
1. The head of marketing **speaks** for about an hour at every team meeting.
2. Arianna and Gabriel **read** their emails first thing every morning.
3. The photocopier **stops** working if we don't load the paper carefully.
4. The owners of the hotel **visit** it at the end of every month.
5. The cleaner **starts** work at 6am every day. The office is always clean in the mornings.

2.9 🔊
1. I work from Monday to Friday.
2. I have a meeting every morning.
3. You work from Monday to Friday.
4. You have a meeting every morning.
5. She works from Monday to Friday.
6. She has a meeting every morning.
7. My manager works from Monday to Friday.
8. My manager has a meeting every morning.

2.10
1. False
2. True
3. True
4. False
5. True
6. False
7. True

4.4 🔊
1. I'm on the **European** sales team.
2. Our **Chilean** office is in Santiago.
3. We sell leather shoes from **Spain**.
4. My job is to watch the **Asian** markets.
5. Book a trip to **Mexico** with us.

4.5
1. India
2. France
3. Asia
4. Italy
5. Africa

4.7 🔊
1. These polo shirts **aren't** made in Vietnam.
2. This restaurant **doesn't** use British meat.
3. The onions in this market **aren't** local.
4. **I'm not** Brazilian, but I work in Brazil.
5. The company **doesn't** have overseas clients.

4.9
1. True
2. False
3. True
4. False
5. False
6. True

6.3 🔊
1. Are the windows open?
2. Is your phone working?
3. Are these your files?
4. Is that drawer locked?
5. Is his desk clean?

6.6 🔊
1. **Does** he have a key for this drawer?
2. **Does** your laptop have a DVD drive?
3. **Do** Jim and Tom have new screens?
4. **Do** you keep pens in your desk drawer?
5. **Does** Sarah write the minutes?
6. **Do** all employees have wall calendars?

6.7
A 3 **B** 4 **C** 1 **D** 5 **E** 2

6.10 🔊
1 **Where** are the cups?
2 **What** is the photocopier code?
3 **How** do I turn off the screen?
4 **Why** is this drawer always locked?
5 **When** does the cafeteria open?
6 **Who** do I ask for printer ink?
7 **What** do you discuss at meetings?

6.11 🔊
1 You need to talk to Anne in HR.
2 It's always full on weekend evenings.
3 So that Marie can control the stock.
4 Turn it on and then select your drink.
5 At 2 o'clock. We usually start on time.

6.12 🔊
1 What can I do to help you?
2 Do you know where the key is?
3 When does the store open?
4 How do I connect the keyboard?
5 Why is her desk always a mess?

6.13 🔊
1 **Where** are the paperclips and pens?
2 **What** is for lunch today?
3 **Why** do we use old computers?
4 **When** do they close the office?

07

7.4
A 2 **B** 5 **C** 3 **D** 1 **E** 4 **F** 6

7.5 🔊
1 Do you **have** a website I can look up?
2 Your job **title** isn't listed here.
3 Just **drop** me a line for more details.
4 How can I **reach** you to follow up?
5 Is this your phone **number**?
6 Here's my **business** card.
7 **Call** me to arrange a meeting.
8 Drop me a **line** to follow up next week.

7.6
1 True
2 False
3 False

4 False
5 False
6 True

7.8 🔊
1 Yes, it is.
2 Yes, they are.
3 Yes, they do.
4 Yes, it does.
5 No, we don't.

7.9 🔊
1 No, it isn't.
2 Yes, they are.
3 Yes, I do.
4 No, it doesn't.
5 Yes, they do.
6 Yes, I do.
7 No, I don't.

08

8.4 🔊
1 They **don't** have interviews today.
2 He **hasn't** got a diploma
3 I **don't have** any experience.
4 Do you **have** good IT skills?
5 We **have** monthly training sessions.
6 He **doesn't** have experience with animals.
7 He **has** a Master's degree.
8 They **have** a lot of inexperienced staff.
9 She's **got** super negotiation skills.

8.5
1 Sam loves working with animals.
2 Sam won a regional competition.
3 Sam organized field trips at college.
4 Sam worked in an office.
5 Sam has excellent photography skills.
6 Sam's degree is in dance and drama.
7 Sam has a photography diploma.

8.8 🔊
1 Oh, yes. I know **the** hotel you mean.
2 Susan has **a** diploma.
3 Is **the** meeting on the second floor?
4 I work for **a** large recruitment agency.
5 There's **an** ad for a chef here.
6 I hired **a** PA to help me out.
7 He works at **the** hospital down the road.
8 Is there **an** office in Mexico?

8.9
A 4 **B** 1 **C** 5 **D** 2 **E** 6 **F** 3

8.11 🔊
1 He was out of the office today.
2 I have excellent people skills.
3 What skills do you need for this job?
4 Have you read the job requirements?
5 She's an architect for a top company.
6 The new designer is very good.

8.12
Dear Mr. Baxter,

I am writing to apply for **the** role of Library Assistant, which I saw advertised on your website. I **have** two years' experience working as a part-time assistant in my local library. **The** job involves working with **a** team of people and the public, so I have **good people skills**. I **do not have** a degree in Library and Information Studies, as **the** ad requested, but I **have** a degree in English Literature.

I look forward to hearing from you.

Yours sincerely,
Judy Stein

10

10.4 🔊
1 She **doesn't like** using computers.
2 He likes **training** new colleagues.
3 I **hate** long meetings.
4 We **don't like** lazy employees.
5 She enjoys **working** in a team.

10.5
1 Dislikes
2 Likes
3 Likes
4 Likes

10.6
1 False
2 True
3 False
4 False
5 True

11.3 🔊
1. There **aren't** any bathrooms on this floor.
2. Is there **a** stationery cabinet in the office?
3. There's **a** staff cafeteria on the third floor.
4. There **isn't** an elevator in this building.
5. **Are** there any places to lock my bicycle here?
6. **Is** there a desk ready for our new designer?
7. **There are** lots of envelopes in the cabinet.

11.4
Model Answers
1. They should leave them in a closet by the main entrance door.
2. There are four desks in Jonathan's office.
3. There is a tea and coffee machine.
4. Staff sign in at reception.

11.5 🔊
1. There is a staff parking lot.
2. There is a business dress code.
3. There are places to relax.
4. There isn't a staff parking lot.
5. There isn't a business dress code.
6. There aren't any places to relax.

13.3
Ⓐ 4 Ⓑ 1 Ⓒ 5 Ⓓ 2 Ⓔ 3

13.4
POSITIVE:
motivated, ambitious, helpful, bright, intelligent
NEGATIVE:
impatient, lazy, impolite, nervous, boring

13.5 🔊
1. My team leader **is impolite** and he is also **very impatient**.
2. My co-workers say that **I am really motivated and ambitious**.
3. The new young intern seems very intelligent and he **is really** polite.
4. I'm very lucky. All my colleagues **are** hardworking and **helpful**.

13.9 🔊
1. Two of the people on **my** team are new to the company, but they're settling in well.
2. **Their** manager is very good with people. They enjoy working with him.
3. The company is very proud of **its** reputation and quality products.
4. Is this **your** phone? It doesn't belong to me but I found it on my desk.

13.12 🔊
1. We hate their product, but we love **ours**.
2. They are proud of **their** project.
3. **Our** clients expect excellent service.
4. This isn't her desk. It's **mine**.
5. This is amazing. Is it **her** project?

13.13 🔊
1. I think these are your files.
2. Is this desk his?
3. These are her pens.
4. Are those products theirs?

13.16 🔊
1. The **interns** work really hard.
2. All the team **members** are intelligent.
3. This big room is my **boss's** office.
4. All the **bosses** have parking spaces.
5. The best thing about this product is **its** strength.

13.17
1. he joined the company
2. Jorge's supervisor
3. Her progress is slow
4. Maria is impatient
5. very intelligent

13.18 🔊
1. You are my manager.
2. You are my assistant.
3. You are Sam's manager.
4. You are Sam's assistant.
5. You are very organized.
6. You are really organized.
7. We are very organized.
8. We are really organized.
9. Katy is my manager.
10. Katy is Sam's manager.
11. Katy is my assistant.
12. Katy is Sam's assistant.
13. Katy is very organized.
14. Katy is really organized.

14.3 🔊
1. That meeting was really **boring**.
2. The printer can be **annoying** at times.
3. By the end of the week, I'm really **tired**.
4. The system is **confusing** at first.
5. I'm very **excited** about my project.
6. The news was **shocking**.
7. I was very **surprised** by my raise!

14.4
1. Not given
2. True
3. False
4. Not given
5. False

14.5 🔊
1. satisfied
2. bored
3. tired
4. confusing
5. annoying
6. interesting
7. excited
8. shocking

14.8 🔊
1. This printer is **faster** than the other, but that one is **more reliable**.
2. This coffee is **stronger** than I normally buy, but it is also **tastier**.
3. This building is **newer** than my last workplace, and the area is **quieter**.
4. This café is **busier** than the other one, so the service is **slower**.
5. My new uniform is **more comfortable** than my old one, but **uglier**.

14.10 🔊
1. Parking is more expensive this year.
2. This system is better than before.
3. I have more work to do than last year.
4. I arrive much earlier than my boss.
5. Every year my raise is smaller.
6. I feel better now that I have a new job.
7. A digital copy is more useful to me.
8. That meeting was worse than usual.

14.11
1 better salary
2 worse overtime pay
3 hourly rate is less
4 shorter commute
5 bigger bonus

14.12 ◀))
1 easy
2 bored
3 stronger
4 lower
5 cheap
6 heavier
7 smaller
8 large
9 worse

14.13
1 friendlier
2 more successful
3 more
4 better
5 longer

14.14 ◀))
1 Now, my vacations are longer **than they used to be**.
2 This new computer system is more **efficient than the old one**.
3 These presentations are making me more **bored than yesterday's**.
4 These new laptops are **lighter than the old ones**.
5 The cafeteria lunches are **tastier than restaurant meals**.

14.15
1 False
2 Not given
3 True
4 False
5 Not given
6 True
7 True

15

15.3 ◀))
1 Lunch is served at noon.
2 Don't leave before Mr. Davies.
3 Never arrive after 9am.

15.5 ◀))
1 Let your manager know if you need to go out **during** the day.
2 My boss is in meetings **for** about four hours every day.
3 I have been here **since** 5am this morning.
4 Do not leave the building **until** you have signed out.
5 The office is closed from Friday **to** Monday.

15.7 ◀))
1 I go by metro.
2 Sometimes I ride my bike to work.
3 I go by train to work.
4 I normally go to work on foot.
5 Sometimes I take a taxi to work.
6 I take the bus.

15.8 ◀))
1 I always **drive** to work.
2 It's usually quicker to **cycle**.
3 When it's sunny, we go on **foot**.
4 I don't like taking the **metro**.
5 I **walk** to work to stay fit.
6 I read a book when I go **by** train.
7 I **take** the bus when it rains.

15.9
A 8 B 1 C 3 D 7 E 2 F 5 G 4 H 6

17

17.2
1 frequently 2 sometimes
3 occasionally 4 never

17.3 ◀))
1 I often do yoga in the evening.
2 We occasionally go to see a play.
3 She often listens to music at work.
4 I always take photos when I go on vacation.

17.8 ◀))
1 This is the best book I've ever read.
2 The piano is the easiest instrument to play.
3 Yannick listens to the loudest music.
4 Shopping is the most expensive hobby I do.
5 That was the worst play I have ever seen.
6 Exercising is the most relaxing thing I do.
7 Let's eat at the closest restaurant.

17.9 ◀))
1 The **most interesting** gallery I've been to is in Paris.
2 I've just finished the **worst** book I've ever read.
3 The **longest** hike I've ever done is 15km.
4 The **farthest** I've ever gone cycling is 50 miles.
5 I think that hiking is the **most exciting** hobby.

18

18.4 ◀))
1 I played soccer after work last night.
2 He didn't walk to work today.
3 I worked from 9 to 5 yesterday.
4 She lived in Paris for four years.
5 I talked to lots of people on my trip.

18.6 ◀))
1 We **arrived** late, but our boss **didn't shout** at us.
2 I **washed** my car, but it **didn't look** clean.
3 I **watched** the film, but I **didn't enjoy** it.
4 It **stopped** raining, but then it **started** snowing.
5 I **didn't walk** to work, I **cycled**.

18.9 ◀))
1 Did you play board games when you were young?
2 Did he cook some pasta for lunch?
3 Did she stay at home and watch TV last night?
4 Did they watch a scary movie at the movie theater?
5 Did they walk home from work together?

18.10
1 True
2 Not given
3 False
4 True
5 Not given

18.11 ◀))
1 They visited a museum.
2 She listened to music.
3 He watched TV.
4 They cooked a meal.
5 They played a board game.

19

19.2 🔊
1. It's two thirty. / It's half past two.
2. It's ten forty-five. / It's (a) quarter to eleven.
3. It's seven. / It's seven o'clock.
4. It's three twenty-five. / It's twenty-five past three.
5. It's eight forty-three pm.

19.5
1. March
2. August
3. 2014
4. May 12

20

20.4 🔊
1. When I was a gardener, I **spent** the majority of my time outside.
2. I **met** lots of famous people when I worked as a reporter.
3. Benjamin **went** to nearly 100 countries as a pilot.
4. In his last job, he **had** a dog as a partner.

20.5 🔊
1. As a police officer, I had a uniform.
2. I met lots of famous musicians.
3. I went to catering school.
4. I spent a lot of time in museums.

20.6
A 3   B 1   C 4   D 5   E 2

20.7
Model Answers
1. Sadim chose to study engineering in college.
2. Sadim thought his father would give him a good job in his company.
3. Sadim felt angry because he wanted a better job.
4. Sadim wrote to his father that he would look for another job.
5. His father said he could be CEO one day.
6. Sadim finally understood what hard work was like in different areas of the company.
7. Sadim's work experience taught him to respect all employees.

8. Sadim's father made him CEO five years ago.
9. Myra began working in the mailroom two months ago.

20.8 🔊
1. I **felt** really happy when I left college with a top degree.
2. My manager **said** that one day I could be CEO of the whole company.
3. My tutor **taught** me that it was important to check my own work.
4. I **made** my girlfriend a big cake to celebrate her new job.

20.9 🔊
Model Answers
1. I saw an ad for the job in the store window.
2. I felt very excited on my first day.
3. I chose the job because I wanted to work with customers.
4. I left my first job five years ago.
5. I left my first job because the hours were long.

21

21.3 🔊
1. We opened our tenth store two months **ago**.
2. The company **recently** merged with one of its competitors.
3. Jane Hunt opened the first Hunt Bags store **in** 1995.
4. A new CEO started working here **last** year.

21.4
A 2   B 3   C 5   D 1   E 4   F 6

21.5
Model Answers
1. Ahmed founded Cake & Crumb in 2003.
2. At first, he worked from the kitchen in his small apartment.
3. In the company's first year, sales remained steady.
4. The company opened its first store in 2005.
5. Cake & Crumb employed 2,000 bakers by 2010.
6. Two years ago, the company launched a catering service for children's parties.

21.7 🔊
1. The number of people going to festivals **went up** last year.
2. Fortunately, the cost of fuel for transportation **stabilized** recently.
3. In the really wet summer of 2010, sales of umbrellas **rose** a lot.
4. The number of people downloading music **stayed the same** last month.
5. The number of students earning MBAs **remained steady** last year.

21.8 🔊
1. **At** first, the value of the company **stayed** the same.
2. Marketing costs **increased** and sales also **rose**.
3. **Last** summer, umbrella sales **increased** because it was rainy.
4. The number of customers **decreased**, but profits **went** up.
5. Two years **ago**, we launched an online delivery service and our sales **rose**.

23

23.4
A 4   B 1   C 6   D 3   E 2   F 8   G 7   H 5

23.5 🔊
1. Sales **are increasing** at the moment, so we **are getting** a bigger bonus.
2. Fashions **are changing**, so we **are adapting** to new trends.
3. Travel costs **are rising** this year, so we **are calling** each other more instead.
4. Profits **are dropping**, so we **are cutting** costs in all areas of the business.
5. We **are selling** a lot to Asia, so we **are planning** to open an office there next year.
6. I can't believe you **are working** late. You **are missing** the staff party!
7. I **am waiting** for my interview to start, and I **am feeling** nervous.
8. The company **is losing** money, so we **are considering** a restructure.

23.8 🔊
1. Are they buying this?
2. Is it working now?
3. Are we selling that?
4. Are you meeting him?
5. Who are they promoting?

23.9 🔊
1. There is no hot water left.
2. That's Giorgio. He's a great speaker.
3. Yes, I'm running two workshops.
4. He's giving a presentation.
5. Yes, I think he is.
6. No, I'm on the bus at the moment.
7. No, it's out of toner. I'm refilling it now.

23.10 🔊
1. Is the company buying everyone new laptops?
2. Is Maria giving her first presentation at the moment?
3. Is Rakesh designing the packaging for the new gadget?
4. Are we all going to the team meeting now?
5. Are they trying to improve sales in North America?

23.12 🔊
1. I'm not coming to work tomorrow.
2. Are you meeting the team today?
3. I can't go. I'm not leaving until 8pm.
4. Are we coming back here next year?
5. Are you coming to the party later?
6. I'm not taking notes today. Are you?
7. I'm having lunch at noon tomorrow.
8. Are you going to Asia this winter?

23.13
1. For 10 days
2. Next Monday morning
3. In the bookstore

23.14 🔊 Model Answers
1. I'm meeting the HR team.
2. I'm going to Paris.
3. I'm traveling by train.
4. I'm getting home at 7.15pm.
5. I'm finishing at 3pm.
6. Monica is leaving work on Friday.

24

24.2
1. Impolite
2. Polite
3. Polite
4. Impolite
5. Impolite
6. Polite
7. Impolite

24.5 🔊
1. Sorry to **interrupt**, but my figures are different.
2. I'm not sure. What do you **think** about new outlets?
3. I'm sorry, but in my **opinion** they will sell well.

24.6
1. False
2. Not given
3. True
4. False
5. True

24.7 🔊
1. **take** the minutes, **review** the minutes
2. **read** the agenda, **work through** the agenda
3. **send** apologies, **announce** apologies
4. **take a** vote, **casting** vote
5. **opening** remarks, **closing** remarks

24.8 🔊
1. environment
2. reduce
3. reuse
4. waste
5. green
6. recycle
7. resources
8. footprint

24.9 🔊
1. Tim **sent** his apologies. He can't come.
2. Let's review our **environmental** strategy.
3. Let's work through the **agenda** quickly.
4. We should look at **reducing** our waste.
5. I'm sorry to **interrupt**, but I disagree.
6. What do you think **about** recycling?
7. Let's **take** a vote on the new policy.
8. The meeting chair has the **casting** vote.
9. I'm **sorry**, but I don't agree.
10. I think it's the best strategy. How **about** you?
11. I just have a few **closing** remarks.

25

25.2 🔊
1. So did I.
2. Me too.
3. So do I.
4. Me neither.
5. Nor did I.

25.3 🔊
1. I suppose you're right, but it was so long!
2. Nor did I. It was too difficult.
3. Yes, I agree. She is very friendly, too.
4. I suppose so, but they are expensive.
5. Me too. They're practical and cheap.
6. Neither did I. He was always moody.
7. So did I. The menu was excellent.

25.5 🔊
1. You could be **right**, but I think it's ugly.
2. I'm **afraid** we disagree about the price.
3. I'm **sorry**, but I don't agree, Jan.
4. I'm afraid I **disagree**. It's too expensive.
5. I'm sorry, Joe, but I don't agree **at** all.

25.6
1. Jeremy strongly disagrees with her.
2. Jeremy agrees with her.
3. Sian disagrees with him.
4. Jeremy strongly agrees with her.

25.7 🔊
1. Yes, I suppose **you're** right about the new design.
2. You **could** be right, but I need to do more research.
3. I'm sorry, but I don't **agree** at all with that comment.
4. I'm **afraid** I don't agree about this one issue.
5. I'm not **sure** about that, Sara. I don't like it.
6. I'm afraid I **totally** disagree. That will never work.

26

26.3 🔊
1. They locked themselves in the fridge.
2. He burned himself on the coffee machine.
3. Both of you, protect yourselves from the sun.
4. We booked ourselves on a fire safety course.
5. I fell and hurt myself on the wet floor.

26.4
1. Not given
2. False
3. True

26.5 🔊
1. assembly point
2. first aid kit
3. fire extinguisher
4. fire exit

26.6 🔊
1. She's cut **herself**. Get the first aid box.
2. They paid for it **themselves**.
3. The machine started **itself**.
4. Please take care of **yourselves**.
5. Make **yourself** aware of the fire exits.

27

27.3 🔊
1. Let's do more promotion on social media.
2. We could redesign the packaging for this product.
3. What about hiring a software consultant?

27.5 🔊
1. You should reset the router.
2. She should tell him before he sees it.
3. I should order some more.
4. We should throw away the food.
5. He should walk around the office.

27.7 🔊
1. I am **unable** to come in the morning. How about the afternoon?
2. I **misspell** words so often. Why don't we get an editor?

3. The machine isn't working. We should **disconnect** it.
4. Are you **unwell**? Why don't we call a doctor for you?
5. These tests are **impossible**. What about doing easier ones?

27.8
Ⓐ 4 Ⓑ 1 Ⓒ 2 Ⓓ 5 Ⓔ 3

27.9 🔊
1. Let's use our old system again. This new one is so **unfamiliar** and slow.
2. How about changing the time so that more people are **able** to come.
3. Let's discuss the negative feedback from people who **disagree** with our plan.
4. What about explaining the delay to stop people from becoming so **impatient**.
5. I love conventions! It's so easy to **connect** with new people.
6. I have no idea how to write this report. It seems **impossible**!

28

28.2 🔊
1. To **start** this talk I will give an overall introduction to the project.
2. **Second**, after the introduction, I'll describe our role in the project.
3. Next, we'll **explore** the benefits of this approach.
4. After **that**, we'll look at the possible difficulties we might have.
5. Then, to **finish** we'll look at what future research we can do.
6. Lastly, I will **answer** any questions that you have for me.

28.4
1. False
2. True
3. Not given

28.5 🔊
1. slide
2. screen
3. projector
4. microphone
5. flipchart

28.7 🔊
1. I'm happy to answer any questions.
2. So, we've covered the main issues.
3. Does anyone have any questions?
4. Would you like to ask anything?
5. In short, next year is important.

28.8
Ⓐ 3 Ⓑ 7 Ⓒ 4 Ⓓ 2 Ⓔ 5 Ⓕ 1 Ⓖ 6

28.9 🔊
1. In **short** we are very proud of our new products.
2. I'd like to **begin** by looking back at past sales.
3. That's all I have to **say** about the advertising campaign.
4. Let's move **on** to talk about the packaging we've designed.
5. Does anyone **have** any questions for me?

29

29.2 🔊
1. It's a special one for fire safety.
2. There's a nice café across the street.
3. We're meeting clients later this afternoon.
4. I have saved all the documents.

29.3 🔊
1. Is your stapler broken? You **can** use mine.
2. She **doesn't have to** come to the training session. She did it last year.
3. You **have to** turn off the light if you're the last person to leave the office.
4. He **has to** test the fire alarm every Wednesday morning.
5. We **don't have to** wear a jacket and tie in the summer months.

29.4
1. Not given
2. False
3. True
4. True
5. False

29.8 🔊
1. Could you **tell** Jan to call me back?
2. Could you **check** this report?
3. Would you mind **ordering** more pens?
4. Could you **mop** the floor, please?

⑤ Could you **come** to today's meeting?
⑥ Would you mind **calling** back later?
⑦ Would you mind **turning** the light off?
⑧ Could you **wash** these cups, please?
⑨ Could you **pass** around the reports?
⑩ Would you mind **booking** me a taxi?
⑪ Could you **show** our clients around?

29.9
① False
② False
③ True
④ True

29.10 ◀))
1. Could you book a meeting room?
2. Could you send Sam Davies an email?
3. Could you call our supplier?
4. Would you mind booking a meeting room?
5. Would you mind sending Sam Davies an email?
6. Would you mind calling our supplier?

31.4 ◀)) Note: Negative sentences can also use the long form "was not."
① Gabino **wasn't listening** during the team meeting this morning.
② The internet **wasn't working** all day yesterday. I had to call my clients.
③ Hannah and Luke **were talking** during the CEO's presentation.
④ I **was forgetting** to do everyday jobs, so I wrote a list.
⑤ I put you on a new team because you **were losing** sales.

31.5
Model Answers
① He wasn't answering important emails.
② He was leaving Maria to reply to all the sales enquiries.
③ The author's advice was to talk to the co-worker.
④ José was feeling tired after lunch every day.
⑤ He changed his diet so that he ate more salads and vegetables.
⑥ He was working until 5pm every day last week.

31.6
Ⓐ 5 Ⓑ 1 Ⓒ 3 Ⓓ 2 Ⓔ 4

31.7 ◀))
① Sales were improving. It was **a win-win** situation.
② It's a difficult task. We must think **outside** the box.
③ The team was throwing money **down** the drain.
④ Was your assistant **pulling** his weight today?
⑤ We were working with a lot of **red** tape.
⑥ Now we're all here, let's get **down** to business.

31.8 ◀))
① The elevator is out of order.
② The printer was going haywire yesterday.
③ Our sales fell last year. Now we're in the red.
④ I'm tied up with these difficult reports.

31.9 ◀))
Model Answers
① Gloria is designing packaging for a health tracker watch.
② The marketing department sends her lots of emails.
③ She doesn't get much work done because she's busy answering emails
④ Mark wants Gloria to take it easy.
⑤ Gloria has written to Faruk to ask for advice.

32.2 ◀))
① Don't worry. I have copies of them here.
② No problem. It's Carson.
③ No need. The signal's always bad here.
④ That's OK. We can have coffee first.
⑤ Never mind. I've got myself another one.

32.3
① Yes ② Yes ③ Yes
④ Yes ⑤ No

32.4 ◀))
① I'm so **sorry** I was late for this morning's meeting.
② I'm afraid that's not good **enough**. I want my money back.
③ I would like to **apologize** for the rudeness of our receptionist.
④ That's OK, but please make **sure** it doesn't happen again.

32.8 ◀))
① She **walked** into the room and saw that Clive **was practicing** his presentation.
② I **was trying** to make an important point when someone's phone **started** to ring.
③ The printer **was working** fine when unfortunately the power **went** off.
④ He **opened** the door and saw that we **were listening** to his conversation.
⑤ We **were eating** lunch in the cafeteria when we **heard** the fire alarm.

32.9
① False
② True
③ False
④ Not given
⑤ True

33.3 ◀))
① Adrian **has made** three flower arrangements already today.
② I **have started** work on the report, but I won't finish it tonight.
③ Leah **has cut** four people's hair so far this afternoon.
④ It's early. We **haven't spoken** to any customers yet.

33.4 ◀))
① I've **just** left work and it's very late.
② We haven't shown this to the public **yet**.
③ Have you **just** started selling this product?
④ She hasn't done her training course **yet**.
⑤ They've **just** opened the store doors.

33.5
① True ② False
③ False ④ True

33.7 ◀))
① **We received** your order two hours ago and sent it about an hour ago.
② I made all those pastries this morning and **I've sold** them all now.
③ **I started** painting Ms. Malone's living room at 7 today, but I haven't finished yet.
④ I emailed the clients yesterday but they **haven't** replied yet.

33.8

1. Some of his new co-workers
2. He had a meeting with his boss
3. She finished her research
4. A marketing conference
5. They both liked his talk

33.9 🔊

1. I **started** in January this year.
2. No, she **hasn't** yet.
3. Yes, I've **just** finished.
4. Not me. I **haven't** been in there.

34

34.4
Model Answers

1. She did not enjoy it.
2. No one responded to her phone calls.
3. The company will ensure every customer is given a second contact number.
4. There wasn't a vegetarian option in the hotel restaurant.
5. The hotel will offer vegetarian and vegan options.
6. The company has given Ms. Chang a voucher.

34.5 🔊

1. We will refund it to your credit card.
2. I'll take it back to the kitchen.
3. We'll replace them with bigger ones.
4. I'll talk to him about his bad attitude.
5. They'll be with you as soon as possible.

34.7 🔊

1. I'm afraid your order **won't** arrive today.
2. We'll **change** your appointment now.
3. I'll **talk** to my manager for you.
4. We'll **send** you a replacement tomorrow.
5. I **will** contact the courier about the delay.
6. I'll **ask** the chef to bring you a new meal.
7. Your delivery will **arrive** later today.

34.8

1. Will
2. Won't
3. Won't
4. Will
5. Will

34.9 🔊

1. I do **apologize**. We'll **replace** the broken part for you.
2. I'm **afraid** it **won't** arrive until Wednesday.
3. We'll **offer** you a **discount** on your next trip.

36

36.4 🔊

1. If you go to China for business, will you visit the Great Wall?
2. If I go to China on business, I won't have time to go sightseeing.
3. If we win the contract, we will go out to celebrate.
4. Will you arrange a taxi if we land late at the airport?
5. We won't get a discount if we don't book now.
6. If you have a lot of luggage, you will need a taxi.

36.5

1. by taxi
2. Business Class
3. a former colleague
4. to do some sightseeing
5. his passport details

36.9 🔊

1. When you book a transfer, a driver meets you.
2. Passengers get annoyed if the plane takes off late.
3. You can order a special meal if you're vegetarian.

36.10 🔊

1. If you buy food on the plane, it **is** quite expensive.
2. If you **are** in a group, it is often cheaper to go by taxi.
3. Will it be cheaper to **buy** a return ticket if I come back the same day?
4. When you book flights early, they **are** usually cheaper.
5. Traveling is boring if you **don't** have anything to do on the plane.

37

37.4 🔊

1. The venue is straight ahead and on **the** left.
2. Excuse **me**, do you where the gym is?
3. Sorry, did you **say** it's on the right?
4. Go straight ahead and **turn** left.
5. The bus stop is in front **of** the park.
6. Do you know the **way** to the post office?
7. The hotel is 50 feet ahead **on** the right.
8. Do you **know** the way to the hotel?
9. **Go** straight ahead and you'll see the sign.
10. The bus stop is directly opposite **the** bank.
11. Turn right at the **intersection**.

37.5 🔊

1. Do you know how to get to Silver Street?
2. It's in front of the red building.
3. Don't take the first right. Take the second.
4. I'll meet you across from the hotel.
5. Go straight ahead and turn left at the lights.
6. The bank is next to the station.

37.6 🔊

1. Sorry, did you say it's opposite the café?
2. Go straight ahead and turn right at the intersection.
3. Do you know how to get to the venue?
4. Go past the post office and it's on the left.

37.7

1. A 2. B 3. B 4. A 5. A

37.8 🔊

1. Take the first **left**, and go **past** the hotel.
2. It's across from the hospital. Take the **second** right.
3. Go straight **ahead**. It's on the **corner**.
4. Take the first **right**, then **go** straight ahead.
5. Just go **straight** ahead and it's on the **left**.

38

38.4 🔊

1. The rooms were cleaned this morning.
2. The key was left in the door.
3. The VIPs were met in the boardroom.
4. Flowers were put in the hotel foyer.

38.5
1. The car was driven by a chauffeur.
2. The key was found by the guest.
3. They were shown around the conference venue.

38.6
Ⓐ 4　Ⓑ 1　Ⓒ 3　Ⓓ 2

38.7
1. False　2. True　3. True
4. False　5. False　6. True

38.8
1. pick up
2. fall apart
3. turn on
4. check out
5. look around

38.9
Ⓐ 2　Ⓑ 4　Ⓒ 5　Ⓓ 1　Ⓔ 3

38.10
1. Breakfast **was served** in the main restaurant.
2. The rooms **were cleaned** every day.
3. The reservation **was made** by my assistant.
4. Yes. Very. They **were decorated** beautifully.

40

40.2
1. Yes, we spoke on the phone.
2. Have you been to Mexico City before?
3. I'll let Mrs. Singh know that you're here.
4. Would you like some tea or coffee?
5. Did you have a good flight?
6. I've been looking forward to this visit.
7. It's great to meet you in person.
8. Did you have any trouble getting here?
9. Can I get you anything?

40.4
1. Would you like **a** cup of tea?
2. Do you take **(any)** sugar?
3. Did you have **a** good trip?
4. Could I have **some** water, please?
5. Here are **some** details about the hotel.

40.5
1. I didn't bring any luggage.
2. Did you have a good flight?
3. Do you need any help?
4. Would you like to meet the team?
5. There will be something to eat.
6. Can I get you anything to drink?
7. Please take a seat and wait here.

40.6
1. The evening before
2. A product launch
3. Social media and marketing

40.7
1. The **keynote** speech will start at 10am.
2. The main **presenter** used a lot of slides.
3. The main sponsor will **launch** a new product.
4. Every attendee gets a **lanyard** and a name tag.
5. In a workshop the **delegates** get involved.
6. There are lots of **networking** opportunities.

40.8
1. They have **some** free food and drinks.
2. Do you have **a** lanyard already?
3. I have **some** business cards to give people.
4. I'd like to see **some** interesting talks.
5. Are you going to **any** talks today?
6. Do you have **a** business card?
7. Are you staying in **a** hotel?
8. They don't have **any** drinks.
9. I'm giving **a** presentation today.

40.9
2

40.10
1. It's Leo Smart. I haven't collected my **lanyard** yet.
2. Yes, here. Please take my **business card**.
3. Yes, and I went to an interesting **workshop** this morning.

41

41.2
1. Would you like to see the dessert menu?
2. Could we have some sparkling water, please?
3. Could I have a receipt for this, please?

41.3
1. The **reservation** was for six, but now there are only five.
2. Is there anything that you **recommend**?
3. Yes. I'm **allergic** to shellfish.
4. It's ok, **but** the food is a little bit cold.

41.5
1. How much rice do you want?
2. I don't need more. There's enough here.
3. There are too many seats here.
4. There's not enough water.
5. $40 for a steak! That's too much.

41.6
1. I've eaten **too** many chocolates.
2. How **many** glasses do we need?
3. There's too **much** sauce on this.
4. How **much** should we tip here?

41.7
1. True
2. True
3. False
4. True
5. Not given

42

42.2
1. Hi, Karl. It's Katie **from** HR.
2. Hi. I'm **calling** about the Wi-Fi.
3. My client is here. I'd **better** be going.
4. Can I ask **who's** calling, please?
5. Is there **anything** else I can do for you?
6. Hello. Olga **speaking**.
7. No, thanks. That's **all**. Bye.

42.3
Ⓐ 2　Ⓑ 6　Ⓒ 4　Ⓓ 1　Ⓔ 5　Ⓕ 3

42.4 🔊
1. Hi. Can I speak **to** Jacob, please?
2. Hello, Sophie. **It's** Ahmed from sales.
3. Could I **ask** who's calling, please?
4. Hi. Adam **speaking**.
5. It's Sandy **from** IT.
6. Hi. **I'm calling** because the elevator is stuck.
7. Bye then. **Speak** to you soon.
8. Can I ask **who's calling**, please?

42.7
1. 6057700930
2. 03069990555
3. 01632960042
4. 01184962027
5. 07700900844
6. 03069690447
7. 01632960177

42.8 🔊
1. **Can** you call Martin at the office? His number's 902-555-4349.
2. You **can** call me on my cell phone any time. My number's 03069 991332.
3. Hi, it's Myra. **Can** you call me back? My number's 07064 881206.
4. **Would** you be able to call me back? I'm at the office. My extension is 8762.
5. If you **want** to contact Samuel later, his number's 01632 960441.
6. I've got a number for Hanna if you **want** to contact her. It's 321-554-8933.

42.9
1. A project selling shoes
2. She cannot connect to the Wi-Fi
3. Enter a different passcode
4. GJ330XS
5. He will fix it

42.12 🔊
1. Anna, can I call you **back** later from the office?
2. Suzanna always takes ages to pick **up** the phone.
3. Ethan, I will get back **to** you later with an answer.
4. I'll put you **through** to Ivor now.
5. If a customer is very rude, you can hang **up**.
6. I'll find out the information and get **back** to you.
7. I'm busy now, Valeria, but I'll call **you** back later.

42.13 🔊
1. I'll put you through to Simone in sales.
2. I will call you back later this afternoon.
3. Sorry about that; we were just cut off.

42.14 🔊
1. get cut off
2. pick up
3. speak up
4. call you back
5. breaking up
6. get back to them

43

43.2 🔊
1. Can you say that I'll arrive late?
2. Could I speak to someone in sales?
3. Can I leave a message for her?
4. Certainly. I'll just put you through.
5. I have a problem with an order.
6. Hello. I wonder if you could help me.

43.3 🔊
1. May I ask who's **calling**?
2. I'll just **put** you through.
3. I'm **afraid** he's away today.
4. **How** can I help you?

43.4
2

43.7 🔊
OPINION:
useful, **awful**
SIZE:
large, **tiny**
AGE:
antique, **new**
COLOR:
blue, **green**
MATERIAL:
wooden, **glass**

43.8 🔊
1. My boss has a **friendly large white** cat.
2. My computer is a **huge old white** desktop from 1995.
3. We're marketing a **clever tiny new** watch that helps keep you fit.
4. Have you seen the **amazing tiny black** briefcase she has?
5. The meeting room has a **very large modern** painting.

43.9
1. False
2. False
3. Not given
4. True
5. False
6. Not given

44

44.2 🔊
1. Personal statement
2. Career summary
3. Professional achievements
4. Education
5. Interests
6. References

44.3 🔊
1. I am **fluent** in Japanese and Mandarin Chinese.
2. I have a great deal of **hands-on** experience in the construction industry.
3. I have an **in-depth** knowledge of hair-coloring techniques.
4. As an ex-car salesman, I have a **service-oriented** background.
5. I am a highly **motivated** librarian and love reading.
6. I am **proficient** in all major types of accounting software.

44.5 🔊
1. Our teams **collaborated** to create the packaging design.
2. We **established** a new headquarters downtown.
3. I **coordinated** a staff training day for all departments.
4. I **volunteered** for a charity and built a classroom.

⑤ I **negotiated** with all our suppliers and cut costs by 15 percent.

44.6
① True
② True
③ False
④ Not given
⑤ False

45

45.4 🔊
Note: Answers to ①, ②, and ④ can also be written in contracted form.
① They **are not going to** invest a lot of money next year.
② He **is going to travel** by plane and then taxi to the meeting.
③ **Are** you **going to meet** with the suppliers next week?
④ We **are going to buy** the best quality business cards we can.

45.5 🔊
① Make sure you have your passports.
② Can you let her know what happens?
③ We should email the printers today.
④ It's good to work with different people.
⑤ He wants to spend more time playing golf.

45.6
Ⓐ 2 Ⓑ 1 Ⓒ 3 Ⓓ 5 Ⓔ 4

45.8 🔊
① Could you come to my office?
② Why don't we discuss this at the meeting?
③ Can you tell me when it's finished, please?
④ Could we move these files?
⑤ Could you send the design to the printers?
⑥ Can you help me with these figures, please?

45.9 🔊
① Can **you help** me move this cupboard?
② Could you **be** a little neater, please?
③ Can you **finish** the design soon, please?
④ Could **we** meet at 5 instead of 6?
⑤ Could you **possibly** send me the report today?
⑥ Can you **clean up** the meeting room?

45.10 🔊
Model Answers
① Sven is going to meet the printers in the afternoon.
② Diane is going to work on the Information Desk.
③ All the delegates are going to wear lanyards during the conference.
④ Simon is going to check that the rooms all have projectors and an internet connection.

47

47.3
① Technology
② Discarded to landfill
③ Purchase it
④ The environment
⑤ In a meeting

47.4 🔊
① Please find your **invoice attached to** this email.
② I am writing to you as the new CEO **at** Yogurt500.
③ I **would appreciate** it if you could reply by 3 o'clock this afternoon.
④ My name's Scott and I work **in** the packaging department.

47.6 🔊
① He is **emailing** all the clients this afternoon.
② She is **going to send** vouchers to all customers.
③ They are **going to meet** in Rome to discuss options.
④ I am **speaking** with our couriers tomorrow.

47.7 🔊
① We hope they're **going to offer** us a discount.
② Our CEO is **going to discuss** a merger.
③ Simone is **sending** your invoice this afternoon.
④ Mark and Johan are **going to answer** the calls later.

47.8
① is going to take place
② Please find attached
③ We are going to
④ in the
⑤ is also attending
⑥ going to discuss

ENGLISH
FOR EVERYONE

COURSE BOOK LEVEL 2

BUSINESS ENGLISH

Level ❷ Contents

01 Introductions

When you first join a company, there are many phrases that you can use to introduce yourself. Other people may also use a variety of phrases to introduce you.

⚙ **New language** Present simple and continuous
Aa Vocabulary Etiquette for introductions
🧩 **New skill** Introducing yourself and others

1.1 KEY LANGUAGE INTRODUCING YOURSELF AND OTHERS

It is common to shake hands with new colleagues and introduce yourself.

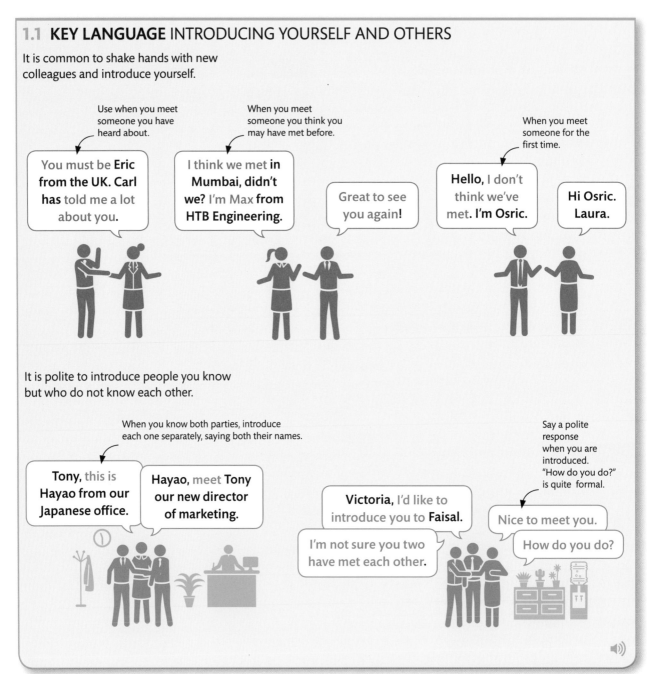

Use when you meet someone you have heard about.

You must be **Eric from the UK. Carl has** told me a lot about you.

When you meet someone you think you may have met before.

I think we met **in Mumbai, didn't we?** I'm Max **from HTB Engineering.**

Great to see you again!

When you meet someone for the first time.

Hello, I don't think we've met. **I'm Osric.**

Hi Osric. Laura.

It is polite to introduce people you know but who do not know each other.

When you know both parties, introduce each one separately, saying both their names.

Tony, this is Hayao from our Japanese office.

Hayao, meet **Tony** our new director of marketing.

Victoria, I'd like to introduce you to **Faisal.**

I'm not sure you two have met each other.

Say a polite response when you are introduced. "How do you do?" is quite formal.

Nice to meet you.

How do you do?

1.2 MATCH THE BEGINNINGS OF THE INTRODUCTIONS TO THE CORRECT ENDINGS

My manager has told me	have met each other before.
① Hi, Katherine. I think I	It's great to see you again.
② I'm not sure whether you	so much about your business!
③ Yes, we met in Barcelona.	Brian, meet Tonya. She's joining our team.
④ You must be Gloria from the design team.	met you at the Market Max conference.
⑤ This is Brian from customer services.	Guvan told me about your great work.

◀))

1.3 FILL IN THE GAPS USING THE WORDS IN THE PANEL

You _____*must*_____ be Joe Smith.

① Did we _____ at a conference?

② Really good to _____ you again.

③ Roula, meet Maria, _____ new assistant.

④ I'd like to _____ you to Karl.

⑤ Have you two _____ each other before?

> ~~must~~   introduce
> meet   our
>   met   see

◀))

1.4 LISTEN TO THE AUDIO AND ANSWER THE QUESTIONS

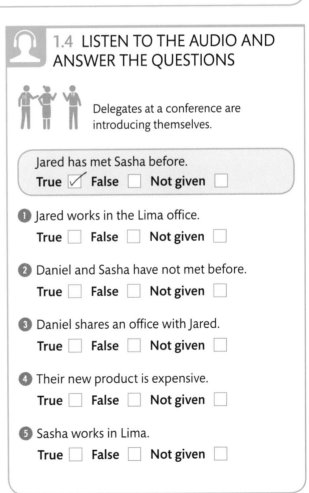

Delegates at a conference are introducing themselves.

Jared has met Sasha before.
True ✓ **False** ☐ **Not given** ☐

① Jared works in the Lima office.
True ☐ **False** ☐ **Not given** ☐

② Daniel and Sasha have not met before.
True ☐ **False** ☐ **Not given** ☐

③ Daniel shares an office with Jared.
True ☐ **False** ☐ **Not given** ☐

④ Their new product is expensive.
True ☐ **False** ☐ **Not given** ☐

⑤ Sasha works in Lima.
True ☐ **False** ☐ **Not given** ☐

1.5 KEY LANGUAGE THE PRESENT SIMPLE AND THE PRESENT CONTINUOUS

The present simple is used to describe something that happens in general, or is part of a routine. The present continuous describes something that is happening right now, and will be continuing for a limited time.

I don't usually enjoy networking, but I'm enjoying this conference.

Present simple is the same as the base form of the verb without "to."

Present continuous is formed by adding "be" before the verb and "-ing" to the verb.

1.6 READ THE ARTICLE AND ANSWER THE QUESTIONS

What word is used for making connections?
Networking ✓ **Sharing** ☐ **Dividing** ☐

❶ What kind of people is the article aimed at?
Shy ☐ **Confident** ☐ **Intelligent** ☐

❷ What types of connections are useful?
New ones ☐ **Good ones** ☐ **Lots of them** ☐

❸ Who might be useful people to talk to?
Ex-colleagues ☐ **Recruiters** ☐ **Family** ☐

❹ What do shy people do a lot?
Lie ☐ **Say sorry** ☐ **Say thank you** ☐

❺ What does apologizing a lot make you seem?
Confident ☐ **Worried** ☐ **Unprofessional** ☐

❻ Where should you look when talking to people?
Their eyes ☐ **Their feet** ☐ **Their mouths** ☐

❼ What should you give contacts?
Money ☐ **Gifts** ☐ **Your business card** ☐

CAREER LADDER

Making connections

How to network better if you're shy

Networking doesn't necessarily mean talking to hundreds of people at a conference. A few good connections are much better than meeting lots of people who you will never hear from again. Start by chatting to ex-colleagues or old friends. Ask what they are doing now and share your experiences.

One common habit of shy people is to constantly apologize for everything. Apologizing all of the time looks unprofessional and shows a lack of confidence in yourself. Instead of saying

sorry, remember to smile, maintain eye contact, ask questions, and, of course, exchange business cards.

1.7 REWRITE THE SENTENCES, CORRECTING THE ERRORS

> I am being happy to finally meet you, Zoe.
> *I'm happy to finally meet you, Zoe.*

❶ Hi James. I'm Vanisha. I don't think we are meeting before.

_____

❷ Ashley, I'd like introduce you to my colleague Neil.

_____

❸ I enjoying the presentations. Are you?

_____

❹ Nice to meet you Bethany. How do you doing?

_____

1.8 CROSS OUT THE INCORRECT WORDS IN EACH SENTENCE, THEN SAY THE SENTENCES OUT LOUD

> I'm sorry, how do you say / ~~are you saying~~ your name again?

❶ Hello Frank. Are you enjoying / do you enjoy the conference?

❷ Wilfred, I'd like you to meet / be meeting Roger, our new press officer.

❸ Serena, it's really great to see / seeing you again after so long.

❹ I usually enjoy workshops, but I am not find / finding this one interesting.

02 Getting to know colleagues

Talking about your past work experience is a good way to get to know your colleagues. Past simple and past continuous tenses are often used to do this.

✿ **New language** Past simple and past continuous
Aa Vocabulary Sharing past experiences
🧩 **New skill** Talking about past experiences

2.1 KEY LANGUAGE THE PAST SIMPLE AND THE PAST CONTINUOUS

Use the past simple to talk about a single, completed action in the past, past habits, or a state that was true for a time in the past.

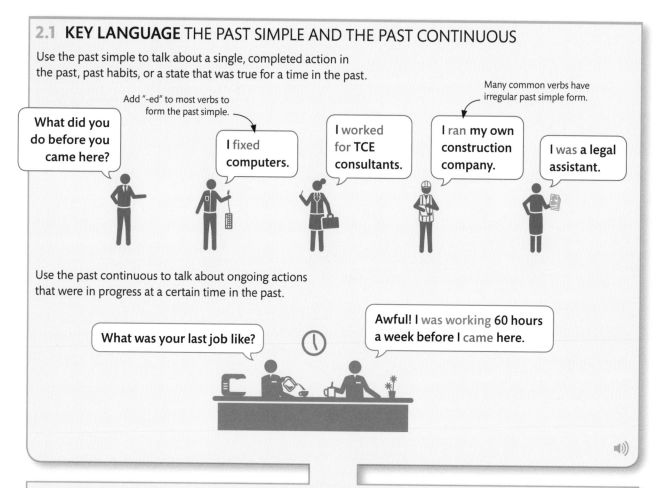

What did you do before you came here?

Add "-ed" to most verbs to form the past simple.

I fixed computers.

I worked for **TCE** consultants.

Many common verbs have irregular past simple form.

I ran **my own** construction company.

I was **a legal** assistant.

Use the past continuous to talk about ongoing actions that were in progress at a certain time in the past.

What was your last job like?

Awful! I was working 60 hours a week before I came here.

2.2 HOW TO FORM THE PAST SIMPLE AND THE PAST CONTINUOUS

The past simple is usually formed by adding "-ed" to the base form of the verb. The past continuous is formed by adding "was" or "were" in front of the verb, and "-ing" to the end of the verb.

SUBJECT	PAST CONTINUOUS	REST OF CLAUSE	PAST SIMPLE
I	was working	60 hours a week	before I came here.

2.3 CROSS OUT THE INCORRECT WORDS IN EACH SENTENCE

I started / ~~was starting~~ my own printing company more than 10 years ago.

1 They **began** / **were beginning** to sell more when the shop suddenly closed last year.

2 I **lost** / **was losing** my job when the factory closed last December.

3 I was delighted when I **got** / **was getting** promoted to senior manager in 2015.

4 We moved here when my wife **was finding** / **found** a new job two years ago.

5 I **was training** / **trained** to be a chef when I was given this award.

6 When I worked 90 hours a week, I **felt** / **was feeling** exhausted all the time.

7 When I was a photographer, I **was meeting** / **met** a lot of famous people through my work.

🔊

2.4 KEY LANGUAGE THE PAST TENSE FOR POLITENESS

You may hear people ask questions about a present situation in the past tense. This makes the question more polite.

"Do" becomes "Did" to make the question in past tense.

Did you want a tour of the office?

The past tense is also sometimes used to make a polite request.

I wanted to ask about the company's history.

🔊

2.5 MARK THE SENTENCES THAT ARE CORRECT

Did you want some more coffee? ✓
Do you wanting some more coffee? ☐

1 I was to look for another job. ☐
I was looking for another job. ☐

2 I was wondering if you could help. ☐
I was wondered if you could help. ☐

3 Were you working as a waiter? ☐
Were you work as a waiter? ☐

4 They weren't employing young people. ☐
They not employing young people. ☐

5 I didn't enjoy my last job. ☐
I didn't enjoying my last job. ☐

6 Did you work in a hotel? ☐
Did you working in a hotel? ☐

🔊

2.6 KEY LANGUAGE THE PRESENT PERFECT SIMPLE

The present perfect simple is used to talk about events in the
recent past that still have an effect on the present moment.

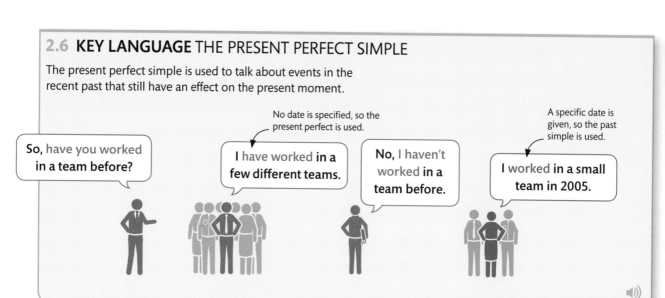

So, have you worked in a team before?

No date is specified, so the present perfect is used.

I have worked in a few different teams.

No, I haven't worked in a team before.

A specific date is given, so the past simple is used.

I worked in a small team in 2005.

2.7 HOW TO FORM THE PRESENT PERFECT SIMPLE

The present perfect simple is formed
with "have" and a past participle.

SUBJECT	"HAVE / HAS" + PAST PARTICIPLE	REST OF SENTENCE
I	have worked	in a few teams.

2.8 FILL IN THE GAPS BY PUTTING THE VERBS IN THE PRESENT PERFECT SIMPLE

Susan _____has worked_____ (work) here since she graduated from college five years ago.

1 He _____ (take) 15 days off sick this year already and it is only May!

2 Julia has a lot of experience. She _____ (manage) this department for years.

3 They _____ (employ) more than 300 people over the years.

4 John _____ (train) lots of young employees across a few different teams.

5 I'm so happy! I _____ (finish) my apprenticeship at last.

6 My manager _____ (approve) my vacation days. I'm going to Italy in July.

2.9 LISTEN TO THE AUDIO AND ANSWER THE QUESTIONS

Two colleagues are discussing their past experience.

2 Suzi has always worked in HR.
True ☐ False ☐ Not given ☐

3 Jack has worked for CIE for six years.
True ☐ False ☐ Not given ☐

This is Suzi's first day at the company.
True ☐ False ☐ Not given ✓

4 Jack has never worked for another company.
True ☐ False ☐ Not given ☐

1 Suzi's previous company was smaller.
True ☐ False ☐ Not given ☐

5 Jack and Suzi always work the same days.
True ☐ False ☐ Not given ☐

2.10 CROSS OUT THE INCORRECT WORDS IN EACH SENTENCE, THEN SAY THE SENTENCES OUT LOUD

I ~~worked~~ / ~~was working~~ / have worked in marketing since 1995.

1 I drove / was driving / have driven taxis when I saw this job advertised.

2 I managed / was managing / have managed accounts for this company for seven years.

3 I bought / was buying / have bought my first business in 2009.

4 I was studying in college when I saw / was seeing / have seen this job.

5 They invested / were investing / have invested in this company since 2010.

6 In 2014, I sold / was selling / has sold the company to an investor.

---

02 ✔ **CHECKLIST**

⚙ Past simple and past continuous ☐   **Aa** Sharing past experiences ☐   ⌘ Talking about past experiences ☐

03 Vocabulary

3.1 DEPARTMENTS

Administration

[deals with organization and internal and external communication]

Research and Development (R&D)

[deals with researching and developing future products for a company]

Human Resources (HR)

[deals with employee relations and matters such as hiring staff]

Accounts / Finance

[deals with money matters, from paying bills to projecting sales]

Marketing

[deals with promoting products]

Public Relations (PR)

[deals with maintaining a positive public image for a company]

Production

[ensures all manufacturing stages run smoothly]

Purchasing

[deals with buying goods and raw materials]

Sales

[deals with selling a finished product to outside markets]

Facilities / Office Services

[ensures the smooth day-to-day running of the practical aspects of a company]

Legal

[ensures that all contracts and company activities are legal]

Information Technology (IT)

[ensures that all technological systems are working and maintained]

3.2 ROLES

employer

Chief Executive
Officer (CEO)

manager

employee

Chief Financial Officer
(CFO)

assistant

3.3 DESCRIBING ROLES

We all work for a large department store.

to work for
[to be employed by a company]

I work in event management.

to work in
[to be employed in a department or area of an industry]

She works as a fashion designer.

to work as
[to have a particular job or role]

He looks after our salaries and wages.

to look after
[to ensure something runs smoothly]

They are responsible for office maintenance.

to be responsible for
[to have the duty of ensuring something is done effectively]

I'm in charge of administration.

to be in charge of
[to have control and authority over something]

04 Talking about changes

There are many ways to talk about changes at work in the past and present. Many of the phrases include "used to," which can have several different meanings.

⚙ New language "Used to," "be / get used to"
Aa Vocabulary Small talk
🧩 New skill Talking about changes at work

4.1 KEY LANGUAGE "USED TO," "GET USED TO," AND "BE USED TO"

"Used" with an infinitive describes a regular habit or state in the past.

"To eat" is the infinitive form of the verb.

Staff used to eat lunch at their desks.

"Get used to" describes the process of becoming familiar with something.

"Get used to" can be followed by a noun or gerund.

It took a while to get used to { **the commute.** **commuting.**

"Be used to" describes being familiar with something.

"Be used to" can be followed by a noun or gerund.

Nowadays I am used to { **waking up early.** **early mornings.**

4.2 FURTHER EXAMPLES "USED TO," "GET USED TO," AND "BE USED TO"

In questions and negatives, there is no "d" after "use."

Did you use to do everything by hand in the factory?

We didn't use to have so much construction in the area.

I don't know that I will ever get used to these uniforms!

After working here for a decade, we are used to the noise.

4.3 MARK THE SENTENCES THAT ARE CORRECT

He is used to working from home. ✓
He is use to working from home. ☐

① I use to travel to work by car. ☐
I used to travel to work by car. ☐

② She's used to giving big presentations. ☐
She's used to give big presentations. ☐

③ I'll get used to my new job eventually. ☐
I get used my new job eventually. ☐

④ We didn't used to get paid a bonus. ☐
We didn't use to get paid a bonus. ☐

⑤ Did he use to work in marketing? ☐
Did he used to work in marketing? ☐

🔊

4.4 LISTEN TO THE AUDIO, THEN NUMBER THE PICTURES IN THE ORDER THEY ARE DESCRIBED

Ⓐ ☐   Ⓑ 1   Ⓒ ☐   Ⓓ ☐

4.5 REWRITE THE SENTENCES, PUTTING THE WORDS IN THE CORRECT ORDER

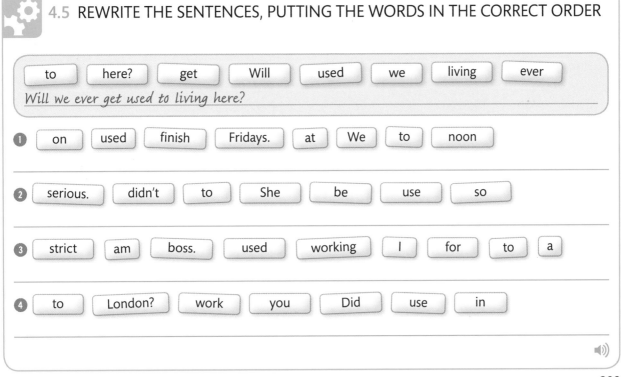

| to | here? | get | Will | used | we | living | ever |

Will we ever get used to living here?

① | on | used | finish | Fridays. | at | We | to | noon |

② | serious. | didn't | to | She | be | use | so |

③ | strict | am | boss. | used | working | I | for | to | a |

④ | to | London? | work | you | Did | use | in |

🔊

4.6 MATCH THE PAIRS OF PHRASES THAT MEAN THE SAME THING

I was a bank employee in the past.

Did he use to work in a bank?

I used to work in a bank.

1 I began working long days early in my career.

You didn't use to work such long hours.

2 He is a qualified lawyer now.

3 I don't usually work short days.

I am used to working long hours.

4 Your working day was shorter in the past.

He didn't use to have a law degree.

5 Has he worked in a bank before?

I got used to long hours in my first job.

4.7 READ THE ARTICLE AND ANSWER THE QUESTIONS

Weather is a common topic for small talk.
True ☑ **False** ☐ **Not given** ☐

1 Being good at small talk can give you an advantage in your job.
True ☐ **False** ☐ **Not given** ☐

2 Sports are the most common topic for small talk.
True ☐ **False** ☐ **Not given** ☐

3 People who are good at small talk are generally disliked.
True ☐ **False** ☐ **Not given** ☐

4 When talking to a colleague, don't look at their face.
True ☐ **False** ☐ **Not given** ☐

5 Not every topic is suitable for small talk.
True ☐ **False** ☐ **Not given** ☐

WORKPLACE ADVICE

It's good to talk

Small talk—chatting about trivial topics such as the weather

"Morning, Sammy. Did you see the game last night?" This kind of small talk happens in every office around the world, every day. People who make an effort to talk to others are more well-liked by their colleagues. When you make small talk, you make the other person feel more relaxed, and form a connection with that person. People who are good at small talk tend to be quick thinkers, and businesses like employees who can think on their feet. So what are the key skills you need to master to be good at small talk? Make eye contact with the other person, and listen. Be interested in what they have to say. Stick to topics such as hobbies, books, films, and the weather. And avoid uncomfortable topics such as politics, religion, and money.

4.8 MARK THE BEST REPLY TO EACH STATEMENT

I'm not used to this heat!

- Would you like something to drink? ✓
- Good afternoon, Mrs. Sullivan.

1

You look tired.

- I feel really hungry. ☐
- I'm not used to starting at 6am! ☐

2

Did you see the game last night?

- I enjoy watching films. ☐
- Yes, what a disappointment! ☐

3

Would you like some of this pizza?

- I didn't use to like it. ☐
- Yes, please. It looks delicious. ☐

4

It takes me 20 minutes to get to work.

- That's a very short commute! ☐
- It's more expensive by train. ☐

5

The sky looks black outside.

- Yes, I think it's going to rain. ☐
- I'm going away this weekend. ☐

🔊

4.9 CROSS OUT THE INCORRECT WORDS IN EACH SENTENCE, THEN SAY THE SENTENCES OUT LOUD

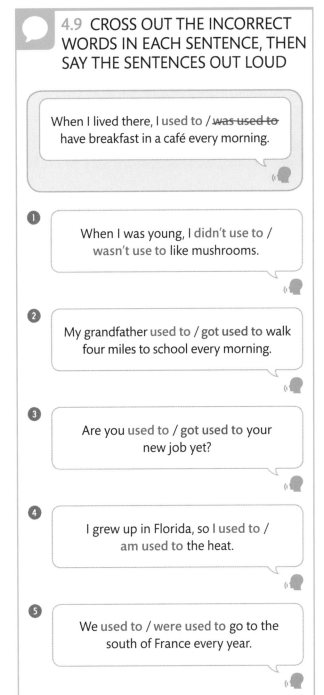

When I lived there, I used to / ~~was used to~~ have breakfast in a café every morning.

1 When I was young, I didn't use to / wasn't use to like mushrooms.

2 My grandfather used to / got used to walk four miles to school every morning.

3 Are you used to / got used to your new job yet?

4 I grew up in Florida, so I used to / am used to the heat.

5 We used to / were used to go to the south of France every year.

🔊

---

05 Delegating tasks

When things get busy, you may want to delegate tasks to colleagues. To do this, different modal verbs are used in English to show the level of obligation.

🔧 **New language** Modal verbs for obligation
Aa Vocabulary Delegation and politeness
🧩 **New skill** Delegating tasks to colleagues

5.1 KEY LANGUAGE MODAL VERBS FOR OBLIGATION

Certain modal verbs can be used to say that someone needs to do something.

 I { **have to / have got to / need to** } **leave this with you.**

"Need" acts like a modal verb here, expressing strong obligation.

 You don't have to deal with this today.

"Don't have to" means that there is no obligation to do something.

 You must complete this project by Monday.

"Must" is a direct, and sometimes impolite, way to say something needs to be done.

You must not go into the testing area.

"Must not" means that something is prohibited.

🔊

5.2 HOW TO FORM MODAL VERBS FOR OBLIGATION

"Must" does not change with the subject, but "have to" becomes "has to" in the third person singular. Both are followed by the base form of the main verb.

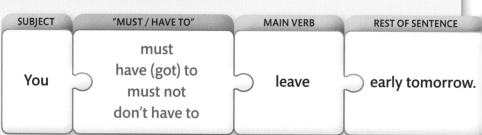

SUBJECT	"MUST / HAVE TO"	MAIN VERB	REST OF SENTENCE
You	must / have (got) to / must not / don't have to	leave	early tomorrow.

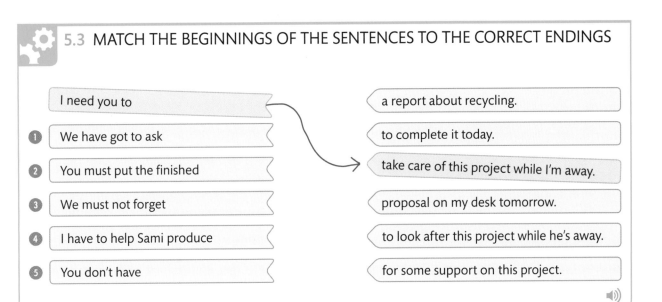

5.3 MATCH THE BEGINNINGS OF THE SENTENCES TO THE CORRECT ENDINGS

I need you to

a report about recycling.

1 We have got to ask

to complete it today.

2 You must put the finished

take care of this project while I'm away.

3 We must not forget

proposal on my desk tomorrow.

4 I have to help Sami produce

to look after this project while he's away.

5 You don't have

for some support on this project.

5.4 MARK THE SENTENCES THAT ARE CORRECT

You have to do this assignment today. ✓
You has to do this assignment today. ☐

1 We need to increase sales to Europe. ☐
We need increase sales to Europe. ☐

2 We can't reveal our new product yet. ☐
We can't to reveal our new product yet. ☐

3 You don't having to work late. ☐
You don't have to work late. ☐

4 I will need the accounts by tomorrow. ☐
I need have the accounts tomorrow. ☐

5 We have get to find a new IT manager. ☐
We have got to find a new IT manager. ☐

6 You must to produce a spreadsheet. ☐
You need to produce a spreadsheet. ☐

7 We must reaching our sales target. ☐
We must reach our sales target. ☐

5.5 LISTEN TO THE AUDIO AND ANSWER THE QUESTIONS

A manager is delegating tasks to an employee at a firm.

The conference takes place once a year.
True ☐ False ☐ Not given ✓

1 The conference will take place in August.
True ☐ False ☐ Not given ☐

2 The conference will take place at the office.
True ☐ False ☐ Not given ☐

3 The manager wants Shona to ask about prices.
True ☐ False ☐ Not given ☐

4 Shona must complete the task by tomorrow.
True ☐ False ☐ Not given ☐

5 Shona's boss often delegates work to her.
True ☐ False ☐ Not given ☐

5.6 KEY LANGUAGE POLITENESS

To maintain a friendly, polite atmosphere, you can use "we" instead of "you" to express obligation.

We have to **finish this project soon**

Other modal verbs can also be used in business to delegate tasks politely.

Could
Would } **you look after this for me?**

"Would" is more formal and is rarely used.

🔊

5.7 REWRITE THE SENTENCES, PUTTING THE WORDS IN THE CORRECT ORDER

you | print | copy? | a | Could | me

Could you print me a copy?

① you | answer | my | Could | phone?

_____

② you | Would | call | the | supplier?

_____

③ We | to | have | today. | finish

_____

④ you | Would | a | book | meeting?

_____

⑤ send | this | Could | you | today?

_____

🔊

5.8 CROSS OUT THE INCORRECT WORDS IN EACH SENTENCE, THEN SAY THE SENTENCES OUT LOUD

Don't worry! You **don't have to** / ~~must not~~ deal with this right now.

① Could / Have you deliver this letter for me, please?

② Must / Would you show the new employee around the office?

③ Jess, I have got / need to leave early today. Could you let Philippe know?

🔊

214

5.9 READ THE ARTICLE AND ANSWER THE QUESTIONS

Team leaders should do everyday tasks.
True ☐ False ☐ Not given ☑

1 A routine task is answering customer enquiries.
True ☐ False ☐ Not given ☐

2 People who don't delegate often feel stressed.
True ☐ False ☐ Not given ☐

3 A team leader has to avoid doing everyday tasks.
True ☐ False ☐ Not given ☐

4 Trust in managers is falling in most companies.
True ☐ False ☐ Not given ☐

5 Team leaders should trust their staff.
True ☐ False ☐ Not given ☐

BUSINESS WEEKLY

Sharing the load

Relieve stress by learning to delegate better

Team leaders must think about goals and how to achieve them. This takes time. You won't have this thinking time if you're busy doing routine tasks and you will feel stressed. You have to let your team members handle the everyday tasks. Show your team members you trust them. Ask them if they could show you a plan of how they can manage their work in their own way. This way you will build a better working relationship.

05 ✓ CHECKLIST

⚙ Modal verbs for obligation ☐   **Aa** Delegation and politeness ☐   🧩 Delegating tasks to colleagues ☐

🔄 REVIEW THE ENGLISH YOU HAVE LEARNED IN UNITS 1–5

NEW LANGUAGE	SAMPLE SENTENCE	☑	UNIT
INTRODUCING YOURSELF AND OTHERS	You must be Eric from the UK. Tony, this is Hayao from our Japanese office.	☐	1.1
THE PAST SIMPLE AND THE PAST CONTINUOUS FOR PAST EXPERIENCES	I was working 60 hours per week when I came here.	☐	2.1
THE PAST TENSE FOR POLITENESS	Did you want a tour of the office?	☐	2.4
TALKING ABOUT THE RECENT PAST WITH THE PRESENT PERFECT SIMPLE	I have worked in a few different teams.	☐	2.6
TALKING ABOUT CHANGES WITH "USED TO" AND "BE / GET USED TO"	Staff used to eat lunch at their desks. It took a while to get used to the commute.	☐	4.1
DELEGATING TASKS WITH MODALS	I have to leave this with you. Could you look after this for me?	☐	5.1, 5.6

6.1 MONEY AND FINANCE

The company's income fell last year.

income
[money coming into a business]

The initial expenditure on technology was huge, but now we can work faster.

expenditure / outlay
[an amount of money spent]

We have a large budget for this movie, so the effects will be amazing.

a budget
[the amount of money that is available to spend on something]

We must do all we can to avoid getting into debt.

to get into debt
[to get into a situation where you owe people money]

The bank charges for overdrafts now.

an overdraft
[extra money the bank allows you to spend]

The profit margin on these T-shirts is huge!

a profit margin
[the difference between the cost of making or buying something and what it's sold for]

We need to sell two cars to break even.

to break even
[to earn just enough to cover the costs of producing a product]

We haven't sold enough pineapples. We've made a loss.

to make a loss
[to lose money by spending more than you earn]

We need to make sure the accounts are always up to date.

accounts
[records of money paid into and out of a business]

High overheads make this business difficult to run.

overheads
[the regular costs of running a business, such as wages]

I'm selling these earrings at cost to attract customers.

cost (US) / cost price (UK)
[a sales price that covers the costs of producing an item without making a profit]

The prices peaked in June, but they're down now.

to peak
[to reach the highest point]

When the CEO left, the company's value dropped.

to drop
[to fall, especially in worth or value]

Changes in the exchange rate make the market uncertain.

the exchange rate
[the amount of one currency that you get when you change it for another]

£ → €
$ → ¥

Thankfully, there was an upturn in the market.

an upturn in the market
[a change to more positive business conditions]

Our clients need to pay now or we will have a cash flow problem.

cash flow
[the rate at which money comes into and goes out of a business]

It's always hard to see a company go out of business.

to go out of business
[to no longer be able to exist as a business]

We need to undercut our competitors or we will lose customers.

to undercut competitors
[to charge less than others who sell the same goods or services as you]

Our sales figures have improved consistently each year.

sales figures
[the amount or value of total sales over a particular period]

Everyone suffered because of the economic downturn last year.

an economic downturn
[a major decline in economic activity]

07 Writing a report

When writing a report, you may need to use different past tenses to show sequences of events. You may also need to use more formal phrasing.

⚙ **New language** Past perfect and past simple
Aa Vocabulary Formal business English
🧩 **New skill** Writing reports

7.1 KEY LANGUAGE PAST PERFECT AND PAST SIMPLE

English uses the past perfect and the past simple together to describe past events that occurred at different times. The past simple describes the event that is closest to the time of speaking.

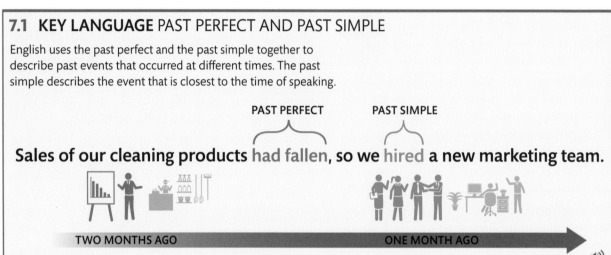

PAST PERFECT · PAST SIMPLE

Sales of our cleaning products had fallen, so we hired a new marketing team.

TWO MONTHS AGO · ONE MONTH AGO

7.2 FURTHER EXAMPLES PAST PERFECT AND PAST SIMPLE

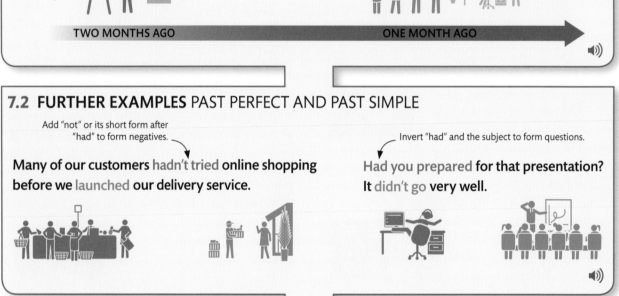

Add "not" or its short form after "had" to form negatives.

Many of our customers hadn't tried online shopping before we launched our delivery service.

Invert "had" and the subject to form questions.

Had you prepared for that presentation? It didn't go very well.

7.3 HOW TO FORM THE PAST PERFECT

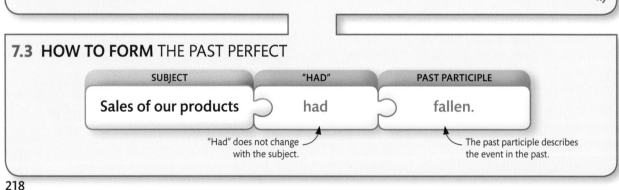

SUBJECT	"HAD"	PAST PARTICIPLE
Sales of our products	had	fallen.

"Had" does not change with the subject.

The past participle describes the event in the past.

7.4 FILL IN THE GAPS BY PUTTING THE VERBS IN THE PAST PERFECT OR PAST SIMPLE

The number of complaints _had risen_ (rise), so we _sent_ (send) our staff for training.

❶ We _____ (change) our logo because a lot of people _____ (complain) about it.

❷ Some of our goods _____ (arrive) broken, so we _____ (ask) for a refund.

❸ There _____ (be) problems in the warehouse because our manager _____ (resign).

❹ Sales of umbrellas _____ (be) poor because we _____ (have) a dry summer.

❺ Our clients _____ (not be) happy because we _____ (miss) our deadline.

❻ Yasmin's presentation _____ (go) very well, so I _____ (give) her a promotion.

❼ Our sales _____ (increase) because we _____ (launch) a new product range.

🔊

7.5 READ THE REPORT AND MARK THE CORRECT SUMMARY

❶ The trial had mostly negative results and the report recommends returning to telephone operators only. ☐

❷ The trial had both positive and negative results and the report recommends maintaining both systems. ☐

❸ The trial had mostly positive results and the report recommends keeping the trial online messaging only. ☐

Replacement of Telephone Operators with Online Messaging

Guil Motors replaced all its telephone operators with online messaging for a trial period.

Benefits:
• Each operator can deal with more than one client
• A written record is kept of each dialogue

Negative effects:
• Significant drop in number of inquiries
• Customer dissatisfaction

Recommendations:
• Offer both phone and online messaging services
• Create positive promotion for online messaging

7.6 KEY LANGUAGE PROJECT REPORTS

Here are some examples of formal language typically found in project reports.

Formal alternative to "This report shows."

The following report presents the results of a client satisfaction survey.

Formal alternative to "said."

Our clients stated that they had been disappointed with the sales figures.

Use the infinitive with "to" to talk about purpose.

The purpose of this report is to review our marketing expenditure.

Formal alternative to "first."

Based on this initial research, we should increase our marketing budget.

Formal reports often use the passive voice.

As can be seen in the table, we spent very little on social media marketing.

Formal alternative to "main."

My principal recommendation is to create and launch a new campaign.

◀))

 ## 7.7 REWRITE THE SENTENCES, CORRECTING THE ERRORS

> Many of our clients was interviewed for this report.
> *Many of our clients were interviewed for this report.*

❶ The purpose of this report is review our sales figures for the last quarter.

_____

❷ Our principle recommendation is to complete the sale of the downtown store.

_____

❸ The follow report presents the results of extensive customer satisfaction research.

_____

❹ Our main client state that the recent changes were beneficial for his business.

_____

◀))

7.8 MATCH THE BEGINNINGS OF THE SENTENCES TO THE CORRECT ENDINGS

The following report presents → our staffing plans for the coming year.

1. As can be seen in the table,

2. It is clear from the research

3. A number of focus groups

4. The purpose of this report is

that there were a number of problems.

to present the findings of our survey.

our staffing plans for the coming year.

the figures for this period were excellent.

were consulted for this report.

7.9 FILL IN THE GAPS USING THE WORDS IN THE PANEL

Our clients _____stated_____ that they had been disappointed with our products.

1. The focus group clients had all _____ both the original and new products.

2. The following chart _____ the sales figures for the two periods.

3. We _____ the customers who had complained why they didn't like the change.

4. The _____ of this report is to present the results of our online trial.

5. We started this online trial after our store costs had _____ by 10 percent.

compares   ~~stated~~   asked   risen   used   purpose

Past perfect and past simple ☐   **Aa** Formal business English ☐   Writing reports ☐

08 Making apologies

The present perfect continuous describes ongoing situations in the past that may affect the present. It can be used in apologies and to give reasons for problems.

⚙ **New language** Present perfect continuous
Aa Vocabulary Apologies
🧩 **New skill** Apologizing on the telephone

8.1 KEY LANGUAGE TELEPHONE APOLOGIES

English uses a variety of phrases for making apologies, offering to investigate a problem, and offering explanations and solutions.

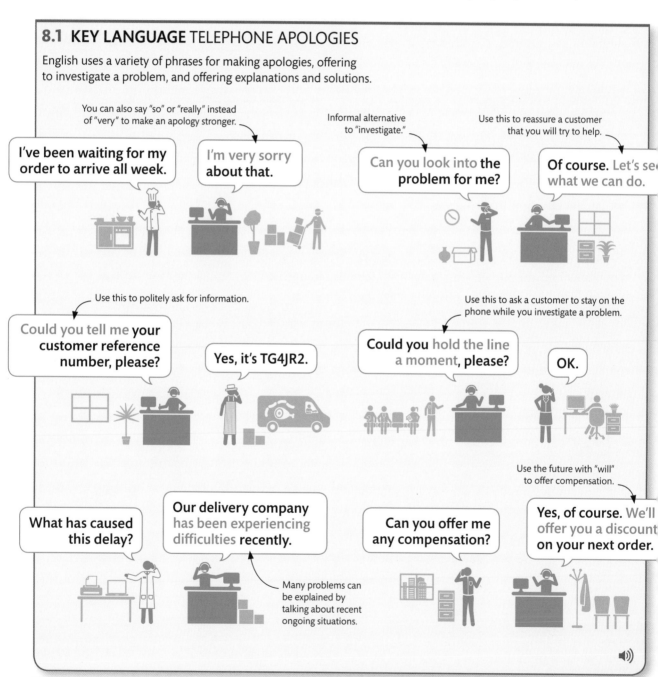

You can also say "so" or "really" instead of "very" to make an apology stronger.

I've been waiting for my order to arrive all week.

I'm very sorry about that.

Informal alternative to "investigate."

Can you look into the problem for me?

Use this to reassure a customer that you will try to help.

Of course. Let's see what we can do.

Use this to politely ask for information.

Could you tell me your customer reference number, please?

Yes, it's TG4JR2.

Use this to ask a customer to stay on the phone while you investigate a problem.

Could you hold the line a moment, please?

OK.

Use the future with "will" to offer compensation.

What has caused this delay?

Our delivery company has been experiencing difficulties recently.

Many problems can be explained by talking about recent ongoing situations.

Can you offer me any compensation?

Yes, of course. We'll offer you a discount on your next order.

Aa 8.2 MATCH THE SENTENCES TO THE CORRECT RESPONSES

Can you look into the problem for me? → Of course. Let's see what we can do.

1. Could I have a refund?
2. Could you tell me your order number?
3. Could you hold the line a moment, please?
4. Why isn't my order here yet?
5. My order arrived dirty and broken.
6. Will you send me a replacement?

Yes, we'll send you a new one tomorrow.

Our courier has been having difficulties.

Of course. Let's see what we can do.

I'm very sorry to hear that, Mrs. Singh.

Yes, we'll give you a full refund.

OK. No problem.

Yes, it's AMLGW14.

8.3 LISTEN TO THE AUDIO, THEN NUMBER THE PHRASES IN THE ORDER YOU HEAR THEM

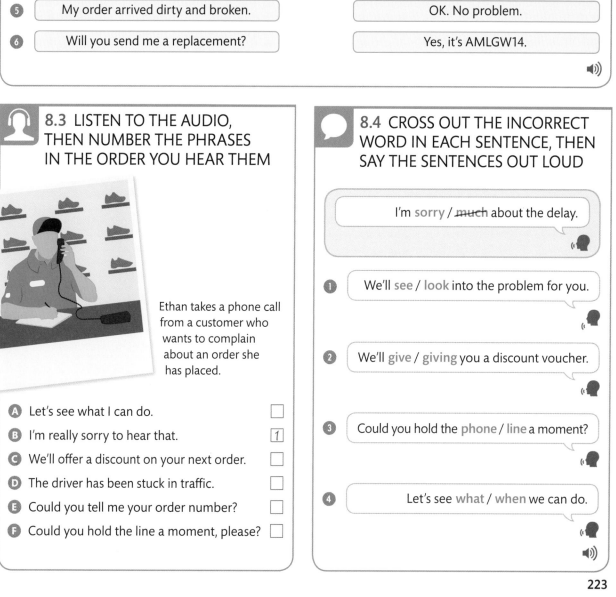

Ethan takes a phone call from a customer who wants to complain about an order she has placed.

A Let's see what I can do. ☐

B I'm really sorry to hear that. ☐ 1

C We'll offer a discount on your next order. ☐

D The driver has been stuck in traffic. ☐

E Could you tell me your order number? ☐

F Could you hold the line a moment, please? ☐

8.4 CROSS OUT THE INCORRECT WORD IN EACH SENTENCE, THEN SAY THE SENTENCES OUT LOUD

I'm sorry / ~~much~~ about the delay.

1. We'll see / look into the problem for you.

2. We'll give / giving you a discount voucher.

3. Could you hold the phone / line a moment?

4. Let's see what / when we can do.

223

8.5 KEY LANGUAGE THE PRESENT PERFECT CONTINUOUS

The present perfect continuous describes an ongoing situation in the past that often affects the present moment. You can use it to offer explanations for problems.

Our delivery company has been experiencing difficulties recently.

PRESENT PERFECT CONTINUOUS

The situation usually affects the present moment or recent past.

8.6 FURTHER EXAMPLES THE PRESENT PERFECT CONTINUOUS

We haven't been getting good feedback lately.

Add "not" or its short form after "have" or "has" to form the negative.

I'm really sorry for the delay. Have you been waiting all morning?

In questions, the subject sits between "have" or "has" and "been."

8.7 HOW TO FORM THE PRESENT PERFECT CONTINUOUS

SUBJECT	"HAS / HAVE"	BEEN	VERB + "-ING"	REST OF SENTENCE
Our delivery company	has	been	experiencing	difficulties.

Use "has" or "have," depending on the subject.

"Been" stays the same for all subjects.

Add "-ing" to the main verb.

8.8 FILL IN THE GAPS BY PUTTING THE VERBS IN THE PRESENT PERFECT CONTINUOUS

Our customers _____*have been complaining*_____ (complain) about our poor service recently.

1. The customers _____ (wait) for us to contact them.

2. Our engineers _____ (work) on the line for two days.

3. What _____ you _____ (do) to solve the problem?

4. I _____ (watch) your program and I want to complain.

5. We _____ (repair) the broken cables this morning.

6. They _____ (update) my software and now it doesn't work.

🔊

8.9 READ THE EMAIL AND ANSWER THE QUESTIONS

The complaint is about train delays.
True ✓   False ☐   Not given ☐

1. RailKo says they are sorry about the delay.
True ☐   False ☐   Not given ☐

2. RailKo says the thieves were found.
True ☐   False ☐   Not given ☐

3. The problem was unexpected for RailKo.
True ☐   False ☐   Not given ☐

4. RailKo offers Ms. Pérez a total refund.
True ☐   False ☐   Not given ☐

5. RailKo will keep passengers up to date with changes.
True ☐   False ☐   Not given ☐

✉

To: Mariana Pérez

Subject: Severe train delay

Dear Ms. Pérez,
Thank you for your email regarding the delay to your trip on July 11th. I've been investigating the problem and see that your train was, indeed, 70 minutes late. We apologize for the inconvenience this caused. We've been upgrading that line for several weeks and unfortunately that morning thieves stole a lot of machinery and it was not safe for trains to travel at their usual speed. As you can imagine, RailKo was unable to predict this event. By way of an apology, however, we'd like to offer you a refund of 50% of the value of your ticket. I've attached the voucher to this email.

Yours sincerely,
Joshua Hawkins

08 ✓ CHECKLIST

⚙ Present perfect continuous ☐   **Aa** Apologies ☐   🧩 Apologizing on the telephone ☐

09 Vocabulary

9.1 COMMUNICATION TECHNOLOGY

I can access my work emails from my home computer.

to access
[to enter or connect to something]

I appear to have lost access to the network again!

a network
[a system of interconnected technology]

As a company we always keep our hardware and apps up to date.

up to date
[current and modern]

We have an automated voicemail system.

automated
[computerized; not operated by a human]

My phone is connected to the network so I can receive emails any time.

connected to
[in communication with]

Most people in the office carry a mobile device with them.

a mobile device
[a small computing device, such as a smartphone or tablet, that is easily carried]

For most of the day I have to work online to access the internet and emails.

to work online
[to work with an internet connection]

I work offline when commuting to work because there is no internet on the train.

to work offline
[to work without an internet connection]

If you download the app, you'll get updates about new products.

to download an app
[to get an application from the internet onto a device or computer]

I automatically back up my documents every 15 minutes.

to back up
[to save an extra copy of a document in case the original is lost]

This new program is very user-friendly.

user-friendly
[easy for the operator to use]

I must have the wrong address. My email has bounced.

an email has bounced
[an email has been automatically returned without reaching the intended recipient]

Our new website works on computers and mobile devices.

a website
[a collection of linked pages accessed through the internet]

I often use social media to look for job vacancies.

social media
[internet-based tools for communicating with friends and communities]

I'm sorry, I can't hear you properly. You're breaking up.

breaking up
[losing a phone or internet connection]

Can you arrange a videoconference with the clients in Sydney?

a videoconference
[a conference by phone or via the internet in which people can see and talk to each other]

Let's arrange a conference call so we can all catch up.

a conference call
[a group conversation held by phone]

Please could you charge the tablet before the meeting?

to charge
[to connect a mobile device to electricity to give it more power]

Our company always uses the latest software.

software
[computer programs]

When you create your account, you get a username and password.

a username and password
[a name and code used to access an account on a computing device]

10 Making plans by email

English uses a variety of phrases to make and check plans with co-workers by email. It is important to ensure that even informal messages are polite.

🔧 **New language** Email language
Aa Vocabulary Meetings and workshops
🧩 **New skill** Making plans

10.1 KEY LANGUAGE EMAILS TO CO-WORKERS

In business emails, it is important to use polite and clear language to exchange information with co-workers. Emails to co-workers are often less formal than emails to clients or senior personnel.

TIP
Keep your style consistent. For example, if you add a comma after your greeting, remember to add one after your sign-off, too.

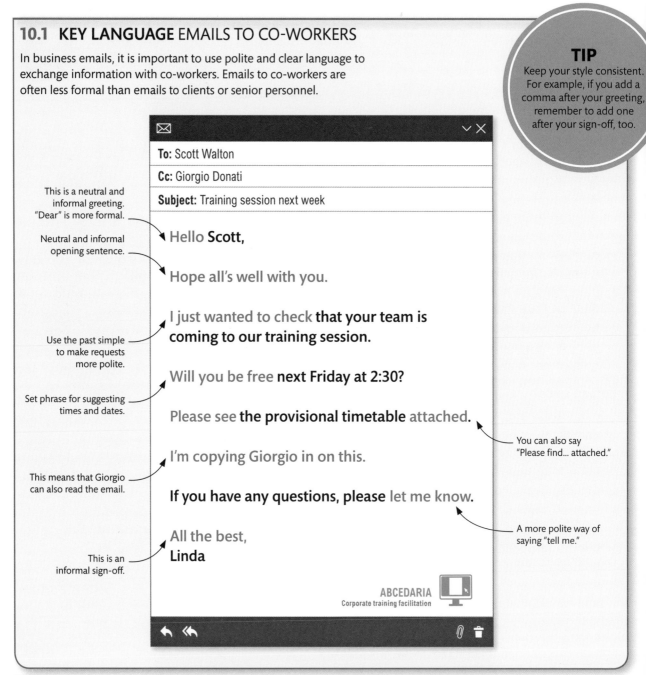

To: Scott Walton

Cc: Giorgio Donati

Subject: Training session next week

This is a neutral and informal greeting. "Dear" is more formal.

Hello **Scott,**

Neutral and informal opening sentence.

Hope all's well with you.

I just wanted to check **that your team is coming to our training session.**

Use the past simple to make requests more polite.

Will you be free **next Friday at 2:30?**

Set phrase for suggesting times and dates.

Please see **the provisional timetable** attached.

You can also say "Please find... attached."

I'm copying Giorgio in on this.

This means that Giorgio can also read the email.

If you have any questions, **please** let me know.

A more polite way of saying "tell me."

All the best,
Linda

This is an informal sign-off.

ABCEDARIA
Corporate training facilitation

10.2 READ THE EMAIL AND MARK THE CORRECT SUMMARY

1 Mira is emailing Catherine to check that she is coming to a sales presentation in Room A. Pauline is also invited to the presentation. ☐

2 Mira wants to meet next Friday to discuss arrangements for the sales presentation. She has asked Pauline to send her the agenda. ☐

3 Mira is inviting Catherine to a meeting to discuss arrangements for the sales presentation. She has sent Catherine and Pauline the timetable and agenda. ☐

4 Mira is emailing to check that Pauline is coming to the sales presentation. Catherine has sent the timetable and agenda. ☐

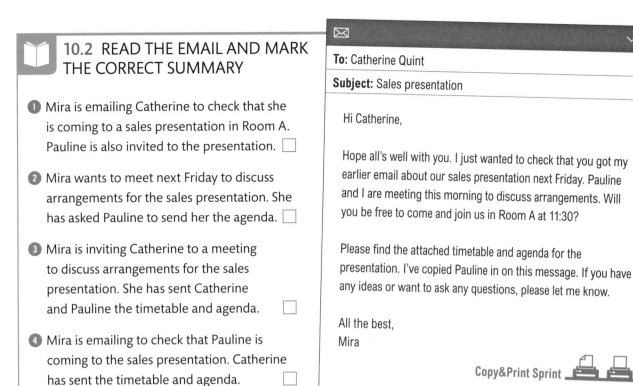

To: Catherine Quint

Subject: Sales presentation

Hi Catherine,

Hope all's well with you. I just wanted to check that you got my earlier email about our sales presentation next Friday. Pauline and I are meeting this morning to discuss arrangements. Will you be free to come and join us in Room A at 11:30?

Please find the attached timetable and agenda for the presentation. I've copied Pauline in on this message. If you have any ideas or want to ask any questions, please let me know.

All the best,
Mira

Copy&Print Sprint

10.3 FILL IN THE GAPS USING THE WORDS IN THE PANEL

Please see the timetable for tomorrow's training course __attached__.

1 I just wanted to _____ that you will be able to make it to the meeting.

2 Don't worry if you have any questions. Just let me _____ .

3 I'm _____ Maxine in on this as she may have some more information.

4 How _____ coming to the restaurant with us this evening?

5 I was _____ if you and Ana could come to the meeting tomorrow.

6 Give me a call if you can't _____ the presentation at 10 o'clock.

know

copying

~~attached~~

wondering

check

about

make

10 ✓ CHECKLIST

 Email language ☐   **Aa** Meetings and workshops ☐   Making plans ☐

229

11 Keeping clients informed

Use the present continuous to inform clients about current situations and future arrangements. Continuous tenses can also soften questions and requests.

🔧 **New language** Continuous tenses
Aa Vocabulary Arrangements and schedules
🧩 **New skill** Keeping clients informed

11.1 KEY LANGUAGE THE PRESENT CONTINUOUS

English uses the present continuous to describe what's happening right now.

Use "still" to emphasize that a situation is ongoing.

We are aiming to give you a full progress report.

We are still waiting for a part from our supplier.

English also uses the present continuous to talk about arrangements for a fixed time in the future.

Use the present continuous with a future time marker to talk about future arrangements.

We are having a meeting with the IT department later today.

Malik is talking to HR next week to discuss the noise issues.

11.2 LISTEN TO THE AUDIO AND MARK WHETHER THE ACTIVITY IN EACH PICTURE TAKES PLACE IN THE PRESENT OR THE FUTURE

Present ☐ Future ✓

① Present ☐ Future ☐

② Present ☐ Future ☐

③ Present ☐ Future ☐

④ Present ☐ Future ☐

11.3 READ THE EMAIL AND WRITE ANSWERS TO THE QUESTIONS AS FULL SENTENCES

What is Janice informing Yasmin about?

She is informing her that her order is delayed.

① What happened to the delivery van?

_____

② When is the company receiving new stock?

_____

③ What is Janice hoping to do next week?

_____

④ How can Yasmin cancel her order?

_____

⑤ Who should Yasmin contact if she has questions?

_____

To: Yasmin Hendricks

Subject: Delay with order TY309

Dear Ms. Hendricks,
I'm sorry to inform you that our delivery van was involved in an accident yesterday. I've obtained a list of affected customers and unfortunately your order was damaged. We're receiving new stock tomorrow and will contact you with a new delivery date. I'm hoping to confirm a new date next week.

We're very sorry about the inconvenience caused, and would like to assure you that you'll receive your order as soon as possible. If you'd prefer to cancel your order, you can do so online. Do not hesitate to contact me if you have any questions.
Best wishes,
Janice Wright

Aa 11.4 MATCH THE DEFINITIONS TO THE CORRECT VERBS

to make a promise

① to delay doing something

② to favor one thing above another

③ to get or find something

④ to say something will definitely happen

⑤ to tell someone something

⑥ to call or email someone

⑦ to ask for something

to prefer

to confirm

to assure

to contact

to request

to hesitate

to inform

to obtain

11.5 KEY LANGUAGE CONTINUOUS TENSES FOR POLITENESS

In correspondence with clients, English often uses continuous tenses to make requests more polite or promises less specific.

PRESENT CONTINUOUS

We are hoping to deliver your order next Monday.

[We intend to deliver your order next Monday.]

PAST CONTINUOUS

The past continuous is only used for politeness here.

I was wondering if we could meet at your office.

[Let's meet at your office.]

FUTURE CONTINUOUS

Use "will," "be," and the verb with "-ing" to form the future continuous.

Will you be attending the launch of our soft drink range?

[We hope you will go to the launch.]

To: Tyson Bailey

Subject: Poster campaign update

Dear Tyson Bailey,

Thanks for your email of December 12th regarding your poster campaign. I aiming to have a final meeting with the designers tomorrow morning, and I is hoping to send you more designs tomorrow afternoon.

We are currently wait for feedback from our focus group, but we expecting to hear from them soon. I was wonder if we could meet at your office to discuss their findings. I ensure you that we doing will be all we can to ensure that the campaign is completed on time. In the meantime, if you have any questions, please do not hesitate contacting me.

Yours,

Darius Gad

I am aiming to have

1. _____
2. _____
3. _____
4. _____
5. _____
6. _____
7. _____

11.7 REWRITE THE SENTENCES, CORRECTING THE ERRORS

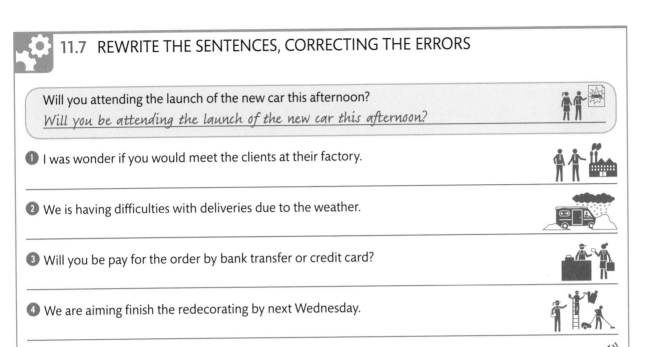

Will you attending the launch of the new car this afternoon?
Will you be attending the launch of the new car this afternoon?

1 I was wonder if you would meet the clients at their factory.

2 We is having difficulties with deliveries due to the weather.

3 Will you be pay for the order by bank transfer or credit card?

4 We are aiming finish the redecorating by next Wednesday.

11.8 REWRITE THE SENTENCES, PUTTING THE WORDS IN THE CORRECT ORDER

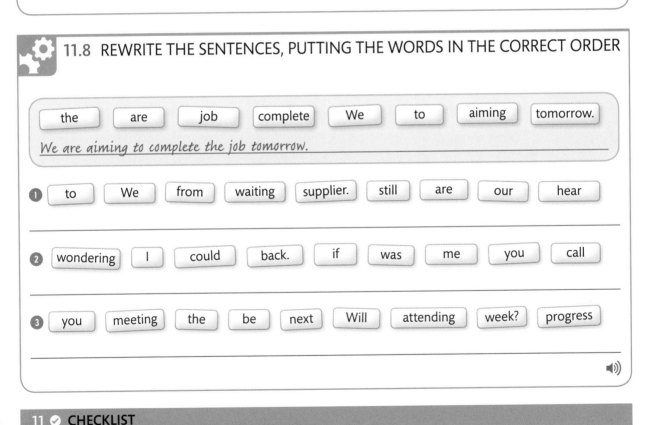

| the | are | job | complete | We | to | aiming | tomorrow. |

We are aiming to complete the job tomorrow.

1 | to | We | from | waiting | supplier. | still | are | our | hear |

2 | wondering | I | could | back. | if | was | me | you | call |

3 | you | meeting | the | be | next | Will | attending | week? | progress |

11 ✓ CHECKLIST

⚙ Continuous tenses ☐   **Aa** Arrangements and schedules ☐   Keeping clients informed ☐

12 Informal communication

Phrasal verbs have two or more parts. They are often used in informal spoken and written English, in things such as messages and requests to co-workers.

⚙ **New language** Phrasal verbs
Aa **Vocabulary** Arrangements and plans
🧩 **New skill** Keeping co-workers informed

12.1 KEY LANGUAGE PHRASAL VERBS

Phrasal verbs consist of a verb followed by at least one particle. Most particles in phrasal verbs are prepositions, and the particle often changes the meaning of the verb.

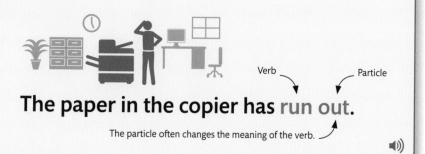

Verb · Particle

The paper in the copier has run out.

The particle often changes the meaning of the verb.

🔊

12.2 FURTHER EXAMPLES PHRASAL VERBS

Could you look into fixing the coffee machine, please?

Welcome back! When would you like to catch up?

Can you deal with the overseas orders?

I'm afraid I have to hang up now.

🔊

12.3 CROSS OUT THE INCORRECT WORDS IN EACH SENTENCE

When should we catch up / ~~off~~ / ~~out~~?

1 I'll look out / up / into the problem now.

2 The printer has run in / out / on of ink.

3 I need to catch / deal / look up with you.

4 Sorry, I have to hang in / up / into now.

5 Could you deal up / out / with this order?

6 I'll see / look / watch into Mr. Li's query.

7 My client just hung / run / ran up on me!

🔊

12.4 LISTEN TO THE AUDIO, THEN NUMBER THE SENTENCES IN THE ORDER YOU HEAR THEM

Nicky leaves a telephone message for her co-worker, Oscar.

A I've got lots to do, so I have to hang up now. ☐

B When one printer runs out of ink, all the others stop working, too. ☐

C It would be nice to meet up sometime soon. ☐

D I just wanted to catch up with you about your problem with the printers. ☑ 1

E I looked into it a bit deeper and discovered the problem. ☐

F It's quite easy to deal with. ☐

Aa 12.5 READ THE EMAIL AND MATCH THE PHRASAL VERBS TO THEIR DEFINITIONS

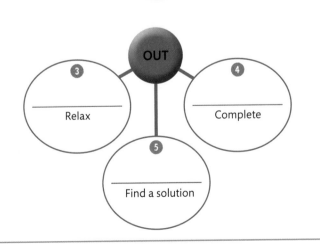

fix up
Arrange

1 _____
Start discussing

2 _____
Arrive

UP

OUT

3 _____
Relax

4 _____
Complete

5 _____
Find a solution

To: André Jennings

Subject: Today

Hi André,

I was just writing to **fix up** a meeting with you to talk about arrangements for next month's sales trip. Maybe we could go for dinner on Friday? We could meet before dinner to **fill out** all the paperwork for the sales meetings and **figure out** the best places to stay during the trip. Then we can **chill out** and eat some food.

We could ask Lucinda to join us. It would be a good opportunity to **bring up** our new sales strategy with her and see what she thinks of it. Hopefully she won't **turn up** late this time!

Let me know your thoughts,
Peter

12.6 KEY LANGUAGE SEPARABLE PHRASAL VERBS

With some phrasal verbs, the object of the sentence can go before or after the particle. The meaning is the same.

The object can go after the particle.

Please could you fill out this form?

Please could you fill this form out?

The object can come between the verb and the particle.

12.7 FURTHER EXAMPLES SEPARABLE PHRASAL VERBS

We have to back up our files every night.
We have to back our files up every night.

Sue's sick today. Let's call off the meeting.
Sue's sick today. Let's call the meeting off.

They're giving out samples of their products.
They're giving samples of their products out.

Please pass on the message to Jess.
Please pass the message on to Jess.

12.8 REWRITE THE SENTENCES BY CHANGING THE POSITION OF THE PARTICLE

Can we **call off** today's meeting?
Can we call today's meeting off?

① James, can you **pass** the message **on** to Zane?

_____

② Welcome to Jo's. Please **fill out** the visitor's form.

_____

③ Can you stand at the exit and **hand out** the leaflets?

_____

④ **Put on** a helmet before entering the site.

_____

⑤ Before I update the software, **back up** your files.

_____

12.9 SAY THE SENTENCES OUT LOUD, FILLING IN THE GAPS USING THE WORDS IN THE PANEL

Every hour I ___back___ my new files ___up___ on my computer.

3 Howard, we should really _____ a meeting _____ for this week.

1 Could you please _____ the message _____ to Gary?

4 After a busy day in the office, I usually _____ _____ at home.

2 I have an important meeting, so I _____ a suit _____ this morning.

| put | chill | ~~back~~ | on | out |
| pass | fix | up | on | ~~up~~ |

---

12 ✓ CHECKLIST

⚙ Phrasal verbs ☐   **Aa** Arrangements and plans ☐   🧩 Keeping co-workers informed ☐

🔄 REVIEW THE ENGLISH YOU HAVE LEARNED IN UNITS 7–12

NEW LANGUAGE	SAMPLE SENTENCE	☑	UNIT
PAST PERFECT AND PAST SIMPLE	Sales of our products had fallen, so we hired a new marketing team.	☐	7.1
PROJECT REPORTS	The following report presents the results of a client satisfaction survey.	☐	7.6
TELEPHONE APOLOGIES	I'm very sorry about the delay. Let's see what we can do.	☐	8.1
PRESENT PERFECT CONTINUOUS	Our delivery company has been experiencing difficulties recently.	☐	8.5
EMAILS TO CO-WORKERS	Please see the timetable for next week's training course attached.	☐	10.1
CONTINUOUS TENSES	We are hoping to give you a full update. I was wondering if we could meet next week.	☐	11.1, 11.5
PHRASAL VERBS	The paper in the copier has run out. Could you please fill this form out?	☐	12.1, 12.6

13.1 PRODUCTION

Everyone on the production line starts and finishes work at the same time.

a production line
[a line of people or machinery in a factory, each making a specific part of a product]

That car was unique. It was a one-off production for a private customer.

a one-off production
[something that is made or produced only once]

The price goes up as the cost of raw materials increases.

raw materials
[the basic substances that are used to make a product]

We can make changes. This is just a prototype.

a prototype
[the first form of a design that can be changed, copied, or developed]

These cars have become much cheaper with mass production.

mass production
[the process of making large numbers of goods, usually in a factory]

These fabrics are much cheaper to manufacture abroad.

to manufacture
[to make a large number of goods, usually in a factory and using machinery]

The bags are expensive because they are all handmade.

handmade
[made by a person without the use of a machine]

The overproduction of these shirts has meant we need to lower the price.

overproduction
[manufacturing too much of something in relation to demand]

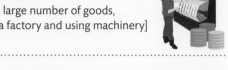

All our toys go through a process of product testing.

product testing
[a process to check that goods meet certain standards]

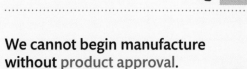

We cannot begin manufacture without product approval.

product approval
[a declaration that a product meets certain standards and is suitable for sale]

The packaging of certain goods is vital for sales.

packaging
[the external wrapping of goods before they are sold]

We arrange shipping all over the world for our clients.

shipping
[moving goods from one place to another]

The painting process starts in this room and takes two days.

a process
[a series of actions or steps that are done in a particular order]

These watches are beautiful, but their production is very labor intensive.

labor intensive
[requiring a lot of human effort to make something]

All the ingredients for this product are ethically sourced.

ethically sourced
[found or bought in a morally acceptable way]

Can you ask the warehouse how many we have available to ship today?

a warehouse
[a place where goods are stored before being shipped to customers or sellers]

We have a lot of stock. We need to sell it before we produce any more.

stock
[goods that a company has made but not yet sold]

With food products, quality control is vital.

quality control
[systems that ensure that products are of a high standard]

The factory makes 200,000 bars of chocolate a day.

a factory
[a building or group of buildings where goods are made]

They have been our main supplier of light bulbs for 20 years.

a supplier
[a company that provides or supplies another company with goods and services]

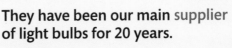

14 Describing a process

The passive voice can be useful when you need to describe how a process works. It emphasizes the action rather than the person or thing doing it.

New language The passive voice
Aa Vocabulary Processes and manufacturing
New skill Discussing how things are done

14.1 KEY LANGUAGE TALKING ABOUT PROCESSES WITH THE PASSIVE VOICE

The present simple passive is formed using "am / is / are" and the past participle.

Our products are designed in London.

The present simple passive describes current or routine events.

The present continuous passive is formed using "am / is / are" plus "being" and the past participle.

The new models are being released before Christmas.

The present continuous passive describes ongoing actions.

The present perfect passive is formed using "have / has" plus "been" and the past participle.

All the latest technologies have been used.

The present perfect passive describes past events that still have an effect on the present.

The past simple passive is formed using "was / were" and the past participle.

Our original model was sold worldwide.

The past simple passive describes a single completed action in the past.

The past continuous passive is formed using "was / were" plus "being" and the past participle.

We tested extensively while it was being redesigned.

The past continuous passive describes ongoing actions in the past.

The past perfect passive describes events that took place before another past event.

The past perfect passive is formed using "had been" and the past participle.

The media had been notified before we announced the launch.

14.2 READ THE ARTICLE AND ANSWER THE QUESTIONS

Potato chips were invented over 100 years ago.
True ✓ False ☐ Not given ☐

1 Chosen potatoes are kept at a steady temperature.
True ☐ False ☐ Not given ☐

2 The biggest potatoes make the best potato chips.
True ☐ False ☐ Not given ☐

3 Potato chips have never come in plastic packaging.
True ☐ False ☐ Not given ☐

4 Chip companies make more money now than ever.
True ☐ False ☐ Not given ☐

5 Chip companies do not monitor packaging styles.
True ☐ False ☐ Not given ☐

BUSINESS TODAY

A slice of history

The essential potato chip: How did we get here?

It is believed that the first potato chips were created at the end of the 19th century. But how are they made? First, golf-ball-sized potatoes are chosen and stored at a constant temperature. The potatoes are then sliced and fried, and additives are used to keep the chips fresh. Potato-chip packaging has been constantly changing. Packets have been made from paper, foil, plastic, and newer, composite materials. The quality of modern packaging is our main focus and is constantly being monitored.

 14.3 CROSS OUT THE INCORRECT WORDS IN EACH SENTENCE

We make everything on site at the Imagicorp plant. All of our products are built / ~~build~~ in Europe.

1 Over the last year, an exciting new line has been developed / develop.

2 This design has been / was patented in 1938. Nobody has ever managed to make a better product!

3 Their new line is being / have been launched next Saturday. Everyone is talking about it.

4 Our factory floor was / is being cleaned before the CEO visited. He was happy things looked good!

5 You don't need to worry about dinner. The food is / had been cooked to order so that it is fresh.

6 The first cars made in this factory were / was sold in the UK in 1972, and worldwide the next year.

7 Our original designers has been / were influenced by Japanese artists.

8 To prepare for the launch, advertising posters are / are being put up around town as we speak.

14.4 KEY LANGUAGE AGENTS IN THE PASSIVE VOICE

"By" can be used to show the person or thing doing the action.

Our CEO will announce the launch soon.

This active sentence emphasizes the person doing the action ("our CEO").

The launch will be announced soon.

In the passive sentence, the action is emphasized and "the launch" is the subject.

The launch will be announced soon by our CEO.

"By" is added to show the person doing the action, while still emphasizing the action itself.

14.5 HOW TO FORM AGENTS IN THE PASSIVE VOICE

SUBJECT	FORM OF "BE"	PAST PARTICIPLE	REST OF SENTENCE	"BY"
The launch	will be	announced	soon	by our CEO.

 14.6 FILL IN THE GAPS USING THE PASSIVE PHRASES IN THE PANEL

How many new models _____*are being produced*_____ ?

1. Their new products _____ on TV now.

2. 80,000 packets _____ in the factory each week.

3. A thousand new cars _____ next week.

4. Our latest gadget _____ by Ronnie Angel.

5. The production line _____ during the summer.

6. Great advances in design _____ recently.

are being promoted

~~are being produced~~

are produced

is stopped

will be sold

have been made

was invented

14.7 REWRITE THE SENTENCES USING THE PASSIVE VOICE, USING "BY" TO SHOW THE AGENT

> Our promotions team markets the product worldwide.
> *The product is marketed worldwide by our promotions team.*

1 Someone checks all the cars before they leave the factory.

_____

2 Maxine invented the new photo app for professional artists.

_____

3 Customers bought all Carl Osric's books on the publication date.

_____

4 Ron buys all our vegetarian ingredients from the market.

_____

5 Samantha checks all of the invoices before they are sent out.

_____

14.8 LISTEN TO THE AUDIO, THEN NUMBER THE PICTURES IN THE ORDER THEY ARE DESCRIBED

A ☐

B ☐ 1

C ☐

D ☐

E ☐

F ☐

G ☐

H ☐

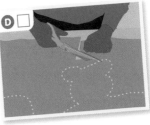

243

14.9 KEY LANGUAGE MODALS IN THE PASSIVE VOICE

Certain modals can be used as set phrases in the passive voice to express ideas such as possibility, ability, likelihood, and obligation.

The importance of product testing can't be overestimated.

[Product testing is very important.]

All products must be approved **before leaving the factory.**

[Products have to meet certain standards before they leave the factory.]

The product must have been damaged **before it was shipped.**

[It seems very likely that the product was broken before it was shipped.]

The shipment could have been packaged **more carefully.**

[The shipment was not packed as carefully as it should have been.]

This device couldn't have been tested **before it went on sale.**

[It seems impossible that the device was tested before it was sold.]

14.10 MATCH THE ACTIVE SENTENCES TO THE PASSIVE SENTENCES WITH THE SAME MEANING

We must not ignore the costs. → The costs can't be ignored.

This picture couldn't have been drawn by Sanjit.

1. Tim must have bought these flowers today.

The price shouldn't have been accepted.

2. You can't mark these down yet. They're new.

These glasses must be packaged carefully.

3. Sanjit could not have drawn this picture.

They can't be marked down yet! They're new.

4. Niamh shouldn't have accepted the price.

The oven has been turned up.

5. You should package these glasses carefully.

These flowers must have been bought today.

6. Nobody should ignore faults in the products.

Faults in the product shouldn't be ignored.

7. Someone has turned the oven up.

14.11 SAY THE SENTENCES OUT LOUD, FILLING IN THE GAPS USING THE WORDS IN THE PANEL

How It's Made

A look at an electric car assembly line.

First, the component parts _____*are delivered*_____ to separate parts of the factory.

1 The chassis parts are placed on the _____ .

2 The engine and radiator _____ by a robot as they are very heavy.

3 The engine and radiator _____ to the chassis by an assembly worker.

4 The bodywork is fully _____ on a separate line.

5 The assembled bodywork is inspected before _____ by a robot.

6 The chassis and bodywork are joined together before the vehicle _____ .

being painted	is checked	~~are delivered~~	assembly line
assembled and welded	are secured		are lifted

15 Describing a product

When describing a product, you will usually use adjectives. You can use more that one adjective, but they must be in a particular order.

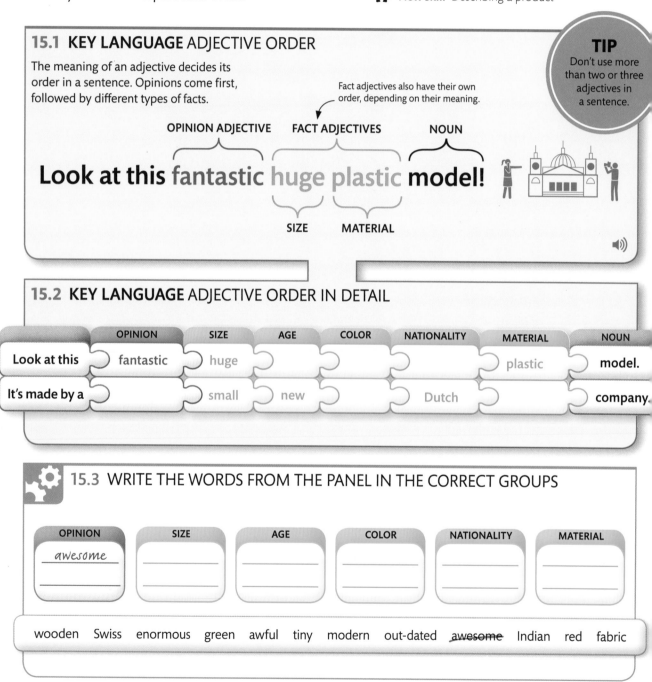

⚙ **New language** Adjective order
Aa Vocabulary Opinion and fact adjectives
🧩 **New skill** Describing a product

15.1 KEY LANGUAGE ADJECTIVE ORDER

The meaning of an adjective decides its order in a sentence. Opinions come first, followed by different types of facts.

Fact adjectives also have their own order, depending on their meaning.

TIP
Don't use more than two or three adjectives in a sentence.

OPINION ADJECTIVE   FACT ADJECTIVES   NOUN

Look at this fantastic huge plastic model!

SIZE   MATERIAL

15.2 KEY LANGUAGE ADJECTIVE ORDER IN DETAIL

	OPINION	SIZE	AGE	COLOR	NATIONALITY	MATERIAL	NOUN
Look at this	fantastic	huge				plastic	model.
It's made by a		small	new		Dutch		company.

15.3 WRITE THE WORDS FROM THE PANEL IN THE CORRECT GROUPS

OPINION	SIZE	AGE	COLOR	NATIONALITY	MATERIAL
awesome					

wooden   Swiss   enormous   green   awful   tiny   modern   out-dated   ~~awesome~~   Indian   red   fabric

15.4 REWRITE THE SENTENCES, PUTTING THE WORDS IN THE CORRECT ORDER

| I | this | blue | version! | new, | love |

I love this new, blue version!

1. | the | you | plastic | seen | Have | desks? | ugly, |

_____

2. | metallic | We're | range | new, | launching | the | tomorrow. |

_____

3. | you | Would | diamond | prefer | ones? | these | tiny, |

_____

15.5 LISTEN TO THE AUDIO AND MARK WHICH THINGS ARE DESCRIBED

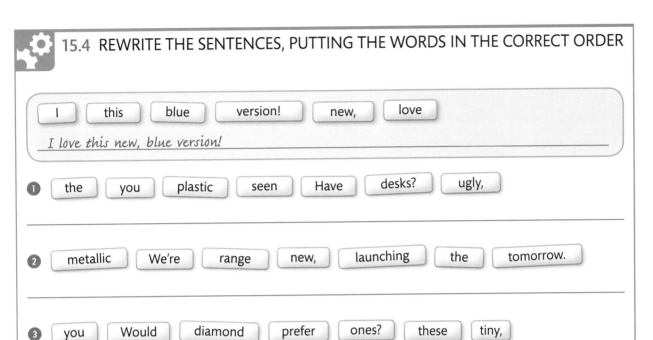

15.6 KEY LANGUAGE SPECIFIC AND GENERAL OPINIONS

General opinion adjectives always come before specific ones. General opinion
adjectives can describe lots of different things. Specific opinion adjectives can
only usually describe a certain type of thing.

OPINION ADJECTIVES   FACT ADJECTIVE

What a nice, friendly new team!

"Nice" is a general opinion
adjective. It can describe
lots of different things.

"Friendly" is a specific opinion
adjective. It usually only
describes people or animals.

15.7 CROSS OUT THE INCORRECT WORD IN EACH SENTENCE

Our catering team is developing a fantastic, ~~friendly~~ / delicious menu for the conference.

1 I'm interested in that incredible / French modern device we saw at the sales fair.

2 Our competitors are still selling those really blue / ugly, large cotton shirts.

3 The office has a profitable / friendly, old black cat that visits regularly.

4 Frances, have you seen these Peruvian silver / small earrings that I brought back?

5 Did you get one of those new plastic / fantastic business cards?

6 A lot of customers have been asking for the new / German red version.

7 My boss has asked me to design a small, paper / fantastic package for the product.

8 I have bought some new leather / large chairs for the boardroom.

White guest towels are cheaper this year.
True ☐ **False** ☐ **Not given** ☑

❶ The Festival towel range is colorful.
True ☐ **False** ☐ **Not given** ☐

❷ There is a discount on Festival towels.
True ☐ **False** ☐ **Not given** ☐

❸ Black tablecloths are a new product.
True ☐ **False** ☐ **Not given** ☐

❹ The kitchen towels are made of paper.
True ☐ **False** ☐ **Not given** ☐

❺ The kitchen towels are made in Egypt.
True ☐ **False** ☐ **Not given** ☐

LARA'S LINEN

We have everything your hotel or restaurant needs, from guest towels through to tablecloths. We are keeping our wonderful, best-selling white guest towels at the same fantastic price as last year. But this year we are also adding a range of stunning, multicolored "Festival" towels to our Hotel range. We are also adding to our wonderful Egyptian cotton tableware range. As well as the usual black and white ranges, we now offer burgundy, brown, and olive-colored tablecloths and napkins. Don't forget to check out our hard-wearing, Turkish, cotton kitchen towels and aprons in the Kitchen section of the brochure.

15.9 SAY THE SENTENCES OUT LOUD, FILLING IN THE GAPS USING THE WORDS IN THE PANEL

His marketing strategy is a _fantastic_ , intelligent idea.

❶ We offer great, _____ food that people can afford.

❷ Look at that _____ new billboard across the street.

❸ I love buying _____ wooden furniture for the office.

❹ My boss drives a tiny _____ car to work. It's definitely easy to spot!

❺ We aim to offer awesome, _____ customer service at all times.

| delicious | enormous | ~~fantastic~~ |
| friendly | green | antique |

16.1 MARKETING AND ADVERTISING

advertising agency

advertisement / ad

copywriter

write copy

brand

logo

slogan / tagline

unique selling point / USP

promote

publicity

press release

door-to-door sales

poster

billboard

sponsor

merchandise

consumer

market research

sales pitch

free sample

special offer

leaflet / flyer

direct mail

coupons

online marketing

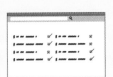
online survey

social media

word of mouth

television advertising

radio advertising

telemarketing

small ads / personal ads

17 Marketing a product

You can use a variety of adjectives and adverbs to describe the key features when marketing a product or service. Not all adjectives can be modified in the same way.

⚙ **New language** Adjectives and adverbs
Aa Vocabulary Descriptive adjectives
🧩 **New skill** Modifying descriptions of products

17.1 KEY LANGUAGE NON-GRADABLE ADJECTIVES

Most adjectives are known as "gradable" adjectives. They can be modified with grading adverbs, such as "slightly," "very," and "extremely." Non-gradable adjectives cannot be modified in this way.

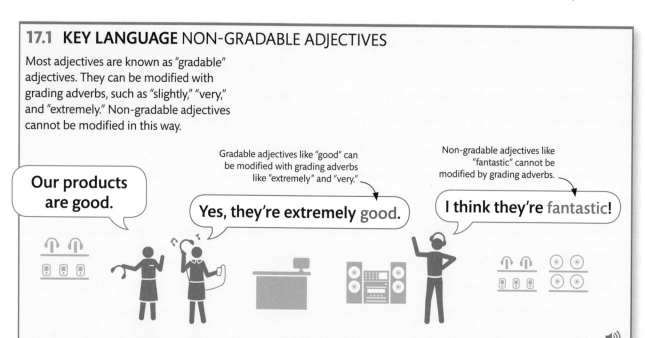

Gradable adjectives like "good" can be modified with grading adverbs like "extremely" and "very."

Non-gradable adjectives like "fantastic" cannot be modified by grading adverbs.

Our products are good.

Yes, they're extremely good.

I think they're fantastic!

17.2 FURTHER EXAMPLES NON-GRADABLE ADJECTIVES

Non-gradable adjectives fall into three categories: extreme, absolute, and classifying.

The demand is enormous.

Extreme adjectives are stronger versions of gradable adjectives. "Enormous" has the sense of "extremely big."

They have a unique design.

Absolute adjectives like "unique" describe fixed qualities or states.

Our customer base is American.

Classifying adjectives are used to say that something is of a specific class or type.

17.3 WRITE THE ADJECTIVES FROM THE PANEL IN THE CORRECT CATEGORIES

EXTREME	ABSOLUTE	CLASSIFYING
awful	*unique*	*organic*
_____ _____	_____ _____	_____ _____
_____ _____	_____ _____	_____ _____

fantastic   ~~awful~~   impossible   tiny   right   digital   ~~organic~~   disgusting

perfect   industrial   wrong   electronic   ~~unique~~   enormous   chemical

🔊

17.4 READ THE ARTICLE AND ANSWER THE QUESTIONS

> The author owns his own marketing company.
> **True** ☐ **False** ☐ **Not given** ☑

1 Give readers a reason for buying your product.
True ☐ **False** ☐ **Not given** ☐

2 Deals of the Day can encourage people to buy.
True ☐ **False** ☐ **Not given** ☐

3 Put key words in a different color text.
True ☐ **False** ☐ **Not given** ☐

4 The article only talks about newsletters.
True ☐ **False** ☐ **Not given** ☐

5 Readers do not trust the words "Free" and "New."
True ☐ **False** ☐ **Not given** ☐

6 The article recommends setting up a website.
True ☐ **False** ☐ **Not given** ☐

MARKETING WEEKLY

Writing for buyers

Rachid Barbery talks about writing effective marketing texts

LIMITED OFFER

DEAL OF THE DAY

Research has shown that there are certain techniques you can use to turn your readers into buyers. First, repeat the positive facts about the product to make them more believable. Make sure you explain why readers would benefit from buying your product compared to others. For example, say that your digital camera weighs 100g less than similar ones and has a unique rubber grip because it makes it easier to carry when traveling. Use the word "you" a lot to help make the connection between the reader and the product. It's also a good idea to promote limited time offers or limited editions as these create an extra reason to buy your product now. This could be a Deal of the Day or Special Edition Color. Using key words in your newsletters and the front pages of your websites or leaflets, such as "Free" and "New" always creates interest and a positive response in readers.

17.5 KEY LANGUAGE NON-GRADING ADVERBS

Some adverbs can be used to qualify non-gradable
adjectives. These are called "non-grading adverbs,"
and often mean "entirely" or "almost entirely."
They cannot usually be used with gradable adjectives.

The demand is
absolutely enormous!

They have a totally
new **design.**

Our customer base is
completely American.

17.6 FURTHER EXAMPLES NON-GRADING ADVERBS

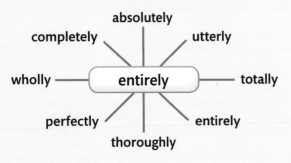

absolutely
completely — utterly
wholly — **entirely** — totally
perfectly — entirely
thoroughly

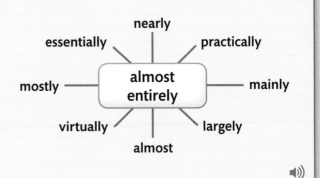

nearly
essentially — practically
mostly — **almost entirely** — mainly
virtually — largely
almost

17.7 MARK THE SENTENCES THAT ARE CORRECT

The product is utterly good. ☐
The product is utterly amazing. ☑

❶ The new gadget is completely digital. ☐
The new gadget is completely bad. ☐

❷ This draft design is practically perfect. ☐
This draft design is practically all right. ☐

❸ The client said it was totally fantastic. ☐
The client said it was totally nice. ☐

❹ His decision to invest was entirely right. ☐
His decision to invest was maybe right. ☐

❺ This area of town is largely industrial. ☐
This area of town is large industrial. ☐

17.8 KEY LANGUAGE "REALLY," "FAIRLY," AND "PRETTY"

A few adverbs can be used with both gradable and non-gradable adjectives. They are "really" (meaning "very much"), and "pretty" and "fairly" (both meaning "quite a lot, but not very").

What you need is a really { good / brilliant } idea.

Gradable

Non-gradable

You need to be fairly { confident / certain } it works.

Inventing a new product is pretty { difficult / impossible } .

17.9 LISTEN TO THE AUDIO AND ANSWER THE QUESTIONS

Two marketing executives are discussing products at a trade fair.

Sales of Vietnamese instant meals are...
quite poor. ☐
fairly good. ☐
really good. ✓

❶ The target market for the instant meal range is...
mainly European. ☐
entirely European. ☐
mostly Asian. ☐

❷ How does Marion feel about selling to the European market?
Really confident ☐
Pretty confident ☐
Totally confident ☐

❸ What does Sean think about the taste of the meals?
Fairly tasty ☐
Pretty tasty ☐
Absolutely delicious ☐

17 ✓ CHECKLIST

⚙ Adjectives and adverbs ☐   **Aa** Descriptive adjectives ☐   Modifying descriptions of products ☐

18 Advertising and branding

When you want to tell people about your company, product, or brand, intensifiers like "enough," "too," "so," and "such" can help communicate your point.

✿ **New language** Intensifiers
Aa Vocabulary "Enough," "too," "so," and "such"
🧩 **New skill** Adding emphasis to descriptions

18.1 KEY LANGUAGE "ENOUGH" AND "TOO"

"Enough" can be used after an adjective or adverb to show that it's the right degree.

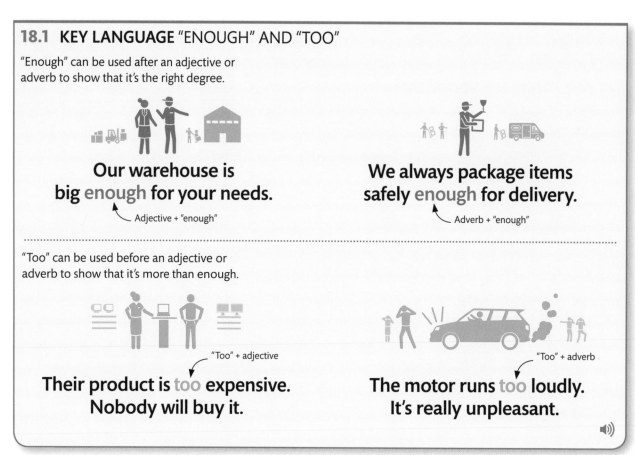

Our warehouse is big enough for your needs.

Adjective + "enough"

We always package items safely enough for delivery.

Adverb + "enough"

"Too" can be used before an adjective or adverb to show that it's more than enough.

"Too" + adjective

"Too" + adverb

Their product is too expensive. Nobody will buy it.

The motor runs too loudly. It's really unpleasant.

🔊

18.2 MARK THE SENTENCES THAT ARE CORRECT

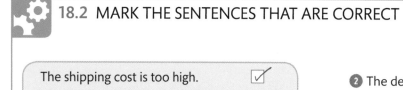

The shipping cost is too high. ✓
The shipping cost is enough high. ☐

❷ The delivery times are too slowly. ☐
The delivery times are too slow. ☐

❶ Is the office big enough for us? ☐
Is the office enough big for us? ☐

❸ Are these shelves strong enough? ☐
Are these shelves too strong? ☐

🔊

256

18.3 LISTEN TO THE AUDIO AND MARK WHICH THINGS ARE DESCRIBED

18.4 READ THE ARTICLE AND ANSWER THE QUESTIONS

The ad suggests images are often too small.
True ☐   False ☐   Not given ☑

❶ Over half of clients view websites on computers.
True ☐   False ☐   Not given ☐

❷ A poor website could mean you lose customers.
True ☐   False ☐   Not given ☐

❸ 50% of consumers shop online.
True ☐   False ☐   Not given ☐

❹ Mobiopt Web focuses on what the website looks like and how it works.
True ☐   False ☐   Not given ☐

❺ You have to pay Mobiopt Web for a quote.
True ☐   False ☐   Not given ☐

Mobiopt Web

HOME | PORTFOLIO | ABOUT | CONTACT

What we do

Have you ever considered what your website looks like on a mobile device? Is the text big enough to read? Are the images too small to showcase your fantastic products? Research says that over 50 percent of your potential clients are likely to use mobile devices to view your site. You need it to look and work perfectly on these devices, otherwise your customer may soon become someone else's.

At Mobiopt Web, we work with you to ensure that not only does your website look great, but that it also does exactly what you and your clients want it to.

Contact us now for a free quotation on your new web design.

18.5 KEY LANGUAGE "SO" AND "SUCH"

"Such" can be added before a noun to add emphasis. It can also be added before an adjective and noun combination.

The new model was such a success.

"Such" + "a/an" + noun

It was such an important meeting.

"Such" + "a/an" + adjective + noun

"So" can be added before an adjective or an adverb to add emphasis.

Initial reviews are so important.

"So" + adjective

The product launch went so well!

"So" + adverb

18.6 REWRITE THE SENTENCES, PUTTING THE WORDS IN THE CORRECT ORDER

| price | The | high! | so | is |

The price is so high!

④ | My | so | is | ambitious. | boss |

_____

① | such | It's | a | product. | great |

_____

⑤ | phones | so | cheap. | Their | are |

_____

② | boring. | was | so | meeting | The |

_____

⑥ | so | Her | is | company | big! |

_____

③ | such | His | was | surprise. | news | a |

_____

⑦ | surprise! | was | such | Our | launch | a |

_____

There is **such** / ~~so~~ a big crowd at the trade fair this year!

1 The slogan is far **such** / too complicated. We need to simplify it.

2 They have created such / **enough** a brilliant poster campaign.

3 We haven't done too / **enough** market research. We need to understand our consumers.

4 Our supervisor is **such** / too a creative person. She designed our new logo.

5 Marion is such / **so** persuasive when she delivers a sales pitch.

---

18 ✔ CHECKLIST

⚙ Intensifiers ☐   **Aa** "Enough," "too," "so," and "such" ☐   🧩 Adding emphasis to descriptions ☐

♻ REVIEW THE ENGLISH YOU HAVE LEARNED IN UNITS 13–18

NEW LANGUAGE	SAMPLE SENTENCE	☑	UNIT
DESCRIBING A PROCESS WITH THE PASSIVE VOICE	**Our products** are designed **in London.** **Our original model** was sold **worldwide.**	☐	14.1
DESCRIBING A PRODUCT WITH CORRECT ADJECTIVE ORDER	**Look at this** fantastic, huge plastic **model!**	☐	15.1, 15.2
SPECIFIC AND GENERAL OPINIONS	**What a** nice, friendly **new team!**	☐	15.6
NON-GRADABLE ADJECTIVES AND NON-GRADING ADVERBS	**They have a** new **design.** **They have a** totally **new design.**	☐	17.1 17.5
"ENOUGH" AND "TOO"	**Our warehouse is big** enough **for your needs.** **Their product is** too **expensive.**	☐	18.1
"SO" AND "SUCH" FOR EMPHASIS	**The new model was** such **a success.** **Initial reviews are** so **important.**	☐	18.5

19 Advice and suggestions

English uses modal verbs such as "could," "should," and "must" for advice or suggestions. They can be used to help co-workers in difficult or stressful situations.

⚙ **New language** Modal verbs for advice
Aa Vocabulary Workplace pressures
🧩 **New skill** Giving advice

19.1 KEY LANGUAGE GIVING ADVICE

English uses "could," "should," and "must" to vary the strength of advice given.

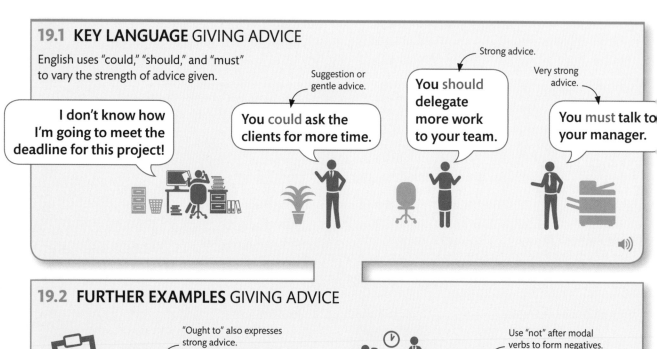

I don't know how I'm going to meet the deadline for this project!

Suggestion or gentle advice.

You could ask the clients for more time.

Strong advice.

You should delegate more work to your team.

Very strong advice.

You must talk to your manager.

19.2 FURTHER EXAMPLES GIVING ADVICE

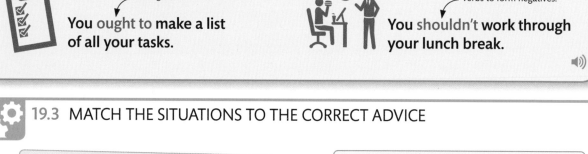

"Ought to" also expresses strong advice.

You ought to make a list of all your tasks.

Use "not" after modal verbs to form negatives.

You shouldn't work through your lunch break.

19.3 MATCH THE SITUATIONS TO THE CORRECT ADVICE

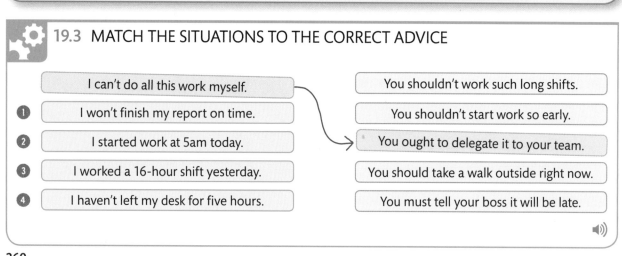

I can't do all this work myself.

You shouldn't work such long shifts.

❶ I won't finish my report on time.

You shouldn't start work so early.

❷ I started work at 5am today.

You ought to delegate it to your team.

❸ I worked a 16-hour shift yesterday.

You should take a walk outside right now.

❹ I haven't left my desk for five hours.

You must tell your boss it will be late.

19.4 FILL IN THE GAPS USING THE PHRASES IN THE PANEL

You really need a break. You _____*shouldn't take*_____ work home.

1 My wife said I _____ yoga and relaxation techniques.

2 You _____ working right away if you feel sick.

3 You _____ a break if you're really tired.

4 You _____ exhausted at the beginning of the week.

5 You _____ some of your work to your assistant.

~~shouldn't take~~

ought to take

could try

shouldn't feel

must delegate

should stop

🔊

19.5 REWRITE THE SENTENCES, CORRECTING THE ERRORS

You **ought** talk to your manager.
You ought to talk to your manager.

1 You **are ought** to relax more.

_____

2 You **must to stop** taking work home every day.

_____

3 He **could trying** to delegate more tasks.

_____

4 You **shouldn't to worry** so much about work.

_____

5 She **shoulds talk** to her colleagues.

_____

6 He **ought to quits** his job if he hates it.

_____

🔊

19.6 LISTEN TO THE AUDIO AND MARK WHETHER KATE ADVISES GIORGOS TO DO THE ACTIVITY IN EACH PICTURE

Yes ✓   No ☐

1 Yes ☐   No ☐

2 Yes ☐   No ☐

3 Yes ☐   No ☐

4 Yes ☐   No ☐

19.7 KEY LANGUAGE MAKING SUGGESTIONS

Use "What about...?" with a gerund or "Why don't we...?" with a base verb to make suggestions.

What about hiring
Why don't we hire } **more staff?**

19.8 HOW TO FORM SUGGESTIONS

"WHAT ABOUT"	GERUND	REST OF SENTENCE
What about	hiring	
"WHY DON'T WE"	BASE VERB	more staff?
Why don't we	hire	

19.9 FURTHER EXAMPLES MAKING SUGGESTIONS

 What about working from home on Fridays?

 Why don't we organize a team lunch?

 What about opening a new store?

 Why don't we file these documents?

19.10 USE THE CHART TO CREATE SIX CORRECT SENTENCES AND SAY THEM OUT LOUD

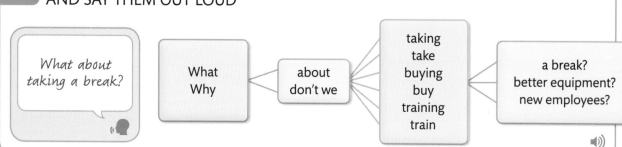

What about taking a break?

What	about	taking	a break?
Why	don't we	take	better equipment?
		buying	new employees?
		buy	
		training	
		train	

19.11 CROSS OUT THE INCORRECT WORD IN EACH SENTENCE

What about ~~train~~ / training our staff better?

1 Why don't we buy / buying new chairs?

2 Why don't we go / going for a walk outside?

3 What about drink / drinking less coffee?

4 Why don't we provide / providing free fruit?

5 What about make / making a list of your tasks?

6 What about delegate / delegating this to Jo?

7 Why don't we ask / asking Paul to help us?

19.12 READ THE ARTICLE AND ANSWER THE QUESTIONS

A heavy workload can affect your health.
True ✓ **False** ☐

1 You must find out what makes you stressed.
True ☐ **False** ☐

2 When you are stressed, you can concentrate.
True ☐ **False** ☐

3 Exercise can help you deal with stress.
True ☐ **False** ☐

4 You should work through your lunch break.
True ☐ **False** ☐

5 It's important to get a good night's sleep.
True ☐ **False** ☐

6 You shouldn't tell people how you feel.
True ☐ **False** ☐

YOUR HEALTH

Stressed out at work?

Our experts give advice about coping with a busy workload

To protect your health from the effects of a heavy workload, you must discover why you feel stressed at work. Then you should learn to recognize signs of excessive stress, such as:
- feeling depressed
- problems sleeping
- difficulty concentrating
- headaches.

Next, you ought to develop positive coping strategies such as exercising and eating well. Have a real break at lunchtime. This in turn will help you sleep better and longer. What about making your night-time routine and your bedroom more relaxing? Sleep is very important, so you shouldn't miss out on it. Finally, you should talk to others about your feelings.

20.1 MANAGEMENT AND LEADERSHIP

Every year I have an appraisal with my manager.

an appraisal / a performance review
[an interview to discuss an employee's performance]

We get a $500 sales bonus if we meet our targets.

a bonus
[money added to a person's wages as a reward for good performance]

I was promoted this year, so I have my own office.

to be promoted
[to be given a more senior position within a company]

My boss is really pleased with my performance this year.

performance
[how well a person carries out tasks]

20.2 SKILLS AND ABILITIES

organization

IT / computing

administration

problem-solving

numeracy

customer service

interpersonal skills

leadership

public speaking

written communication

initiative

telephone manner

Our manager has to approve this before it goes to the client.

to approve
[to officially confirm something meets the required standards]

My team leader allocates tasks at the beginning of each week.

to allocate a task
[to give a task to somebody]

I like to delegate tasks to give my co-workers a variety of work.

to delegate
[to give work or tasks to a person in a position junior to you]

I have to designate a colleague as the main first aider in the office.

to designate
[to choose somebody to take on a particular role]

data analysis

decision-making

teamwork

fast learner

research

fluent in languages

attention to detail

negotiating

work well under pressure

able to drive

project management

time management

21 Talking about abilities

To talk about people's skills, for example in a performance review, you can use various modal verbs to express present, past, and future ability.

⚙ **New language** Modal verbs for abilities
Aa Vocabulary Workplace skills
🧩 **New skill** Describing abilities

21.1 KEY LANGUAGE TALKING ABOUT PRESENT ABILITY

Use "can," "can't," and "cannot" to talk about people's skills and abilities in the present.

Jasmine's team **can finish** the job really quickly.

21.2 FURTHER EXAMPLES TALKING ABOUT PRESENT ABILITY

Umar **can create** beautiful flower arrangements.

Stuart **can't cook** in a professional kitchen.

Negative form of "can." English also uses "cannot."

I **can fix** your car by the end of the day.

They **can't work** together without arguing.

21.3 FILL IN THE GAPS USING "CAN" OR "CAN'T"

Alastair has excellent IT skills. He _____*can*_____ create computer programs and apps.

① She doesn't like meeting new people. She _____ work in the HR department.

② Shaun _____ work really well with new employees, so he should help run our training course.

③ Have you seen her brilliant photographs? She _____ create our posters and flyers.

④ Lydia failed her driving test, so, unfortunately, she _____ drive the delivery van.

21.4 KEY LANGUAGE TALKING ABOUT PAST ABILITY

Use "could" to talk about abilities in the past.
The negative form is "couldn't" or "could not."

My old team could work really well, but my new team can't concentrate.

PAST   NOW

I used to be so nervous that I couldn't speak in public, but now I can give presentations.

PAST   NOW

🔊

 21.5 REWRITE THE SENTENCES, CORRECTING THE ERRORS

> For years she can't drive but now she has passed her test.
> *For years she couldn't drive but now she has passed her test.*

❶ Peter can't use the new coffee machine. He didn't know how it worked.

_____

❷ Varinder could write reports very well at first, but she can now that she's had more practice.

_____

❸ No one in the office can read his handwriting. It was awful.

_____

❹ Bill was the only person who can't figure out how to use the photocopier.

_____

🔊

21.6 KEY LANGUAGE TALKING ABOUT FUTURE POTENTIAL

English uses "could" to talk about people's future abilities and potential. In this context, "could" can be followed by most English verbs.

Use "could" before most verbs to talk about possible future situations.

If Felipe keeps on working hard, he could become head chef.

Jenny could reach the top of our company's sales rankings.

You can also use "would" followed by "do," "make," or "be" to talk about future potential. "Would" is stronger than "could," and suggests that something is more likely to happen.

Use "do" or "make" after "would" to talk about future potential.

Kim is good at training people. She would make an excellent team leader.

Liz is really polite. She would do well in the customer services department.

21.7 MARK WHETHER THE STATEMENTS REFER TO PAST OR FUTURE ABILITY

You could be head of your department.
Past ☐ **Future** ☑

1 She would make a great team leader.
Past ☐ **Future** ☐

2 He couldn't cook before his training.
Past ☐ **Future** ☐

3 He would do well in a smaller team.
Past ☐ **Future** ☐

4 Ray could get along with the old CEO.
Past ☐ **Future** ☐

5 Fiona could do better if she tried.
Past ☐ **Future** ☐

21.8 LISTEN TO THE AUDIO AND ANSWER THE QUESTIONS

Shona is having her annual performance review with her manager.

Shona's manager wants to talk about her past.
True ☐ **False** ☐ **Not given** ☑

① Nick is pleased with Shona's work.
True ☐ **False** ☐ **Not given** ☐

② Shona has worked there for five years.
True ☐ **False** ☐ **Not given** ☐

③ Shona will get a $500 bonus.
True ☐ **False** ☐ **Not given** ☐

④ Shona can't work well with new staff.
True ☐ **False** ☐ **Not given** ☐

⑤ Shona wouldn't be a good team leader.
True ☐ **False** ☐ **Not given** ☐

21.9 CROSS OUT THE INCORRECT WORD IN EACH SENTENCE, THEN SAY THE SENTENCES OUT LOUD

You're an excellent sales assistant, and you ~~can't~~ / would do well in the marketing team.

① James's team was weak, but he's trained them well and now they can / can't do anything.

② We think that you are really creative and couldn't / would make a great addition to the PR team.

③ I don't know what is wrong with me today. I can / can't get anything finished.

④ My confidence is much better now. Before, I would / couldn't talk in public.

21 ✓ CHECKLIST

⚙ Modal verbs for abilities ☐   **Aa** Workplace skills ☐   🧩 Describing abilities ☐

22 Comparing and contrasting

In team discussions, discourse markers can ease the flow of conversation. They can help link similar or contrasting ideas, or connect an action to a result.

⚙ **New language** Discourse markers
Aa Vocabulary Teamwork and team building
🧩 **New skill** Expressing your ideas

22.1 KEY LANGUAGE EXPRESSING SIMILAR IDEAS

Some discourse markers link ideas that are similar to each other.

This training is useful for your day-to-day work. It is also fun.

Team A completed the task very quickly. Team B were equally successful.

Laziness is a terrible trait for a team member. Dishonesty is very bad, too.

It is important to say what we all think. We should listen to each other as well.

22.2 KEY LANGUAGE EXPRESSING CONTRASTING IDEAS

Some discourse markers link contrasting ideas.

The training today was useful. However, yesterday's task was pointless.

Although Team A completed the task quickly, Team B didn't finish it.

Some people want to run a team, while others want to be team members.

Laziness is a terrible trait in a team, whereas hard work is excellent.

22.3 CROSS OUT THE INCORRECT WORD IN EACH SENTENCE

All staff should follow the dress code for the training. Please be on time, ~~while~~ / too.

 ❶ **Although** / **Equally** I attended the training session, I'm not sure I learned very much.

 ❷ You got a high score for the IT test, and you've done **equally** / **while** well on the team-building course.

 ❸ Team A built a small boat out of plastic bottles, **as well** / **whereas** Team B used wood to make theirs.

 ❹ The training day is a great way to learn new skills. It's **also** / **however** a good way to get to know people.

22.4 LISTEN TO THE AUDIO AND ANSWER THE QUESTIONS

 A team-building coach is giving feedback on two teams' performances.

The coach says the team-building days are...
challenging and tiring. ☐
challenging but rewarding. ☐
challenging and fun. ☑

❶ At the beginning of the team-building day, the participants...
walked across bridges over a river. ☐
walked across bridges high in the air. ☐
made ladders to climb up trees. ☐

❷ This task challenged the participants to...
overcome fear and help each other. ☐
deal with a fear of heights. ☐
learn how to build rope bridges. ☐

 ❸ Members of Team Bear were...
the tallest and the quickest. ☐
the tallest and the most scared. ☐
the tallest, whereas Team Lion were slowest. ☐

❹ Members of Team Bear helped each other while members of Team Lion...
disagreed with each other. ☐
worked too slowly. ☐
raced each other to the finish. ☐

❺ In the future, Team Lion should...
help Team Bear to be less afraid. ☐
argue less and work faster. ☐
work more slowly and listen to their teammates. ☐

22.5 KEY LANGUAGE TALKING ABOUT RESULTS

Some discourse markers link an action or situation with its result.

Less formal discourse markers.

The training days are useful. { As a result, For this reason, Consequently, As a consequence, } everyone attends them.

More formal discourse markers.

22.6 MARK THE SENTENCES THAT ARE CORRECT

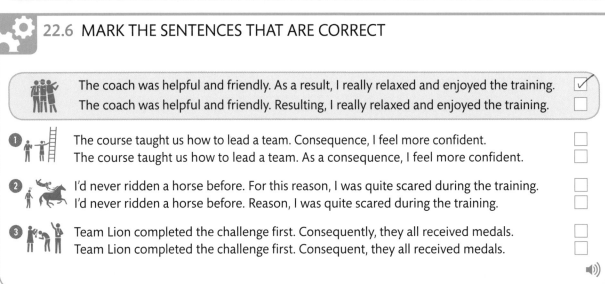

The coach was helpful and friendly. As a result, I really relaxed and enjoyed the training. ✓
The coach was helpful and friendly. Resulting, I really relaxed and enjoyed the training. ☐

❶ The course taught us how to lead a team. Consequence, I feel more confident. ☐
The course taught us how to lead a team. As a consequence, I feel more confident. ☐

❷ I'd never ridden a horse before. For this reason, I was quite scared during the training. ☐
I'd never ridden a horse before. Reason, I was quite scared during the training. ☐

❸ Team Lion completed the challenge first. Consequently, they all received medals. ☐
Team Lion completed the challenge first. Consequent, they all received medals. ☐

22.7 MATCH THE BEGINNINGS OF THE STATEMENTS TO THE CORRECT ENDINGS

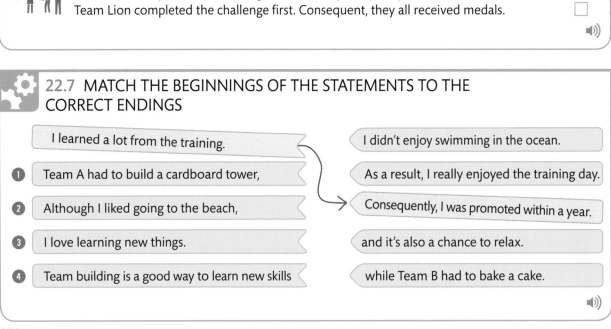

I learned a lot from the training.

❶ Team A had to build a cardboard tower,

❷ Although I liked going to the beach,

❸ I love learning new things.

❹ Team building is a good way to learn new skills

I didn't enjoy swimming in the ocean.

As a result, I really enjoyed the training day.

Consequently, I was promoted within a year.

and it's also a chance to relax.

while Team B had to bake a cake.

22.8 READ THE ARTICLE AND ANSWER THE QUESTIONS

BUILDING A TEAM

CEO Lucia Gomez talks to us about team building

We send all our employees on team-building courses at least once a year. Our staff have gone on team-building treasure hunts, and they've also completed obstacle courses. However, what activity they

Activities are good for morale

do isn't so important. What matters is that they get out of the office and do something that requires them to communicate effectively, and support and help each other, too. It's quite easy to spot employees who are natural-born leaders during these activities. We sometimes identify future managers in this way and put them on our fast-track management-training program.

> Lucia's staff do team building every year.
> **True** ☑ **False** ☐ **Not given** ☐

❶ Lucia's staff have learned how to sail.
True ☐ **False** ☐ **Not given** ☐

❷ Team building takes place away from work.
True ☐ **False** ☐ **Not given** ☐

❸ The choice of activity is very important.
True ☐ **False** ☐ **Not given** ☐

❹ During team building, staff work with new people.
True ☐ **False** ☐ **Not given** ☐

❺ Lucia can identify which employees are leaders.
True ☐ **False** ☐ **Not given** ☐

22.9 SAY THE SENTENCES OUT LOUD, CORRECTING THE ERRORS

> This task is useful. It's however fun.
>> *This task is useful. It's also fun.*

❶ This course will teach you new skills. It will help you to get to know each other whereas.

❷ Equally Team B completed the task first, they had some major communication problems.

❸ By doing this task, we'll not only identify the team's weaknesses, but while its strengths.

❹ Team A worked together very well. Team B were whereas cooperative.

---

22 ✓ CHECKLIST

⚙ Discourse markers ☐   **Aa** Teamwork and team building ☐   🧩 Expressing your ideas ☐

23 Planning events

Many English verbs that are used to give opinions or talk about plans, intentions, and arrangements are followed by a gerund or an infinitive.

⚙ **New language** Verb patterns
Aa Vocabulary Corporate entertainment
🧩 **New skill** Talking about business events

23.1 KEY LANGUAGE VERBS AND GERUNDS / INFINITIVES

Some English verbs are followed by gerunds.

Verb ⟶   Gerund ⟶

I really enjoy entertaining new clients at our company parties.

Other verbs, often those that express plans or intentions, are followed by an infinitive.

Verb ⟶   Infinitive ⟶

Our clients expect to have high-quality accommodation.

23.2 HOW TO FORM VERBS AND GERUNDS / INFINITIVES

START OF SENTENCE	VERB	GERUND	REST OF SENTENCE
I really	enjoy	entertaining	new clients.

START OF SENTENCE	VERB	INFINITIVE	REST OF SENTENCE
Our clients	expect	to have	high-quality accommodation.

23.3 FURTHER EXAMPLES VERBS AND GERUNDS / INFINITIVES

 I'll consider organizing the refreshments for our guests.

 We must keep reminding clients of our product range.

 Sandeep has offered to welcome our visitors.

 We hope to impress our clients at the product launch.

23.4 CROSS OUT THE INCORRECT WORDS IN EACH SENTENCE

You need ~~being~~ / to be very organized to plan a successful business event.

1. Mara has offered organizing / to organize the accommodation for our guests.

2. I keep suggesting / to suggest that our company should organize a golf day, but my boss disagrees.

3. We like offering / to offer our clients a wide range of food at our conferences.

4. I enjoy helping / to help out at company open days because I get to meet lots of people.

5. Before I start planning, I usually make a list of all the customers I want inviting / to invite.

6. I expect staying / to stay late tonight to help Martina decorate the conference hall.

23.5 READ THE ADVERTISEMENT AND WRITE ANSWERS TO THE QUESTIONS AS FULL SENTENCES

Which city is the SmartTech Fair in?
The SmartTech Fair is in Tokyo.

1. What year did the SmartTech Fair open?

2. What is smart health technology helping to do?

3. What could self-driving cars do?

4. How can you show interest in attending an event?

5. How can you buy tickets in advance?

TECHNOLOGY WEEKLY

Don't miss this year's SmartTech Fair!

Based in Tokyo, SmartTech Fair is one of the biggest IT fairs in the world. Established in 1987, each year's show is bigger and better than the last!

Don't miss out on these exciting seminars

CompuHealth seminar: Our industry expert examines how smart technology is helping us to live healthier lives.

Self-driving cars: Learn how these cutting-edge vehicles could shape the future of the car industry.

Register your interest online, and buy tickets in advance from the SmartTech website.

23.6 KEY LANGUAGE VERBS PLUS GERUND OR INFINITIVE (CHANGE IN MEANING)

Some verbs change their meaning depending
on the form of the verb that follows them.

**You remember meeting David, don't
you? He's the CEO of Unodom.**

[You have met David before. Do you remember?]

**You must remember to meet David to
make plans for the conference.**

[You must remember that you have to meet David.]

23.7 FURTHER EXAMPLES VERBS PLUS GERUND OR INFINITIVE (CHANGE IN MEANING)

In general, the gerund is often used for an action that happens before,
or at the same time as, that of the main verb. The infinitive is used to
describe an action that happens after the main verb's action.

VERB + GERUND	VERB + INFINITIVE

**I stopped reading the timetable
because my manager called me.**

[I was reading the timetable, but then I stopped.]

**I stopped to read the timetable
for our team training day.**

[I stopped what I was doing to read the timetable.]

**Sally went on talking all evening.
I hope you weren't bored.**

[Sally was talking for a long time.]

**Sally prepared her presentation, and went on
to talk about the company's new branding.**

[Sally gave the talk after she had prepared it.]

**I regret telling you that I can't come to dinner
with the clients. I can see that you're angry.**

[I wish I hadn't told you that I can't come to dinner.]

**I regret to tell you that I can't come to dinner
with the clients. I'm really sorry.**

[I'm sorry, but I can't come to dinner.]

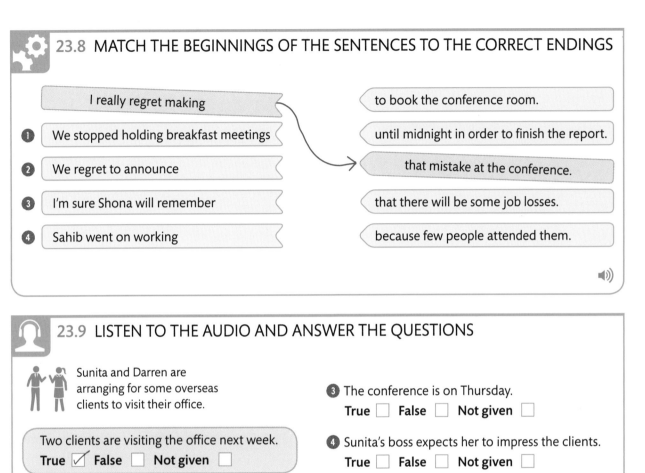

23.8 MATCH THE BEGINNINGS OF THE SENTENCES TO THE CORRECT ENDINGS

I really regret making → that mistake at the conference.

1 We stopped holding breakfast meetings

2 We regret to announce

3 I'm sure Shona will remember

4 Sahib went on working

to book the conference room.

until midnight in order to finish the report.

that mistake at the conference.

that there will be some job losses.

because few people attended them.

23.9 LISTEN TO THE AUDIO AND ANSWER THE QUESTIONS

Sunita and Darren are arranging for some overseas clients to visit their office.

Two clients are visiting the office next week.
True ✓ False ☐ Not given ☐

1 Darren is not going to the meetings.
True ☐ False ☐ Not given ☐

2 The conference is about healthcare products.
True ☐ False ☐ Not given ☐

3 The conference is on Thursday.
True ☐ False ☐ Not given ☐

4 Sunita's boss expects her to impress the clients.
True ☐ False ☐ Not given ☐

5 It is Mr. Yamada's first visit to the US.
True ☐ False ☐ Not given ☐

6 They may go sightseeing with the clients.
True ☐ False ☐ Not given ☐

23.10 USE THE CHART TO CREATE NINE CORRECT SENTENCES AND SAY THEM OUT LOUD

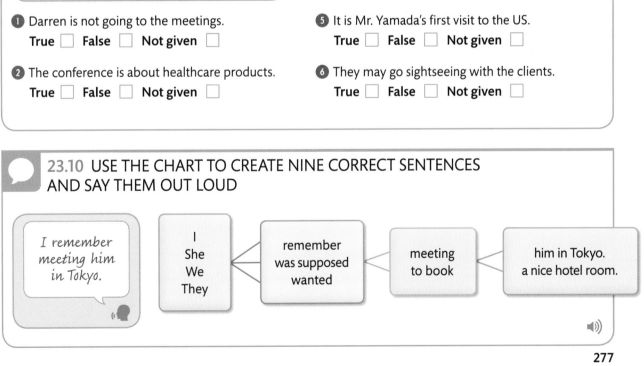

I remember meeting him in Tokyo.

| I / She / We / They | remember / was supposed / wanted | meeting / to book | him in Tokyo. / a nice hotel room. |

23.11 KEY LANGUAGE VERB + OBJECT + INFINITIVE

Some verbs, particularly ones that express orders or requests, can be followed by an object and another verb in the infinitive.

We expect all our staff **to attend a party with our clients.**

Verb ↗   Object ↗   ↖ Infinitive

🔊

23.12 HOW TO FORM VERB + OBJECT + INFINITIVE

SUBJECT	VERB	OBJECT	INFINITIVE	REST OF SENTENCE
We	expect	all our staff	to attend	a party with our clients.

23.13 FURTHER EXAMPLES VERB + OBJECT + INFINITIVE

I've invited our new clients **to have lunch with us.**

My manager asked me **to book the conference room.**

23.14 FILL IN THE GAPS USING THE PHRASES IN THE PANEL

We ___*want all our staff*___ to feel happy at work.

1 My boss asked me _____ a meeting with our clients.

2 Our clients _____ to visit them in Paris.

3 We expect all our staff _____ on time.

4 We _____ to attend our end-of-year party.

5 I expect my manager _____ me a promotion soon.

---

asked us

to arrange

to give

~~want all our staff~~

invited all our clients

to arrive

🔊

278

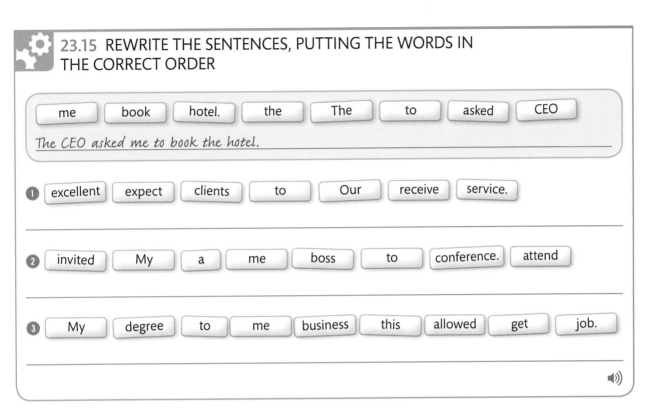

23.15 REWRITE THE SENTENCES, PUTTING THE WORDS IN THE CORRECT ORDER

| me | book | hotel. | the | The | to | asked | CEO |

The CEO asked me to book the hotel.

① | excellent | expect | clients | to | Our | receive | service. |

_____

② | invited | My | a | me | boss | to | conference. | attend |

_____

③ | My | degree | to | me | business | this | allowed | get | job. |

_____

🔊

23 ✓ CHECKLIST

⚙ Verb patterns ☐   **Aa** Corporate entertainment ☐   🧩 Talking about business events ☐

🔄 REVIEW THE ENGLISH YOU HAVE LEARNED IN UNITS 19–23

NEW LANGUAGE	SAMPLE SENTENCE	☑	UNIT
GIVING ADVICE	You should **ask the clients** for more time. You must **talk to your manager.**	☐	19.1
MAKING SUGGESTIONS	What about hiring **more staff?** Why don't we open **a new store?**	☐	19.7
TALKING ABOUT ABILITIES	Jasmine's team can **finish a job quickly.** I couldn't **give presentations five years ago.**	☐	21.1, 21.5, 21.6
COMPARING AND CONTRASTING IDEAS	This task is useful. It is also **fun.** Team A won the task, whereas **Team B lost.**	☐	22.1, 22.2
VERBS WITH GERUNDS AND INFINITIVES	I really enjoy entertaining **clients.** Sandeep has offered to welcome **our guests.**	☐	23.1, 23.3, 23.6
VERB + OBJECT + INFINITIVE	We expect all our staff to attend **the party.**	☐	23.11

24 Vocabulary

24.1 MEETINGS

Lee, could you send out the agenda **for Friday's meeting, please?**

to send out an agenda
[to send a plan for what will be discussed]

The main objective **of this meeting is to agree on a budget.**

main objective
[the primary aim]

Yolanda is sick, so she will be absent **from the meeting today.**

to be absent
[to be not present]

Can we have a show of hands **for those who agree with the proposal?**

a show of hands
[a vote made by raising hands in the air to show agreement]

Francesca will give a presentation **on health and safety.**

to give a presentation
[to present information to a group of people]

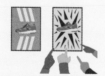

Today we need to look at **our sales figures for the last year.**

to look at
[to consider or focus on something]

If we can't reach a consensus, **we will have a vote.**

to reach a consensus
[to come to an agreement about an issue]

We reached a unanimous agreement **on the plan.**

unanimous agreement
[when everyone agrees]

We will have another meeting next week because we have run out of time.

to run out of time
[to have no more time left to do something]

We will take questions **at the end of the meeting.**

to take questions
[to answer questions]

We need someone to take minutes during the meeting.

to take minutes
[to write a record of what was said during a meeting]

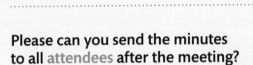

Did you manage to review the minutes from the last meeting?

to review the minutes
[to look again at the written record of a past meeting]

Please can you send the minutes to all attendees after the meeting?

attendees
[people who have been to or are going to a meeting]

We need a strategy for increasing sales to young buyers.

a strategy
[a plan for achieving a particular goal]

Let's discuss the options for the new logo.

to discuss
[to talk about something]

I suggest that we use this new design.

to suggest / propose
[to put forward an idea or plan for others to discuss]

It's nearly lunchtime. Let's wrap up the meeting.

to wrap up
[to conclude or finish something]

I'm sorry to interrupt, but I have some more recent figures.

to interrupt
[to say something before someone else has finished speaking]

So to sum up, we really need to increase sales next month.

to sum up
[to conclude]

Excellent, we have three clear action points to work on.

action points
[proposals for specific action to be taken]

25 What people said

When telling co-workers what someone else said, you can take what they said (direct speech) and rephrase it accurately and clearly. This is called reported speech.

⚙ **New language** Reported speech
Aa Vocabulary Meetings
🧩 **New skill** Reporting what someone said

25.1 KEY LANGUAGE REPORTED SPEECH

The main verb in reported speech is usually "said." The reported verb is usually in a different tense from the direct speech.

Direct speech uses the present simple.

I can't come to the meeting. I'm too busy.

Luke said that he was **too busy to come to the meeting.**

"That" is usually added after "said" in reported speech.

Reported speech uses the past simple for the reported verb.

🔊

25.2 KEY LANGUAGE REPORTED SPEECH IN DIFFERENT TENSES

The tense used in reported speech is usually one tense back in time from the tense in direct speech.

I'm working in New York.

⬇

She said she was working in New York.
— Past continuous replaces present continuous.

I will call you soon.

⬇

He said he would call them soon.
— "Would" replaces "will."

I've been to China twice.

⬇

He said that he'd been **to China twice.**
— Past perfect replaces present perfect.

We can speak Japanese.

⬇

They said that they could speak **Japanese.**
— "Could" replaces "can."

🔊

25.3 KEY LANGUAGE REPORTED SPEECH AND THE PAST SIMPLE

The past simple in direct speech can either stay as the past simple or change to the past perfect in reported speech. The meaning is the same.

I **arrived** in Delhi on Saturday.

He said { he arrived / he'd arrived } in Delhi on Saturday.

25.4 MATCH THE DIRECT SPEECH TO THE REPORTED SPEECH

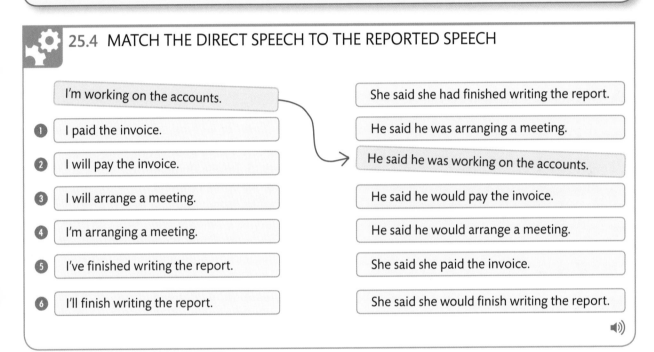

I'm working on the accounts. → He said he was working on the accounts.

1. I paid the invoice.
2. I will pay the invoice.
3. I will arrange a meeting.
4. I'm arranging a meeting.
5. I've finished writing the report.
6. I'll finish writing the report.

She said she had finished writing the report.

He said he was arranging a meeting.

He said he was working on the accounts.

He said he would pay the invoice.

He said he would arrange a meeting.

She said she paid the invoice.

She said she would finish writing the report.

25.5 REWRITE THE SENTENCES, PUTTING THEM INTO REPORTED SPEECH

I need to send an email.
He _said that he needed to send an email._

1. I will interview the candidates.
She _____

2. I met the CEO on Monday.
He _____

3. I can book the meeting room.
He _____

4. I'm writing a press release.
She _____

5. I can use design software.
He _____

283

25.6 KEY LANGUAGE TIME AND PLACE REFERENCES

If speech is reported some time after it was said, words used to talk about times and places may need to change.

I went to work yesterday.

The time reference is "yesterday" in direct speech.

She said she'd been to work the day before.

The time reference is "the day before" in reported speech.

MAY 15   MAY 16   MAY 17

25.7 FURTHER EXAMPLES TIME AND PLACE REFERENCES

I'll call you tomorrow. ➡ **He said he'd call me the following day.**

The weather is nice here. ➡ **He told me the weather was nice there.**

We'll be closed this weekend. ➡ **They said they'd be closed that weekend.**

I saw you last week. ➡ **She said she'd seen me the week before.**

25.8 LISTEN TO THE AUDIO, THEN NUMBER THE REPORTED SENTENCES IN THE ORDER YOU HEAR THEM AS DIRECT SPEECH

Ⓐ Jack said he would send me the proposal the following day. ☐

Ⓑ Jack said he had got promoted the week before. ☐

Ⓒ Jack said he enjoyed working there. ☐

Ⓓ Jack said he'd be going to Dubai the following weekend. ☐ 1

Ⓔ Jack said he had gone to the London office the day before. ☐

25.9 KEY LANGUAGE OTHER CHANGES IN REPORTED SPEECH

In reported speech, pronouns may also need to be changed
to ensure they refer to the correct person or thing.

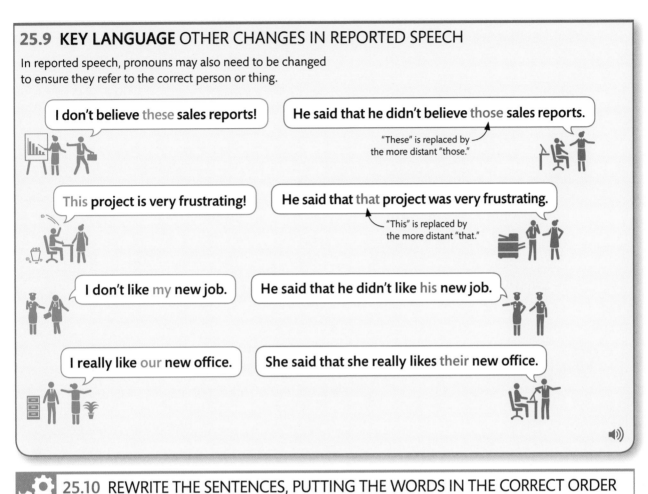

I don't believe these sales reports!

He said that he didn't believe those sales reports.

"These" is replaced by the more distant "those."

This project is very frustrating!

He said that that project was very frustrating.

"This" is replaced by the more distant "that."

I don't like my new job.

He said that he didn't like his new job.

I really like our new office.

She said that she really likes their new office.

25.10 REWRITE THE SENTENCES, PUTTING THE WORDS IN THE CORRECT ORDER

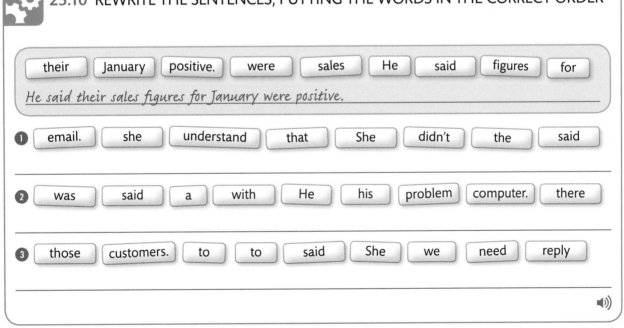

| their | January | positive. | were | sales | He | said | figures | for |

He said their sales figures for January were positive.

1. | email. | she | understand | that | She | didn't | the | said |

2. | was | said | a | with | He | his | problem | computer. | there |

3. | those | customers. | to | to | said | She | we | need | reply |

285

25.11 KEY LANGUAGE "TELL" IN REPORTED SPEECH

In reported speech, "tell" can also be used as the main verb. It must be followed by an object, which shows who someone is talking to.

I have to change the meeting date.

He told me that he had to change the meeting date

Unlike "say," "tell" must be followed by an object.

🔊))

25.12 KEY LANGUAGE REPORTING VERBS WITH "THAT"

"Say" and "tell" do not give any information about the speaker's manner. They can be replaced with other verbs that suggest the speaker's mood or reason for speaking.

I'm not very good at sales.

Neil admitted that he wasn't very good at sales.

"Admit" suggests a confession on the part of the speaker.

🔊))

25.13 FURTHER EXAMPLES REPORTING VERBS WITH "THAT"

We have to close the building for security tests.

They explained that the building had to be closed for security tests.

Your office is huge! It has a nice view, too.

Rohit admired our office, and added that it had a nice view.

That's right! Our profits have risen this year.

Jeremy confirmed that our profits had risen this year.

🔊))

25.14 REPORT THE DIRECT SPEECH IN THE AUDIO OUT LOUD, FILLING IN THE GAPS USING THE WORDS IN THE PANEL

I am not the person in charge of this project.

He _____*denied*_____ that he was the person in charge of that project.

1 Yes, that's right. The sales figures will be ready by 5pm.

Sharon _____ that the sales figures would be ready by 5pm.

2 Don't worry. I'll definitely stay late to help you finish the report.

Lilia _____ that she would stay late to help me finish the report.

3 We have beaten our sales target for the year.

Mr. Lee _____ that we had beaten our sales target for the year.

4 The coffee from the machine tastes awful.

Ben _____ that the coffee from the machine tasted awful.

5 Perhaps you could ask your boss about a raise.

She _____ that I could ask my boss about a raise.

complained	announced	confirmed	suggested	~~denied~~	promised

26 What people asked

You can use reported questions to tell someone what someone else has asked. Direct questions and reported questions have different word orders.

- ⚙ **New language** Reported questions
- **Aa Vocabulary** "Have," "make," "get," "do"
- 🧩 **New skill** Reporting what someone asked

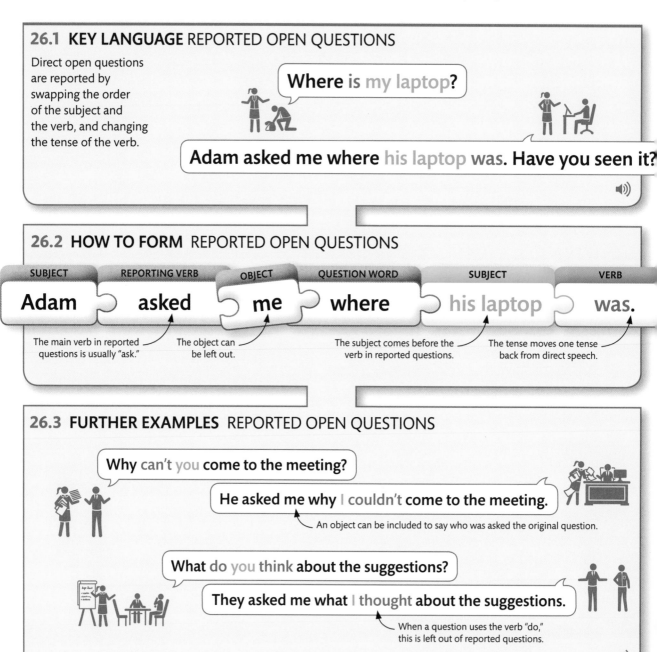

26.1 KEY LANGUAGE REPORTED OPEN QUESTIONS

Direct open questions are reported by swapping the order of the subject and the verb, and changing the tense of the verb.

Where is my laptop?

Adam asked me where his laptop was. Have you seen it?

26.2 HOW TO FORM REPORTED OPEN QUESTIONS

SUBJECT	REPORTING VERB	OBJECT	QUESTION WORD	SUBJECT	VERB
Adam	asked	me	where	his laptop	was.

The main verb in reported questions is usually "ask."

The object can be left out.

The subject comes before the verb in reported questions.

The tense moves one tense back from direct speech.

26.3 FURTHER EXAMPLES REPORTED OPEN QUESTIONS

Why can't you come to the meeting?

He asked me why I couldn't come to the meeting.

An object can be included to say who was asked the original question.

What do you think about the suggestions?

They asked me what I thought about the suggestions.

When a question uses the verb "do," this is left out of reported questions.

26.4 REWRITE THE SENTENCES, PUTTING THE WORDS IN THE CORRECT ORDER

me | where | was. | Sasha | the | asked | conference

Sasha asked me where the conference was.

1. asked | me | I | late | again. | why | was | He
   _____

2. was. | me | Lara | asked | the | meeting | where
   _____

3. asked | interview. | I | me | missed | She | the | why | had
   _____

4. asked | who | had | minutes. | taken | He | me | the
   _____

◀))

26.5 LISTEN TO THE AUDIO AND ANSWER THE QUESTIONS

Two co-workers, Krista and Mandy, are discussing a launch.

Krista said they're launching a new phone.
True ☐ False ☐ Not given ✓

1. Krista asked Mandy about the press release.
   True ☐ False ☐ Not given ☐

2. Mandy hasn't finished writing the press release.
   True ☐ False ☐ Not given ☐

3. Journalists are coming to the press launch.
   True ☐ False ☐ Not given ☐

4. Mandy has a good relationship with ABC TV.
   True ☐ False ☐ Not given ☐

5. Mandy asked what to do with the speech.
   True ☐ False ☐ Not given ☐

6. Krista told Mandy to email the speech to her.
   True ☐ False ☐ Not given ☐

7. Mandy usually makes a lot of changes.
   True ☐ False ☐ Not given ☐

26.6 READ THE ARTICLE AND ANSWER THE QUESTIONS

You must have meetings in order to do business.
True ☐ **False** ☐ **Not given** ☑

1. You should limit the number of things to discuss.
True ☐ **False** ☐ **Not given** ☐

2. There is no need to share the agenda.
True ☐ **False** ☐ **Not given** ☐

3. Let attendees know how long the lunch break is.
True ☐ **False** ☐ **Not given** ☐

4. People tend to take a long break after a meeting.
True ☐ **False** ☐ **Not given** ☐

5. People rarely forget to organize the meeting location.
True ☐ **False** ☐ **Not given** ☐

6. A good meeting room has plenty of light.
True ☐ **False** ☐ **Not given** ☐

BUSINESS TIPS

Preparation is key

CEO David Moss explains how to have successful meetings

It is important to decide your main objectives before the meeting. Create an agenda and send it to all attendees so they can prepare in advance. Set a date and time for your meeting. Decide when you will have a break, and how long you will give attendees to have lunch. If you don't do this, people might take long breaks, reducing your meeting time! Last of all, this sounds simple, but it's easy to forget to make arrangements for the meeting location, especially if you're very busy. Get the room ready with the right amount of chairs and refreshments, and your laptop or any other necessary equipment.

Aa 26.7 FILL IN THE GAPS USING THE WORDS IN THE PANEL TO CREATE MORE COLLOCATIONS WITH "HAVE," "MAKE," "GET," AND "DO"

Suzi suggested that in a couple of years, I could [**get** *a job*] in the Paris office.

1. The boss is angry with Max. He told him to [**do**] before he leaves.

2. Mr. Tan promised that I would [**get**] to manager if I worked hard.

3. Could you [**do**] ? Could you make 20 copies of this, please?

4. Can I [**make**] ? Finish the proposal first, then work on the spreadsheet.

5. Paola said that she usually [**gets**] from work at 6:30pm.

6. Paul said that he [**had**] with his boss, but he was really late.

his work   a suggestion   a̶ ̶j̶o̶b̶   me a favor   an appointment   home   promoted

🔊

290

26.8 KEY LANGUAGE REPORTED CLOSED QUESTIONS

If the answer to a question is "yes" or "no," "if" or "whether" is used to report the question.

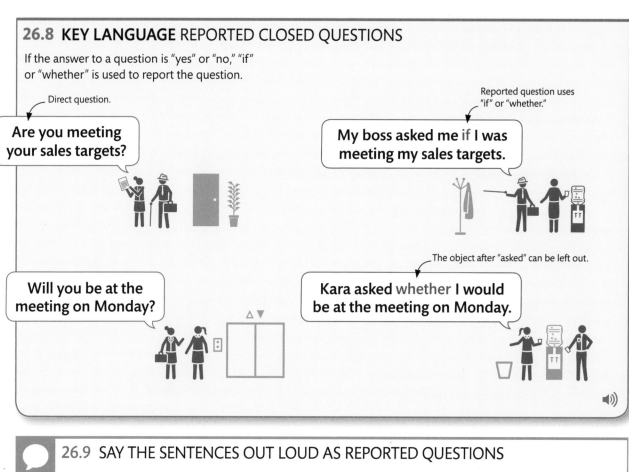

Direct question.

Are you meeting your sales targets?

Reported question uses "if" or "whether."

My boss asked me if I was meeting my sales targets.

The object after "asked" can be left out.

Will you be at the meeting on Monday?

Kara asked whether I would be at the meeting on Monday.

26.9 SAY THE SENTENCES OUT LOUD AS REPORTED QUESTIONS

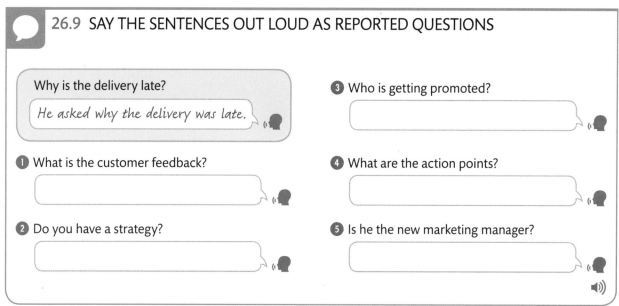

Why is the delivery late?

He asked why the delivery was late.

❶ What is the customer feedback?

❷ Do you have a strategy?

❸ Who is getting promoted?

❹ What are the action points?

❺ Is he the new marketing manager?

26 ⊘ CHECKLIST

⚙ Reported questions ☐   Aa "Have," "make," "get," "do" ☐   🧩 Reporting what someone asked ☐

27 Reporting quantities

In presentations and reports, you may need to talk about how much of something there is. The words you can use to do this depend on the thing you are describing.

⚙ **New language** "Few," "little," and "all"
Aa Vocabulary Meetings
🧩 **New skill** Talking about quantity

27.1 KEY LANGUAGE "FEW" FOR SMALL NUMBERS

"Few" is used with plural countable nouns to say that there are not many of something. It emphasizes how small the number is.

> few = not many

 There have been few new customers this quarter.

"A few" is used with countable nouns to mean "some." It emphasizes that the number, though small, is enough.

> a few = some

 I have a few suggestions for how to improve sales.

"Few" can also be used as a pronoun to mean "not many."

 So few are willing to spend money for the deluxe range.

"Very" can be used to stress that the number of something is even smaller.

 We have very few items left in stock.

◀))

27.2 MARK THE SENTENCES THAT ARE CORRECT

> You'll be glad to hear that we still have a few options available to us this year. ☑
> You'll be glad to hear that we still have few options available to us this year. ☐

1 We'll have to reduce the price. A few customers have bought our new jeans. ☐
We'll have to reduce the price. Very few customers have bought our new jeans. ☐

2 So few people pay by check these days that we no longer accept this form of payment. ☐
A few people pay by check these days that we no longer accept this form of payment. ☐

3 Unfortunately, we've had a few inquiries about our new spa treatments. ☐
Unfortunately, we've had few inquiries about our new spa treatments. ☐

◀))

27.3 KEY LANGUAGE "LITTLE" FOR SMALL AMOUNTS

"Little" is used with uncountable nouns to say that there is not much of something in UK English. It emphasizes how small the amount is.

"A little" is used with uncountable nouns to mean "some." It emphasizes that the amount, though small, is enough.

> little = not much

I have little doubt that next year will be challenging.

> a little = some

The summer should offer a little boost to sales.

"Little" can also be used as a pronoun to mean "not much."

Very little can be done to improve the short-term performance.

Informally, "a (little) bit of" can be used instead of "a little."

There's a little bit of time left to discuss our options.

27.4 CROSS OUT THE INCORRECT WORD IN EACH SENTENCE, THEN SAY THE SENTENCES OUT LOUD

I'm afraid that there are ~~little~~ / few options left for us to explore.

1. Unfortunately, there is a little / little chance of us winning this contract.

2. I have a few / few ideas that I really think could improve our brand image.

3. There is still a little / a few time left before we need to submit the report.

4. Kelvin has little / few understanding of accountancy.

5. So few / a few people have bought this TV that we're going to stop production.

27.5 KEY LANGUAGE "ALL" AS A PRONOUN

"All" can sometimes be used as a pronoun to mean either "everything" or "the only thing."

all = everything

I hope all goes well in the presentation.

all = the only thing

All we can do is hope that they like the product.

27.6 REWRITE THE SENTENCES, PUTTING THE WORDS IN THE CORRECT ORDER

about | told | all | you | I | know | have | it. | I

I have told you all I know about it.

1. do | can | is | your | mistake. | apologize | All | for | you

---

2. expect | I | is | tasks. | to | All | complete | for | staff | their

---

3. sure | be | the | I'm | will | interview. | well | in | all

---

4. I | is | All | raise. | want | a

---

5. all | have | information | We | the | need. | we

294

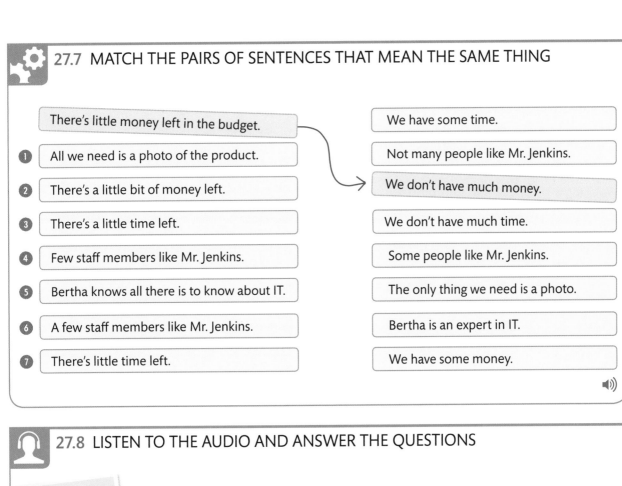

27.7 MATCH THE PAIRS OF SENTENCES THAT MEAN THE SAME THING

There's little money left in the budget. →

1 All we need is a photo of the product.

2 There's a little bit of money left.

3 There's a little time left.

4 Few staff members like Mr. Jenkins.

5 Bertha knows all there is to know about IT.

6 A few staff members like Mr. Jenkins.

7 There's little time left.

We have some time.

Not many people like Mr. Jenkins.

We don't have much money.

We don't have much time.

Some people like Mr. Jenkins.

The only thing we need is a photo.

Bertha is an expert in IT.

We have some money.

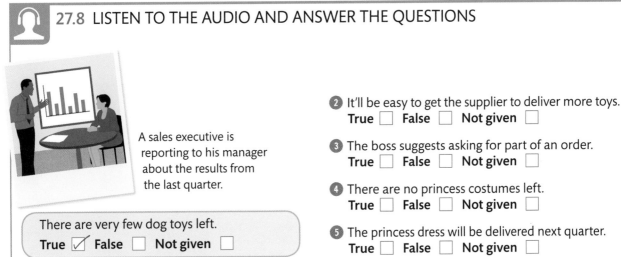

27.8 LISTEN TO THE AUDIO AND ANSWER THE QUESTIONS

A sales executive is reporting to his manager about the results from the last quarter.

There are very few dog toys left.
True ☑ False ☐ Not given ☐

1 The Woof Doggy toy is a new product.
True ☐ False ☐ Not given ☐

2 It'll be easy to get the supplier to deliver more toys.
True ☐ False ☐ Not given ☐

3 The boss suggests asking for part of an order.
True ☐ False ☐ Not given ☐

4 There are no princess costumes left.
True ☐ False ☐ Not given ☐

5 The princess dress will be delivered next quarter.
True ☐ False ☐ Not given ☐

6 The camping kit has been very popular.
True ☐ False ☐ Not given ☐

27 ✓ CHECKLIST

⚙ "Few," "little," and "all" ☐   **Aa** Meetings ☐   🧩 Talking about quantity ☐

28 Checking information

Sometimes you may need to clarify whether you have understood a point. There are a number of ways to politely check information in conversation.

⚙ **New language** Subject questions, question tags
Aa Vocabulary Polite checks and echo questions
🧩 **New skill** Checking information

28.1 KEY LANGUAGE SUBJECT QUESTIONS

In English, most questions ask about the person or thing receiving that action (the object). If you want to find out or confirm who or what did an action, you can use subject questions.

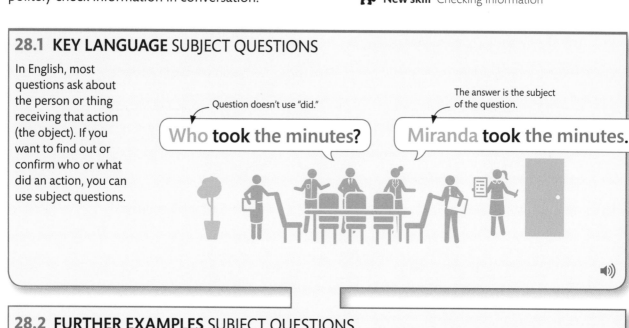

Question doesn't use "did."

Who took the minutes?

The answer is the subject of the question.

Miranda took the minutes.

28.2 FURTHER EXAMPLES SUBJECT QUESTIONS

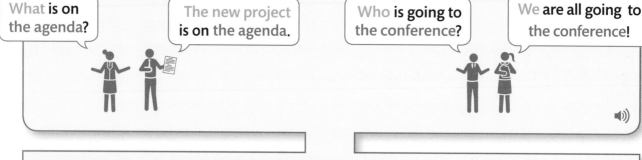

What is on the agenda?

The new project is on the agenda.

Who is going to the conference?

We are all going to the conference!

28.3 HOW TO FORM SUBJECT QUESTIONS

"Who" (for people) and "what" (for things) are the most common pronouns used in subject questions.

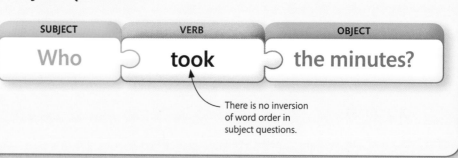

SUBJECT	VERB	OBJECT
Who	took	the minutes?

There is no inversion of word order in subject questions.

28.4 REWRITE THE QUESTIONS, PUTTING THE WORDS IN THE CORRECT ORDER

the · is · problem? · What

What is the problem?

1 manager? · Who · the · is

_____

2 the · What's · in · report?

_____

3 answers · telephone? · Who · the

_____

4 approves · Who · annual · vacation?

_____

5 is · What · deadline? · the

_____

6 wrote · the · ad? · Who

_____

7 take · Who · questions? · will

_____

8 are · the · What · objectives?

_____

9 the · What's · about? · complaint

_____

28.5 MARK THE BEST QUESTION FOR EACH SITUATION

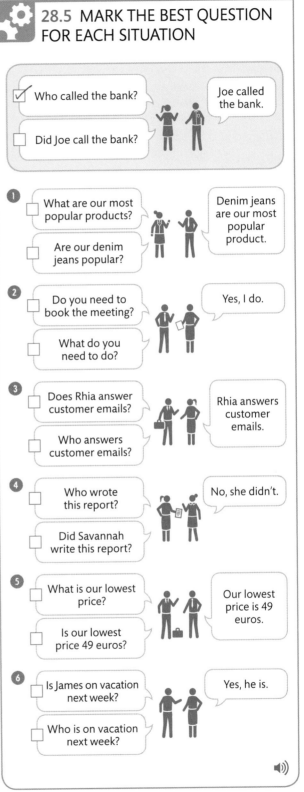

☑ Who called the bank?
☐ Did Joe call the bank?
Joe called the bank.

1
☐ What are our most popular products?
☐ Are our denim jeans popular?
Denim jeans are our most popular product.

2
☐ Do you need to book the meeting?
☐ What do you need to do?
Yes, I do.

3
☐ Does Rhia answer customer emails?
☐ Who answers customer emails?
Rhia answers customer emails.

4
☐ Who wrote this report?
☐ Did Savannah write this report?
No, she didn't.

5
☐ What is our lowest price?
☐ Is our lowest price 49 euros?
Our lowest price is 49 euros.

6
☐ Is James on vacation next week?
☐ Who is on vacation next week?
Yes, he is.

297

28.6 KEY LANGUAGE QUESTION TAGS

Another way to check information is by using question tags. The simplest question tags use the verb "be" with a pronoun matching the subject of the sentence.

STATEMENT **QUESTION TAG**

Hi everyone! I'm late, aren't I?

For statements with "I," "aren't I?" is used in the negative question tag, not "amn't I?"

For most verbs other than "be," a present simple statement is followed by a question tag with "do" or "does."

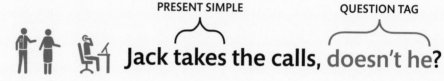

PRESENT SIMPLE **QUESTION TAG**

Jack takes the calls, doesn't he?

A past simple statement is followed by a question tag with "did."

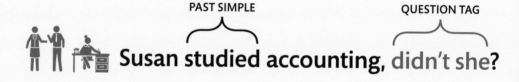

PAST SIMPLE **QUESTION TAG**

Susan studied accounting, didn't she?

A statement with an auxiliary verb is followed by a question tag with the same auxiliary.

AUXILIARY VERB **MAIN VERB** **QUESTION TAG**

You haven't seen my laptop, have you?

Auxiliary verb

Main verb describes the action.

Question tag uses the same auxiliary verb.

Statements with modal verbs such as "could," "would," and "should" are followed by question tags with the same modal.

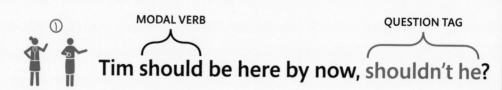

MODAL VERB **QUESTION TAG**

Tim should be here by now, shouldn't he?

298

28.7 HOW TO FORM QUESTION TAGS

A positive statement is followed by a negative question tag,
and a negative statement is followed by a positive question tag.

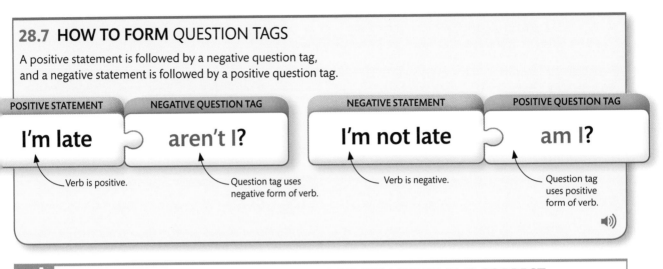

POSITIVE STATEMENT

I'm late

Verb is positive.

NEGATIVE QUESTION TAG

aren't I?

Question tag uses
negative form of verb.

NEGATIVE STATEMENT

I'm not late

Verb is negative.

POSITIVE QUESTION TAG

am I?

Question tag
uses positive
form of verb.

28.8 MATCH THE BEGINNINGS OF THE SENTENCES TO THE CORRECT QUESTION TAGS

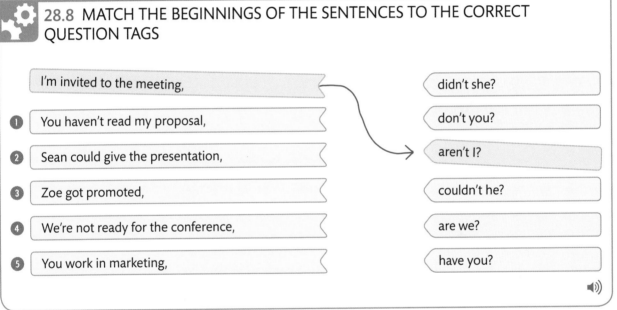

I'm invited to the meeting,

didn't she?

1 You haven't read my proposal,

don't you?

2 Sean could give the presentation,

aren't I?

3 Zoe got promoted,

couldn't he?

4 We're not ready for the conference,

are we?

5 You work in marketing,

have you?

28.9 FILL IN THE GAPS USING THE CORRECT QUESTION TAGS

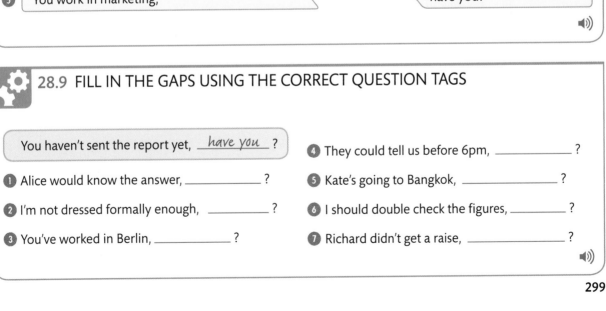

You haven't sent the report yet, _have you_ ?

1 Alice would know the answer, _____ ?

2 I'm not dressed formally enough, _____ ?

3 You've worked in Berlin, _____ ?

4 They could tell us before 6pm, _____ ?

5 Kate's going to Bangkok, _____ ?

6 I should double check the figures, _____ ?

7 Richard didn't get a raise, _____ ?

299

28.10 VOCABULARY POLITE CHECKS AND ECHO QUESTIONS

There are also certain set phrases you can use to politely check information.

Pardon?

Could you say that again? I didn't catch it.

What was the last figure? I didn't hear it.

Sorry, I missed that.

Be careful not to say "What?" too directly, as it can sound rude.

You can also repeat the important word or phrase you want to check, or echo part or all of the sentence with a question word or phrase at the end.

We sold $40,000 of stock to Japan last month.

To Japan?

We sold $40,000 of stock to where?

28.11 LISTEN TO THE AUDIO AND ANSWER THE QUESTIONS

A sales assistant is calling her manager to check a few details and confirm information.

The standard discount offered is 30%.
True ☐   False ☐   Not given ☑

1 Discounts are offered to long-term customers.
True ☐   False ☐   Not given ☐

2 If a customer buys 1,000 units, they get 15% off.
True ☐   False ☐   Not given ☐

3 A new customer in Thailand sent an inquiry.
True ☐   False ☐   Not given ☐

4 They already work with companies in Asia.
True ☐   False ☐   Not given ☐

5 Julian will find out more about the new customer.
True ☐   False ☐   Not given ☐

28.12 CROSS OUT THE INCORRECT WORDS IN EACH SENTENCE, THEN SAY THE SENTENCES OUT LOUD

We've made good progress, haven't / ~~have~~ we?

1. What was the name of the company? I didn't listen / hear.

2. Who / What is working on the project for the new office?

3. You identified the mistake, haven't you / didn't you?

4. Could you repeat that, please? I didn't catch / grab it.

5. Where / What is the theme of this year's conference?

---

28 ✓ CHECKLIST

⚙ Subject questions, question tags ☐   **Aa** Polite checks and echo questions ☐   🧩 Checking information ☐

♻ REVIEW THE ENGLISH YOU HAVE LEARNED IN UNITS 24-28

NEW LANGUAGE	SAMPLE SENTENCE	☑	UNIT
REPORTED SPEECH	Luke said that he felt sick. She said she'd been to work the day before.	☐	25.1, 25.6, 25.9
REPORTING VERBS	Jeremy confirmed that our profits had risen.	☐	25.12
REPORTED QUESTIONS	Adam asked me where his laptop was.	☐	26.1, 26.8
"FEW," "LITTLE," AND "ALL"	I have a few suggestions. Very little can be done. I hope all goes well.	☐	27.1, 27.3, 27.5
CHECKING INFORMATION WITH SUBJECT QUESTIONS AND QUESTION TAGS	Who took the minutes? I'm late, aren't I?	☐	28.1, 28.6
POLITE CHECKS AND ECHO QUESTIONS	Sorry, I missed that. We sold $40,000 of stock to where?	☐	28.10

29 Vocabulary

Aa 29.1 INDUSTRIES

education

healthcare

catering / food

chemical

construction

agriculture / farming

energy

electronics

entertainment

fashion

finance

fishing

hospitality

journalism

manufacturing

advertising

mining

petroleum

pharmaceutical

real estate (US) / property (UK)

recycling

shipping

tourism

transportation

Aa 29.2 PROFESSIONAL ATTRIBUTES

accurate

adaptable

ambitious

calm

confident

creative

customer-focused

determined

efficient

energetic

flexible

hardworking

honest

independent

innovative

motivated

organized

patient

practical

professional

punctual

reliable

responsible

team player

303

30 Job descriptions

English uses "a" or "an" in descriptions of jobs and to introduce new information. The zero article refers to general things, and "the" refers to specific things.

⚙ New language Articles
Aa Vocabulary Job descriptions and applications
🧩 New skill Describing a job

30.1 KEY LANGUAGE "A" AND "AN"

Use "a" or "an" to introduce new information. Use "the" when the reader or listener already knows what you are talking about.

Use "a" because this is the first time "job" is mentioned.

Use "an" before a vowel sound.

I applied for a job last week as an engineer.
The application form was really long.

Use "the" because it is clear from the context that this is the application form for the engineer job.

🔊

30.2 CROSS OUT THE INCORRECT WORDS IN EACH SENTENCE

~~A~~ / ~~An~~ / The salary for this job is really good.

1 A / An / The deadline for applications is Friday.

2 This job is based in a / an / the Berlin office.

3 We are recruiting a / an / the new designer.

4 I've got a / an / the interview for a new job.

5 A / An / The application form for this job is long.

6 Please complete a / an / the form on our website.

7 A / An / The ideal candidate enjoys teamwork.

8 There's an ad for a / an / the English teacher.

🔊

30.3 LISTEN TO THE AUDIO, THEN NUMBER THE PICTURES IN THE ORDER THEY ARE DESCRIBED

A ☐   B ☐1   C ☐   D ☐   E ☐

30.4 KEY LANGUAGE ZERO AND DEFINITE ARTICLES (PLURALS)

With plurals, English uses no article (zero article) to talk about things in general. Use "the" (definite article) to talk about specific things.

General

Catering jobs are very well paid at the moment.

Specific

The catering jobs at this café are really well paid.

30.5 FURTHER EXAMPLES ZERO AND DEFINITE ARTICLES (PLURALS)

Accountants have to work very hard.
The accountants at my office work long hours.

Managers don't always listen to their staff.
The managers here can't run a team.

Noriko loves giving **presentations**.
The presentations she gave last week were great.

30.6 MARK THE SENTENCES THAT ARE CORRECT

Most doctors have to work long hours. They are very dedicated people. ✓

Most the doctors have to work long hours. They are the very dedicated people. ☐

① The jobs I'm really interested in are based in Los Angeles. They're in IT. ☐
Jobs I'm really interested in are based in Los Angeles. They're in the IT. ☐

② People who interviewed me for the job were really nice. They were managers. ☐
The people who interviewed me for the job were really nice. They were the managers. ☐

③ Clients can be very demanding. The clients I met today had lots of complaints. ☐
The clients can be very demanding. Clients I met today had lots of the complaints. ☐

30.7 KEY LANGUAGE MORE USES OF THE ZERO ARTICLE

Use the zero article to talk about company names, place names
(including most countries and continents), and languages.

Apollo AV is looking to recruit an International Marketing Manager.

The successful candidate must speak excellent **French** and **Italian**.

The role involves travel to **France** and all over **Europe**.

30.8 KEY LANGUAGE MORE USES OF THE DEFINITE ARTICLE

Use "the" to talk about specific roles and departments
within a company, and for international organizations.

I applied for a job in **the finance department** at your company.

I have an interview with **the Head of HR** and **the CEO**.

The United Nations is recruiting a scientific researcher.

30.9 REWRITE THE SENTENCES, CORRECTING THE ERRORS

She works in design department.
She works in the design department.

❶ I often travel to the Hong Kong on business.

_____

❷ The Zenith Accounting has three job openings.

_____

❸ I have a meeting with company director.

_____

❹ He works for World Health Organization.

_____

❺ I'm a strong candidate because I speak the Russian.

_____

30.10 REWRITE THE HIGHLIGHTED PHRASES, CORRECTING THE ERRORS

Golden Wings Ltd. _____

1 _____

2 _____

3 _____

4 _____

5 _____

FLIGHT ATTENDANT

The Golden Wings Ltd. is hiring! Our airline flies throughout the Europe and Asia, and we have a opening for a bright, enthusiastic flight attendant. Have you go what it takes? A Flight attendants must be polite, hard-working and presentable. If this sounds like you, then we'd love to hear from you. An hours can be long, but the job is well paid, and you will have the

chance to stay in the best hotels and locations across the world. This is a once-in-a-lifetime opportunity to see the world and build the career. Apply now!

30.11 CROSS OUT THE INCORRECT WORDS IN EACH SENTENCE, THEN SAY THE SENTENCES OUT LOUD

Salary in this job / The salary in this job is really good.

1 Your meeting is with HR manager / the HR manager.

2 We're recruiting more staff in France / the France.

3 I'm looking for a job as education consultant / an education consultant.

4 We need someone who can speak the Italian / Italian.

5 Omnitech / The Omnitech is advertising several vacancies in its marketing department.

6 I work in sales department / the sales department of a large company.

---

30 ✓ CHECKLIST

✿ Articles ☐   **Aa** Job descriptions and applications ☐   🧩 Describing a job ☐

Cover letters for job applications should sound fluent and confident. Using the correct prepositions after verbs, nouns, and adjectives can help you achieve this.

New language Dependent prepositions
Aa Vocabulary Cover-letter vocabulary
New skill Writing a cover letter

31.1 KEY LANGUAGE DEPENDENT PREPOSITIONS

Some English words cannot be used on their own. They need to be followed by specific "dependent" prepositions.

"Apply" cannot be paired with any other preposition in this context.

I am writing to apply for the position of Senior Police Officer.

31.2 FURTHER EXAMPLES DEPENDENT PREPOSITIONS

 I graduated from college in June 2015.

 He is highly trained in all aspects of catering.

 At college, I focused on mechanical engineering.

 As Deputy Director, I reported to the CEO.

31.3 CROSS OUT THE INCORRECT WORDS IN EACH SENTENCE

In my role as Senior Production Manager, I reported ~~in~~ / ~~by~~ / to the Production Director.

1 In our department, we focus at / on / to sales and marketing.

2 Katrina graduated at / in / from college with a degree in Biological Sciences.

3 Our technicians are fully trained to / with / in all aspects of health and safety.

4 I've applied at / to / for a job in the IT department of a big company in Los Angeles.

31.4 READ THE COVER LETTER AND ANSWER THE QUESTIONS

> Sasha heard about the job on the radio.
> **True** ☐ **False** ☐ **Not given** ☑

1 Sasha is currently a senior travel executive.
True ☐ **False** ☐ **Not given** ☐

2 She has worked for the same company for 10 years.
True ☐ **False** ☐ **Not given** ☐

3 She is responsible for travel to Southeast Asia.
True ☐ **False** ☐ **Not given** ☐

4 She is tired of working in the travel industry.
True ☐ **False** ☐ **Not given** ☐

5 She would like to learn new skills.
True ☐ **False** ☐ **Not given** ☐

6 She has provided written recommendations with her application.
True ☐ **False** ☐ **Not given** ☐

Dear Mr. Goméz,

I am writing to apply for the position of Senior Travel Representative, as advertised in Go Travel! magazine.

I have worked in the travel industry for more than 10 years, and have experience handling both package vacations and tailor-made trips. In my current position, I am responsible for travel to Southeast Asia, and last year I was responsible for more than 15,000 customers. My sales figures amounted to more than $12 million.

I am passionate about working in the travel industry and would welcome the opportunity to learn new skills and broaden my experience. I'm extremely reliable and hard-working.

Please find attached my résumé and references. I look forward to hearing from you.

Yours sincerely,

Sasha Mailovitch

Aa 31.5 MATCH THE PHRASES THAT MEAN THE SAME

to have a job in a particular industry	to be responsible for something
1 to look after something	to be passionate about
2 to be excited about a future event	to work in
3 to equal a total number	experience in something
4 to make an official request for a job	to amount to
5 to have strong enthusiasm for	to look forward to something
6 skill gained through time spent in a job	to apply for a job

🔊

31.6 KEY LANGUAGE DEPENDENT PREPOSITIONS (CHANGE IN MEANING)

Some words can be paired with different dependent prepositions.
Their meaning changes depending on which preposition is used.

**I worked with the head chef
in a busy restaurant.**

[The head chef was a colleague.]

**I worked for the head chef
in a busy restaurant.**

[The head chef was my boss.]

31.7 FURTHER EXAMPLES DEPENDENT PREPOSITIONS (CHANGE IN MEANING)

I heard about the job on your website.

[I heard that the job was open.]

I look forward to hearing from you.

[I look forward to you responding to me.]

I was responsible for a rise in sales.

[I was responsible for sales going up.]

Last year, there was a rise of 40 percent.

[Sales went up by 40 percent.]

31.8 FILL IN THE GAPS WITH THE CORRECT PREPOSITION

Jake and I are both trainee hairdressers. I have been working ____*with*____ him for two months.

❶ When can I expect to hear _____ you about the job?

❷ Unfortunately, there has been a rise _____ complaints from customers.

❸ I work _____ the CEO of a big IT company. I'm her assistant.

❹ I heard _____ the job through a friend who works at the company.

❺ Our profits went up last year. There was a rise _____ about five percent.

Aa 31.9 USING THE CLUES, WRITE THE WORDS FROM THE PANEL IN THE CORRECT PLACES ON THE GRID

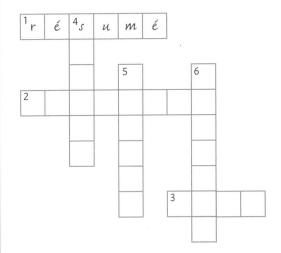

ACROSS

1 A document detailing your qualifications

2 Honest and trustworthy

3 The group of people you work with

DOWN

4 A set of abilities resulting from experience

5 A fixed regular payment

6 A person who gives a formal recommendation

| skills | salary | ~~résumé~~ |
| team | referee | reliable |

31.10 READ THE COVER LETTER AND CROSS OUT THE INCORRECT WORDS

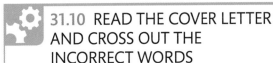

64 Elm Tree Way
West Clinton
PO13 4JS

Dear Mr. Khan,
I am writing to apply for / apply with the position / positioning of head web designer with your company.

I have experience at / experience in managing large commercial websites. Last year, sales from the website that I designed for a major online store amounted at / amounted to more than $6 million.

I am eager to develop my skilful / skills and broaden my knowledge of other industries / industrial.
I believe this job would be a fantastic opponent / opportunity for me, and I'd add a great deal to your company. I am enthusiastic and passionate for / passionate about being at the cutting edge of web development. I'm also very reliability / reliable and I enjoy working in a team.

I have attached my résumé / cover letter and details of my referees. I look forward to hearing to / hearing from you.

Yours sincerely,
Amy Quah

32 Job interviews

In a job interview, it is important to describe your achievements in a specific and detailed way. You can use relative clauses to do this.

⚙️ **New language** Relative clauses
Aa **Vocabulary** Job interviews
🧩 **New skill** Describing your achievements in detail

32.1 KEY LANGUAGE DEFINING RELATIVE CLAUSES

Defining relative clauses give essential information that helps to identify a person or thing. Here, the defining relative clause gives essential information about a thing.

> **Could you tell me more about yourself?**

MAIN CLAUSE | DEFINING RELATIVE CLAUSE

This is the product that I designed last year.

In defining relative clauses, this is the relative pronoun for things.

Here, the defining relative clause gives essential information about people.

MAIN CLAUSE | DEFINING RELATIVE CLAUSE

I work with clients who expect excellent service.

This relative pronoun is used for people.

The defining relative clause can also go in the middle of the main clause.

MAIN CLAUSE | DEFINING RELATIVE CLAUSE | RETURN TO MAIN CLAUSE

The clients who came to my product launch **were very impressed.**

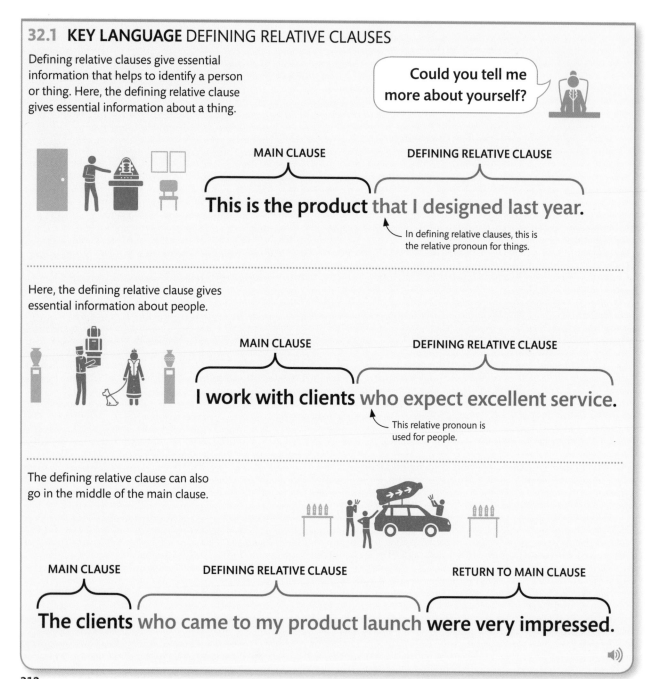

32.2 MATCH THE BEGINNINGS OF THE SENTENCES TO THE CORRECT ENDINGS

The main thing that I enjoy → about my job is my wonderful team.

① The office that I work in — is modern and open-plan.

② The customers who gave us — say they enjoy working with me.

③ One thing that I don't like — is already selling very well.

④ The people who are on my team — feedback were all very positive.

⑤ The product that we've just launched — about my job is the long hours.

32.3 CROSS OUT THE INCORRECT WORDS IN EACH SENTENCE

This is the product ~~who~~ / that / ~~what~~ I designed earlier this year. It is selling very well.

① The main thing that / who / where I hope to gain by working here is more experience.

② The area when / that / who I live in is very close to the bus routes into the business district.

③ The tasks who / when / that I perform best usually involve customer relations.

④ The exams why / that / where I passed last year mean that I am now fully qualified.

⑤ The person which / where / who I have learned the most from is my college professor.

⑥ The countries who / that / where order most of our umbrellas are in Europe.

⑦ The achievement that / who / where I am most proud of is winning "employee of the year."

313

32.4 KEY LANGUAGE NON-DEFINING RELATIVE CLAUSES

Non-defining relative clauses give extra information about situations, people, or things.

MAIN CLAUSE   NON-DEFINING RELATIVE CLAUSE

I worked in a café, which taught me a lot about customer service.

Relative pronoun for situations in non-defining relative clauses.

Non-defining relative clauses can also go in the middle of a sentence.

MAIN CLAUSE   NON-DEFINING RELATIVE CLAUSE   RETURN TO MAIN CLAUSE

In my previous job, which was in IT, I learned how to develop apps.

Relative pronoun for things in non-defining relative clauses.

The relative pronoun for people is "who" in non-defining relative clauses.

MAIN CLAUSE   NON-DEFINING RELATIVE CLAUSE   RETURN TO MAIN CLAUSE

My clients, who have high standards, said my work was excellent.

Relative pronoun for people.

32.5 REWRITE THE SENTENCES, CORRECTING THE ERRORS

> In my current job which I have been in for three years I often give presentations.
> *In my current job, which I have been in for three years, I often give presentations.*

1 I have completed all the training, who means you wouldn't need to train me.

2 My boss, which is very talented, always encourages me not to work too late.

3 IT development, what is my favorite part of the job, is very fast-paced.

4 My co-workers who are all older than me, have taught me a lot.

5 I worked at the reception desk, that taught me how to deal with customers.

6 I take my job very seriously which means I always follow the company dress code.

7 In my last job, who was in Paris, I learned to speak French fluently.

 ## 32.6 LISTEN TO THE INTERVIEW, THEN NUMBER THE SENTENCES IN THE ORDER YOU HEAR THEM

A I work about 35 hours a week, and I love it. ☐

B I think I'm really good at understanding people's goals and aims. ☐

C I'd like to join a bigger gym so I have the opportunity to build my career. ☐

D I have 40 regular clients, who I spend 30–60 minutes with each session. ☐

E I can see you have some experience already. ☐ `1`

F There are only about 100 clients, so there are only two trainers. ☐

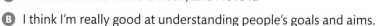

32.7 KEY LANGUAGE MORE RELATIVE PRONOUNS

Relative clauses can use other relative pronouns, depending on the nouns they refer to.

Last summer, when I had just graduated, I did an internship at a law firm.

Use "when" to refer to a time.

The fashion industry is where I would hope to expand your client base.

Use "where" to refer to a place, industry, or sector.

My team, whose members are very motivated, always meet their targets.

Use "whose" to refer to a person, company, or department.

32.8 FILL IN THE GAPS USING THE WORDS IN THE PANEL

 My apprenticeship, _____which_____ I completed in 2016, was in car manufacturing.

① The place _____ I can concentrate the best is at home.

② The person _____ career inspires me the most is Muhammad Ali.

③ Last year, _____ I was an intern, I learned how to give presentations.

④ My parents, _____ are both doctors, inspired me to study medicine.

where	when	~~which~~	who	whose

32.9 RESPOND OUT LOUD TO THE AUDIO, FILLING IN THE GAPS USING THE PHRASES IN THE PANEL

What would you say is your biggest weakness?

People ___*who know*___ me well say that I'm sometimes impatient.

1 What do you think of your current salary?

My current salary, _____ $20,000 a year, is not very high.

2 What do you like most about your job?

The thing _____ me excited about my job is seeing our products on sale.

3 Do you think you are a good team leader?

Yes. I always know _____ the responsibility for getting a task done on my team.

4 What benefits do you think you would bring to our company?

I can identify things _____ to change, to make your business more efficient.

5 How soon can you start, supposing we offer you the job?

My boss, _____ quite flexible, would allow me to leave after six weeks' notice.

| that need | that gets | who is | ~~who know~~ | which is | who has |

---

32 ✓ CHECKLIST

⚙ Relative clauses ☐   **Aa** Job interviews ☐   Describing your achievements in detail ☐

33 Vocabulary

33.1 BUSINESS IDIOMS

Our company is always ahead of the game in the latest technology.

to be ahead of the game
[to be ahead of your competitors in a certain field]

I just want to check that we are all on the same page.

to be on the same page
[to be in agreement about something]

I know it's always difficult to fill someone's shoes.

to fill someone's shoes
[to start doing a job or role that someone else has just left]

They haven't signed the contract yet, but at least I have a foot in the door.

to get / have a foot in the door
[to gain a small initial advantage at the beginning of a longer process]

It's important to go the extra mile for these customers.

to go the extra mile
[to make more effort than is usually expected]

This is a big contract. Make sure you do everything by the book.

to do something by the book
[to do something strictly according to the rules]

There's been a change of pace in the company since our product launch.

a change of pace
[an increase or decrease in speed from what is normal]

The design is flawed. We'll have to go back to square one.

to go back to square one
[to return to the start position]

Don't complicate things. Tell me the facts in a nutshell.

in a nutshell
[simply and succinctly]

It's essential that we get the campaign up and running this week.

up and running
[operating properly]

I need an update on this project. Let's touch base next week.

to touch base
[to talk to someone briefly in order to catch up or get an update]

Everyone was pleased when Simon clinched the deal last week.

to clinch the deal
[to confirm or settle an agreement or contract]

I don't know the exact price, but I can you give you a ballpark figure.

a ballpark figure
[a rough estimate]

We're not sure which new product to launch this month. It's all up in the air.

up in the air
[uncertain and undecided]

My boss and I see eye to eye on most things.

to see eye to eye
[to agree totally]

It's getting late. I think we should call it a day.

to call it a day
[to stop the current activity]

We want to corner the market in street fashion by next year.

to corner the market
[to have control of a particular market]

Food quality is extremely important in this restaurant. We can't cut corners.

to cut corners
[to do something in a cheaper or easier way, at the expense of high standards]

We're really behind on this project now, Tony. What's the game plan?

a game plan
[a strategy worked out beforehand]

This chair design is totally groundbreaking, Ceri.

groundbreaking
[original and a big departure from what was there before]

34 Working relationships

Phrasal verbs are commonly used to talk about relationships with co-workers and clients. It is important to use the correct word order with phrasal verbs.

🔧 **New language** Three-word phrasal verbs
Aa Vocabulary Social media
🧩 **New skill** Social networking

34.1 KEY LANGUAGE THREE-WORD PHRASAL VERBS

Three-word phrasal verbs consist of a verb and two particles. The particles usually change the meaning of the verb.

VERB AND PARTICLES

It's important to get along with clients. 🔊

34.2 FURTHER EXAMPLES THREE-WORD PHRASAL VERBS

 I look up to **my manager**.

 Caitlin looks down on her co-workers.

 Sadiq comes up with **great ideas**.

 I can't put up with his loud music! 🔊

Aa 34.3 MATCH THE DEFINITIONS TO THE PHRASAL VERBS

to accept a problem or situation ————→ to face up to something

① to be as good as promised — to live up to something

② to be excited about something yet to happen — to keep up with someone

③ to create a particular impression — to get away with something

④ to escape punishment — to run out of something

⑤ to use all of something and not have any left — to look forward to something

⑥ to go at the same speed as someone else — to come across as something

🔊

34.4 READ THE ARTICLE AND ANSWER THE QUESTIONS

The benefits of social media were recognized quickly.
True ☐ **False** ☐ **Not given** ☑

❶ Not all companies think social media is useful.
True ☐ **False** ☐ **Not given** ☐

❷ Some companies think social media costs too much.
True ☐ **False** ☐ **Not given** ☐

❸ Companies who don't use social media can compete.
True ☐ **False** ☐ **Not given** ☐

❹ Customers are irritated by ads on social media.
True ☐ **False** ☐ **Not given** ☐

❺ Social media increases awareness of brands.
True ☐ **False** ☐ **Not given** ☐

❻ It doesn't matter if customers aren't loyal.
True ☐ **False** ☐ **Not given** ☐

BUSINESS FORUM

Using social media
How social networking can benefit your company

Some companies have been slow to recognize the benefits of social media in business. Some even look down on social media, and doubt that it has any serious purpose or value. But ignore social media at your peril, because you can be sure your competitors are using it. And if you don't keep up with the competition, you'll never corner the market.

Using social media platforms can increase awareness of your company. Your brand becomes more familiar and more recognizable. If customers feel that they are keeping up with all your news and developments, they feel like they have a relationship with the company. As a result they become more loyal, and loyal customers make repeat purchases.

34.5 FILL IN THE GAPS USING THE WORDS IN THE PANEL

I look up _____up_____ to Yohann. He works hard and always goes the extra mile.

❶ Please could you _____ up with a proposal on how to improve punctuality?

❷ I can't _____ up with Thom when he goes through the accounts. He's too quick.

❸ Liza comes _____ as very serious, but outside of work she's a lot of fun.

❹ The two interns don't get _____ with each other very well. They don't see eye to eye.

❺ I'm really looking _____ to welcoming our new clients to London.

| come | ~~up~~ | across | keep | forward | along |

🔊

34.6 KEY LANGUAGE SEPARABLE PHRASAL VERBS WITH PRONOUNS

Some phrasal verbs are separable, which means the particle does not have to sit immediately after the verb. If the object of the sentence with a separable phrasal verb is a pronoun, it must go between the verb and the particle.

I'm **looking up** our competitors on social media. ✓

I'm **looking them up** on social media. ✓

I'm **looking** our competitors **up** on social media. ✓

I'm **looking up them** on social media. ✗

34.7 FURTHER EXAMPLES SEPARABLE PHRASAL VERBS WITH PRONOUNS

Here's a new form.
Please can you **fill it in**?

This is a difficult task.
Can you **take it on**?

They have a great website.
You must **check it out**.

Our clients are relying on you.
Don't **let them down**.

34.8 REWRITE THE SENTENCES USING OBJECT PRONOUNS

Jayne really let her co-workers down.
Jayne really let them down.

❶ Can you take on the presentation?

_____

❷ We're giving away free bags.

_____

❸ Let's look up this company on social media.

_____

❹ I think we should call off the meeting.

_____

❺ Can we talk over your sales proposal?

_____

34.9 LISTEN TO THE AUDIO AND ANSWER THE QUESTIONS

Leah and Tariq are discussing how to market their products on social media.

Tariq's idea involves...

a sports event.	☑
an online survey.	☐
an advertising campaign.	☐

❶ Tariq says the company...

should spend more on advertising.	☐
needs a modern image.	☐
needs to employ more people.	☐

❷ The company could use social media to...

increase awareness of health.	☐
tell people about their products.	☐
advertise the event.	☐

❸ The event would...

encourage people to become fitter.	☐
benefit the local environment.	☐
increase awareness of the company.	☐

❹ Who will take on the work?

Tariq volunteers to do it.	☐
Leah will find a team to work on it.	☐
Leah will do the organizing.	☐

34.10 SAY THE SENTENCES OUT LOUD, CORRECTING THE ERRORS

This is a difficult task. Can you take on it?

> This is a difficult task.
> Can you take it on?

❶ I need the report today. Please don't let down me.

❷ Josef complains a lot. I can't put with it.

❸ I'm looking forward finishing my training.

❹ If you have a problem, we can talk over.

❺ Don't look down to Rachel. She's still new.

❻ Our company is giving off three cars.

34 ✔ CHECKLIST

⚙ Three-word phrasal verbs ☐   **Aa** Social media ☐   🧩 Social networking ☐

323

35 Career outcomes

To talk about possible future events, such as career development and promotion, use "will," "might," and "won't" to say how likely something is to happen.

⚙ **New language** Modal verbs for possibility
Aa Vocabulary Career development
🧩 **New skill** Talking about the future

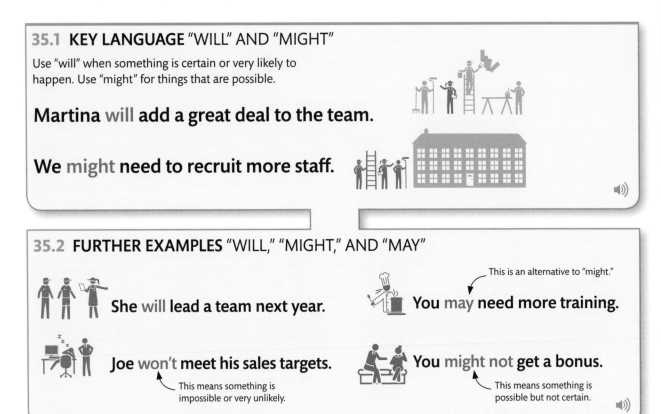

35.1 KEY LANGUAGE "WILL" AND "MIGHT"

Use "will" when something is certain or very likely to happen. Use "might" for things that are possible.

Martina will add a great deal to the team.

We might need to recruit more staff.

35.2 FURTHER EXAMPLES "WILL," "MIGHT," AND "MAY"

She will lead a team next year.

You may need more training.
This is an alternative to "might."

Joe won't meet his sales targets.
This means something is impossible or very unlikely.

You might not get a bonus.
This means something is possible but not certain.

35.3 MATCH THE PAIRS OF SENTENCES

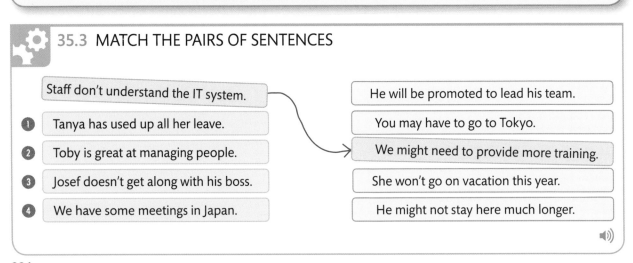

Staff don't understand the IT system. —→ We might need to provide more training.

1. Tanya has used up all her leave. — She won't go on vacation this year.
2. Toby is great at managing people. — He will be promoted to lead his team.
3. Josef doesn't get along with his boss. — He might not stay here much longer.
4. We have some meetings in Japan. — You may have to go to Tokyo.

He will be promoted to lead his team.

You may have to go to Tokyo.

We might need to provide more training.

She won't go on vacation this year.

He might not stay here much longer.

35.4 MARK THE SENTENCES THAT ARE CORRECT

Pam has more than 10 years' experience and she wills lead our sales department. ☐
Pam has more than 10 years' experience and she will lead our sales department. ✓

1 We can't hire any staff at the moment, so you don't might get an assistant until May. ☐
We can't hire any staff at the moment, so you might not get an assistant until May. ☐

2 You're great with new staff, so we may ask you to become a mentor. ☐
You're great with new staff, so we ask may you to become a mentor. ☐

3 It's been a bad year for the company, so you won't get a raise. ☐
It's been a bad year for the company, so you not will get a raise. ☐

4 This report needs to be finished by Friday. You need might to work overtime. ☐
This report needs to be finished by Friday. You might need to work overtime. ☐

5 If Lucinda's work doesn't improve, we may have to fire her. ☐
If Lucinda's work doesn't improve, we won't have to fire her. ☐

35.5 READ THE PERFORMANCE REVIEW AND ANSWER THE QUESTIONS

Performance Review:
Paula Stannard

Paula has worked in our customer relations department for two years. She will be promoted to assistant manager at the beginning of next year.

After her promotion, Paula will be in charge of about 45 people. We may need to give her additional training, but I am confident that she will perform well in this role. Paula will receive a 10 percent raise in her new position. We might consider providing her with a company car, as she will need to go out and visit clients.

Paula works in accounts. **True** ☐ **False** ✓

1 Paula will be promoted next year. **True** ☐ **False** ☐

2 Paula will be head of her department. **True** ☐ **False** ☐

3 Paula will manage more than 40 people. **True** ☐ **False** ☐

4 She won't need any extra training. **True** ☐ **False** ☐

5 Her boss thinks she will perform well. **True** ☐ **False** ☐

6 Paula's salary will not increase. **True** ☐ **False** ☐

7 Paula may get a company car. **True** ☐ **False** ☐

8 Paula will stay in the office all the time. **True** ☐ **False** ☐

35.6 KEY LANGUAGE "DEFINITELY" AND "PROBABLY"

Use "definitely" with "will" and "won't" to talk about things that are certain, and "probably" for things that are likely.

TIP
"Definitely" and "probably" are placed after "will" in a sentence, but before "won't."

You will definitely **be promoted.**

What are my chances of being promoted this year?

You will probably **be promoted.**

You probably won't **be promoted.**

You definitely won't **be promoted.**

35.7 REWRITE THE SENTENCES, CORRECTING THE ERRORS

> You **will probable** move to the new office.
> _You will probably move to the new office._

❶ He **don't definitely** get the job.
_____

❷ You probably **don't will need** any training.
_____

❸ We **will hire probably** some more staff soon.
_____

❹ She **will definite** get a raise.
_____

❺ I **definitely not will** move to the head office.
_____

❻ I **not probably will** go on vacation this year.
_____

35.8 SAY THE SENTENCES OUT LOUD, PUTTING THE MODIFIER IN THE CORRECT PLACE

> You won't get a new laptop. [definitely]
>
> _You definitely won't get a new laptop._

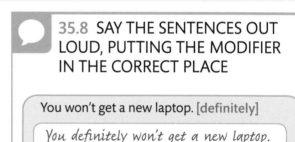

❶ We will get a thank-you gift. [probably]

❷ I won't change jobs this year. [definitely]

❸ You will get a bonus. [definitely]

❹ We won't invite him to the meeting. [probably]

35.9 LISTEN TO THE AUDIO AND MATCH THE IMAGES TO THE CORRECT PHRASES

| definitely won't happen | will definitely happen | may happen | might not happen | probably won't happen |

35 ✓ CHECKLIST

⚙ Modal verbs for possibility ☐   **Aa** Career development ☐   🧩 Talking about the future ☐

🔄 REVIEW THE ENGLISH YOU HAVE LEARNED IN UNITS 30–35

NEW LANGUAGE	SAMPLE SENTENCE	☑	UNIT
"A" AND "THE"	I applied for a job as a nurse. The application form was really long.	☐	30.1
DEFINITE AND ZERO ARTICLES FOR PLURALS	Accountants work very hard. The accountants in my office work long hours.	☐	30.4, 30.5
DEPENDENT PREPOSITIONS	I worked with the head chef in a restaurant.	☐	31.1, 31.6
RELATIVE CLAUSES	This is the product that I designed last year. I worked in a café, which was a lot of fun.	☐	32.1, 32.5
THREE-WORD PHRASAL VERBS	It's important to get along with clients.	☐	34.1
PHRASAL VERBS WITH PRONOUNS	Here's a form. Please can you fill it in?	☐	34.6, 34.7
TALKING ABOUT POSSIBILITIES	We might have to recruit more staff. You will definitely be promoted.	☐	35.1, 35.6

36.1 OFFICE AND PRESENTATION EQUIPMENT

computer

screen

keyboard

mouse

laptop

tablet

touch screen

cursor

power button

charger

power cable

low battery

USB drive / flash drive

hard drive

router

laminator

scanner

webcam

video camera

voice recorder

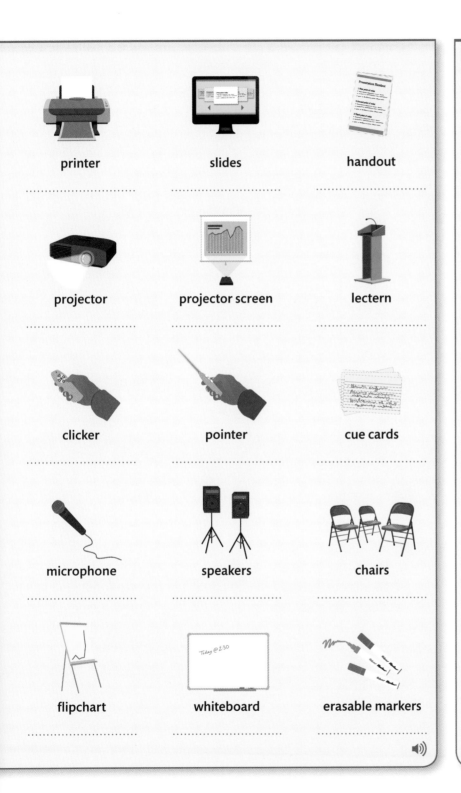

printer

slides

handout

projector

projector screen

lectern

clicker

pointer

cue cards

microphone

speakers

chairs

flipchart

whiteboard

erasable markers

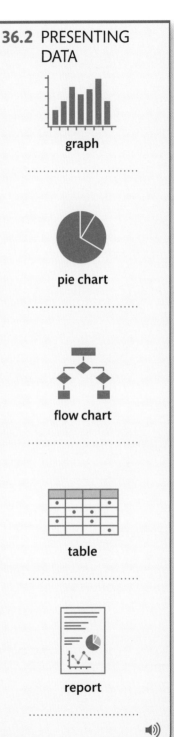

graph

pie chart

flow chart

table

report

37 Structuring a presentation

When you are presenting to an audience, it is important to structure your talk in a way that is clear and easy to understand. Certain set phrases can help you do this.

New language Signposting language
Aa Vocabulary Presentation equipment
New skill Structuring a presentation

37.1 KEY LANGUAGE SIGNPOSTING LANGUAGE

You can signal (or "signpost") what you are going to talk about with particular phrases. Using these lets your audience know what to expect.

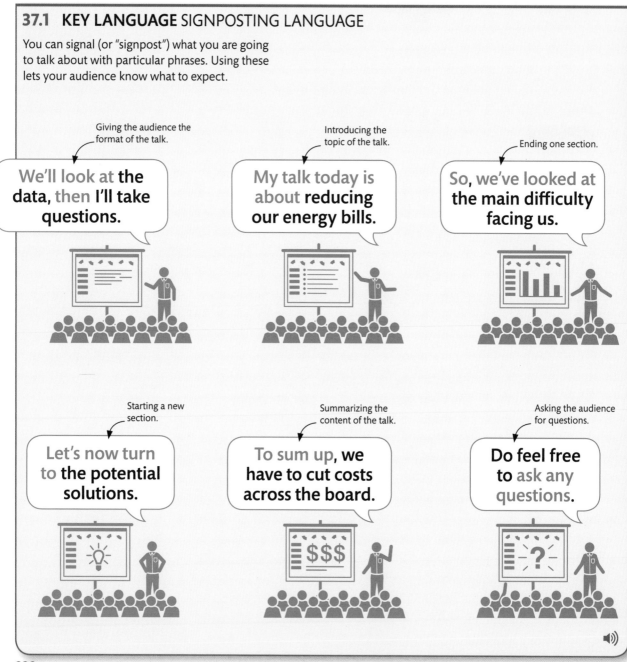

Giving the audience the format of the talk.

We'll look at **the data,** then **I'll take questions.**

Introducing the topic of the talk.

My talk today is about **reducing our energy bills.**

Ending one section.

So, we've looked at **the main difficulty facing us.**

Starting a new section.

Let's now turn to **the potential solutions.**

Summarizing the content of the talk.

To sum up, **we have to cut costs across the board.**

Asking the audience for questions.

Do feel free to **ask any questions.**

37.2 LISTEN TO THE AUDIO AND ANSWER THE QUESTIONS

The owner of a café is presenting proposals for the future to the investors.

The speaker invites questions during the talk.	True ☐	False ☑	Not given ☐
❶ The café is not very successful.	True ☐	False ☐	Not given ☐
❷ One option is adding 20 more tables.	True ☐	False ☐	Not given ☐
❸ Any expansion would require more restrooms.	True ☐	False ☐	Not given ☐
❹ The choice is to expand or close the café.	True ☐	False ☐	Not given ☐
❺ The speaker wants to expand the café.	True ☐	False ☐	Not given ☐

37.3 REWRITE THE SENTENCES, PUTTING THE WORDS IN THE CORRECT ORDER

talk.   end   my   That   me   brings   the   to   of

That brings me to the end of my talk.

❶ up,   bright   To   a   future.   sum   have   we   very

_____

❷ ask   questions.   feel   me   Do   to   any   free

_____

❸ the   figures.   turn   predicted   Let's   sales   to

_____

❹ we've   alternatives.   looked   all   So,   at   main   the

_____

331

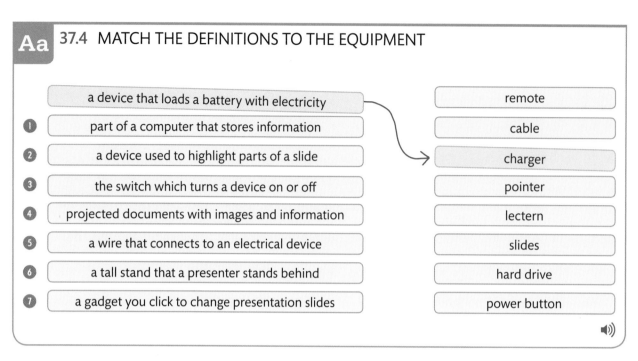

Aa 37.4 MATCH THE DEFINITIONS TO THE EQUIPMENT

a device that loads a battery with electricity — charger

1. part of a computer that stores information
2. a device used to highlight parts of a slide
3. the switch which turns a device on or off
4. projected documents with images and information
5. a wire that connects to an electrical device
6. a tall stand that a presenter stands behind
7. a gadget you click to change presentation slides

remote
cable
charger
pointer
lectern
slides
hard drive
power button

37.5 SAY THE SENTENCES OUT LOUD, FILLING IN THE GAPS WITH THE WORDS IN THE PANEL

You can ask for copies of the _____slides_____ after the talk.

1. Be careful of the _____ in front of the stage.

2. I will return to the _____ to answer questions.

3. If you follow my _____, you can see the graph.

4. I'll use my _____ to forward to the final slide.

5. This projector's noisy. I'll turn the _____ off.

cable   ~~slides~~   lectern   pointer   remote   power button

332

37.6 READ THE ARTICLE AND ANSWER THE QUESTIONS

> We often see similar pictures in presentations.
> True ☑ False ☐ Not given ☐

1 Images always make presentations exciting.
True ☐ False ☐ Not given ☐

2 The writer often gives presentations himself.
True ☐ False ☐ Not given ☐

3 Slides can add extra meaning to the presentation.
True ☐ False ☐ Not given ☐

4 It can be better to use your own images.
True ☐ False ☐ Not given ☐

5 It is better to have a lot of text on slides.
True ☐ False ☐ Not given ☐

6 You must have slides to give a good presentation.
True ☐ False ☐ Not given ☐

PRESENTATIONS AND TALKS

Visual Aids: tips and tricks

Make the most of the images you use in your presentations

The internet contains millions of images and yet, when we sit through presentations, we often see the same old pictures of cogs and handshakes. These images add little value to any presentation. Here are some simple tips for using visual aids in presentations. First, use clear slides with simple images that add to the meaning of the presentation. Also, don't forget that you can use your own photographs, rather than the impersonal images taken from the internet. Next, ensure that slides are not covered in lots of tiny text that is either difficult to read, or that you intend to read out anyway. Finally, consider if you need slides at all. If they don't add anything, you may be better off without them.

37.7 LISTEN TO THE AUDIO, THEN NUMBER THE SENTENCES IN THE ORDER YOU HEAR THEM

A My talk today is about the advertising budget for the next year. ☐

B Let's now turn to the advertising plans for next year. ☐

C Do feel free to ask any questions or for more information. ☐

D Good morning. Thank you for coming to my presentation this morning. ☐ *1*

E So, we've looked at last year's advertising successes and failures. ☐

F To sum up, we will have even more publicity for less money. ☐

G If you follow my pointer, you'll see last year's figures on the left. ☐

H I'll quickly go through the figures and then I'll take any questions. ☐

37 ✓ CHECKLIST

⚙ Signposting language ☐   **Aa** Presentation equipment ☐   👥 Structuring a presentation ☐

38 Developing an argument

When you are giving a presentation, there are several key phrases you can use to develop your argument, and make your audience aware of what is coming.

🔧 **New language** Useful presentation language
Aa Vocabulary Presentations
🧩 **New skill** Developing an argument

38.1 KEY LANGUAGE GENERALIZING, MAKING EXCEPTIONS, AND FOCUSING

If you have specific figures, it may be useful to give them. However, you may need to use more general terms if you do not have the figures or you want to avoid repetition.

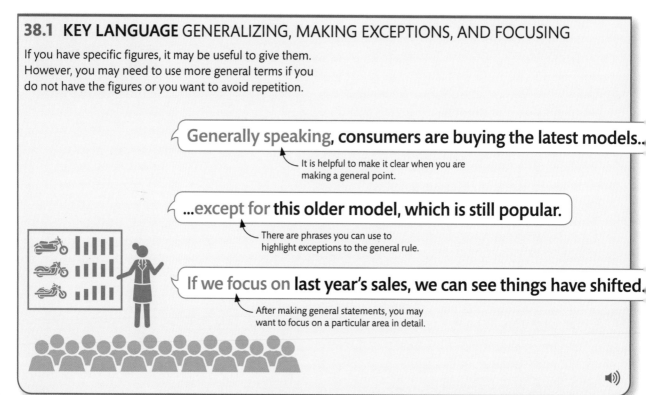

Generally speaking, consumers are buying the latest models..

It is helpful to make it clear when you are making a general point.

...except for this older model, which is still popular.

There are phrases you can use to highlight exceptions to the general rule.

If we focus on last year's sales, we can see things have shifted.

After making general statements, you may want to focus on a particular area in detail.

38.2 WRITE THE PHRASES FROM THE PANEL IN THE CORRECT CATEGORIES

GENERALIZING	EXCEPTIONS	FOCUSING
on the whole		

except for   with the exception of

generally   if we focus on

aside from   ~~on the whole~~

if we home in on   excepting

concentrating on   focusing on

in general   by and large

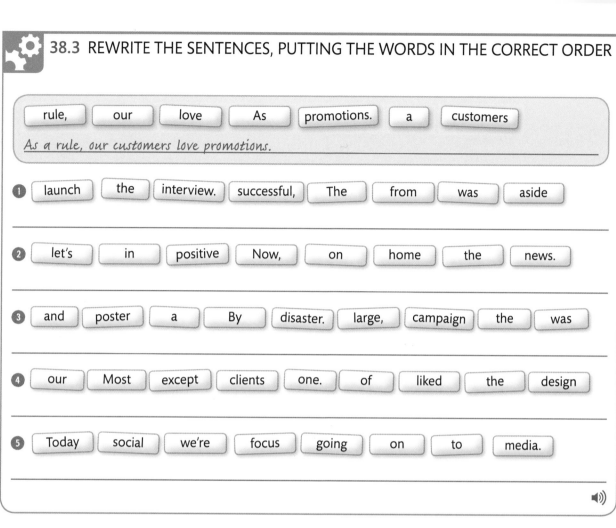

rule, | our | love | As | promotions. | a | customers

As a rule, our customers love promotions.

1. launch | the | interview. | successful, | The | from | was | aside

2. let's | in | positive | Now, | on | home | the | news.

3. and | poster | a | By | disaster. | large, | campaign | the | was

4. our | Most | except | clients | one. | of | liked | the | design

5. Today | social | we're | focus | going | on | to | media.

38.4 LISTEN TO THE AUDIO AND ANSWER THE QUESTIONS

A brand manager is talking to an audience about a new range of products.

ValenTova's is going to take over Tina's.
True ☐ **False** ☐ **Not given** ☑

1. Both brands have a good reputation.
True ☐ **False** ☐ **Not given** ☐

2. The new partnership will have a website.
True ☐ **False** ☐ **Not given** ☐

3. You can only buy Tina's in London.
True ☐ **False** ☐ **Not given** ☐

4. They will sell mail order chocolate.
True ☐ **False** ☐ **Not given** ☐

5. The ice cream will be called Valentina's.
True ☐ **False** ☐ **Not given** ☐

335

38.5 KEY LANGUAGE GIVING EXAMPLES

When you have focused your argument, you may want to give examples to explain your point.

"For instance" can go at the beginning, middle, or (less commonly) end of a sentence.

For instance, our new distribution method has been a huge success.

You can also say "As an illustration..." at the start of a sentence.

As an example, our products have been very popular in Asia.

We've made progress in new sectors such as the travel market.

"Such as" comes in the middle of a sentence before the noun it is illustrating.

38.6 KEY LANGUAGE COUNTERING THE GENERAL OPINION

To counter something that has been stated as, or is understood as, the general opinion there are a number of set phrases you can use.

These phrases tend to go at the beginning of sentences.

In fact...

Actually...

As a matter of fact...

In actual fact...

In reality...

However...

38.7 READ THE ARTICLE AND ANSWER THE QUESTIONS

The article is about creating slides.	**True** ☐	**False** ☑

1 Start with a joke. **True** ☐ **False** ☐

2 Research each audience. **True** ☐ **False** ☐

3 You should not stay still. **True** ☐ **False** ☐

4 You should look serious. **True** ☐ **False** ☐

15 LIFE HACKS

PRESENTING

We put a lot of effort into writing presentations, so it's important to keep the audience's attention. Start with a good, relevant story and include facts and images that are aimed directly at your audience. This shows you have researched them and their needs. Use the space that you have and move around the stage. Lastly, make sure that you look up regularly and smile.

38.8 RESPOND OUT LOUD TO THE AUDIO, FILLING IN THE GAPS USING THE WORDS IN THE PANEL

How do our customers spend their free time?

Our research shows that, _____ *as a rule* _____ , they are very active.

1 So, were all the media campaigns failures?

No. _____ the posters, we can see they were very successful.

2 Did all the stores improve sales last year?

Yes, _____ our Madrid store.

3 So, it was yet another poor year for the company.

_____ it was very successful.

4 Where do you think we should open the next store?

Cities _____ Seoul and Busan could have successful stores.

5 Have sales increased after the launch of our new TV advert?

They haven't yet. _____ , it's too soon to see what the impact will be.

| If we focus on | As a matter of fact | However | ~~as a rule~~ | such as | with the exception of |

---

38 ✓ CHECKLIST

⚙ Useful presentation language ☐   **Aa** Presentations ☐   🧩 Developing an argument ☐

39 Pitching a product

When describing a product to a potential client, it is useful to compare the product with competitors using comparative and superlative adjectives.

⚙ **New language** Comparatives and superlatives
Aa Vocabulary Product marketing
🧩 **New skill** Comparing products

39.1 KEY LANGUAGE COMPARATIVE AND SUPERLATIVE ADJECTIVES

Regular comparative adjectives are formed by adding "-er" to the adjective. Regular superlatives are formed by adding "the" before and "-est" after the adjective.

Comparative

Our competitors might offer cheaper broadband, but ours is the fastest.

Superlative

For some two-syllable adjectives, and all adjectives with more than two syllables, add "more" before the adjective to make the comparative, and "the most" to make the superlative.

This sports car is more stylish than anything else on the market, and the most beautiful car on sale today.

🔊

39.2 FURTHER EXAMPLES COMPARATIVE AND SUPERLATIVE ADJECTIVES

Our new widescreen TV is bigger than any other flatscreen TV.

We offer better customer service than any of our competitors.

These are the easiest tents to put up and take down.

Nevastick 3000 is, quite simply, the best frying pan I've ever used.

🔊

39.3 REWRITE THE SENTENCES, CORRECTING THE ERRORS

> Our phones are much more reliabler than our competitors' phones.
> *Our phones are much more reliable than our competitors' phones.*

1 Our new smartwatch is easyer to operate than the old one.

_____

2 Our new designer jeans are stylish than last year's products.

_____

3 Our tablet is cheapest on the market.

_____

4 This is the more beautiful dress in our range.

_____

5 This is the goodest laptop I have ever owned.

_____

◀))

39.4 LISTEN TO THE AUDIO AND MATCH THE PRODUCTS TO THE PHRASES THAT DESCRIBE THEM

| the most reliable | the thinnest | more affordable | lighter | more comfortable |

39.5 KEY LANGUAGE "AS... AS" COMPARISONS

English uses "as... as" with an adjective to compare things that are similar.

Our laptops are as fast as our competitors' laptops, but are much cheaper.

39.6 FURTHER EXAMPLES "AS... AS" COMPARISONS

Use "just as... as" to emphasize the similarity between two things.

Our new watch is just as light as any other design on the market.

Use "not as... as" to contrast things that are different.

This drill is not as noisy as many existing brands.

This sports drink is as healthy as the leading brand, but much cheaper.

Our washing machine is as quick as more expensive models.

39.7 MARK THE SENTENCES THAT ARE CORRECT

These energy-efficient light bulbs are just as effective as the old ones. ☑
These energy-efficient light bulbs are as just effective as the old ones. ☐

❶ Our new phone is cheap as existing models, but has a much wider range of features. ☐
Our new phone is as cheap as existing models, but has a much wider range of features. ☐

❷ Our latest DVD is as more exciting as anything I've ever seen. ☐
Our latest DVD is as exciting as anything I've ever seen. ☐

❸ Our chairs are excellent value, and just as comfortable as more expensive models. ☐
Our chairs are excellent value, and as just as comfortable as more expensive models. ☐

39.8 READ THE ADVERTISEMENT AND ANSWER THE QUESTIONS

ORGANIC VEG BOX

Perfect organic goodness, delivered to your door

In our veg box, you'll find the freshest lettuce, picked the day before delivery, and delicious, ripe, seasonal fruit. You and your family will love it!

Our vegetables are just as cheap as supermarket produce. And we deliver them free to your door every week!

Vegetables in the box are grown in the UK.
True ☐ **False** ☐ **Not given** ☑

1. The ad claims that the fruit tastes delicious.
True ☐ **False** ☐ **Not given** ☐

2. The veg box contains apples.
True ☐ **False** ☐ **Not given** ☐

3. Vegetables in the supermarket are cheaper.
True ☐ **False** ☐ **Not given** ☐

4. There is no extra charge for home delivery.
True ☐ **False** ☐ **Not given** ☐

5. The box is available in different sizes.
True ☐ **False** ☐ **Not given** ☐

39.9 CROSS OUT THE INCORRECT WORDS IN EACH SENTENCE, THEN SAY THE SENTENCES OUT LOUD

This car is ~~reliabler~~ / **more reliable** than other models, and good value for money.

1. Our new laptop is much **lighter** / **more light** than its competitors.

2. This fitness tracker is **just effective as** / **just as effective as** more expensive models.

3. Organic fruit is not **as cheap** / **as cheap as** supermarket fruit, but it tastes better.

4. A consumer survey voted our pizzas the **tastiest** / **most tastyest** on the market.

39 ✓ CHECKLIST

⚙ Comparatives and superlatives ☐   **Aa** Product marketing ☐   🧩 Comparing products ☐

40 Talking about facts and figures

When you are making a presentation or writing a report, it is important to describe changes and trends with precise language that sounds natural.

⚙ **New language** Collocations
Aa Vocabulary Business trends
🧩 **New skill** Describing facts and figures

40.1 KEY LANGUAGE DESCRIBING TRENDS WITH COLLOCATIONS

You can use a verb modified with an adverb to describe the speed or size of a change. Some of these pairings are collocations that sound "right" to fluent speakers.

TIP
Collocations are often formed of two words, but can contain more. Using them will make you a more fluent English speaker.

VERB　　　ADVERB

Sales have declined considerably.

House prices are fluctuating wildly.

Public interest has fallen steadily.

The markets have rallied slightly.

Some collocations to describe trends are adjectives followed by a noun.

ADJECTIVE　　NOUN

There was a steady increase **last quarter.**

We expect a considerable drop **in the new year.**

After the news, there was a dramatic spike **in sales.**

There was a sharp rise **in profits over the winter.**

40.2 LISTEN TO THE AUDIO, THEN NUMBER THE TRENDS IN THE ORDER THEY ARE DESCRIBED

A ☐

B ☑

C ☐

D ☐

E ☐

F ☐

G ☐

H ☐

40.3 MATCH THE PAIRS OF SENTENCES THAT MEAN THE SAME THING

Profits are going to increase a lot.

We've had a sharp rise in customer numbers.

Sales of our bags have rallied slightly.

We expect a sharp rise in profits.

1. Our share value has increased gradually.

2. There was much less interested in our bags.

3. There have been many more customers.

4. Sales increased suddenly in May.

5. People are a bit more interested in our bags.

6. There's been a steady decline in share value.

7. The dollar's value is going up and down.

8. The value of the dollar increased a lot.

The value of the dollar saw a dramatic spike.

Interest in our bags declined considerably.

The value of the dollar is fluctuating wildly.

There was a dramatic spike in sales in May.

The value of our shares has fallen steadily.

There was a steady increase in our share value.

🔊

40.4 VOCABULARY DESCRIBING FIGURES USING PREPOSITIONS

Between **25** and **30** percent of our stock is seasonal.

....

Sales have fallen **by 40** percent in **the** last quarter.

....

There was an increase **of 5** percent, with profits peaking **at** $20 per unit.

....

We are increasing our fleet **from 20** cars **to** 35.

....

◀))

 ## 40.5 CROSS OUT THE INCORRECT WORD IN EACH SENTENCE

We expect the price to stay ~~from~~ / at $500.

1 Returns have increased **by** / at 10 percent.

2 Prices fell between 30 **and** / of 45 percent.

3 We're shrinking our staff **from** / at 800 to 650.

4 Year-end profit stands in / **at** 8 percent.

5 Salaries will increase **by** / of 2 percent.

6 We have **between** / after 1,100 and 1,200 staff.

7 There was a decrease **of** / on 5 percent.

8 Profits have fallen for / **by** 15 percent.

9 We are lowering the price **to** / at 30 euros.

10 The price peaked in / **at** £19.99.

◀))

40.6 READ THE REPORT AND ANSWER THE QUESTIONS

The share price has fallen a lot.
True ✓ **False** ☐ **Not given** ☐

1 The share price was £22 when the markets closed.
True ☐ **False** ☐ **Not given** ☐

2 There was a small increase in share prices after 11am.
True ☐ **False** ☐ **Not given** ☐

3 RedJet's tickets are likely to become more expensive.
True ☐ **False** ☐ **Not given** ☐

4 RedJet's tickets are 10 percent cheaper than average.
True ☐ **False** ☐ **Not given** ☐

26 **BUSINESS TODAY**

FLIGHT FRIGHT

S hare prices in the aviation company RedJet plummeted overnight after news emerged that its home airport—Stanmore—will be tightening security further, making it difficult for the company to offer as many flights. The company's share price dropped by 27 percent to £22 when the markets opened. Confidence had returned slightly by 11am, when the price climbed slightly to £23.50.

Stanmore airport has also said that it will increase the landing fee it charges RedJet from £1,100 to £1,300 per plane. This means the low-budget airline will almost certainly have to increase ticket prices by between 5 and 10 percent.

40.7 SAY THE SENTENCES OUT LOUD, FILLING IN THE GAPS USING THE WORDS IN THE PANEL

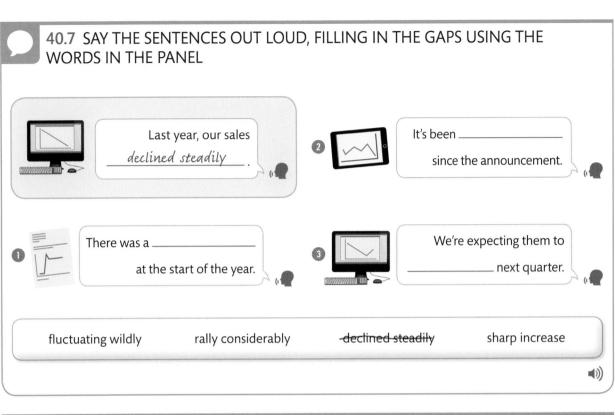

Last year, our sales _declined steadily_ .

It's been _____ since the announcement.

1 There was a _____ at the start of the year.

3 We're expecting them to _____ next quarter.

| fluctuating wildly | rally considerably | ~~declined steadily~~ | sharp increase |

---

40 ⊘ CHECKLIST

⚙ Collocations ☐   **Aa** Business trends ☐   🧩 Describing facts and figures ☐

↻ REVIEW THE ENGLISH YOU HAVE LEARNED IN UNITS 36–40

NEW LANGUAGE	SAMPLE SENTENCE	☑	UNIT
STRUCTURING A PRESENTATION	So, we've looked at **the main difficulty facing us.** Let's now turn to **some solutions.**	☐	37.1
GENERALIZING, MAKING EXCEPTIONS, AND FOCUSING	Generally speaking, **customers are buying the latest models,** except for **this old model.**	☐	38.1
GIVING EXAMPLES AND COUNTERING	For instance, **our new distribution model has been a huge success.**	☐	38.5, 38.6
PITCHING A PRODUCT WITH COMPARATIVES AND SUPERLATIVES	**Our competitors might offer** cheaper **broadband, but ours is** the fastest.	☐	39.1, 39.5
DESCRIBING TRENDS	**Sales have** declined considerably. **There was a** steady increase.	☐	40.1
DESCRIBING FIGURES USING PREPOSITIONS	Between **25 and 30 percent of our stock is** seasonal.	☐	40.4

41 Plans and suggestions

English uses modal verbs to make suggestions, and indirect questions or the passive voice to politely request information or point out a mistake.

⚙ **New language** Indirect questions
Aa Vocabulary Business negotiations
🧩 **New skill** Negotiating politely

41.1 KEY LANGUAGE NEGOTIATION AND SUGGESTIONS

One way of making language for negotiation more polite and indirect is to use modal verbs or the past continuous.

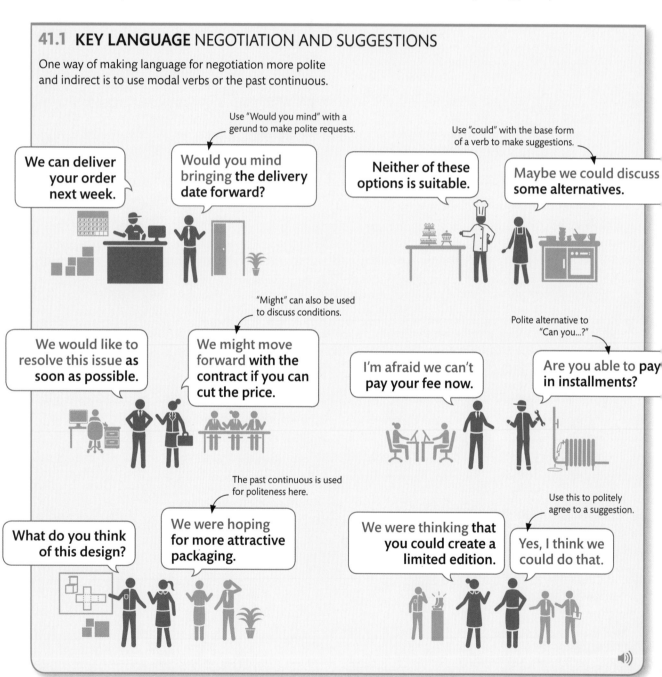

We can deliver your order next week.

Use "Would you mind" with a gerund to make polite requests.

Would you mind bringing **the delivery date forward?**

Neither of these options is suitable.

Use "could" with the base form of a verb to make suggestions.

Maybe we could discuss **some alternatives.**

We would like to resolve this issue **as soon as possible.**

"Might" can also be used to discuss conditions.

We might move forward **with the contract if you can cut the price.**

I'm afraid we can't pay your fee now.

Polite alternative to "Can you...?"

Are you able to **pay in installments?**

What do you think of this design?

The past continuous is used for politeness here.

We were hoping **for more attractive packaging.**

We were thinking **that you could create a limited edition.**

Use this to politely agree to a suggestion.

Yes, I think we could do that.

I'm afraid we're not going to meet your deadline.

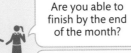

Are you able to finish by the end of the month? ✓

That's terrible news. ☐

1

We were thinking that you could design a gift box.

Yes, I think we could do that. ☐

That sounds complicated. ☐

2

I would like to resolve the issue right away.

We can't agree anything without a delivery date. ☐

We might move forward if we can agree on a delivery date. ☐

3

Our client doesn't like these colors.

We'll have to start again. ☐

Maybe we could consider different colors. ☐

4

My payment terms are 30 days.

I can't pay you until next month. ☐

Would you mind waiting until next month for payment? ☐

5

What do you think of our new product?

We were hoping it would be more innovative. ☐

It's too old-fashioned. ☐

🔊

Kevin is negotiating with Jamila, whose catering company might provide refreshments for an event.

How many people will be at the party?
100 people ☐
150 people ✓
200 people ☐

1 What is the maximum number of people the company can cater for?
500 ☐
1,000 ☐
1,500 ☐

2 What does Kevin say the problem with the price is?
It doesn't include drinks ☐
It is for 35 people ☐
It is too high ☐

3 What else does Kevin ask the company to supply for the party?
A cake ☐
A design ☐
A table layout ☐

4 When will Kevin talk to Jamila again?
Tomorrow ☐
Next week ☐
Next month ☐

41.4 KEY LANGUAGE INDIRECT QUESTIONS

Indirect questions start with a polite opening phrase. Unlike with direct questions, the verb sits after the subject in indirect questions.

Indirect questions start with a polite opening phrase.

Could you tell me when my order will be ready?

[When will my order be ready?]

Direct questions and indirect questions follow a different word order.

41.5 FURTHER EXAMPLES INDIRECT QUESTIONS

If the opening phrase is "Could you tell me," the indirect question ends with a question mark.

If the opening phrase is "I was wondering," the indirect question ends with a period (full stop).

Could you tell me **how much your product** costs?

Indirect questions leave out the auxiliary verb "do."

I was wondering **what time your store** closes.

Could you tell me **when we** can **expect payment?**

I was wondering **if you** are **free for a meeting.**

41.6 HOW TO FORM INDIRECT QUESTIONS

OPENING PHRASE	QUESTION WORD	SUBJECT	VERB
Could you tell me	when	the store	closes?

You can also use "I was wondering."

In indirect questions, the verb follows the subject.

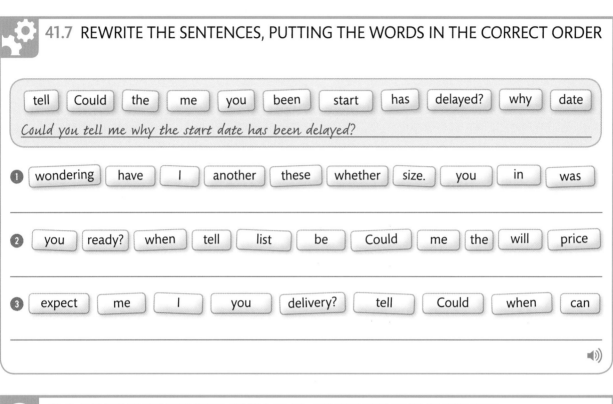

41.7 REWRITE THE SENTENCES, PUTTING THE WORDS IN THE CORRECT ORDER

tell | Could | the | me | you | been | start | has | delayed? | why | date

Could you tell me why the start date has been delayed?

1. wondering | have | I | another | these | whether | size. | you | in | was

_____

2. you | ready? | when | tell | list | be | Could | me | the | will | price

_____

3. expect | me | I | you | delivery? | tell | Could | when | can

_____

41.8 SAY THE SENTENCES OUT LOUD, CORRECTING THE ERRORS

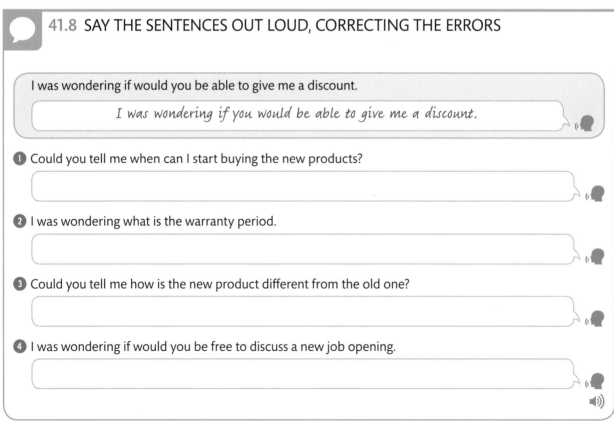

I was wondering if would you be able to give me a discount.

I was wondering if you would be able to give me a discount.

1. Could you tell me when can I start buying the new products?

_____

2. I was wondering what is the warranty period.

_____

3. Could you tell me how is the new product different from the old one?

_____

4. I was wondering if would you be free to discuss a new job opening.

_____

41.9 KEY LANGUAGE THE PASSIVE VOICE

In formal or written negotiations or complaints, you can use
the passive voice to be polite and avoid sounding too critical.

It seems that a mistake has been made.

[You made a mistake.]

Complaints using the passive voice often
start with a polite opening phrase.

I'm afraid the invoice was not paid on time.

[You didn't pay the invoice on time.]

It looks as if your staff are
not very well trained.

[You don't train your staff very well.]

 ## 41.10 REWRITE THE SENTENCES USING THE PASSIVE VOICE

I'm afraid you delivered our order several days late.
I'm afraid our order was delivered several days late.

❶ Could you tell me whether you have changed the delivery date?

❷ I was wondering whether you have paid my invoice.

❸ It seems that you sent the wrong product.

❹ It looks as if that you did not fully understand my complaint.

❺ It seems that you did not calculate the price correctly.

41.11 MATCH THE BEGINNINGS OF THE SENTENCES TO THE CORRECT ENDINGS

We would like to resolve	the sales start?
❶ I'm afraid I can't access	the discount has not been applied.
❷ It looks as if	this issue as soon as possible.
❸ I was wondering why the	the computer system right now.
❹ Could you tell me when	has been contacted.
❺ It seems that the wrong customer	deadline has been missed.

41.12 READ THE EMAIL AND ANSWER THE QUESTIONS

Bettina's order arrived on May 5.
True ☐   False ☐   Not given ☑

❶ The shipments from Ms. Liang are often late.
True ☐   False ☐   Not given ☐

❷ Ms. Liang said the order was sent before April 26.
True ☐   False ☐   Not given ☐

❸ Bettina has the shipping information.
True ☐   False ☐   Not given ☐

❹ Ms. Liang won't be charged for the late delivery.
True ☐   False ☐   Not given ☐

❺ Bettina will cancel her next order.
True ☐   False ☐   Not given ☐

✉

To: Jennifer Liang

Subject: Shipment of jeans overdue

Dear Ms. Liang,

I'm afraid we have still not received the shipment of jeans that was due to arrive on May 5. I contacted you on April 26, when you confirmed that the order had been sent and would arrive on time. Could you please send me the shipping information and tell me when the order will arrive?

I'm afraid we will have to make a deduction from your final invoice to compensate us for the late delivery.

I look forward to hearing from you,
Bettina Koehl

41 ✓ CHECKLIST

⚙ Indirect questions ☐   **Aa** Business negotiations ☐   🧩 Negotiating politely ☐

42 Emphasizing your opinion

There are many English phrases for politely emphasizing your point of view. These are useful when you are dealing with disagreement in the workplace.

⚙ **New language** Discourse markers for emphasis
Aa Vocabulary Workplace disagreement
🧩 **New skill** Emphasizing your opinion

42.1 KEY LANGUAGE DISCOURSE MARKERS FOR EMPHASIS

There are a variety of words and phrases that you can use to make your position more emphatic without being rude.

> Is there any reason why you can't sign the contract today?

> What we need is **an assurance from you about the future.**

42.2 FURTHER EXAMPLES DISCOURSE MARKERS FOR EMPHASIS

> Could we see some more options for the design tomorrow?

> **Actually,** we are very short-staffed at the moment. Would next week be OK?

> I'm afraid your asking price is too high.

> If you ask me, **this is a good deal for you.**

42.3 CROSS OUT THE INCORRECT WORDS IN EACH SENTENCE

> What I'm ~~needing~~ / saying / ~~telling~~ is that we need to increase sales by at least five percent.

1. If you ask I / **me** / us, we might be better to wait until the summer.

2. Which / Who / **What** we need is proof that your business is profitable.

3. **Actually** / Actual / Actionally, we'd like to reach an agreement by the end of the day.

4. The **main** / most / minor thing is that we agree on a price that everyone is happy with.

42.4 LISTEN TO THE NEGOTIATION, THEN NUMBER THE SENTENCES IN THE ORDER YOU HEAR THEM

A If you ask me, these colors are quite bright already. ☐

B We need assurance that you can supply 1,000 umbrellas a month. ☐

C Actually, we're worried about the colors. ☐ 1

D The main thing is that our company logo should really stand out. ☐

E What I'm saying is I can send you samples in brighter colors next week. ☐

42.5 RESPOND OUT LOUD TO THE AUDIO, FILLING IN THE GAPS USING THE WORDS IN THE PANEL

Is there any chance you could reduce your asking price?

I'm afraid not. If _____*you ask me*_____ , you won't find a lower price.

1 Are you ready to sign the contract?

Not quite. _____ some references from your customers.

2 I'm afraid I can't start on this job until December.

That's OK. The _____ we find the right person to do the work.

3 Is it possible for you to offer free delivery?

_____ , our quote already includes free delivery.

| What we need are | ~~you ask me~~ | Actually | main thing is that |

42 ✓ CHECKLIST

⚙ Discourse markers for emphasis ☐   **Aa** Workplace disagreement ☐   Emphasizing your opinion ☐

43 Discussing conditions

English often uses the first and second conditionals for negotiating with clients and co-workers, and the zero conditional to talk about general truths.

⚙ **New language** Conditionals
Aa Vocabulary Negotiating and bargaining
🧩 **New skill** Discussing possibilities

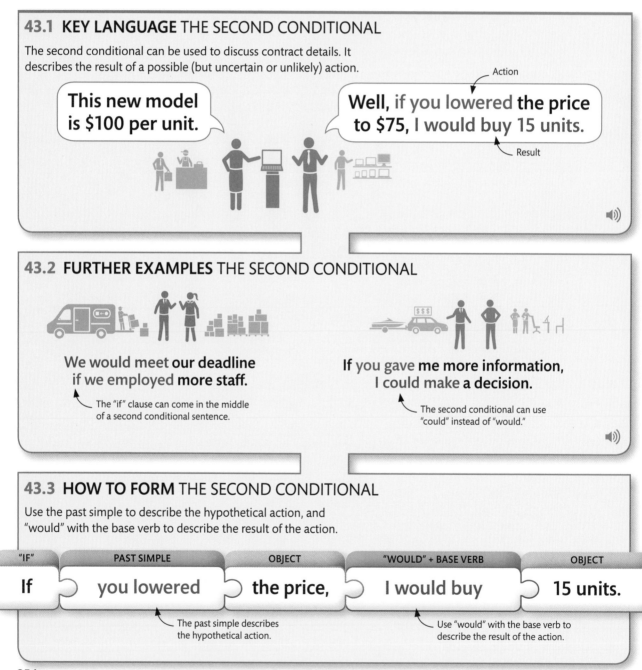

43.1 KEY LANGUAGE THE SECOND CONDITIONAL

The second conditional can be used to discuss contract details. It describes the result of a possible (but uncertain or unlikely) action.

Action

This new model is $100 per unit.

Well, if you lowered the price to $75, I would buy 15 units.

Result

43.2 FURTHER EXAMPLES THE SECOND CONDITIONAL

We would meet our deadline if we employed more staff.

The "if" clause can come in the middle of a second conditional sentence.

If you gave me more information, I could make a decision.

The second conditional can use "could" instead of "would."

43.3 HOW TO FORM THE SECOND CONDITIONAL

Use the past simple to describe the hypothetical action, and "would" with the base verb to describe the result of the action.

"IF"	PAST SIMPLE	OBJECT	"WOULD" + BASE VERB	OBJECT
If	you lowered	the price,	I would buy	15 units.

The past simple describes the hypothetical action.

Use "would" with the base verb to describe the result of the action.

43.4 REWRITE THE SECOND CONDITIONAL SENTENCES, CORRECTING THE ERRORS

> If you give me a discount, I would book.
> *If you gave me a discount, I would book.*

❶ I would placed an order if they delivered sooner.

_____

❷ If your product is cheaper, we would buy it.

_____

❸ If you moved the deadline, we could to meet it.

_____

❹ I work with them if they answered my questions.

_____

❺ If they would check their work, I would use them.

_____

🔊

43.5 LISTEN TO THE AUDIO AND ANSWER THE QUESTIONS

Diane is negotiating a better price for her office supplies with Josef, an office stationery salesman.

> Diane has talked to another company.
> **True** ☑ **False** ☐ **Not given** ☐

❶ Diane is impressed with Office Hub's offers.
True ☐ **False** ☐ **Not given** ☐

❷ Diane has always bought stationery from Josef.
True ☐ **False** ☐ **Not given** ☐

❸ Josef can't offer free next-day delivery.
True ☐ **False** ☐ **Not given** ☐

❹ Josef offers free delivery after four days.
True ☐ **False** ☐ **Not given** ☐

❺ The two-for-one deal is a new offer.
True ☐ **False** ☐ **Not given** ☐

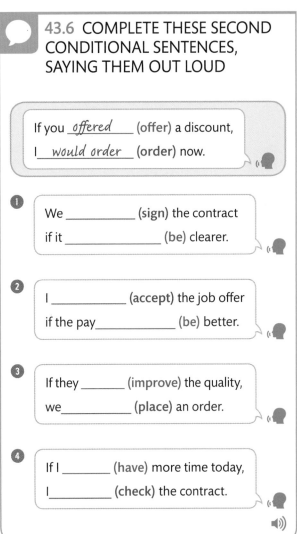

43.6 COMPLETE THESE SECOND CONDITIONAL SENTENCES, SAYING THEM OUT LOUD

> If you _offered_ (offer) a discount,
> I _would order_ (order) now.

❶ We _____ (sign) the contract
if it _____ (be) clearer.

❷ I _____ (accept) the job offer
if the pay_____ (be) better.

❸ If they _____ (improve) the quality,
we_____ (place) an order.

❹ If I _____ (have) more time today,
I_____ (check) the contract.

🔊

355

43.7 KEY LANGUAGE ZERO AND FIRST CONDITIONALS

THE ZERO CONDITIONAL

Use the zero conditional to talk about things that
are generally true. The present simple describes
the action and the result.

PRESENT SIMPLE   **PRESENT SIMPLE**

If customers buy our products in bulk, we reduce our prices.

↳ Action   ↳ Result

THE FIRST CONDITIONAL

The first conditional uses the present simple
and the future with "will" to talk about the
likely results of things that might happen.

PRESENT SIMPLE   **FUTURE WITH "WILL"**

If you are not satisfied, we will give you a refund.

↳ Action   ↳ Result

43.8 FURTHER EXAMPLES ZERO AND FIRST CONDITIONALS

Zero conditional sentences can
use "when" instead of "if."

**When we work too late,
we're tired the next day.**

Conditional sentences can
start with the result clause.

**You'll get a bonus if your
presentation goes well.**

**Products don't sell well
if they're poor quality.**

**If you don't plan ahead,
you won't have enough stock.**

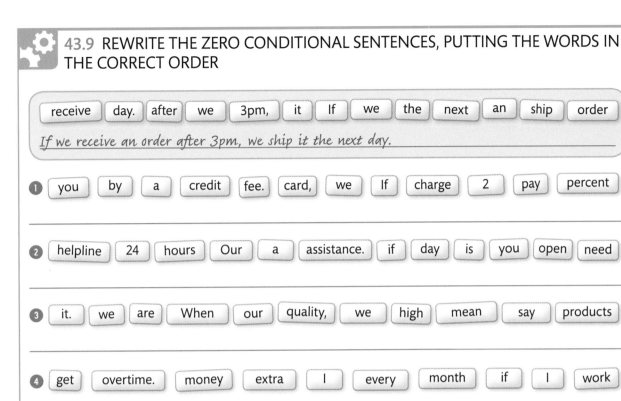

43.9 REWRITE THE ZERO CONDITIONAL SENTENCES, PUTTING THE WORDS IN THE CORRECT ORDER

receive | day. | after | we | 3pm, | it | If | we | the | next | an | ship | order

If we receive an order after 3pm, we ship it the next day.

1. you | by | a | credit | fee. | card, | we | If | charge | 2 | pay | percent

_____

2. helpline | 24 | hours | Our | a | assistance. | if | day | is | you | open | need

_____

3. it. | we | are | When | our | quality, | we | high | mean | say | products

_____

4. get | overtime. | money | extra | I | every | month | if | I | work

_____

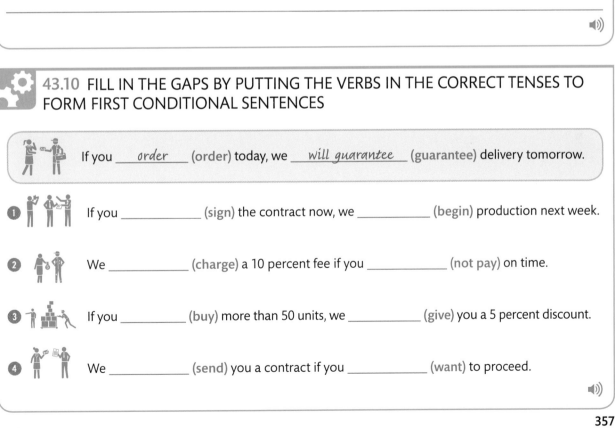

43.10 FILL IN THE GAPS BY PUTTING THE VERBS IN THE CORRECT TENSES TO FORM FIRST CONDITIONAL SENTENCES

If you _____order_____ (order) today, we _____will guarantee_____ (guarantee) delivery tomorrow.

1. If you _____ (sign) the contract now, we _____ (begin) production next week.

2. We _____ (charge) a 10 percent fee if you _____ (not pay) on time.

3. If you _____ (buy) more than 50 units, we _____ (give) you a 5 percent discount.

4. We _____ (send) you a contract if you _____ (want) to proceed.

43.11 KEY LANGUAGE ZERO, FIRST, AND SECOND CONDITIONALS OVERVIEW

ZERO CONDITIONAL

Use the zero conditional to talk about general truths and things that always happen.

If employees are friendly to clients, they get better tips.

FIRST CONDITIONAL

Use the first conditional to talk about things that are likely to happen.

If Lisa's meeting goes well, she will get a raise.

SECOND CONDITIONAL

Use the second conditional to talk about things that are unlikely to happen, but are still possible.

If Ethan was more polite to clients, he would be promoted.

🔊

 43.12 MATCH THE BEGINNINGS OF THE SENTENCES TO THE CORRECT ENDINGS

If a customer makes a complaint,   if you leave a message.

① We will return your call ASAP   if our products were more popular there.

② We would open stores in the US   → we always take it seriously.

③ If you need more training,   if we had more staff.

④ We would increase production   if you return your product within 28 days.

⑤ We will issue a full refund   you can contact the HR department.

🔊

43.13 READ THE WEB PAGE AND WRITE ANSWERS TO THE QUESTIONS AS FULL SENTENCES

Business Tips

HOME | ENTRIES | ABOUT | CONTACT

EFFECTIVE NEGOTIATION

Many businesspeople are required to handle negotiations, but few receive any training in how to do it. Here are my top negotiating tips.

Before negotiating
- Do your research. Find out about your business partner. If you understand the other party, you'll understand his or her strengths and weaknesses.
- Before the meeting, decide what you can compromise on. For example, if your business partner offered you Deal A, would you accept it? If not, what would you accept?

During the negotiation
- If you haven't met your business partner before, hold the meeting face to face. Research has shown that meetings in person help to build rapport, so the other party will be more likely to meet you halfway.
- Don't talk more than is necessary. If you talk too much, you run the risk of revealing information that could be useful to the other party.
- Remember, if you keep the meeting professional and listen to each other, you'll reach the goal of any negotiation: finding common ground so that you can reach an agreement and close the deal.

Why might you need negotiation advice?
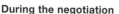
Few businesspeople are trained to negotiate.

❶ Why should you understand the other party?
_____

❷ What should you decide before negotiating?
_____

❸ Why are face-to-face meetings important?
_____

❹ Why shouldn't you talk too much?
_____

❺ What is the goal of any negotiation?
_____

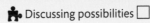

43 ✓ CHECKLIST

⚙ Conditionals ☐   **Aa** Negotiating and bargaining ☐   🧩 Discussing possibilities ☐

Discussing problems

English uses the third conditional to talk about an unreal past, or events that did not happen. This is useful for talking about workplace mistakes.

⚙ **New language** Third conditional
Aa Vocabulary Workplace mistakes
🧩 **New skill** Talking about past mistakes

44.1 KEY LANGUAGE THE THIRD CONDITIONAL

In third conditional sentences, the past perfect describes something that did not happen, and the "would" clause describes the unreal result.

If you had paid **on time,** we would have sent **the goods to you.**

└ Past perfect   └ Past participle

🔊

44.2 HOW TO FORM THE THIRD CONDITIONAL

"IF"	PAST PERFECT	REST OF CLAUSE	"WOULD" + "HAVE" + PAST PARTICIPLE	REST OF SENTENCE
If	you had paid	on time,	we would have sent	the goods.

44.3 FURTHER EXAMPLES THE THIRD CONDITIONAL

Third conditional sentences can start with the result. ↘

I wouldn't have missed **the meeting if I** had left **earlier.**

The third conditional can use the short form of "had." ↘

If you'd checked **your work, the clients** wouldn't have **complained.**

If we had wanted **a smaller model, we** would have asked **for one.**

If your staff hadn't been **so rude, we** would have signed **the contract.**

🔊

44.4 FILL IN THE GAPS BY PUTTING THE VERBS IN THE CORRECT FORMS TO MAKE THIRD CONDITIONAL SENTENCES

If you ___had spoken___ (speak) more calmly, people ___would have listened___ (listen) to you.

1 If he _____ (use) the correct figures, his report _____ (not be) so out of date.

2 The boss _____ (not shout) if you _____ (admit) your mistake earlier.

3 If you _____ (run) a spell check, the report _____ (not contain) so many errors.

4 We _____ (not embarrass) ourselves if we _____ (research) local customs before our trip.

5 I _____ (work) late last night if I _____ (know) our deadline was so soon.

◀))

44.5 LISTEN TO THE AUDIO AND MARK WHICH THINGS ACTUALLY HAPPENED

44.6 KEY LANGUAGE FIRST CONDITIONAL WITH "UNLESS"

You can use "unless" instead of "if...not" in first conditional sentences. In sentences with "unless," the result only happens if the action does not take place.

We will cancel the contract { **if you don't** / **unless you** } **repair the copier tomorrow.**

Result — Action

44.7 FURTHER EXAMPLES FIRST CONDITIONAL WITH "UNLESS"

We won't be able to offer you a discount unless you order more units.

Elena will get a verbal warning unless her work improves.

44.8 REWRITE THE SENTENCES USING "UNLESS"

> If you don't place the order before 3pm, we won't be able to deliver tomorrow.
> *Unless you place the order before 3pm, we won't be able to deliver tomorrow.*

❶ Tony is not going to meet the deadline if he doesn't work overtime.
_____

❷ If I don't get a good performance review, I won't get a raise this year.
_____

❸ I'm afraid we can't track your order if you can't give us your customer reference number.
_____

❹ If we can't offer a better price, we won't win the contract.
_____

44.9 READ THE REPORT AND ANSWER THE QUESTIONS

Customer response to the product was as expected.
True ☐ **False** ☐ **Not given** ☑

1 Avatar has been a competitor for a long time.
True ☐ **False** ☐ **Not given** ☐

2 It was known when Avatar would launch its product.
True ☐ **False** ☐ **Not given** ☐

3 Vivo knew how much Avatar's watch cost.
True ☐ **False** ☐ **Not given** ☐

4 The Avatar watch is cheaper than the Vivo watch.
True ☐ **False** ☐ **Not given** ☐

5 The new watch will be ready in six months.
True ☐ **False** ☐ **Not given** ☐

VIVO PRODUCT LAUNCH REPORT

Six months ago we launched our new smartwatch, the Vivo. Sales have been very disappointing and interest in the product is low.

WHY?

Our main competitor, Avatar, launched its new smartwatch one week after us. If we had known this, we would have launched our product later. Furthermore, they priced their smartwatch $50 lower than our product. We would have priced our watch lower if we had known about their competitive price.

WHAT NOW?

Unless we reduce the price of our product to match Avatar's watch, we won't make many sales. I suggest we reduce the price to $125. Furthermore, we need to develop a new, better product. We won't beat Avatar unless we can offer a more functional, better-looking watch.

44 ✓ CHECKLIST

⚙ Third conditional ☐   **Aa** Workplace mistakes ☐   🧩 Talking about past mistakes ☐

🔄 REVIEW THE ENGLISH YOU HAVE LEARNED IN UNITS 41–44

NEW LANGUAGE	SAMPLE SENTENCE	☑	UNIT
INDIRECT QUESTIONS	Could you tell me **when my order will be ready?**	☐	41.4
THE PASSIVE VOICE FOR POLITENESS	**It seems that a mistake** has been made.	☐	41.9
EMPHASIZING YOUR OPINION	What we need is **an assurance from you about the future.**	☐	42.1
SECOND CONDITIONAL	If you lowered **the price,** I would order **more units.**	☐	43.1
THIRD CONDITIONAL	If you had paid **on time,** we would have delivered **the goods.**	☐	44.1
FIRST CONDITIONAL WITH "UNLESS"	**We will cancel the contract** unless **you repair the copier tomorrow.**	☐	44.6

Answers

1.2 🔊
1. Hi, Katherine. I think I **met you at the Market Max conference**.
2. I'm not sure whether you **have met each other before**.
3. Yes, we met in Barcelona. **It's great to see you again.**
4. You must be Gloria from the design team. **Guvan told me about your great work.**
5. This is Brian from customer services. **Brian, meet Tonya. She's joining our team.**

1.3 🔊
1. Did we **meet** at a conference?
2. Really good to **see** you again.
3. Roula, meet Maria, **our** new assistant.
4. I'd like to **introduce** you to Karl.
5. Have you two **met** each other before?

1.4
1. False
2. True
3. Not given
4. Not given
5. True

1.6
1. Shy
2. Good ones
3. Ex-colleagues
4. Say sorry
5. Unprofessional
6. Their eyes
7. Your business card

1.7 🔊
1. Hi James. I'm Vanisha. I don't think **we've met** before.
2. Ashley, I'd like **to** introduce you to my colleague Neil.
3. I **am** enjoying the presentations. Are you?
4. Nice to meet you Bethany. How do you **do**?

1.8 🔊
1. Hello Frank. **Are you enjoying** the conference?
2. Wilfred, I'd like you to **meet** Roger, our new press officer.
3. Serena, it's really great to **see** you again after so long.
4. I usually enjoy workshops, but I am not finding this one interesting.

2.3 🔊
1. They **were beginning** to sell more when the shop suddenly closed last year.
2. I **lost** my job when the factory closed last December.
3. I was delighted when I **got** promoted to senior manager in 2015.
4. We moved here when my wife **found** a new job two years ago.
5. I **was training** to be a chef when I was given this award.
6. When I worked 90 hours a week, I **felt** exhausted all the time.
7. When I was a photographer, I **met** a lot of famous people through my work.

2.5 🔊
1. I was looking for another job.
2. I was wondering if you could help.
3. Were you working as a waiter?
4. They weren't employing young people.
5. I didn't enjoy my last job.
6. Did you work in a hotel?

2.8 🔊
1. He **has taken** 15 days off sick this year and it is only May!
2. Julia has a lot of experience. She **has managed** this department for years.
3. They **have employed** more than 300 people over the years.
4. John **has trained** lots of young employees across a few different teams.
5. I'm so happy! I **have finished** my apprenticeship at last.
6. My manager **has approved** my vacation days. I'm going to Italy in July.

2.9 🔊
1. True
2. False
3. Not given
4. True
5. Not given

2.10 🔊
1. I **was driving** taxis when I saw this job advertised.
2. I **have managed** accounts for this company for seven years.
3. I **bought** my first business in 2009.
4. I was studying in college when I **saw** this job.
5. They **have invested** in this company since 2010.
5. In 2014, I sold the company to an investor.

4.3 🔊
1. I used to travel to work by car.
2. She's used to giving big presentations.
3. I'll get used to my new job eventually.
4. We didn't use to get paid a bonus.
5. Did he use to work in marketing?

4.4
- **(A)** 2
- **(B)** 1
- **(C)** 4
- **(D)** 3

4.5 🔊
1. We used to finish at noon on Fridays.
2. She didn't use to be so serious.
3. I am used to working for a strict boss.
4. Did you use to work in London?

4.6 🔊
1. I got used to long hours in my first job.
2. He didn't use to have a law degree.
3. I am used to working long hours.
4. You didn't use to work such long hours.
5. Did he use to work in a bank?

4.7
1. True
2. Not given
3. False
4. False
5. True

4.8 🔊
1. I'm not used to starting at 6am!
2. Yes, what a disappointment!
3. Yes, please. It looks delicious.
4. That's a very short commute!
5. Yes, I think it's going to rain.

4.9 🔊
1. When I was young, I **didn't use to** like mushrooms.
2. My grandfather **used to** walk four miles to school every morning.
3. Are you **used to** your new job yet?
4. I grew up in Florida, so I **am used to** the heat.
5. We **used to** go to the south of France every year.

05

5.3 🔊
1. We have got to ask **for some support on this project**.
2. You must put the finished **proposal on my desk tomorrow**.
3. We must not forget **to look after this project while he's away**.
4. I have to help Sami produce **a report about recycling**.
5. You don't have **to complete it today**.

5.4 🔊
1. We need to increase sales to Europe.
2. We can't reveal our new product yet.
3. You don't have to work late.
4. I will need the accounts by tomorrow.
5. We have got to find a new IT manager.
6. You need to produce a spreadsheet.
7. We must reach our sales target.

5.5
1. True
2. False
3. False
4. False
5. Not given

5.7 🔊
1. Could you answer my phone?
2. Would you call the supplier?
3. We have to finish today.
4. Would you book a meeting?
5. Could you send this today?

5.8 🔊
1. **Could** you deliver this letter for me, please?
2. **Would** you show the new employee around the office?
3. Jess, I **need to** leave early today. Could you let Philippe know?

5.9
1. Not given
2. True
3. True
4. Not given
5. True

07

7.4 🔊
1. We **changed** our logo because a lot of people **had complained** about it.
2. Some of our goods **had arrived** broken, so we **asked** for a refund.
3. There **were** problems in the warehouse because our manager **had resigned**.
4. Sales of umbrellas **were** poor because we **had had** a dry summer.
5. Our clients **were not** happy because we **had missed** our deadline.
6. Yasmin's presentation **had gone** very well, so I **gave** her a promotion.
7. Our sales **increased** because we **had launched** a new product range.

7.5
2.

7.7 🔊
1. The purpose of this report is **to** review our sales figures for the last quarter.
2. Our **principal** recommendation is to complete the sale of the downtown store.
3. The **following** report presents the results of extensive customer satisfaction research.
4. Our main client **stated** that the recent changes were beneficial for his business.

7.8 🔊

① As can be seen in the table, **the figures for this period were excellent.**
② It is clear from the research **that there were a number of problems**.
③ A number of focus groups **were consulted for this report**.
④ The purpose of this report is **to present the findings of our survey**.

7.9 🔊

① The focus group clients had all **used** both the original and new products.
② The following chart **compares** the sales figures for the two periods.
③ We **asked** the customers who had complained why they didn't like the change.
④ The **purpose** of this report is to present the results of our online trial.
⑤ We started this online trial after our store costs had **risen** by 10 percent.

08

8.2 🔊

① Yes, we'll give you a full refund.
② Yes, it's AMLGW14.
③ OK. No problem.
④ Our courier has been having difficulties.
⑤ I'm very sorry to hear that, Mrs. Singh.
⑥ Yes, we'll send you a new one tomorrow.

8.3

Ⓐ 3
Ⓑ 1
Ⓒ 6
Ⓓ 5
Ⓔ 2
Ⓕ 4

8.4 🔊

① We'll **look** into the problem for you.
② We'll **give** you a discount voucher.
③ Could you hold the **line** a moment?
④ Let's see **what** we can do.

8.8 🔊

① The customers **have been waiting** for us to contact them.
② Our engineers **have been working** on the line for two days.
③ What **have** you **been doing** to solve the problem?
④ I **have been watching** your program and I want to complain.
⑤ We **have been repairing** the broken cables this morning.
⑥ They **have been updating** my software and now it doesn't work.

8.9

① True ② Not given ③ True
④ False ⑤ Not given

10

10.2

③

10.3 🔊

① I just wanted to **check** that you will be able to make it to the meeting.
② Don't worry if you have any questions. Just let me **know**.
③ I'm **copying** Maxine in on this as she may have some more information.
④ How **about** coming to the restaurant with us this evening?
⑤ I was **wondering** if you and Ana could come to the meeting tomorrow.
⑥ Give me a call if you can't **make** the presentation at 10 o'clock

11

11.2

① Present ② Future
③ Future ④ Present

11.3

Model Answers
① The delivery van was involved in an accident yesterday.
② The company is receiving new stock tomorrow.
③ She is hoping to confirm a new delivery date next week.
④ She can cancel her order online.
⑤ Yasmin should contact Janice if she has any questions.

11.4 🔊

① to hesitate ② to prefer ③ to obtain
④ to confirm ⑤ to inform
⑥ to contact ⑦ to request

11.6

① I am hoping
② We are currently waiting
③ we are expecting
④ I was wondering
⑤ I assure you
⑥ We will be doing
⑦ please do not hesitate to contact me

11.7 🔊

① I was **wondering** if you would meet the clients at their factory.
② We **are** having difficulties with deliveries due to the weather.
③ Will you be **paying** for the order by bank transfer or credit card?
④ We are aiming **to** finish the redecorating by next Wednesday.

11.8 🔊
1 We are still waiting to hear from our supplier.
2 I was wondering if you could call me back.
3 Will you be attending the progress meeting next week?

12

12.3 🔊
1 I'll look **into** the problem now.
2 The printer has run **out** of ink.
3 I need to **catch** up with you.
4 Sorry, I have to hang **up** now.
5 Could you deal **with** this order?
6 I'll **look** into Mr. Li's query.
7 My client just hung **up** on me!

12.4
Ⓐ 6
Ⓑ 3
Ⓒ 5
Ⓓ 1
Ⓔ 2
Ⓕ 4

12.5 🔊
1 bring up   2 turn up   3 chill out
4 fill out   5 figure out

12.8 🔊
1 James, can you **pass on** the message to Zane?
2 Welcome to Jo's. Please **fill** the visitor's form **out**.
3 Can you stand at the exit and **hand** the leaflets **out**?
4 **Put** a helmet **on** before entering the site.
5 Before I update the software, **back** your files **up**.

12.9 🔊
1 Could you please **pass** the message **on** to Gary?
2 I have an important meeting, so I **put** a suit **on** this morning.
3 Howard, we should really **fix** a meeting **up** for this week.
4 After a busy day in the office, I usually **chill out** at home.

14

14.2
1 True
2 False
3 False
4 Not given
5 False

14.3 🔊
1 Over the last year, an exciting new line has been **developed**.
2 This design **was** patented in 1938. Nobody has ever managed to make a better product!
3 Their new line **is being** launched next Saturday. Everyone is talking about it.
4 Our factory floor **was** cleaned before the CEO visited. He was happy things looked good!
5 You don't need to worry about dinner. The food **is** cooked to order so that it is fresh.
6 The first cars made in this factory **were** sold in the UK in 1972, and worldwide the next year.
7 Our original designers **were** influenced by Japanese artists.
8 To prepare for the launch, advertising posters **are being** put up around town as we speak.

14.6 🔊
1 Their new products **are being promoted** on TV now.
2 80,000 packets **are produced** in the factory each week.
3 A thousand new cars **will be sold** next week.
4 Our latest gadget **was invented** by Ronnie Angel.
5 The production line **is stopped** during the summer.
6 Great advances in design **have been made** recently.

14.7 🔊
1 All the cars are checked by someone before they leave the factory.
2 The new photo app for professional artists was invented by Maxine.
3 All Carl Osric's books were bought by customers on the publication date.
4 All our vegetarian ingredients are bought from the market by Ron.
5 All of the invoices are checked by Samantha before they are sent out.

14.8
Ⓐ 3
Ⓑ 1
Ⓒ 6
Ⓓ 2
Ⓔ 7
Ⓕ 8
Ⓖ 4
Ⓗ 5

14.10 🔊
1 These flowers must have been bought today.
2 They can't be marked down yet! They're new.
3 This picture couldn't have been drawn by Sanjit.
4 The price shouldn't have been accepted.
5 These glasses must be packaged carefully.
6 Faults in the product shouldn't be ignored.
7 The oven has been turned up.

14.11 🔊
1 The chassis parts are placed on the **assembly line**.
2 The engine and radiator **are lifted** by a robot as they are very heavy.
3 The engine and radiator **are secured** to the chassis by an assembly worker.
4 The bodywork is fully **assembled and welded** on a separate line.
5 The assembled bodywork is inspected before **being painted** by a robot.
6 The chassis and bodywork are joined together before the vehicle **is checked**.

15

15.3 🔊
OPINION:
awesome, awful
SIZE:
enormous, tiny
AGE:
modern, out-dated
COLOR:
green, red
NATIONALITY:
Swiss, Indian
MATERIAL:
wooden, fabric

15.4 🔊
1 Have you seen the ugly, plastic desks?
2 We're launching the new, metallic range tomorrow.
3 Would you prefer these tiny, diamond ones?

15.5
1 B 2 A 3 A
4 A 5 B

15.7 🔊
1 I'm interested in that **incredible** modern device we saw at the sales fair.
2 Our competitors are still selling those really **ugly**, large cotton shirts.
3 The office has a **friendly**, old black cat that visits regularly.
4 Frances, have you seen these Peruvian **silver** earrings that I brought back?
5 Did you get one of those new **plastic** business cards?
6 A lot of customers have been asking for the **new** red version.
7 My boss has asked me to design a small, **paper** package for the product.
8 I have bought some new **leather** chairs for the boardroom.

15.8
1 True
2 Not given
3 False
4 False
5 False

15.9 🔊
1 We offer great, **delicious** food that people can afford.
2 Look at that **enormous** new billboard across the street.
3 I love buying **antique** wooden furniture for the office.
4 My boss drives a tiny **green** car to work. It's definitely easy to spot!
5 We aim to offer awesome, **friendly** customer service at all times.

17

17.3 🔊
EXTREME:
awful, fantastic, tiny, disgusting, enormous
ABSOLUTE:
unique, impossible, right, perfect, wrong
CLASSIFYING:
organic, digital, industrial, electronic, chemical

17.4
1 True
2 True
3 Not given
4 False
5 False
6 Not given

17.7 🔊
1 The new gadget is completely digital.
2 This draft design is practically perfect.
3 The client said it was totally fantastic.
4 His decision to invest was entirely right.
5 This area of town is largely industrial.

17.9
1 mainly European
2 pretty confident
3 absolutely delicious

18

18.2 🔊
1 Is the office big enough for us?
2 The delivery times are too slow.
3 Are these shelves strong enough?

18.3
1 B
2 A
3 A
4 A
5 B

18.4
1 False
2 True
3 Not given
4 True
5 False

18.6 ◀))
1 It's such a great product.
2 The meeting was so boring.
3 His news was such a surprise.
4 My boss is so ambitious.
5 Their phones are so cheap.
6 Her company is so big!
7 Our launch was such a surprise!

18.7 ◀))
1 The slogan is far **too** complicated. We need to simplify it.
2 They have created **such** a brilliant poster campaign.
3 We haven't done **enough** market research. We need to understand our consumers.
4 Our supervisor is **such** a creative person. She designed our new logo.
5 Marion is **so** persuasive when she delivers a sales pitch.

19

19.3 ◀))
1 You must tell your boss it will be late.
2 You shouldn't start work so early.
3 You shouldn't work such long shifts.
4 You should take a walk outside right now.

19.4 ◀))
1 My wife said I **could try** yoga and relaxation techniques.
2 You **should stop** working right away if you feel sick.
3 You **ought to take** a break if you're really tired.
4 You **shouldn't feel** exhausted at the beginning of the week.
5 You **must delegate** some of your work to your assistant.

19.5 ◀))
1 You **ought to** relax more.
2 You **must stop** taking work home every day.
3 He **could try** to delegate more tasks.
4 You **shouldn't worry** so much about work.
5 She **should talk** to her colleagues.
6 He **ought to quit** his job if he hates it.

19.6
1 No
2 Yes
3 Yes
4 Yes

19.10 ◀))
1. What about taking a break?
2. What about buying better equipment?
3. What about training new employees?
4. Why don't we take a break?
5. Why don't we buy better equipment?
6. Why don't we train new employees?

19.11 ◀))
1 Why don't we **buy** new chairs?
2 Why don't we **go** for a walk outside?
3 What about **drinking** less coffee?
4 Why don't we **provide** free fruit?
5 What about **making** a list of your tasks?
6 What about **delegating** this to Jo?
7 Why don't we **ask** Paul to help us?

19.12
1 True
2 False
3 True
4 False
5 True
6 False

21

21.3 ◀))
1 She doesn't like meeting new people. She **can't** work in the HR department.
2 Shaun **can** work really well with new employees, so he should help run our training course.
3 Have you seen her brilliant photographs? She **can** create our posters and flyers.
4 Lydia failed her driving test, so, unfortunately, she **can't** drive the delivery van.

21.5 ◀))
1 Peter **couldn't** use the new coffee machine. He didn't know how it worked.
2 Varinder **couldn't** write reports very well at first, but she can now that she's had more practice.
3 No one in the office **could** read his handwriting. It was awful.
4 Bill was the only person who **couldn't** figure out how to use the photocopier.

21.7 ◀))
1 Future
2 Past
3 Future
4 Past
5 Future

21.8
1. True
2. Not given
3. True
4. False
5. False

21.9 🔊
1. James's team was weak, but he's trained them well and now they **can** do anything.
2. We think that you are really creative and **would** make a great addition to the PR team.
3. I don't know what is wrong with me today. I **can't** get anything finished.
4. My confidence is much better now. Before, I **couldn't** talk in public.

22

22.3 🔊
1. **Although** I attended the training session, I'm not sure I learned very much.
2. You got a high score for the IT test, and you've done **equally** well on the team-building course.
3. Team A built a small boat out of plastic bottles, **whereas** Team B used wood to make theirs.
4. The training day is a great way to learn new skills. It's **also** a good way to get to know people.

22.4
1. Walked across bridges high in the air
2. Overcome fear and help each other
3. The tallest and the most scared
4. Disagreed with each other
5. Work more slowly and listen to their teammates

22.6 🔊
1. The course taught us how to lead a team. As a consequence, I feel more confident.
2. I'd never ridden a horse before. For this reason, I was quite scared during the training.
3. Team Lion completed the challenge first. Consequently, they all received medals.

22.7 🔊
1. Team A had to build a cardboard tower, **while Team B had to bake a cake**.
2. Although I liked going to the beach, **I didn't enjoy swimming in the ocean**.
3. I love learning new things. **As a result, I really enjoyed the training day**.
4. Team building is a good way to learn new skills **and it's also a chance to relax**.

22.8
1. Not given
2. True
3. False
4. Not given
5. True

22.9 🔊
Model Answers
1. This course will teach you new skills. It will help you to get to know each other, **too**.
2. **Although** Team B completed the task first, they had some major communication problems.
3. By doing this task, we'll not only identify the team's weaknesses, but **also** its strengths.
4. Team A worked together very well. Team B were **equally** cooperative.

23

23.4 🔊
1. Mara has offered **to organize** the accommodation for our guests.
2. I keep **suggesting** that our company should organize a golf day, but my boss disagrees.
3. We like **to offer** our clients a wide range of food at our conferences.
4. I enjoy **helping** out at company open days because I get to meet lots of people.
5. Before I start planning, I usually make a list of all the customers I want **to invite**.
6. I expect **to stay** late tonight to help Martina decorate the conference hall.

23.5
Model Answers
1. The SmartTech Fair opened in 1987.
2. It is helping us to live healthier lives.
3. They could shape the future of the car industry.
4. You can register your interest online.
5. You can buy tickets from the SmartTech website.

23.8 🔊
1. We stopped holding breakfast meetings **because few people attended them**.
2. We regret to announce **that there will be some job losses**.
3. I'm sure Shona will remember **to book the conference room**.
4. Sahib went on working **until midnight in order to finish the report**.

23.9
1. False
2. Not given
3. False
4. Not given
5. True
6. True

23.10 🔊
1. I remember meeting him in Tokyo.
2. I was supposed to book a nice hotel room.
3. I wanted to book a nice hotel room.
4. She was supposed to book a nice hotel room.
5. She wanted to book a nice hotel room.
6. We remember meeting him in Tokyo.
7. We wanted to book a nice hotel room.
8. They remember meeting him in Tokyo.
9. They wanted to book a nice hotel room.

23.14 🔊
❶ My boss asked me **to arrange** a meeting with our clients.
❷ Our clients **asked us** to visit them in Paris.
❸ We expect all our staff **to arrive** on time.
❹ We **invited all our clients** to attend our end-of-year party.
❺ I expect my manager **to give** me a promotion soon.

23.15 🔊
❶ Our clients expect to receive excellent service.
❷ My boss invited me to attend a conference.
❸ My business degree allowed me to get this job.

25

25.4 🔊
❶ She said she paid the invoice.
❷ He said he would pay the invoice.
❸ He said he would arrange a meeting.
❹ He said he was arranging a meeting.
❺ She said she had finished writing the report.
❻ She said she would finish writing the report.

25.5 🔊
❶ She **said (that) she would interview the candidates**.
❷ He **said (that) he met the CEO on Monday**. / He **said (that) he'd met the CEO on Monday**.
❸ He **said (that) he could book the meeting room**.
❹ She **said (that) she was writing a press release**.
❺ He **said (that) he could use design software**.

25.8
Ⓐ 2
Ⓑ 4
Ⓒ 5
Ⓓ 1
Ⓔ 3

25.10 🔊
❶ She said that she didn't understand the email.
❷ He said there was a problem with his computer.
❸ She said we need to reply to those customers.

25.14 🔊
❶ Sharon **confirmed** that the sales figures would be ready by 5pm.
❷ Lilia **promised** that she would stay late to help me finish the report.
❸ Mr. Lee **announced** that we had beaten our sales target for the year.
❹ Ben **complained** that the coffee from the machine tasted awful.
❺ She **suggested** that I could ask my boss about a raise.

26

26.4 🔊
❶ He asked me why I was late again.
❷ Lara asked me where the meeting was.
❸ She asked me why I had missed the interview.
❹ He asked me who had taken the minutes.

26.5
❶ True
❷ False
❸ True
❹ Not given
❺ True
❻ False
❼ Not given

26.6
❶ Not given
❷ False
❸ True
❹ Not given
❺ False
❻ Not given

26.7 🔊
❶ The boss is angry with Max. He told him to **do his work** before he leaves.
❷ Mr. Tan promised that I would **get promoted** to manager if I worked hard.
❸ Could you **do me a favor**? Could you make 20 copies of this, please?
❹ Can I **make a suggestion**? Finish the proposal first, then work on the spreadsheet.
❺ Paola said that she usually **gets home** from work at 6:30pm.
❻ Paul said that he **had an appointment** with his boss, but he was really late.

26.9 🔊
Model Answers
① She asked (me) what the consumer feedback was.
② He asked (me) whether I had a strategy. / He asked (me) if I had a strategy.
③ She asked (me) who was getting promoted.
④ He asked (me) what the main points were.
⑤ She asked (me) if he was the new marketing manager. / She asked (me) whether he was the new marketing manager.

27

27.2 🔊
① We'll have to reduce the price. Very few customers have bought our new jeans.
② So few people pay by check these days that we no longer accept this form of payment.
③ Unfortunately, we've had few inquiries about our new spa treatments.

27.4 🔊
① Unfortunately, there is **little** chance of us winning this contract.
② I have **a few** ideas that I really think could improve our brand image.
③ There is still **a little** time left before we need to submit the report.
④ Kelvin has **little** understanding of accountancy.
⑤ So **few** people have bought this TV that we're going to stop production.

27.6 🔊
① All you can do is apologize for your mistake.
② All I expect is for staff to complete their tasks.
③ I'm sure all will be well in the interview.
④ All I want is a raise.
⑤ We have all the information we need.

27.7 🔊
① The only thing we need is a photo.
② We have some money.
③ We have some time.
④ Not many people like Mr. Jenkins.
⑤ Bertha is an expert in IT.
⑥ Some people like Mr. Jenkins.
⑦ We don't have much time.

27.8
① Not given
② False
③ True
④ True
⑤ False
⑥ False

28

28.4 🔊
① Who is the manager?
② What's in the report?
③ Who answers the telephone?
④ Who approves annual vacation?
⑤ What is the deadline?
⑥ Who wrote the ad?
⑦ Who will take questions?
⑧ What are the objectives?
⑨ What's the complaint about?

28.5 🔊
① What are our most popular products?
② Do you need to book the meeting?
③ Who answers customer emails?

④ Did Savannah write this report?
⑤ What is our lowest price?
⑥ Is James on vacation next week?

28.8 🔊
① You haven't read my proposal, **have you**?
② Sean could give the presentation, **couldn't he**?
③ Zoe got promoted, **didn't she**?
④ We're not ready for the conference, **are we**?
⑤ You work in marketing, **don't you**?

28.9 🔊
① Alice would know the answer, **wouldn't she**?
② I'm not dressed formally enough, **am I**?
③ You've worked in Berlin, **haven't you**?
④ They could tell us before 6pm, **couldn't they**?
⑤ Kate's going to Bangkok, **isn't she**?
⑥ I should double check the figures, **shouldn't I**?
⑦ Richard didn't get a raise, **did he**?

28.11
① Not given
② False
③ False
④ True
⑤ True

28.12 🔊
① What was the name of the company? I didn't **hear**.
② **Who** is working on the project for the new office?
③ You identified the mistake, **didn't you**?
④ Could you repeat that, please? I didn't **catch** it.
⑤ **What** is the theme of this year's conference?

30.2 🔊
1 **The** deadline for applications is Friday.
2 This job is based in **the** Berlin office.
3 We are recruiting **a** new designer.
4 I've got **an** interview for a new job.
5 **The** application form for this job is long.
6 Please complete **the** form on our website.
7 **The** ideal candidate enjoys teamwork.
8 There's an ad for **an** English teacher.

30.3
Ⓐ 2
Ⓑ 1
Ⓒ 4
Ⓓ 3
Ⓔ 5

30.6 🔊
1 The jobs I'm really interested in are based in Los Angeles. They're in IT.
2 The people who interviewed me for the job were really nice. They were the managers.
3 Clients can be very demanding. The clients I met today had lots of complaints.

30.9 🔊
1 I often travel to **Hong Kong** on business.
2 **Zenith Accounting** has three job openings.
3 I have a meeting with **the company director**.
4 He works for **the World Health Organization**.
5 I'm a strong candidate because I speak **Russian**.

30.10
1 Europe
2 an opening
3 Flight attendants
4 The hours
5 build a career

30.11 🔊
1 Your meeting is with **the HR manager**.
2 We're recruiting more staff in **France**.
3 I'm looking for a job as **an education consultant**.
4 We need someone who can speak **Italian**.
5 **Omnitech** is advertising several vacancies in its marketing department.
6 I work in **the sales department** of a large company.

31.3 🔊
1 In our department, we focus **on** sales and marketing.
2 Katrina graduated **from** college with a degree in Biological Sciences.
3 Our technicians are fully trained **in** all aspects of health and safety.
4 I've applied **for** a job in the IT department of a big company in Los Angeles.

31.4
1 Not given
2 Not given
3 True
4 False
5 True
6 True

31.5 🔊
1 to be responsible for something
2 to look forward to something
3 to amount to
4 to apply for a job
5 to be passionate about
6 experience in something

31.8 🔊
1 When can I expect to hear **from** you about the job?
2 Unfortunately, there has been a rise **in** complaints from customers.
3 I work **for** the CEO of a big IT company. I'm her assistant.
4 I heard **about** the job through a friend who works at the company.
5 Our profits went up last year. There was a rise **of** about five percent.

31.9
1 résumé
2 reliable
3 team
4 skills
5 salary
6 referee

31.10

Dear Mr. Khan,

I am writing to **apply for** the **position** of head web designer with your company.

I have **experience in** managing large commercial websites. Last year, sales from the website that I designed for a major online store **amounted to** more than $6 million.

I am eager to develop my **skills** and broaden my knowledge of other **industries**. I believe this job would be a fantastic **opportunity** for me, and I'd add a great deal to your company. I am enthusiastic and **passionate about** being at the cutting edge of web development. I'm also very **reliable** and I enjoy working in a team.

I have attached my **résumé** and details of my referees. I look forward to **hearing from** you.

Yours sincerely,
Amy Quah

32

32.2 ◀))
1 The office that I work in **is modern and open-plan**.
2 The customers who gave us **feedback were all very positive**.
3 One thing that I don't like **about my job is the long hours**.
4 The people who are on my team **say they enjoy working with me**.
5 The product that we've just launched **is already selling very well**.

32.3 ◀))
1 The main thing **that** I hope to gain by working here is more experience.
2 The area **that** I live in is very close to the bus routes into the business district.
3 The tasks **that** I perform best usually involve customer relations.
4 The exams **that** I passed last year mean that I am now fully qualified.
5 The person **who** I have learned the most from is my college professor.
6 The countries **that** order most of our umbrellas are in Europe.
7 The achievement **that** I am most proud of is winning "employee of the year."

32.5 ◀))
1 I have completed all the training, **which** means you wouldn't need to train me.
2 My boss, **who** is very talented, always encourages me not to work too late.
3 IT development, **which** is my favorite part of the job, is very fast-paced.
4 My co-workers, who are all older than me, have taught me a lot.
5 I worked at the reception desk, **which** taught me how to deal with customers.
6 I take my job very seriously, which means I always follow the company dress code.
7 In my last job, **which** was in Paris, I learned to speak French fluently.

32.6
Ⓐ 3
Ⓑ 6
Ⓒ 5
Ⓓ 2
Ⓔ 1
Ⓕ 4

32.8 ◀))
1 The place **where** I can concentrate the best is at home.
2 The person **whose** career inspires me the most is Muhammad Ali.
3 Last year, **when** I was an intern, I learned how to give presentations.
4 My parents, **who** are both doctors, inspired me to study medicine.

32.9 ◀))
1 My current salary, **which is** $20,000 a year, is not very high.
2 The thing **that gets** me excited about my job is seeing our products on sale.
3 Yes. I always know **who has** the responsibility for getting a task done on my team.
4 I can identify things **that need** to change, to make your business more efficient.
5 My boss, **who is** quite flexible, would allow me to leave after six weeks' notice.

34

34.3 ◀))
1 to live up to something
2 to look forward to something
3 to come across as something
4 to get away with something
5 to run out of something
6 to keep up with someone

34.4
1 True
2 Not given
3 False
4 Not given
5 True
6 False

34.5 🔊
① Please could you **come** up with a proposal on how to improve punctuality?
② I can't **keep** up with Thom when he goes through the accounts. He's too quick.
③ Liza comes **across** as very serious, but outside of work she's a lot of fun.
④ The two interns don't get **along** with each other very well. They don't see eye to eye.
⑤ I'm really looking **forward** to welcoming our new clients to London.

34.8 🔊
① Can you **take it on**?
② We're **giving them away**.
③ Let's **look it up** on social media.
④ I think we should **call it off**.
⑤ Can we **talk it over**?

34.9
① Needs a modern image
② Advertise the event
③ Increase awareness of the company
④ Tariq volunteers to do it

34.10 🔊
① I need the report today. Please don't let **me down**.
② Josef complains a lot. I can't put **up** with it.
③ I'm looking **forward** to finishing my training.
④ If you have a problem, we can talk **it** over.
⑤ Don't look down **on** Rachel. She's still new.
⑥ Our company is giving **away** three cars.

35

35.3 🔊
① Tanya has used up all her leave. **She won't go on vacation this year**.
② Toby is great at managing people. **He will be promoted to lead his team**.
③ Josef doesn't get along with his boss. **He might not stay here much longer**.
④ We have some meetings in Japan. **You may have to go to Tokyo**.

35.4 🔊
① We can't hire any staff at the moment, so you might not get an assistant until May.
② You're great with new staff, so we may ask you to become a mentor.
③ It's been a bad year for the company, so you won't get a raise.
④ This report needs to be finished by Friday. You might need to work overtime.
⑤ If Lucinda's work doesn't improve, we may have to fire her.

35.5
① True
② False
③ True
④ False
⑤ True
⑥ False
⑦ True
⑧ False

35.7 🔊
① He **definitely won't** get the job.
② You probably **won't need** any training.
③ We **will probably hire** some more staff soon.
④ She **will definitely** get a raise.
⑤ I **definitely won't** move to the head office.
⑥ I **probably won't** go on vacation this year.

35.8 🔊
① We will **probably** get a thank-you gift.
② I **definitely** won't change jobs this year.
③ You will **definitely** get a bonus.
④ We **probably** won't invite him to the meeting.

35.9
① may happen
② might not happen
③ probably won't happen
④ definitely won't happen

37

37.2
① False
② True
③ True
④ False
⑤ Not given

37.3 🔊
① To sum up, we have a very bright future.
② Do feel free to ask me any questions.
③ Let's turn to the predicted sales figures.
④ So, we've looked at all the main alternatives.

37.4 🔊
① hard drive
② pointer
③ power button
④ slides
⑤ cable
⑥ lectern
⑦ remote

37.5 🔊
1 Be careful of the **cable** in front of the stage.
2 I will return to the **lectern** to answer questions.
3 If you follow my **pointer**, you can see the graph.
4 I'll use my **remote** to forward to the final slide.
5 This projector's noisy. I'll turn the **power button** off.

37.6
1 False
2 Not given
3 True
4 True
5 False
6 False

37.7
Ⓐ 2
Ⓑ 6
Ⓒ 8
Ⓓ 1
Ⓔ 5
Ⓕ 7
Ⓖ 4
Ⓗ 3

38

38.2 🔊
GENERALIZING:
on the whole, generally, in general, by and large
EXCEPTIONS:
except for, with the exception of, aside from, excepting
FOCUSING: **if we focus on, if we home in on, concentrating on, focusing on**

38.3 🔊
1 The launch was successful, aside from the interview.
2 Now, let's home in on the positive news.
3 By and large, the poster campaign was a disaster.
4 Most of our clients liked the design except one.
5 Today we're going to focus on social media.

38.4
1 True
2 Not given
3 False
4 Not given
5 True

38.7
1 False
2 True
3 True
4 False

38.8 🔊
1 No. **If we focus on** the posters, we can see they were very successful.
2 Yes, **with the exception of** our Madrid store.
3 **As a matter of fact** it was very successful.
4 Cities **such as** Seoul and Busan could have successful stores.
5 They haven't yet. **However**, it's too soon to see what the impact will be.

39

39.3 🔊
1 Our new smartwatch is **easier** to operate than the old one.
2 Our new designer jeans are **more** stylish than last year's products.
3 Our tablet is **the** cheapest on the market.
4 This is the **most** beautiful dress in our range.
5 This is the **best** laptop I have ever owned.

39.4
1 more comfortable
2 the most reliable
3 lighter
4 more affordable

39.7 🔊
1 Our new phone is as cheap as existing models, but has a much wider range of features.
2 Our latest DVD is as exciting as anything I've ever seen.
3 Our chairs are excellent value, and just as comfortable as more expensive models.

39.8
1 True   2 Not given   3 False
4 True   5 Not given

39.9 🔊
1 Our new laptop is much **lighter** than its competitors.
2 This fitness tracker is **just as effective as** more expensive models.
3 Organic fruit is not **as cheap as** supermarket fruit, but it tastes better.
4 A consumer survey voted our pizzas the **tastiest** on the market.

40.2
Ⓐ 6
Ⓑ 1
Ⓒ 2
Ⓓ 7
Ⓔ 5
Ⓕ 8
Ⓖ 3
Ⓗ 4

40.3 ◀))
❶ There was a steady increase in our share value.
❷ Interest in our bags declined considerably.
❸ We've had a sharp rise in customer numbers.
❹ There was a dramatic spike in sales in May.
❺ Sales of our bags have rallied slightly.
❻ The value of our shares has fallen steadily.
❼ The value of the dollar is fluctuating wildly.
❽ The value of the dollar saw a dramatic spike.

40.5 ◀))
❶ Returns have increased **by** 10 percent.
❷ Prices fell between 30 **and** 45 percent.
❸ We're shrinking our staff **from** 800 to 650.
❹ Year-end profit stands **at** 8 percent.
❺ Salaries will increase **by** 2 percent.
❻ We have **between** 1,100 and 1,200 staff.
❼ There was a decrease **of** 5 percent.
❽ Profits have fallen **by** 15 percent.
❾ We are lowering the price **to** 30 euros.
❿ The price peaked **at** £19.99.

40.6
❶ False
❷ True
❸ True
❹ Not given

40.7 ◀))
❶ There was a **sharp increase** at the start of the year.
❷ It has been **fluctuating wildly** since the announcement.
❸ We're expecting them to **rally considerably** next quarter.

41.2 ◀))
❶ Yes, I think we could do that.
❷ We might move forward if we can agree on a delivery date.
❸ Maybe we could consider different colors.
❹ Would you mind waiting until next month for payment?
❺ We were hoping it would be more innovative.

41.3
❶ 1,000
❷ It is too high
❸ A cake
❹ Next week

41.7 ◀))
❶ I was wondering whether you have these in another size.
❷ Could you tell me when the price list will be ready?
❸ Could you tell me when I can expect delivery?

41.8 ◀))
❶ Could you tell me when **I can** start buying the new products?
❷ I was wondering **what the warranty period is**.
❸ Could you tell me how **the new product is** different from the old one?
❹ I was wondering if **you would** be free to discuss a new job opening.

41.10 ◀))
❶ Could you tell me whether **the delivery date has been changed**?
❷ I was wondering whether **my invoice has been paid**.
❸ It seems that **the wrong product was sent**.
❹ It looks as if **my complaint was not fully understood**.
❺ It seems that **the price was not calculated correctly**.

41.11 ◀))
❶ I'm afraid I can't access **the computer system right now**.
❷ It looks as if **the discount has not been applied**.
❸ I was wondering why the **deadline has been missed**.
❹ Could you tell me when **the sales start**?
❺ It seems that the wrong customer **has been contacted**.

41.12
❶ Not given
❷ True
❸ False
❹ False
❺ Not given

42.3 🔊

1 If you ask **me**, we might be better to wait until the summer.
2 **What** we need is proof that your business is profitable.
3 **Actually**, we'd like to reach an agreement by the end of the day.
4 The **main** thing is that we agree on a price that everyone is happy with.

42.4

Ⓐ 2
Ⓑ 4
Ⓒ 1
Ⓓ 3
Ⓔ 5

42.5 🔊

1 Not quite. **What we need are** some references from your customers.
2 That's OK. The **main thing is that** we find the right person to do the work.
3 **Actually**, our quote already includes free delivery.

43.4 🔊

1 I would **place** an order if they delivered sooner.
2 If your product **was** cheaper, we would buy it.
3 If you moved the deadline, we **could meet** it.
4 I **would** work with them if they answered my questions.
5 If they **checked** their work, I would use them.

43.5

1 True
2 Not given
3 True
4 False
5 Not given

43.6 🔊

1 We **would sign** the contract if it **was** clearer.
2 I **would accept** the job offer if the pay **was** better.
3 If they **improved** the quality, we **would place** an order.
4 If I **had** more time today, I **would check** the contract.

43.9 🔊

1 If you pay by credit card, we charge a 2 percent fee.
2 Our helpline is open 24 hours a day if you need assistance.
3 When we say our products are high quality, we mean it.
4 I get extra money every month if I work overtime.

43.10 🔊

Note: All answers can also use the short form of the future with "will."
1 If you **sign** the contract now, we **will begin** production next week.
2 We **will charge** a 10 percent fee if you **don't pay / do not pay** on time.
3 If you **buy** more than 50 units, we **will give** you a 5 percent discount.
4 We **will send** you a contract if you **want** to proceed.

43.12 🔊

1 We will return your call ASAP **if you leave a message**.
2 We would open stores in the US **if our products were more popular there**.
3 If you need more training, **you can contact the HR department**.
4 We would increase production **if we had more staff**.
5 We will issue a full refund **if you return your product within 28 days**.

43.13

Model Answers
1 You will understand his or her strengths and weaknesses.
2 You should decide what you can compromise on.
3 They help to build rapport if you don't know your business partner.
4 If you talk too much, you run the risk of revealing useful information.
5 To find a common ground so that you can reach an agreement.

44.4 🔊

Note: All answers can also be written in contracted form.
1 If he **had used** the correct figures, his report **would not have been** so out of date.
2 The boss **would not have shouted** if you **had admitted** your mistake earlier.
3 If you **had run** a spell check, the report **would not have contained** so many errors.
4 We **would not have embarrassed** ourselves if we **had researched** local customs before our trip.
5 I **would have worked** late last night if I **had known** our deadline was so soon.

44.5
1 B
2 A
3 A
4 B
5 A

44.8 🔊
1 Tony is not going to meet the deadline **unless he works overtime**.
2 **Unless I get** a good performance review, I won't get a raise this year.
3 I'm afraid we can't track your order **unless you can** give us your customer reference number.
4 **Unless we can** offer a better price, we won't win the contract.

44.9
1 Not given
2 False
3 False
4 True
5 Not given

Index

Subjects are indexed by unit number. Entries beginning with **L1** refer to units in level **1**. Entries beginning with **L2** refer to units in level **2**. (For example, **L1-8** refers to unit **8** in level **1**.) Entries in **bold** indicate the unit with the most information.

Acknowledgments

The publisher would like to thank:
Amy Child, Dominic Clifford, Devika Khosla, and Priyansha Tuli for design assistance; Dominic Clifford and Hansa Babra for additional illustrations; Sam Atkinson, Vineetha Mokkil, Antara Moitra, Margaret Parrish, Nisha Shaw, and Rohan Sinha for editorial assistance; Elizabeth Wise for indexing; Jo Kent for additional text; Scarlett O'Hara, Georgina Palffy, and Helen Ridge for proofreading; Christine Stroyan for project management; ID Audio for audio recording and production; David Almond, Gillian Reid, and Jacqueline Street-Elkayam for production assistance.

DK would like to thank the following for their kind permission to use their photographs:
25 **Fotolia**: semisatch (center).
37 **Fotolia**: Leonid Smirnov (bottom center).
55 **Dorling Kindersley**: NASA (top right).
257 **Fotolia**: Maksym Dykha (bottom right).
336 **Alamy**: MBI (bottom right).
All other images are copyright DK.
For more information, please visit **www.dkimages.com**.